# THE LAW OF HAZARDOUS WASTES AND TOXIC SUBSTANCES

# IN A NUTSHELL®

THIRD EDITION

JOHN G. SPRANKLING
Distinguished Professor of Law
University of the Pacific
McGeorge School of Law

RACHAEL E. SALCIDO
Professor of Law
University of the Pacific
McGeorge School of Law

WEST ACADEMIC PUBLISHING

444 Cedar Street, Suite 700
St. Paul, MN 55101
1-877-888-1330



Printed in the United States of America

**ISBN:** 978-1-68328-210-5

*For Gail, Tom and Alexis, and Doug*
J.G.S.

*For Phil and Natalie*
R.E.S.

# PREFACE

The "law of hazardous wastes and toxic substances" has now emerged as a subject of law school courses and as a field of specialization for attorneys. The law in this area is extraordinarily complex and rapidly evolving. Part of its attraction undoubtedly lies in the overlap of law, science, economics, and public policy which it presents. In addition, its rapid development has generated a growing demand for attorneys who are able to navigate its perils.

This book is primarily designed to provide law students with a concise and coherent overview of the subject. It may also be useful to attorneys seeking an introduction to the area. As with any book that attempts to simplify a complex subject, much has necessarily been summarized. The text of the principal federal statutes addressed in this book occupy over 1,000 single-spaced pages in West's *Selected Environmental Law Statutes*. In turn, these statutes are interpreted by thousands of pages of regulations, judicial opinions, administrative decisions, and guidance documents. Although this book addresses the basic legal components in the area, many details have been omitted and some topics (e.g., the special problems of nuclear materials) are mentioned only briefly.

Consistent with the custom among courts and attorneys in the field, this book generally uses the popular names of the key federal statutes rather than their more formal names (e.g., the "Clean Water Act" rather than the "Federal Water Pollution Control Act"). Also, it generally cites to sections of the uncodified bills rather than to the codified versions (e.g., "Clean Water Act § 311" rather than "33 U.S.C. § 1321"). Finally, as used in the book "EPA" refers to the federal Environmental Protection Agency, not to a state agency with a similar name.

Many people helped make this book possible. We particularly wish to thank Dean Michael Hunter Schwartz and Associate Dean Michael Colatrella for their constant support. We also thank our student research assistants, Ana Gonzalez (Class of 2018), Uri Grant (Class of 2019), and Trevor Wong (Class of 2019). Most importantly, we thank our families for their encouragement and patience.

JOHN G. SPRANKLING
RACHAEL E. SALCIDO

Sacramento, California
January 2018

# OUTLINE

# TABLE OF CASES

**References are to Pages**

---

# TABLE OF STATUTES

**References are to Pages**

---

# TABLE OF REGULATIONS

**References are to Pages**

# THE LAW OF HAZARDOUS WASTES AND TOXIC SUBSTANCES

## IN A NUTSHELL®

THIRD EDITION

# CHAPTER 1
# INTRODUCTION

Humans and the environment are routinely exposed to potentially dangerous substances. Even such basic activities as breathing air and drinking water expose us to chemical products, byproducts, and wastes. Over 10 million chemical compounds are known to exist. Minute amounts of some chemicals are known to cause death or substantial bodily harm to humans. However, the risks which most chemicals pose are unknown. Despite our twenty-first century technology, many people fear that we are slowly poisoning both ourselves and the planet. Indeed, scientific advances in biotechnology, nanotechnology, and other areas increasingly raise new dangers.

These *hazardous wastes* and *toxic substances* are primarily regulated under a complex network of federal statutes, supplemented by regulations and case law. In general, these statutes empower federal agencies (notably EPA) to regulate a dangerous substance at every point in its life cycle, including its manufacture, distribution, use, disposal, and cleanup.

## A. REGULATORY BACKGROUND: A TOXIC LEGACY

The problem presented by widespread exposure to hazardous wastes and toxic substances is comparatively new. In the distant past, their danger was experienced only rarely, from naturally-occurring substances. For example, primitive tribes learned that some plants were unsafe to eat; lead water pipes killed thousands of Romans; and English hat makers injured by work place exposure to mercury prompted the phrase "mad as a hatter." After World War II, however, a veritable tidal wave of new synthetic chemical substances was released into the environment. Some of these substances were valuable products (e.g., pesticides); others were wastes or byproducts from manufacturing, petroleum refining, and other industrial processes.

One event awakened the nation to the dangers of these new chemical substances: the 1962 publication of *Silent Spring*, Rachel Carson's famous attack on DDT. Hailed as a "miracle" pesticide, DDT had saved millions of human lives by controlling insects which spread malaria and other fatal diseases; and it had dramatically increased the world's food supply by killing crop-destroying pests. But Carson revealed that DDT imperiled humans and other species as well. It killed fish, birds, and other wildlife, threatening a spring which would be truly silent. More ominous still, high levels of DDT were commonly detected in human tissue (and even in human breast milk), the result of eating fruits, vegetables, milk, meats, and other foods bearing DDT residues. Based on the limited scientific data available, Carson suggested that DDT might cause cancer and other life-threatening diseases. *Silent Spring* sparked an intense national debate on the dangers which chemical substances pose to human health and the environment.

## 1. WIDESPREAD EXPOSURE TO CHEMICALS

Even today, with extensive federal legislation in place, the scale of the problem staggers the imagination. As a practical matter, we depend on potentially dangerous chemical substances in all facets of everyday living, including food, clothing, housing, entertainment, and transportation. For example, one toxic chemical alone—benzene—is used in products which make up 10% of the nation's gross domestic product. Any return to a prehistoric, pristine world is impossible.

Inevitably, humans and the environment in general will continue to be exposed to millions of chemical compounds. According to EPA's "Toxic Release Inventory," each year large industrial facilities in the United States release over 4 billion pounds of toxic chemicals into the environment. Billions of pounds more are incorporated into products or generated as wastes. Thus, for example, humans are widely exposed to dioxin, which one court called the "most acutely toxic substance yet synthesized by man." United States v. Vertac Chemical Corp., 489 F.Supp. 870 (E.D.Ark.1980). One ounce of dioxin is capable of killing over 100,000 people. Yet dioxin is encountered in cigarette smoke, vehicle emissions, fireplace smoke, barbecued steaks, and even in the air which the reader is now breathing.

## 2. INSUFFICIENT DATA ON EFFECTS OF CHEMICALS

Another facet of the problem is even more troubling: we do not have enough data to understand the risks which most of these chemicals pose. At some level, nearly everything is toxic to living organisms. For example, a certain quantity of ordinary table salt can kill a human being. But scientists lack basic information about the toxicity—at different dosages and over different time periods—of most of the chemicals synthesized since World War II. In particular, what level of exposure to the substance is "safe"? The long-term effects of low dosage human exposure to many modern chemicals are only now beginning to be understood. In addition, not enough is known about their persistence in the environment; their potential to accumulate in the food chain; and their potential to combine with other substances to produce a more potent effect.

For example, does long term exposure to chemicals in the environment cause cancer? According to studies reported by the federal Agency for Toxic Substances and Disease Registry, merely living near a hazardous waste site poses a small-to-moderate increased risk of certain types of cancer; and over 10 million people live within one mile of the over 1,300 hazardous waste sites listed for priority cleanup under federal law. The National Cancer Institute also found increased incidents of certain cancers in sample populations who lived within one kilometer of a chemical, petroleum, rubber, or plastics manufacturing plant. Many scientists now believe that chemical exposure causes at least some cancer cases. Yet the identity of the responsible chemicals, the minimum dosage levels, the minimum exposure periods, and the precise methods of causation are still largely unknown.

## B. DEFINING "HAZARDOUS WASTES" AND "TOXIC SUBSTANCES"

As the title of this book suggests, the law governing dangerous substances distinguishes broadly between *hazardous wastes* and *toxic substances*. In a sense, both are encompassed within the broader universe of "hazardous substances." But the law regulating hazardous substances has developed along two major lines. First, major portions of the law are meant to be *prospective*; they control the manufacture, use, and allowable release of *toxic substances* in order to minimize human and environmental exposure. Yet prophylactic schemes are often imperfect, and those concerning toxic substances are no exception. As a result, a second, *retrospective* branch of the law has developed. It regulates the disposal and cleanup of those hazardous substances known as *hazardous wastes*.

The terminology in this area is far from uniform and, as discussed below, each statute typically describes its regulated substances differently (e.g., "toxic pollutants," "toxic materials," "extremely hazardous substances," "hazardous substances," and "hazardous wastes"). Broadly speaking, however, *toxic substances* and *hazardous wastes* are conventionally used to refer to the materials regulated under the two branches.

## 1. WHAT ARE "TOXIC SUBSTANCES"?

In general, a *toxic substance* is a material which can cause death or serious injury to humans, or significant damage to the environment, in relatively *small* quantities. For example, one ounce of dioxin is capable of killing over 100,000 people. Beyond this general definition, there are many specific ways in which a toxic substance may harm a living organism; for example, it may induce cancer (a "carcinogen"), cause birth defects (a "teratogen"), produce mutations (a "mutagen"), or damage nerve systems (a "neurotoxin"). Recognizing the variety of ways in which a substance may endanger living organisms, the statutory definitions of "toxic substances" are often quite broad. For example, Clean Water Act § 502(13) defines "toxic pollutants" as those:

> which after discharge and upon exposure, ingestion, inhalation or assimilation into any organism, either directly from the environment or indirectly by ingestion through food chains, will * * * cause death, disease, behavioral abnormalities, cancer, genetic mutations, physiological malfunctions (including malfunctions in reproduction) or physical deformations, in [any] organisms or their offspring.

Examples of toxic substances include asbestos, creosote, formaldehyde, PCBs, and vinyl chloride. In recent years, the definition of toxic substances has been broadened to include certain genetically-engineered microorganisms, and this trend is expected to continue as technology advances.

On the other hand, for example, carbon dioxide and other greenhouse gases that contribute to global climate change are not toxic substances. Certainly, as the Supreme Court recognized in Massachusetts v. EPA, 549 U.S. 497, 127 S.Ct. 1438, 167 L.Ed.2d 248 (2007), the "harms associated with climate change are serious and well recognized." But these harms are caused by extremely *large* quantities of greenhouse gases, unlike toxic substances where only a small quantity will cause injury.

### 2. WHAT ARE "HAZARDOUS WASTES"?

In contrast, *hazardous wastes* refer to discarded toxic or hazardous substances that pose a threat to human health or the environment under certain conditions. For example, an abandoned barrel of *toxic substances* will be considered a *hazardous waste*. Wastes may be considered hazardous because of their potential to destroy property as well as life. Thus, corrosive, reactive, and ignitable materials are frequently treated as hazardous wastes apart from their impact on living organisms. These materials are not inherently toxic, but may become dangerous if improperly treated, transported, disposed of, or stored.

Most specifically, *hazardous wastes* refers to the materials that are regulated under Subtitle C of the Resource Conservation and Recovery Act (RCRA).

Similarly, although the Comprehensive Environmental Response, Compensation, and Liability Act (CERCLA) regulates cleanup of the somewhat broader universe of "hazardous substances," it is primarily concerned with hazardous wastes which have been released into the environment.

## C. REGULATION OF HAZARDOUS WASTES AND TOXIC SUBSTANCES

The law governing hazardous wastes and toxic substances is principally set forth in a series of complicated federal statutes. About a dozen major statutes, and a number of minor statutes, collectively provide the statutory framework. In almost all instances, Congress has asked EPA to flesh out these statutes with implementing regulations. This proliferation of different statutes—each with its own definitional and regulatory provisions—often produces overlap, inconsistency, and disharmony. Moreover, roughly every decade, Congress adds to the confusion by substantially amending each of the major statutes.

### 1. REGULATORY STRUCTURE: A LIFE CYCLE APPROACH

The key to understanding this complex, fragmented system is to focus on the "life cycle" of a sample chemical substance. For example, consider a hypothetical new chemical known as "kylonite," used in making cell phone components. Assume that kylonite is a toxic substance. Each pound of kylonite has a predictable, five stage life cycle, beginning with its birth (manufacture) and ending with its death (cleanup):

- *Production/Sale:* First, it will be manufactured by a chemical company and distributed through interstate commerce to a component factory.
- *Use*: At the component factory, the kylonite will be incorporated into telephones which are sold to consumers across the nation.
- *Releases*: Small amounts of kylonite will be released into the air and water incident to the production process at both the chemical company and the component factory.
- *Disposal*: Kylonite wastes from the chemical plant and the component factory will be discarded.
- *Cleanup*: Finally, any kylonite wastes which were improperly disposed of will be cleaned up.

Like pieces of a jigsaw puzzle fitting together, the various federal statutes regulating toxic substances and hazardous wastes make more sense if they are viewed as efforts to regulate different stages in a chemical's life cycle. Accordingly, the chapters in this book are organized around this life cycle approach.

- *Production/Sale*: Two key federal statutes govern the access of chemical products to the market, as discussed in Chapter 3. The

Federal Insecticide, Fungicide, and Rodenticide Act (FIFRA) regulates pesticides, while the Toxic Substances Control Act (TSCA) regulates other chemical substances. Kylonite might be banned or restricted under TSCA.

- *Use*: A number of statutes regulate chemical use, as covered in Chapter 4. The workers in the chemical plant and component factory might be protected from exposure to kylonite by safety equipment mandated under the Occupational Safety and Health Act (OSHA). If the kylonite-containing telephones are dangerous to consumers, this use of kylonite might be restricted under the Hazardous Substances Act (HSA) or the Consumer Products Safety Act (CPSA).

- *Releases*: Three main federal statutes address the release of chemicals into the air and water, as explained in Chapter 5: the Clean Air Act (CAA), the Clean Water Act (CWA), and the Safe Drinking Water Act (SDWA). Thus, for example, the kylonite emissions into the air might be controlled by the CAA, while the water pollution would be addressed under the CWA and the SWDA.

- *Disposal*: The disposal of hazardous wastes is governed by the Resource Conservation and Recovery Act (RCRA), addressed in Chapter 6. If the kylonite wastes are toxic, RCRA will control their storage, treatment, and ultimate disposal.

- *Cleanup*: The Comprehensive Environmental Response, Compensation, and Liability Act (CERCLA) is the main federal statute authorizing the cleanup of hazardous substances which were disposed of improperly, as discussed in Chapters 7–12. Thus, if kylonite wastes were abandoned on a stranger's farm, CERCLA might empower EPA to clean up the site. RCRA also contains important cleanup authority, as explained in Chapter 12.

## 2. OTHER REGULATORY THEMES

Other common themes which bind this disparate group of statutes together include the following:

- **Human Health Focus:** In practice, these statutes are largely enforced to protect human health. Although the statutory language frequently expresses concern for environmental quality in general and empowers EPA to protect the environment even absent human health risks, this strand of the law is largely ignored.

- **Regulatory Implementation:** EPA implements the governing statutes in three principal ways. First and foremost, it promulgates regulations which have the force of law, binding both EPA and the regulated public. Second, EPA issues interpretive rulings, policy statements, and guidance documents. These materials provide a wealth of information about the EPA's regulatory priorities. Finally, EPA can bring enforcement actions; these can set administrative and judicial precedent in their interpretation of the law. In addition to these formal regulatory tools, EPA maintains an enormous database of useful information. It is generally accessible to the public through publications, telephone "hot lines," and, increasingly, the Internet.

- **Limited Judicial Role:** Courts play a comparatively minor role in shaping policy in this area. In general, the courts show great deference to EPA's expertise in fashioning the details of regulation. They will uphold the agency's action unless it is "arbitrary and capricious" or lacks "substantial evidence." They will, however, scrutinize carefully the *process* by which EPA implemented the statute; many regulations have been overturned on procedural grounds. Only rarely, however, will the courts upset an EPA interpretation of an enabling statute. In two areas, however, the courts have continued to play the principal role in shaping the law. First, under CERCLA, the courts have largely fashioned the standards governing liability for remediation of sites contaminated with hazardous substances. Similarly, in a direct link with traditional tort practice, courts continue to develop the rules governing the compensability of personal injuries and property damage caused by such substances.

- **Role for State Law:** Because the problems of hazardous wastes and toxic substances implicate important national interests, Congress has legislated extensively in this area. As a result, the statutory framework is largely federal. In two areas, however, state law remains of primary importance. First, for the most part, federal law merely sets the *floor* below which the states may not fall. The states have frequently enacted stricter requirements. Preemption of more stringent state regulation in this area is rare. Second, there is almost no federal law governing liability for personal injuries or property damages caused by toxic substances or hazardous wastes. As a result, this area remains governed almost exclusively by state law.

- **State Enforcement:** States retain an important enforcement role. In many of the federal regulatory programs (particularly those regulating the emissions of toxic substances into the air, water, and drinking water, and those governing the treatment, storage, and disposal of hazardous wastes) EPA has authorized many of the states to act as the primary enforcement agents for the statutory schemes. EPA retains primary enforcement authority, and can intervene if a state fails to act appropriately. But the vast bulk of the enforcement under such statutes is done by the authorized states.

- **Private Enforcement:** In addition to state enforcement possibilities, virtually all of the key federal statutes contain citizens' suit provisions. These allow individual citizens or citizen groups to sue private parties for violations of the given statutory and regulatory schemes. Additional provisions in all of the Acts allow a citizen to sue EPA for violating statutory directives.

- **Technological Change:** The technology in this area is developing more quickly than the statutes that are intended to regulate it. For example, the rapidly-developing field of biotechnology may conceivably produce new hybrid organisms that threaten the environment. Because Congress has not enacted legislation specifically designed to govern this area, EPA has tried to utilize TSCA or FIFRA for this purpose, even though TSCA was drafted to regulate toxic chemical substances and FIFRA pesticides.

# CHAPTER 2

# RISK AND SCIENTIFIC UNCERTAINTY

## A. OVERVIEW

Life is full of risks. As the Supreme Court observed in Industrial Union Department, AFL-CIO v. American Petroleum Institute, 448 U.S. 607, 100 S.Ct. 2844, 65 L.Ed.2d 1010 (1980), "[t]here are many activities that we engage in every day—such as driving a car or even breathing city air—that entail some risk of accident or material health impairment."

Yet the unique risks posed by hazardous wastes and toxic substances have generated extraordinary public fear. Why? Part of the answer, of course, is the severity of the harm which these substances can cause: death or serious injury to humans (and the environment) on a large scale. A single release of toxic gas, for example, killed thousands of people in Bhopal, India. Similarly, these substances cause innumerable cancer cases throughout the world each year. The rest of the answer is found in factors which affect the public's perception of this risk. In general, people tend to overestimate the likelihood that hazardous wastes and toxic substances will actually harm them. This is because: (1) the risk is unfamiliar to them; (2) they have not voluntarily chosen to encounter it; and (3) they have little ability to control it.

The regulatory response to this public concern encounters a major obstacle: scientific uncertainty. Little is known about the effects of chemical substances on humans and the environment. For example, a National Academy of Sciences study found insufficient data to assess the health risks posed by over 86% of the commercially-used chemicals it surveyed. Accordingly, science is often unable to answer two key questions:

- Which chemical substances are hazardous to humans and the environment?
- What level of exposure to hazardous chemicals is "safe"?

Only limited data is available, for example, concerning the cancer risks that chemical substances present; non-cancer human health risks and environmental risks have received even less study. Moreover, even if a chemical is known to cause death or serious injury in high doses, the effect of small doses over a long time period is typically unknown. The uncertainty problem is compounded by technological advances which allow scientists to detect extremely low levels of chemical substances (i.e., parts per trillion). In short, our ability to *detect* chemicals far surpasses our ability to *predict* their danger.

Given scientific uncertainty, how should the legal system respond to these risks? One option is to defer any response until a particular chemical causes serious, demonstrable harm (e.g., hundreds of human deaths). But the human suffering which this approach entails is not tolerable; the goal of regulation is to *prevent harm* from occurring in the first place. A second option—at the opposite extreme—is to ban all potentially dangerous chemicals. But such a draconian rule would bring modern industrial society to a standstill. In everyday life, people rely on chemicals for food, medicine, housing, clothing, and transportation. Manufacturing, mining, agriculture, and other vital industries depend on thousands of chemical substances which are known or suspected to be harmful; and the byproducts and wastes which these industries generate pose similar threats. Thus, humans and the environment are exposed to a variety of potentially dangerous substances.

Regulation of hazardous wastes and toxic substances steers a middle course between these two options. On the one hand, it is generally *preventive regulation*. The principal goal of the federal regulatory framework is to prevent harm from occurring, not to remediate past harm. Even CERCLA, the key federal statute governing hazardous waste cleanup, is premised on the need to avoid future injury to humans and the environment. Thus, almost by definition, regulatory decisions must often be based on incomplete, ambiguous, and imprecise information. On the other hand, it is *selective regulation*. In general, federal authorities determine whether to regulate chemicals on a case-by-case basis, considering the existing scientific data and other information. Moreover, once the decision is made to regulate a particular chemical, the manner of regulation varies according to circumstances. Complete bans are rare. Less restrictive techniques tailored to the particular chemical (e.g., quantity limits, use conditions, and warning requirements) are almost always employed.

This chapter surveys the response of the legal system to the interrelated problems of risk and scientific uncertainty. After a brief look at the common law approach to risk, it focuses on risk assessment techniques and risk management approaches currently used by federal agencies in regulating chemical substances. It then examines the general judicial response to risk regulation by federal agencies.

## B. THE COMMON LAW APPROACH TO RISK

Nuisance and other common law doctrines failed to protect the public from the dangers of hazardous wastes and toxic substances. As a result, this area is now dominated by federal statutes; common law doctrines play only a supporting role, as discussed in Chapter 13. In part, the common law failed because of its simplistic approach to risk.

The common law system is primarily attuned to resolving disputes concerning actual past events, not potential future risks. Most importantly, the system assumes that sufficient information exists to establish truth. For example, consider a simple traffic accident. Suppose A is driving north and B is driving east. After their cars collide, A sues B; each claims he entered the intersection on a green light. Only one light could have been green, but which one? The common law functions well in such a situation. Its goal is to ascertain a historic fact—to determine the color of each light at a particular time in the past. Information sufficient to establish this fact (e.g., percipient witnesses, photos, or skid marks) already exists. It can be gathered by able counsel and readily understood by judges and juries lacking technical expertise. Alternatively, suppose that A sued B *before* any accident occurred and asked the court to protect him against the *risk* of being hit by B's car. Would the common law provide a theory for A's suit? How could this risk be ascertained? In particular, how could A prove the likelihood of a future event?

The foundational assumption of the common law system—that information existed to determine truth—did not apply in the special case of the risks posed by hazardous wastes and toxic substances. These substances presented the problem of scientific uncertainty. In many cases, the data necessary to evaluate the health and environmental risks of a particular substance simply *did not exist*; they lay beyond the frontiers of human knowledge. Moreover, when information was available it was often incomplete and inconsistent. Yet the common law system largely ignored this dilemma, taking refuge in familiar concepts such as the burden of proof.

The common law approach focused almost exclusively on proving the *probability of harm*. Thus, the plaintiff seeking to prevent risk from hazardous wastes or toxic substances was bound by the normal evidentiary standard applicable to all civil cases. She was required to *prove* by a preponderance of the evidence that harm *would* actually occur in the future. In contrast, this approach largely ignored the *severity of harm* which the risk posed. The law provided no protection against low probability/high severity risks. Thus, conduct proven to have a 51% probability of causing temporary disease in a few people might be enjoined. Yet a 10% probability that a toxic substance would kill hundreds of people would not justify relief.

The common law approach to risk is well-illustrated by the Supreme Court's 1906 decision in Missouri v. Illinois, 200 U.S. 496, 26 S.Ct. 268, 50 L.Ed. 572 (1906). Claiming a public nuisance, Missouri sought to enjoin Chicago from discharging typhoid-contaminated sewage into a tributary of the Mississippi River, which allegedly tainted the water supply used by St. Louis residents. Hundreds of St. Louis residents died each year from typhoid fever. The main question was whether the water-borne typhoid bacillus was still potent enough to cause disease when it reached Missouri. Writing for the Court, Justice Holmes stressed that contamination could not "be detected by the unassisted senses—no visible increase of filth, no new smell. * * * The plaintiff's case depends on an inference of the unseen." Each party submitted expert testimony in favor of its position, leading Holmes to conclude that "there is a categorical contradiction between the experts on the two sides." Confronted with this conflicting testimony, the Court reasoned that

Missouri had failed to meet its burden of proof and refused to restrain Chicago's discharges.

## C. THE REGULATORY APPROACH TO RISK

In contrast to the common law view, the regulatory approach to risk focuses on preventing potential harm from occurring. Thus, Congress addressed the risk posed by hazardous wastes and toxic substances by empowering EPA and other federal agencies to regulate them without conclusive evidence of proven harm to human health or to the environment. The typical federal statute in this area vests broad discretion in the responsible agency to determine both: (1) which substances to regulate; and (2) which regulatory tools to use. For example, suppose that EPA is concerned about the health risks of "exomine," a hypothetical chemical used in maintaining bakery equipment. Using the standards contained in the Toxic Substances Control Act (see Chapter 3) or other applicable federal statutes, EPA could decide whether to regulate exomine and, if so, how.

The process of risk regulation is commonly divided into two stages: (1) risk assessment and (2) risk management. Initially, *risk assessment* evaluates the risk which a particular chemical poses. Once the risk is known, *risk management* addresses how the legal system should regulate the risk. In theory, there is a clear separation between risk assessment and risk management: risk assessment is a purely scientific endeavor performed by scientists and other technical experts, while risk management is exclusively a public policy question resolved by legislatures and regulatory agencies. In practice, however, it is extremely difficult to separate the two. For example, risk assessment inevitably raises important policy questions (e.g., what assumptions should be made about the shape of the dose-response curve at low doses?). Similarly, agencies trying to reach risk management decisions must frequently act on the basis of incomplete and imperfect data. Thus, the problem of scientific uncertainty pervades both stages.

## 1. THE RISK ASSESSMENT PROCESS

How much risk does a particular substance pose? The risk assessment process seeks to answer this question. It is the principal tool used to determine if a substance merits regulation. The most difficult risk assessment questions concern whether small amounts of a particular substance will adversely affect human health over a long time period.

The regulatory approach defines risk as the product of two factors: *probability of harm* (how likely is harm to occur?) and *magnitude of harm* (if harm occurs, how severe will it be?). *In short, risk equals probability times magnitude.* Thus, for example, a 10% likelihood that 200 people will die is considered a greater risk than a 50% chance that 5 people will catch the flu. This quantitative risk assessment, then, attempts to determine the *actual risk* which a chemical poses. (Although this process remains the dominant model, many argue that it is incomplete because it fails to consider the public's reaction to the hazard, known as the "outrage" factor. In assessing risk, members of the public take into account more than mere probability and magnitude. For example, people underestimate the actual risk of hazards which are familiar, voluntarily encountered, and perceived as controllable, such as driving a car. Conversely, using the same factors, people tend to overestimate the quantitative risk posed by hazardous wastes and toxic substances. Under this alternative view, *risk equals probability times magnitude, plus outrage*.)

In discussing risk, it is important to distinguish between *background risk* and *additional risk*. For example, each person already has a pre-existing, *background risk* of contracting cancer during his lifetime; this risk is about 250,000 in 1,000,000. The risk assessment process asks how much *additional risk* is created by exposure to the suspect substance (e.g., an increased cancer risk of 1 in 1,000,000?).

The risk assessment approach used by EPA and other regulatory agencies is founded on a landmark 1983 study performed by the National Research Council entitled "Risk Management in the Federal Government: Managing the Process" (the "Red Book"). This approach involves four steps: (1) hazard identification; (2) dose-response assessment; (3) exposure assessment; and (4) overall risk characterization. The risk assessment process is discussed below, using the hypothetical "exomine" problem discussed above. How will EPA assess its risks?

### a. Hazard Identification: Does the Substance Adversely Affect Human Health or the Environment?

EPA must first determine whether exomine can harm human health or the environment. Although the most accurate tool for assessing harm to human health would be laboratory studies which expose human subjects to a suspect chemical, such experimentation is ethically proscribed. Thus, scientists must use alternative methods, principally epidemiologic studies and animal bioassays. The reliability of these methods is often disputed.

- *Epidemiologic Studies*: Epidemiologists attempt to identity the factors which cause a disease by analyzing statistical data. They seek a correlation between the occurrence of the disease and a particular risk factor (e.g., between lung cancer and smoking). In a "cohort study," for example, scientists would determine whether the disease rates of a population incidentally exposed to exomine in everyday life (e.g., in the work place) were statistically greater than the parallel rates of an unexposed population. Alternatively, in a "case control study," scientists would assess whether disease victims received significantly greater exposure to exomine than unaffected persons. Well-conducted epidemiologic studies can provide valuable evidence of human risk. Yet such studies suffer from various weaknesses: (1) it is often difficult to isolate the impact of one substance from the effects of other agents; (2) the latency period between exposure and disease may be long (up to 40 years); (3) data may be difficult to collect, especially where the exposed population is small; (4) it is often difficult to extrapolate findings based on high doses to low dose situations; and (5) the technique cannot evaluate new chemical substances because it is based on historic exposure data.

- *Animal Bioassays*: The most common technique used in hazard identification is the animal bioassay, in which laboratory animals are exposed to a suspect chemical under controlled conditions. For example, to evaluate exomine scientists might expose a rodent population to the substance over a multi-year period and then compare the incidence of cancer and other diseases with that found in a control group. Positive results in test animals are generally (but cautiously) accepted as signaling risk for humans. Interspecies comparisons, however, are not uniformly reliable. Moreover, animal bioassays are costly (over $2 million), lengthy (over two years), and produce limited data (usually only a few exposure levels can be tested).

- *Other Techniques*: Because many mutagenic substances (i.e., those that damage DNA) are also carcinogens, short-term tests which establish that a particular chemical is a mutagen may suggest that it is also a carcinogen. In addition, scientists sometimes compare the molecular structure of a suspect substance to the structure of known carcinogens. Although both of these techniques are relatively quick and inexpensive, they are far less reliable than epidemiologic studies or animal bioassays.

### b. Dose-Response Assessment: What Level of Exposure to the Substance ("Dose") Produces Adverse Effects ("Response")?

Assuming that exomine can harm humans or the environment, EPA must next determine the dose at which harm first occurs. Epidemiologic data is usually far too vague to establish the minimum exposure level which causes a disease. Accordingly, scientists typically rely on extrapolations from animal bioassay data to predict the dose-response relationship. For example, if 100 rodents each ingest 20 micrograms of exomine per week, and 5 later develop "excess" cancer tumors (that is, excess above the number of expected background cases), then an inference arises that the 20 microgram/week dose produces cancer in rodents. It is difficult, however, to translate this finding into data relevant to humans. Humans who ingest 20 micrograms or more of exomine each week might well suffer no adverse effects, due to differences in weight, metabolism, immune systems, and related factors.

Another problem involves extrapolation from high doses to low doses. Laboratory animals are commonly exposed to test substances at levels much greater than actual human exposure, in order to ensure that the test results are statistically significant (i.e., not caused by chance). Suppose that in the hypothetical exomine test described above, 5% of rodents receiving the 20 microgram/week dose developed "excess" tumors, but all rodents receiving a 10 microgram/week dose remained healthy. Three interpretations of this result are possible. First, there might be a "threshold dose" somewhere between 10 and 20 micrograms/week, below which no cancer is caused. See, e.g., Chlorine Chemistry Council v. EPA, 206 F.3d 1286 (D.C.Cir.2000) (invalidating EPA rule on chloroform contamination that assumed dose-response curve was linear, because evidence showed threshold effect). Second, the increased risk caused by low doses might be too small to detect given the number of test animals involved (e.g., 1 in 1,000). Finally, the study period might be too short to evaluate the effects of long-term exposure. Without more study, scientists will not know which of these explanations is correct.

### c. Exposure Assessment: To What Extent Are Humans and the Environment Actually Exposed to the Substance?

EPA must next identify the extent to which humans and the environment are actually exposed to exomine. Attempts to assess exposure are usually plagued by incomplete data. For example, suppose EPA evaluates the exposure of consumers to exomine. Assume that the average concentration level of exomine in bread can be measured. The amount of exomine ingested from this source will vary substantially with each person's diet. Moreover, some population groups (e.g., infants, pregnant women, and the elderly) may be more vulnerable than others to adverse health impacts, even assuming equal doses of exomine. Finally, the combination of exomine with other carcinogens might enhance the risk of cancer far beyond what mere addition would suggest; data on such synergistic effects, however, are difficult to obtain. EPA would also consider the exomine exposure of groups other than consumers (e.g., workers manufacturing exomine, bakery workers using exomine, and persons exposed to exomine wastes).

#### d. Risk Characterization: What Is the Overall Nature of the Risk?

Finally, EPA must assess the overall nature of the risk. It combines the hazard identification, dose-response assessment, and exposure assessment data to reach a final conclusion. The overall risk may be expressed in qualitative (e.g., high risk) or quantitative (e.g., 10 additional cancer cases per year) terms. Based on the hypothetical exomine data above, suppose that EPA concludes exomine *probably* will cause .2 human deaths per year (i.e., 1 death every 5 years) in the United States.

## 2. RISK MANAGEMENT: HOW SAFE IS SAFE?

Risk management examines how the legal system should respond to a known risk. Even assuming that exomine will cause 1 death every 5 years, is this risk significant enough to merit regulation? If so, what regulatory tool is appropriate to reduce the exomine risk to an acceptable level? Alternatively, one might ask: (1) is the substance "safe"?; and (2) if not, how can we make it "safe"? Both questions raise a fundamental policy issue: "how safe is 'safe' "? Or, in the context of hazardous waste cleanup, "how clean is 'clean' "?

Our nation lacks a uniform policy on risk management. Indeed, there is widespread disagreement over such fundamental issues as: (1) what goals should risk management serve? (2) how strictly should we regulate a known risk? and (3) which risks merit regulation? Because our approaches toward risk management are badly fragmented, none of these questions can be readily answered in general terms. Rather, the federal statutes governing hazardous wastes and toxic substances reflect three broad approaches to risk management, with considerable variation within the statutes under each approach. Depending on the context, Congress directs federal agencies to use: (1) health-based standards; (2) feasibility standards; or (3) cost-benefit analyses. Thus, whether and how exomine is regulated will turn on the specific provisions of each potentially applicable statute.

### a. Health-Based Standards

Risk management is sometimes governed by the overriding goal of public health protection. Health-based standards reflect the view that risk to human life can never be justified by economic, social, or other factors. Accordingly, some federal statutes mandate regulation of chemicals to the extent appropriate to protect human health, regardless of the ensuing social or economic consequences. The Food Quality Protection Act of 1996, for example, requires EPA to set ceiling levels for pesticide residues on foods which "ensure that there is a reasonable certainty that no harm will result to infants and children from aggregate exposure." 21 U.S.C. § 346a(b)(2)(C)(ii)(I). Other examples of health-based standards include:

- Clean Air Act levels for criteria pollutants (§ 109(b)(1): standards "requisite to protect the public health"); and
- Safe Drinking Water Act maximum contaminant level goals (§ 1412(b)(4): "level at which no known or anticipated adverse effects on the health of persons occur and which allows an adequate margin of safety").

Probably the best known health-based standards are portions of the Food, Drug, and Cosmetic Act known as "Delaney clauses" which prohibit the use of certain food additives "found * * * to induce cancer in man or animal," regardless of the magnitude of the risk or the benefits of the substance. As discussed in Chapter 4, this absolutist standard is quite controversial.

In the abstract, health-based standards provide optimum protection for public health by ignoring non-health concerns. In the hypothetical discussed above, the application of health-based standards would result in a de facto ban on exomine use in bakeries, even if it forced most bakeries to close and required the surviving bakeries to treble bread prices. Because exomine is known to cause cancer in laboratory animals, bread containing exomine would be deemed "adulterated"—and thus unsaleable under federal law—pursuant to the above "Delaney clause." Yet economic, social, and political concerns often undermine the efficacy of health-based standards. For example, as discussed in Chapter 5, the original hazardous air pollutants section of the Clean Air Act—which relied on health-based standards—was notably unsuccessful. Aware that implementation of the section would shut down major segments of American industry, EPA largely circumvented it by refusing to designate pollutants as "hazardous." Broadly speaking, the last two decades have seen a shift away from reliance on health-based standards.

### b. Feasibility Standards

A second risk management approach is to safeguard public health, but only so far as is "feasible" given technological, economic, and other constraints. This view is reflected in a variety of federal statutes, including the:

- Clean Water Act standards for toxic water pollutants (§ 301(b)(2)(A): use of "the best available technology economically achievable");
- Clean Air Act standards for hazardous air pollutants (§ 112(d)(2): the "maximum degree of reduction * * * achievable");
- Occupational Safety and Health Act standards for "toxic materials" (§ 6(b)(5): regulation which "most adequately assures, to the extent feasible, * * * that no employee will suffer material impairment of health or functional capacity").

These standards typically protect public health only within the statutorily-defined limit of "feasibility." For example, under the feasibility approach used by the Occupational Safety and Health Act to ensure work place safety (discussed in Chapter 4), a ban on exomine use in bakeries might not be economically feasible; a ban would bankrupt most bakeries. Conversely, this approach might mandate the installation of new, expensive technology capable of reducing exomine concentrations which harm bakery workers. Although this requirement would increase the price of bread, it is both technologically and economically feasible.

Feasibility standards are sometimes attacked as condoning avoidable health risks. Yet because they are more easily implemented than health-based standards, many commentators conclude that feasibility standards ultimately provide better health protection.

### c. Cost-Benefit Standards

Under the cost-benefit analysis approach, regulation is appropriate only when its benefits outweigh its costs. It is the predominant risk management standard encountered in federal environmental law, particularly statutes governing hazardous wastes and toxic substances. Thus, for example, as discussed in Chapter 3, cost-benefit analysis is the basic approach utilized by FIFRA in deciding to allow market access for pesticides. Similarly, as explained in Chapter 9, although public health protection and a number of other goals must normally be considered in determining the level of required cleanup under CERCLA, the particular remedy selected must also be "cost-effective."

Despite its widespread use, cost-benefit analysis suffers from several weaknesses. The underlying assumption that all benefits and risks can be quantified is often flawed, due to lack of data, scientific uncertainty, or other causes. Moreover, in most cases, the costs of regulation (e.g., expense of adding new equipment or changing production methods) are comparatively easier to compute than health benefits; the risk posed by hazardous wastes and toxic substances is often difficult to establish. This disparity tends to skew the analysis against regulation.

Most fundamentally, any attempt to weigh financial costs against human health benefits (or environmental protection) presents the extraordinarily difficult policy question of where to strike the balance. For example, is regulation of exomine justified if it costs $50 million for each human life saved? Alternatively, if an exomine ban would save an endangered frog species but cost $100 million, how should EPA respond?

## D. THE JUDICIAL REACTION TO RISK REGULATION

The actions of EPA and other agencies in regulating the risks posed by hazardous wastes and toxic substances are, of course, subject to judicial review. Yet courts have proven far more supportive of such regulation than the traditional common law approach might suggest. Two factors explain this difference. First, courts acknowledge that the federal statutes on the subject were intended by Congress as preventive legislation. Thus, they will uphold administrative regulation even where the likelihood of future harm cannot be proven. Second, the judicial function in this arena is usually to review administrative action, not to make an independent decision. Thus, consistent with standard administrative law doctrine, courts typically use a deferential standard of review in evaluating agency decisions.

The D.C. Circuit's 1976 decision in Ethyl Corp. v. EPA, 541 F.2d 1 (D.C.Cir.1976) symbolized the new judicial willingness to protect against risk. Applying a health-based Clean Air Act standard, which allowed regulation of substances that "will endanger the public health or welfare," EPA ordered a reduction in the amount of lead in gasoline. Challenging the order, manufacturers of lead additives argued that this section allowed EPA to regulate only if it could prove that the lead emissions in auto exhaust caused actual harm. The court responded:

> Case law and dictionary definition agree that endanger means something less than actual harm. * * * A statute allowing for regulation in the face of danger is, necessarily, a precautionary statute. Regulatory action must be taken before the threatened harm occurs. * * * Where a statute is precautionary in nature, the evidence difficult to come by, uncertain, or conflicting because it is on the frontiers of scientific knowledge, the regulations designed to protect the public health, and the decision that of an expert administrator, we will not demand rigorous step-by-step proof of cause and effect.

See also Reserve Mining Co. v. EPA, 514 F.2d 492 (8th Cir.1975) (holding, in part, that discharges of wastes containing asbestos-like fibers into Lake Superior should be enjoined under a similar health-based Clean Water Act provision, even though "it cannot be said that the probability of harm is more likely than not").

Despite that promising beginning, the extent of judicial deference to regulatory actions concerning chemical substances remains largely uncharted. Indeed, as discussed in more detail in later chapters, courts have invalidated many high-profile regulatory efforts in the area. For example, the Consumer Product Safety Commission's ban on urea-formaldehyde foam insulation—the product of a 6 year investigation—was annulled in Gulf South Insulation v. CPSC, 701 F.2d 1137 (5th Cir.1983). EPA's asbestos ban—which resulted from a 10 year study—was invalidated in Corrosion Proof Fittings v. EPA, 947 F.2d 1201 (5th Cir.1991). And the Supreme Court canceled the Occupational Safety and Health Administration's benzene restrictions in Industrial Union Department, AFL-CIO v. American Petroleum Institute, 448 U.S. 607, 100 S.Ct. 2844, 65 L.Ed.2d 1010 (1980).

Yet the Supreme Court's 2007 decision in Massachusetts v. EPA, 549 U.S. 497, 127 S.Ct. 1438, 167 L.Ed.2d 248 (2007), may signal a new judicial approach to scientific uncertainty. There, EPA refused to regulate greenhouse gases, in part because of incomplete data. The Court responded: "Nor can EPA avoid its statutory obligation [to regulate] by noting the uncertainty surrounding various aspects of climate change and concluding that it would therefore be better not to regulate at this time. If the scientific uncertainty is so profound that it precludes EPA from making a reasoned judgment as to whether greenhouse gases contribute to global warming, EPA must say so. That EPA would prefer not to regulate greenhouse gases because of some residual uncertainty . . . is irrelevant." See also Gulf Restoration Network v.

McCarthy, 783 F.3d 227, 239 (9th Cir. 2015) (observing that EPA cannot "resort to general claims of scientific uncertainty—if it justifies its refusal to make a threshold determination on that basis, it must be explicit about what uncertainty is present").

# CHAPTER 3

# REGULATING THE PRODUCTION AND SALE OF TOXIC SUBSTANCES

## A. OVERVIEW

The foundation of toxic substance regulation is market access control. Pesticides and many other toxic substances are manufactured as valuable products. Consider lemdipyle, a hypothetical pesticide that is successfully used to eradicate aphids, beetles, moths, and similar insects from almost 100 food crops. Yet lemdipyle is so toxic to humans and other mammals that even a comparatively low dose can cause death; it is a leading cause of farm worker poisoning. Under what circumstances should we allow the manufacture and sale of deadly products like lemdipyle?

Two key federal statutes regulate the entry of toxic substances into the market: the Federal Insecticide, Fungicide, and Rodenticide Act (FIFRA), dealing with pesticides, and the Toxic Substances Control Act (TSCA), covering most other chemical substances. Despite significant differences, these "gatekeeper" statutes share certain features:

- both require notice to EPA before manufacture of the product may begin;
- both provide for the submission of test data and other product information to EPA; and
- both permit EPA to prohibit or restrict market access for new and existing products.

Most federal environmental law is oriented toward dealing with toxic substances as *wastes* (e.g., under RCRA, CERCLA, the Clean Water Act, and the Clean Air Act). Market access control statutes such as FIFRA and TSCA focus instead on *products*. This focus offers several advantages as a strategy for regulating toxic substances. In many instances, it is the most effective means to prevent irreparable "downstream" injury such as loss of human life or major environmental degradation; if a product never reaches the market, it cannot cause harm. This approach also reduces the burden of hazardous waste cleanup; if a product never reaches the market, it cannot become a waste. Enforcement is facilitated because the number of producers is small; and local political opposition is minimized because this technique does not involve land use restrictions. Finally, because market access is inextricably linked to interstate commerce, the constitutional basis for federal regulation is well-established. Despite the theoretical strengths of the technique, however, in practice both FIFRA and TSCA have proven disappointing.

## B. PESTICIDES: THE FEDERAL INSECTICIDE, FUNGICIDE, AND RODENTICIDE ACT (FIFRA)

### 1. INTRODUCTION

Pesticide regulation presents a classic paradox: to what extent should we *protect* the environment against substances designed to *alter* the environment? Pesticides are specialized toxic substances which are intentionally introduced into the environment in order to kill or otherwise affect particular plant or animal species. Most pesticides, however, are toxic to both the "target pests" and a wide spectrum of non-target species, sometimes including humans. Over *a billion pounds* of pesticides are used in the United States each year.

Pesticide use in the United States escalated rapidly after World War II as DDT and similar products resulting from wartime research dramatically increased crop yields. In 1947, Congress enacted the Federal Insecticide, Fungicide, and Rodenticide Act, 7 U.S.C.A. § 136 et seq. Like its ancestor, the Insecticide Act of 1910, FIFRA was first enacted as a consumer protection measure, with no concern for environmental protection. This original FIFRA was designed to serve two goals: (1) ensuring that the pesticide performed its intended function (e.g., that it was sufficiently toxic to kill the target pest); and (2) protecting the health of the pesticide user through label instructions. In effect, the statute assumed that pesticides endangered only farmers or other users. Although FIFRA required that pesticide products be "registered" with the Department of Agriculture, this requirement was toothless; the Department did not have the legal right to refuse registration. Little was known at this time about the long term effects of pesticides on human health and the environment in general. For example, in Murphy v. Benson, 164 F.Supp. 120 (E.D.N.Y.1958), a federal district court refused to enjoin the aerial spraying of DDT over suburbs of Long Island, New

York despite the vigorous protests of affected residents.

In 1962, Rachel Carson's landmark book *Silent Spring* awakened the American public to both the dangers of pesticides and the inadequacy of existing law. Congress added teeth to FIFRA in 1964 by empowering the Department of Agriculture to refuse registration or to cancel existing registrations. Enforcement authority was transferred to the new Environmental Protection Agency in 1970. A series of later amendments—most notably the Federal Environmental Pesticide Control Act of 1972—reshaped FIFRA into its present form: the main federal statute regulating pesticides to protect human health and the environment.

FIFRA is now primarily a *product licensing statute*. Just as a person cannot drive a car without obtaining a license, § 3(a) provides that a pesticide may not be sold or distributed in the United States unless it is "registered" with EPA. The registration decision hinges on cost-benefit analysis. Thus, EPA will safeguard public health and the environment by denying or conditioning registration when the benefits of regulation exceed its costs.

FIFRA's most innovative feature is its approach to the problem of scientific uncertainty: *it assigns the burden of proving the safety of a pesticide to the applicant*. This provides industry with an incentive to develop new data, imposes the costs of producing data on the applicant, and permits EPA to protect against unknown risks by refusing registration if adequate data cannot be developed. In this way, scientific uncertainty cuts against market access under FIFRA.

FIFRA contains two other main components:

- *Labeling Requirements*: Each pesticide must bear an EPA-approved label that describes the risks it poses, instructions on proper use, and other information.
- *Use Restrictions*: FIFRA regulates the use of pesticides in several ways. First, use of a pesticide in a manner inconsistent with the label directions is illegal. Second, particularly hazardous pesticides are registered for "restricted use" only; they may be applied only by "certified applicators." Finally, regulations promulgated under FIFRA mandate procedures to protect farm workers from pesticide exposure.

At bottom, FIFRA is an uneasy compromise between two fundamentally opposite views. Its original version was devoted to conquering nature by ensuring that pesticides were sufficiently deadly; thus, one strand of FIFRA, as Professor William Rodgers observed, "perceives nature as the enemy." The 1972 FIFRA amendments, in contrast, were oriented toward environmental protection; they added a new FIFRA strand which views nature as inherently valuable. FIFRA's efficacy as an environmental protection statute remains handicapped by this internal tension.

## 2. WHAT IS A "PESTICIDE"?

The jurisdictional heart of FIFRA is the term "pesticide." FIFRA regulates "pesticides," while the sale and distribution of other chemical substances are governed by parallel legislation, most notably TSCA. (Although FIFRA also regulates "devices" which have the same purpose as pesticides—for example, rodent traps—the discussion below focuses on pesticides.) Section 2(u) broadly defines a pesticide as including "any substance or mixture of substances" which is: (1) "intended for preventing, destroying, repelling, or mitigating any pest;" or (2) "intended for use as a plant regulator, defoliant, or desiccant." Thus, this definition concerns only the *intended use* of the substance, not its *inherent toxicity*.

Two key parts of this standard merit discussion: "pest" and "intended." Reflecting FIFRA's agricultural heritage, "pest" is defined in § 2(t) to include any insect, rodent, nematode (a type of worm), fungus, or weed. In addition, FIFRA grants EPA the power to designate almost *any living thing* as a pest. EPA has exercised this authority not by issuing a list of individual "pests," but rather by declaring almost every plant and animal species (other than humans) to be a "pest" when it exists under circumstances that make it "deleterious" to humans or the environment. Thus, for example, crop-damaging insects, household cockroaches, swimming pool algae, garden-eating snails, and natural vegetation which hinders agriculture are all "pests." Genetically modified organisms intended for pesticidal use are also included within this definition.

Unfortunately, FIFRA fails to explain the meaning of "intended," the second key term in the definition of pesticide. Two questions thus arise: (1) whose intent is relevant? and (2) what is intent? Regulations adopted by EPA specify that this element concerns the intent of the manufacturer, seller, or distributor, not the intent of the product user. Further, these regulations expand the meaning of "intent" to include mere knowledge of pesticidal use. Thus, any of the following establishes the requisite intent: (1) the statement or implication (from labeling or otherwise) that the product can be used as a pesticide; (2) the product's lack of any significant commercially valuable use other than as a pesticide; or (3) actual or constructive knowledge that the product will be used as a pesticide. As the Third Circuit explained in N. Jonas & Co., Inc. v. EPA, 666 F.2d 829 (3d Cir.1981), under FIFRA the manufacturer "intends those uses to which the reasonable consumer will put its products."

In short, the definition of pesticide under FIFRA extends well beyond the agricultural context. Using the standards discussed above, products such as household air purifiers and swimming pool additives have been held to be pesticides subject to FIFRA regulation. Over 16,000 pesticide products are currently registered under FIFRA.

## 3. THE REGISTRATION PROCESS

### a. Registration Procedure

Registration is the core of FIFRA. It allows EPA to control whether a pesticide is distributed or sold—and thus used—in the United States.

The registration process begins with the submission of an application to EPA. In addition to basic information about the applicant and the pesticide, the application must include (1) the proposed labeling and (2) enough scientific data to allow EPA to determine whether the pesticide meets the standards for registration. Such scientific data may consist of *either* the results of testing performed by the applicant *or* citations to data already available to EPA (in public literature or in other applications previously submitted). Although § 3(c)(3) requires EPA to rule on applications "as expeditiously as possible," the process often requires years to complete.

The type of scientific data required depends on the proposed use, e.g., terrestrial food crop use, aquatic non-crop use, or forestry use. 40 C.F.R. § 158.202 et seq. The typical applicant must submit data on the toxicity of the product to humans and domestic animals, including the results from acute (high dose, short-term exposure), chronic (prolonged and repeated exposure), and subchronic (repeated exposure over short period) testing. The applicant may also be required to provide information on the following aspects of its product: (a) residue chemistry (the amount of pesticide residue which will remain on crops); (b) environmental fate (including exposure rate of non-target organisms); (c) reentry protection (data needed to assess hazards to farm employees from reentry into treated areas); (d) spray drift evaluation; and (e) toxicity to non-target organisms. In general, FIFRA allows the applicant to rely on the scientific data base which EPA has established containing information submitted in past applications. Data submitted by one applicant is often relevant to evaluating a later application by a second applicant, such as when the two pesticides are similar in content and use. An applicant can avoid sharing trade secrets and other "confidential business information," however, by complying with procedures outlined in § 10.

To avoid concern that the data sharing program violates the Fifth Amendment as an uncompensated taking of property rights in information, under some circumstances FIFRA requires the new applicant to compensate the original data submitter for use of the information. The Supreme Court upheld the constitutionality of these provisions in Ruckelshaus v. Monsanto Co., 467 U.S. 986, 104 S.Ct. 2862, 81 L.Ed.2d 815 (1984). Although acknowledging the trial court's finding that development of a potential commercial pesticide "typically requires the expenditure of $5 million to $15 million annually for several years," the Court dismissed Monsanto's claim that FIFRA did not ensure it full compensation. The Court reasoned that Monsanto chose to develop and submit its data with full knowledge of these provisions, and thus did not have "reasonable investment-backed expectations" at stake. Further, the Court observed that because the conditions under which FIFRA data was submitted were rationally related to the legitimate government purpose of pesticide regulation, Monsanto's "voluntary submissions of data * * * in exchange for the economic advantages of a registration can hardly be called a taking."

## b. New Registrations

A pesticide containing a new active ingredient is the most difficult to register. Because EPA typically lacks enough existing data to evaluate the environmental effects of a wholly new product, the registration process can be both expensive and lengthy. The development of test data alone may cost up to $5 million for the average new pesticide. Even when the required testing is complete, as a general rule EPA will only register a new pesticide on a conditional basis. The 1996 amendments added a new registration category qualifying for expedited review—the "minor use" registration. The registration of a new pesticide for a minor use must be approved or denied within 12 months after the application is complete.

Two other types of new product registrations, however, are easier to secure: the "new use" registration and the "me too" registration. The "new use" registration arises when a new pesticide contains an active ingredient which is already registered but for a different use than that proposed for the product. For example, an active ingredient registered for use in forests might be incorporated into a pesticide intended for use in wetlands. Under these circumstances, EPA refers to existing information to help evaluate the application. Also, when a new product and its proposed use are identical or substantially similar to a currently registered pesticide, EPA can rely on the existing data base to evaluate the product's effects; the process for such a "me too" registration is comparatively simple.

### 4. REGISTRATION STANDARDS

EPA must register a pesticide under § 3(c)(5) if four requirements are met:

- its composition warrants the proposed claims for it;
- its labeling and other submitted material comply with FIFRA standards;
- it will perform its intended function without causing "unreasonable adverse effects on the environment;" and
- when used in accordance with widespread and commonly recognized practice, it will not generally cause "unreasonable adverse effects on the environment."

As noted above, the applicant has the burden of proving that its pesticide meets these standards.

#### a. Product Composition

The first requirement—that the composition of the pesticide warrants the claims proposed for it—

reflects FIFRA's consumer protection origin; it has little connection with environmental quality. The central question is whether the product is as effective in controlling pests as the proposed labeling asserts (e.g., as deadly as advertised).

### b. Labeling

The labeling requirement is the historic cornerstone of FIFRA. Although its efficacy has been strongly questioned, in theory labeling serves the twin goals of consumer protection and environmental conservation. It informs the pesticide user how to apply the product for maximum pest control with minimum personal risk. However, EPA's approval of a label is not a representation that the pesticide is safe. See, e.g., In re StarLink Corn Products Liability Litigation, 212 F.Supp.2d 828 (N.D.Ill.2002). Labeling also sets forth any warnings or restrictions on pesticide use which EPA has imposed to protect the environment (e.g., a prohibition on aquatic use). Because FIFRA mandates that the pesticide user follow the label instructions, labeling allows EPA to regulate pesticide use.

Under § 2(p), "labeling" includes any written, printed, or graphic matter on, attached to, or accompanying the pesticide, its wrapping, or its container. Extensive regulations promulgated under FIFRA impose precise, detailed labeling standards. For example, when use of the pesticide might pose a hazard to non-target organisms or the environment in general, the label must include specific warnings describing the nature of the hazard and the appropriate precautions to avoid injury. Similarly, the label's use directions must describe the target pests, the appropriate application sites, the dosage rates, the method and timing of application, storage instructions, and any other statement which EPA deems proper to prevent unreasonable adverse effects. The labeling requirements for "restricted use" pesticides are more extensive than those for "general use" pesticides.

### c. Effect on the Environment

FIFRA's environmental protection mandate is expressed in the last two § 3(c)(5) criteria. Collectively, they require that the pesticide, when used in accordance with "widespread and commonly recognized practice," perform its intended function without causing "unreasonable adverse effects on the environment." § 3(c)(5)(C), (D). The phrase "unreasonable adverse effects on the environment" is in turn defined by § 2(bb) as "any unreasonable risk to man or the environment, taking into account the economic, social, and environmental costs and benefits" of using the pesticide. This definition is the source of FIFRA's cost-benefit standard. A cost-benefit analysis is required to determine whether the adverse environmental effects of a pesticide are "unreasonable." Under this test, even a pesticide which will clearly injure the environment may still be registered if its anticipated harm is outweighed by economic, social, or other benefits.

Two exceptions to this standard were added through amendments in 1996. One exception involves food safety; if the pesticide residues in or on any food exceed the tolerance levels set forth in 21 U.S.C.A. § 346a (part of the Federal Food, Drug, and Cosmetics Act, discussed in Chapter 4), this presents a "human dietary risk." Such a dietary risk is deemed an "unreasonable adverse effect on the environment" based on health considerations alone, without cost-benefit analysis. The second exception relates to "public health pesticides," defined as any "minor use" pesticide used predominantly in public health programs; in evaluating whether such a pesticide produces an unreasonable adverse effect, EPA must weigh any risks of the pesticide against the health risks stemming from non-use (e.g., diseases transmitted by the insect or other "vector" which the pesticide controls).

## 5. TERMINATING REGISTRATIONS

Registration does not confer a perpetual license. Environmental risk may justify temporary suspension and permanent cancellation of a registration. Indeed, public awareness of FIFRA largely stems from a series of high-profile disputes concerning efforts to suspend or cancel the registrations for pesticides such as DDT, aldrin, dieldrin, heptachlor, and chlordane. Although these controversies have generated most of the appellate decisions interpreting FIFRA, only a small number of registrations have actually been canceled or suspended due to environmental risk.

Section 3(g) requires EPA to "periodically review" each registration to determine if cancellation is warranted; the current goal is to review each registration every 15 years.

### a. Suspension

A suspension is a temporary order which bans the sale or distribution of a pesticide until a cancellation hearing can occur; it is analogous to the preliminary injunction in civil litigation. Suspension is appropriate only when necessary to prevent an "imminent hazard" before the cancellation hearing. § 6(c)(1). Under § 2(*l*), an imminent hazard exists if interim use of the pesticide would be likely to result in "unreasonable adverse effects on the environment." This is the same cost-benefit standard utilized in evaluating applications for initial registration. In addition, an imminent hazard will be found if such interim use would present an "unreasonable hazard" to the survival of species deemed endangered or threatened under the Endangered Species Act, 16 U.S.C.A. § 1531 et seq. A suspension order does not take effect until at least five days after the registrant has received notice of the intended suspension and an opportunity for an administrative hearing. The registrant's request for a hearing will stay the suspension order. Suspension hearings are required to be "expedited," but in practice can take months to complete.

The suspension process is illustrated by Environmental Defense Fund, Inc. v. EPA, 548 F.2d 998 (D.C.Cir.1976), which affirmed an EPA order suspending the registrations of heptachlor and chlordane. There, a pesticide manufacturer attacked EPA's reliance on laboratory studies which demonstrated that high doses of these pesticides caused cancer in rodents; it argued that animal study data could not be applied to humans. The D.C. Circuit reasoned, however, that EPA's showing that the pesticides caused cancer in laboratory animals—coupled with the widespread presence of these pesticides in human tissue—created an inference that they posed a cancer hazard to humans; the burden then shifted to the manufacturer to rebut this inference. In short, an "imminent hazard" is a risk—not a certainty—that harm will occur. Similarly, the court noted that once risk was shown, "the responsibility to demonstrate that the benefits outweigh the risk is upon the proponents of continued registration."

In an emergency, § 6(c)(3) allows EPA to issue a suspension order without prior notice to the applicant. See, e.g., Dow Chemical Co. v. Blum, 469 F.Supp. 892 (E.D.Mich.1979) (finding that EPA made no "clear error of judgment" in its analysis, court affirms emergency ban of two herbicides).

### b. Cancellation

Because cancellation is the mirror image of registration, the cancellation standard in § 6(b) essentially duplicates the two key elements in the initial registration standard. EPA may cancel a pesticide registration if either: (1) its labeling fails to comply with FIFRA requirements; or (2) when used in accordance with "widespread and commonly recognized practice," it "generally causes unreasonable adverse effects on the environment." In addition, EPA must consider the impact of cancellation on the production and prices of agricultural commodities, including retail food prices.

The most common basis for seeking cancellation is the pesticide's effect on the environment. The vague cost-benefit standard outlined above gives EPA broad discretion in the cancellation process. The leading decision interpreting this standard is Ciba-Geigy Corp. v. EPA, 874 F.2d 277 (5th Cir.1989). In that case, a manufacturer challenged EPA's decision to cancel the registration of diazinon for controlling insects on golf courses and sod farms due to concern about its effect on birds. The manufacturer argued that the term "generally" in the statutory standard meant that cancellation was appropriate only if the pesticide caused adverse effects "most of the time it is used." The Fifth Circuit rejected this assertion and concluded that cancellation is proper if a pesticide commonly causes a significant probability that adverse consequences may occur. Thus, a "significant risk of bird kills, even if birds are actually killed infrequently, may justify the Administrator's decision to ban or restrict diazinon use."

### 6. REPORTING REQUIREMENTS

Once a pesticide is registered, § 6(a)(2) directs the registrant to report to EPA any later information it obtains regarding whether the product causes unreasonable adverse effects on the environment. In theory, EPA can then consider this information in deciding whether to suspend or cancel the registration.

For example, if new toxicological or epidemiological studies indicate that a pesticide presents a greater risk than previously believed, this data must be reported. Further, consumer complaints or other information indicating that the pesticide has caused injury to humans or non-target species must similarly be reported to EPA, unless they are "demonstrably inaccurate."

### 7. ENFORCEMENT

Under § 23(a), EPA has delegated its enforcement authority to most states pursuant to cooperative agreements. Thus, state government typically has the principal responsibility to enforce FIFRA. In such states, EPA takes enforcement action only in emergency situations or when the state has failed to act after receiving notice of a violation.

Unlike most other federal environmental statutes, FIFRA does not contain an express citizens' suit provision. After exploring the legislative history of FIFRA, the Ninth Circuit held in Fiedler v. Clark, 714 F.2d 77 (9th Cir.1983) that members of the public cannot enforce it through direct suit against violators. However, citizens generally may sue EPA in federal district court to challenge its non-discretionary decisions under FIFRA. § 16(a). But federal courts of appeals have exclusive jurisdiction over controversies concerning the validity of pesticide registration orders under some circumstances, such as where registration follows a public hearing. Center for Biological Diversity v. EPA, 861 F.3d 174 (D.C. Cir.2017).

The three most commonly used FIFRA remedies—notices of warning; civil penalties; and stop sale, use, or removal orders—require only administrative action. EPA normally issues a notice of warning for minor violations, such as those which do not result in health or environmental damage. For significant violations, EPA typically files administrative proceedings under § 14(a), seeking civil penalties which range up to $5,000 per violation. In addition, if inspection or testing gives EPA reason to believe that FIFRA has been violated, it may issue a § 13(a) stop sale, use, or removal order. This prevents the affected person from selling, using, or removing the pesticide except in compliance with the order. Although FIFRA authorizes EPA to sue violators in district court for an injunction (§ 16(c)) or seizure order (§ 13(b)), this procedure is rarely used. The stop sale, use, or removal order is easier to obtain and provides essentially the same relief.

Further, § 14(b) provides that a person who "knowingly" violates FIFRA may be subject to criminal penalties of up to a $50,000 fine plus one year in prison. In United States v. Corbin Farm Service, 444 F.Supp. 510 (E.D.Cal.1978), where defendants killed over 1,000 waterfowl by applying a pesticide in violation of its label instructions, the court interpreted "knowingly" to require only general intent. Thus, the United States was required to prove only that defendants knew they were spraying a pesticide on the field, not that the defendants also knew they were violating the label instructions.

## 8. EVALUATING FIFRA

In practice, FIFRA has proven a somewhat effective tool for pesticide regulation. On the positive side, the systematic evaluation of environmental effects which it mandates, together with allocation of the proof burden to the applicant, have certainly prohibited or restricted dangerous products. Further, its mere existence has reoriented industry efforts toward the development of more environmentally-protective pesticides.

Yet experience has also demonstrated FIFRA's shortcomings. The pace of regulation is slow: EPA has suspended, canceled, or restricted only a handful of pesticides over FIFRA's entire history.

Another controversial aspect of FIFRA is that most of its provisions do not apply to pesticides manufactured for export. Even pesticides whose sale or distribution is illegal in the United States can be produced here for sale abroad, with minimal restrictions. In recent years, up to 25% of exported pesticides were either unregistered or prohibited for use in the United States.

## C. PESTICIDES: STATE AND LOCAL REGULATION

State and local laws regulating pesticides have proliferated in recent years, especially in light of FIFRA's perceived weaknesses. FIFRA § 24(a) generally allows states to regulate the sale or use of pesticides more strictly than federal law. Some states have established pesticide registration systems which impose more rigorous standards than FIFRA. However, to avoid undue burden on interstate commerce, § 24(b) prohibits state regulation concerning labeling. The preemptive reach of FIFRA, as explored in numerous decisions, is relatively short.

The boundary between "sale/use" and "labeling" regulation has proven elusive. For example, in Chemical Specialties Manufacturers Association, Inc. v. Allenby, 958 F.2d 941 (9th Cir.1992), a trade organization argued that FIFRA preempted California's Proposition 65, a statute which requires businesses to warn consumers of the risks of certain toxic substances, including many pesticides (see Chapter 4). The Ninth Circuit observed, however, that the statutory definition of "labeling" did not "encompass every type of written material accompanying the pesticide." Because the required warning could be provided through signs posted in the store, newspaper advertisements, and other non-labeling methods, the court upheld the state law.

The Supreme Court considered the permissible scope of non-federal sale and use regulation in

Wisconsin Public Intervenor v. Mortier, 501 U.S. 597, 111 S.Ct. 2476, 115 L.Ed.2d 532 (1991). There, a Wisconsin town enacted an ordinance which required a permit for certain pesticide uses within its borders. Plaintiff Mortier sued after the town denied his permit application and argued that FIFRA preempted the local ordinance. The Court concluded, however:

> [T]he statute leaves ample room for States and localities to supplement federal efforts * * *. * * * FIFRA nowhere seeks to establish an affirmative permit system for the actual use of pesticides. It certainly does not equate registration and labeling requirements with a general approval to apply pesticides throughout the Nation without regard to regional and local factors like climate, population, geography, and water supply.

The Court further noted that the preemption standards in § 24(a) applied only to states, not to local governments. Thus, it reasoned that FIFRA did not expressly or impliedly supersede local regulation of pesticide use.

In Bates v. Dow Agrosciences LLC, 544 U.S. 431, 125 S.Ct. 1788, 161 L.Ed.2d 687 (2005), the Supreme Court brought new clarity to the scope of federal preemption. In this case, a pesticide intended to kill weeds also injured the users' peanut crops. When the plaintiffs sued on a variety of state law theories—including strict liability, negligent manufacture, negligent failure to warn, fraud, and breach of warranty—the defendant manufacturer asserted that all these claims were preempted by the § 24(b) prohibition on state labeling requirements. Defendant's theory was that an adverse judgment would force it to alter its product label, an indirect form of state regulation. The Court explained that for a state law to be preempted, it must be (a) a requirement for "labeling or packaging" that (b) imposed a requirement "in addition to or different from" those required under FIFRA. Under this standard, the Court found that the state laws governing strict liability, negligent manufacture, and breach of warranty were not preempted, simply because they did not *require* manufacturers to label or package their products in any particular manner. Conversely, it concluded that the fraud and failure to warn claims were based on common law rules that did qualify as requirements for labeling and packaging; however, it remanded the case on these claims to determine if the second preemption element was satisfied.

## D. OTHER CHEMICAL SUBSTANCES: THE TOXIC SUBSTANCES CONTROL ACT (TSCA)

### 1. INTRODUCTION

The Toxic Substances Control Act, 15 U.S.C.A. § 2601 et seq., was enacted in 1976 as the first comprehensive statute to regulate the manufacture, distribution, and processing of chemical substances, in order to protect public health and the environment. It was intended to fill the regulatory gaps left by FIFRA and similar federal statutes, which concerned only particular categories of chemical products. TSCA is a classic "catch all" statute; if no other federal law regulates market access for a chemical substance, it is regulated under TSCA.

TSCA, as amended by the Frank R. Lautenberg Chemical Safety for the 21st Century Act in 2016, authorizes EPA to regulate new chemicals and evaluate the safety of existing chemicals. With these amendments, Congress significantly expanded EPA's authority in order to overcome problems that had hindered effective regulation of chemicals for decades. Under the revised TSCA, EPA must make an affirmative determination on the safety of a new chemical or significant new use of a chemical *before* it is allowed into the marketplace, bringing TSCA more in line with FIFRA. Moreover, EPA is empowered to determine if a proposed new chemical or use presents an "unreasonable risk" of injury to health or the environment *without* consideration of costs or other non-risk factors. Cost and availability of alternatives are considered later in the process, when EPA determines what actions to take to address any identified risks.

## 2. WHAT IS A "CHEMICAL SUBSTANCE"?

The jurisdictional reach of TSCA is extraordinarily broad, extending to any "chemical substance" or "mixture." Section 3(2) defines "chemical substance" as "any organic or inorganic substance of a particular molecular identity * * *." It then excludes substances already regulated under other federal statutes such as pesticides (FIFRA), foods, drugs, and cosmetics (FFDCA), nuclear material (AEA), and "mixtures" from the definition. Section 3(8) defines "mixture" as "any combination of two or more chemical substances" which does not occur in nature and is not the result of a chemical reaction. In effect, TSCA is potentially applicable to almost *every form of matter*, whether natural or artificial, except for certain substances regulated elsewhere. Thus, water would be considered a "chemical substance" under the above definition. For convenience, the discussion below uses the phrase "chemical substance" as shorthand for both "chemical substance" and "mixture." Literally, of course, "chemical substance" also includes life forms, and thus TSCA applies to genetically-modified organisms produced through biotechnology.

TSCA divides all chemical substances into two categories: existing chemical substances and "new chemical substances." As initially enacted, § 8(b) directed EPA to compile and maintain a list of all chemical substances that were "manufactured or processed" in the United States. When completed in 1980, the inventory included approximately 62,000 existing substances. Any substance that was first manufactured or processed after 1980 (and thus not included in the initial TSCA inventory) was deemed a "new chemical substance," subject to more stringent regulation. Since 1980, over 32,000 new chemical substances have been added to the inventory. Yet many of the chemicals in this inventory are no longer used in commerce. Accordingly, the revised TSCA directed EPA to (1) identify which chemicals in the inventory are active or inactive, and (2) subsequently keep these designations current. § 8(b)(4), (5). The TSCA Inventory Reset, as it is known, is intended to allow EPA to focus its regulatory efforts on "active" chemicals—those in commerce today—and to identify chemical substances for which claims of confidential business information are no longer relevant.

An important 2016 amendment addresses risks to vulnerable subpopulations. It defines "potentially exposed or susceptible subpopulations" to include "infants, children, pregnant women, women, the elderly," who may be at greater risk from chemicals due to either greater susceptibility or greater exposure. § 3(12). EPA is obligated to ensure that restrictions are sufficient to protect these subpopulations when it (1) evaluates new chemical substances under § 5 and (2) regulates existing chemical substances under § 6. §§ 5(e)(1)(A), 5(f)(1), 6(a), 6(b)(4)(A).

## 3. REGULATED PERSONS

The two main categories of actors regulated by TSCA are "manufacturers" and "processors." A "manufacturer" is a person who produces or manufactures a chemical substance in, or imports such a substance into, the United States. The definition of "processor" is much broader, extending to a wide range of non-chemical manufacturers and other businesses. Under § 3(13), "process" includes the "preparation" of a chemical substance or mixture for "distribution in commerce" either in "the same form or physical state as, or in a different form or physical state from, that in which it was received by the person so preparing such substance or mixture," or as "part of an article containing" the substance or mixture. Thus, for example, a paper towel manufacturer which incorporates formaldehyde into its product would be considered a "processor." Some sections of TSCA also apply to persons who "distribute" chemical substances in commerce.

## 4. THE TESTING PROGRAM

TSCA arms EPA with formidable powers to regulate the sale and distribution of chemical substances and mixtures. The 2016 amendments place new pressure on EPA to actually exercise these powers by imposing deadlines for it to both (1) test chemical substances and (2) take action when testing shows that a substance presents an "unreasonable risk."

Before the 2016 amendments, EPA rarely exercised its power to mandate testing. In fact, during the first three decades after TSCA was enacted, EPA required testing for fewer than 200 of the 62,000 existing chemicals in the inventory. Instead, it preferred to reach voluntary testing consent agreements with manufacturers and processors. As a result, the pace of regulation was slow.

Suppose that today EPA is considering restrictions on zaline, a hypothetical existing chemical substance. How can EPA obtain the test data necessary to determine, for example, whether zaline presents an "unreasonable risk" such that it can be regulated?

Under TSCA, EPA can require testing if it establishes that the threshold standards of § 4 are met in the individual case. If so, EPA may require the manufacturer or processor to test zaline according to EPA standards and to submit the resulting test data on health and environmental effects; the manufacturer or processor bears the expense of testing. EPA then uses this data in deciding whether to regulate the substance. EPA bears the burden of proving the need for both initial testing and ultimate regulation. Under the TSCA amendments, EPA must make regulatory decisions "based on the weight of the scientific evidence," in a manner "consistent with the best available science." § 26(h), (i).

Before the 2016 amendments, EPA had to adopt a rule in order to force a manufacturer to test a particular substance; such rulemaking was slow and costly. But the amendments significantly reduced this burden. Section 4(a) now provides that EPA shall **by rule, order, or consent agreement** require testing of a substance like zaline if:

- the manufacture, distribution, processing, use, or disposal of the substance or mixture "may present an unreasonable risk of injury to health or the environment,"

- there are insufficient data and experience upon which the effects of the manufacturing, distribution, processing, use, or disposal of the substance or mixture on health or the environment can be predicted; and
- testing of such substance or mixture is necessary to develop this data.

In contrast, EPA must follow the rulemaking approach if:

- the substance or mixture is, or will be, produced in substantial quantities and may enter the environment in substantial quantities or there may be significant human exposure to it;
- there are insufficient data and experience upon which the effects of the manufacturing, distribution, processing, use, or disposal of the substance or mixture on health or the environment can be predicted; and
- testing of such substance or mixture with respect to such effects is necessary to develop such data; and
- in the case of a mixture, the effects of a mixture's distribution, processing, use or disposal or combination thereof impacts on health or the environment may not be reasonably predicted by testing the chemical substances of the mixture.

Similarly, the amendments allow EPA to require the development of new information by rule, order, or consent agreement if necessary to review a notice under § 5, implement requirements under § 5(e) or § 5(f), perform a risk evaluation under § 6(b), and prioritize a chemical substance under § 6(b) within certain limitations. § 4(a)(2).

In the past, EPA rules mandating testing were regularly challenged by the affected manufacturers. In part, cost plays a role in motivating such challenges; the required tests may be quite expensive, ranging up to $2 million per substance. More fundamentally, however, given budget constraints, EPA may not be able to gather sufficient information to regulate a substance unless it can force testing by industry. Manufacturers accordingly have an incentive to resist required testing in order to escape regulation.

The leading decision interpreting former § 4 is Chemical Manufacturers Association v. EPA, 859 F.2d 977 (D.C.Cir.1988), where an industry group attacked an EPA rule requiring testing of 2-ethylhexanoic acid (EHA). The D.C. Circuit resoundingly rejected plaintiffs' challenge to the EPA finding that EHA presented an unreasonable risk of injury to health. *Chemical Manufacturers Association* sanctioned the broad exercise of EPA's § 4 authority by deferring to its interpretation on three central points:

- To establish an unreasonable risk EPA need merely demonstrate "a more-than-theoretical basis for suspecting" that humans are exposed to the substance and that the substance is sufficiently toxic at that exposure level to present such a risk.

- In this process, EPA is not required to produce direct evidence documenting human exposure; exposure may be inferred from the circumstances under which the substance is manufactured and used.
- Rare, brief human exposure may be enough to support a test rule; accordingly, a national survey which suggested that roughly 50 individuals might have occasional skin contact with EHA was sufficient to demonstrate exposure.

## 5. REGULATION OF EXISTING CHEMICAL SUBSTANCES

### a. Existing Substances Presenting an "Unreasonable Risk of Injury"

EPA's principal TSCA weapon for regulating existing chemical substances is § 6(a). When TSCA was enacted, it was believed that EPA would use this authority to review the 62,000 chemical substances already in use and impose appropriate restrictions. Yet during TSCA's first 28 years, EPA imposed restrictions on only *five* such substances (PCBs, CFCs, dioxin, hexavalent chromium, and asbestos). Moreover, the Fifth Circuit's decision in Corrosion Proof Fittings v. EPA, 947 F.2d 1201 (5th Cir.1991)—which largely invalidated EPA's asbestos ban by seizing on the statutory language that regulation must be the "least burdensome"—

severely undercut the practical utility of the section. This led many to question the viability of the entire program.

Therefore, one of the most significant changes in the 2016 amendments was a re-working of § 6. As amended, it imposes deadlines for prioritizing chemical substances for risk evaluation, for the completion of risk evaluations, for the adoption of regulations for chemicals presenting an unreasonable risk, and for compliance with these regulations. Moreover, Congress explicitly rejected the prior requirement that EPA use the regulatory technique that imposes the "least burdensome requirements." Instead, EPA must make regulatory decisions "based on the weight of the scientific evidence." § 26(i).

### *i. Prioritization and Risk Evaluation*

Due to shifting priorities, EPA's work on chemical regulation has been inconsistent. Under the prioritization framework mandated by the 2016 amendments, EPA was required to adopt a risk-based screening process within one year and use the process to identify chemical substances as (1) high-priority for risk evaluations or (2) low-priority for which no risk evaluation is currently warranted. §§ 6(b)(1)(A), (B). EPA adopted a final rule, Procedures for Prioritization of Chemicals for Risk Evaluation Under the Toxic Substances Control Act, which went into effect on Sept. 18, 2017, to implement prioritization. 82 Fed. Reg. 33753 (July 20, 2017). The rule has been challenged by various environmental and health advocate groups as failing to sufficiently uphold the best available science provisions in the revised TSCA.

The TSCA Work Plan for Chemical Assessments identifies existing chemicals having the highest potential for hazard and exposure, most recently updated in 2014. Section 6(b)(2)(A) requires that within six months after enactment of the 2016 amendments, EPA must be conducting risk evaluations for 10 chemicals from its 2014 Work Plan. Within three and a half years after enactment, EPA must be conducting risk evaluations on at least 20 high-priority substances, and have designated at least 20 chemical substances as low-priority. At least half of all the risk evaluations being conducted must be from the 2014 Work Plan. Risk evaluations are to be conducted on all high-priority chemical substances. § 6(b)(3). The risk evaluation process must be complete "as soon as practicable" but no later than three years after initiation, and the deadline can only be extended for a maximum of six months. §§ 6(b)(4)(G)(i), (ii). The law ensures ongoing designations by requiring that EPA "shall designate at least one high-priority substance upon the completion of each risk evaluation." § 6(b)(3)(C). To implement this program, EPA adopted a final rule, Procedures for Chemical Risk Evaluation Under the Amended Toxic Substances Control Act, which became effective Sept. 18, 2017. 82 Fed. Reg. 22726 (July 20, 2017). The rule has also been challenged by various environmental and health advocate groups for failing to follow the best available science standard in the revised TSCA.

### *ii. Promulgation of Rules*

Formerly EPA had authority to regulate chemical substances that posed an unreasonable risk, but action was not mandatory. The 2016 amendments provide that if EPA determines a chemical substance presents an unreasonable risk through the risk evaluation process, it *must* take action; specifically, it is required to impose restrictions (potentially including phase-outs or bans) "to the extent necessary so that the chemical no longer present such risk." § (6)(a). The amendments also impose deadlines for EPA to take action in this situation. After the final risk evaluation is published, EPA has one year to propose a rule under § 6(a), and two years to publish a final rule. §§ 6(c)(1)(A), (B). These deadlines may be extended for not more than two years. In addition, the deadlines for certain chemicals—those that (1) are persistent and bioaccumulate or (2) are on the 2014 Work Plan—cannot be extended unless EPA can demonstrate that additional information is needed to complete the regulatory process. § 6(c)(1)(C). These deadlines should put pressure on EPA to timely adopt rules.

Section 6(c) identifies the process for promulgating § 6(a) rules. Formerly EPA had to select the technique which will protect adequately against the risk "using the least burdensome requirements." Corrosion Proof Fittings v. EPA, 947 F.2d 1201 (5th Cir.1991). This standard severely hampered EPA's regulatory efforts. As amended in 2016, § 6(c)(2)(A) requires that in proposing and issuing a rule, EPA must publish a statement that addresses:

- Effects on human health and magnitude of exposure of human beings to the chemical substance or mixture;
- Effects on the environment and magnitude of exposure of the environment of the chemical substance or mixture;
- Benefits of the of the chemical substance or mixture;
- Economic effects of the rule, including
    - effects on the national economy, small business, innovation, health and environment;
    - costs and benefits of the proposed and final regulation and one or more alternatives;
    - cost effectiveness of the proposed and final regulation and one or more alternatives.

EPA must consider these factors "to the extent practicable" when selecting the appropriate regulatory technique. § 6(c)(2)(B). Section 6(a) directs that EPA regulate "to the extent necessary" so that the chemical substance no longer presents an unreasonable risk. When considering whether to phase out or ban a use of a substance, EPA is required to consider "whether technically and economically feasible alternatives that benefit health or the environment, compared to the use so proposed to be prohibited or restricted, will be reasonable available as a substitute." § 6(c)(2)(C).

Finally, compliance deadlines require that any rule should take effect "as soon as practicable." In no event can a deadline be set more than five years after the rule is finalized. § 6(d)(2).

### b. "Imminently Hazardous" Substances

In emergency situations, EPA can seek immediate judicial relief. Section 7 authorizes EPA action against "imminently hazardous" chemical substances and mixtures—those that present "an imminent and unreasonable risk of serious or widespread injury to health or the environment, notwithstanding costs or other nonrisk factors." § 7(f). By revising the definition of "imminently hazardous" substances, the 2016 amendments clarified that costs or nonrisk factors play no role in defining an imminent hazard. If the manufacture, processing, distribution, use or disposal of such a substance or mixture is likely to result in such injury before a rule can be issued under § 6, then EPA may bring a civil action, seeking relief that may include seizure, notice to purchasers, notice to the public, and recall, replacement or repurchase of the article. Section 7(b)(1) empowers the court to grant "such temporary or permanent relief as may be necessary" to protect public health or the environment.

Despite its similarity to FIFRA § 6(c)(1) (which allows the suspension of a registration when a pesticide poses an "imminent hazard"), EPA rarely used its TSCA § 7 authority before the 2016 amendments. Hopefully the amendments will encourage EPA to utilize § 7 more frequently.

### c. "Significant New Uses" of Existing Substances

Even though the historic uses of a substance may be innocuous, a new use of the substance may endanger human health or the environment. Accordingly, § 5(a) requires that a "significant new use notice" (SNUN) be submitted to EPA 90 days before manufacturing or processing certain substances for new uses, together with supporting test data. This requirement is triggered only if EPA has issued a regulation requiring notice for the category of new use involved, called a "significant new use rule" (SNUR).

EPA is required to make an affirmative risk determination for all new significant uses within this 90-day period. In theory, this period enables EPA to analyze whether any restrictions on the proposed new use are appropriate to avoid unreasonable risk to human health or the environment, pursuant to its § 6(a) or § 5(f) authority. Alternatively, EPA could determine more information is required to make an evaluation of risk and take action under § 5(e) by limiting or prohibiting the manufacture pending the development of further information. In practice, however, the 90-day period has proven too short to permit thorough evaluation by EPA in the past.

### d. Special Rules for PCBs

In enacting TSCA, Congress was aware that PCBs posed an immediate threat to humans and the environment. At the peak of production, about 80 million pounds of PCBs were manufactured each year in the United States for use as fire retardants or plastics components. Large quantities of PCBs were released into the environment annually, where they proved to be unusually persistent, bioaccumulative, and toxic. Accordingly, § 6(e) generally prohibits the manufacture, processing, distribution, or use of PCBs "in any manner other than a totally enclosed manner."

### e. Persistent, Bioaccumulative, and Toxic (PBT) Chemical Substances

Congress took aim at chemicals that are persistent, bioaccumulative, and toxic (PBT) in § 6(h) of revised TSCA. It requires EPA to take expedited action to propose rules for these substances within three years of enactment. § 6(h)(1). The rules must address the risk of injury to health or the environment that these chemical substances present and reduce exposure to such substances to the extent practicable. § 6(h)(4). The substances covered by this requirement are those in the 2014 TSCA Work Plan that meet two criteria:

- EPA has a reasonable basis to conclude they are toxic, and they score high for persistence or bioaccumulation; and

- Exposure is likely to the general population, or to a potentially exposed or susceptible subpopulation, or the environment. §§ 6(h)(1)(A) & (B).

## 6. REGULATION OF NEW CHEMICAL SUBSTANCES

EPA's power to regulate *new* chemical substances is broader than its authority over *existing* substances. In general, anyone who plans to produce a new chemical substance must provide EPA with a "premanufacture notice" (PMN) 90 days before manufacturing begins. § 5(a). During the 90-day period EPA decides whether to prohibit or restrict manufacturing, processing, distribution, use, or disposal of the substance. The 2016 amendments require that EPA review each PMN and make a determination that either (1) triggers action under §§ 6(b), 5(e), 5(f) *or* (2) supports the commencement of manufacturing.

### a. Premanufacture Notice

The PMN must set forth basic information concerning the new substance, including its chemical identity, trade name, anticipated maximum production volume, and intended types of uses. 40 C.F.R. § 720.45. In addition, the PMN must be accompanied by test data which demonstrates that the manufacture, processing, distribution, use and disposal of the new substance will not present an unreasonable risk of injury to health or the environment, but only if such data is already available to the submitter. EPA does not mandate that specific toxicity data be supplied with a PMN, and such information is rarely submitted. However, as previously noted, § 4 authorizes EPA to require testing by rule, order, or consent agreement when needed to assess a PMN under this section. EPA is required to make an affirmative determination that the chemical substance does not present an unreasonable risk before manufacturing can commence. § 5(a)(3). Short of this finding, EPA must use its other tools to regulate new chemical substances, as discussed below.

The information contained in a PMN and accompanying test data often includes trade secrets and other confidential material; § 14(c) allows the PMN submitter to protect such data from public disclosure by designating it as confidential. The amended TSCA limits presumptions of protection to the period before chemical substances enter the market; claims after market entry must be substantiated and reviewed by EPA. §§ 14(c)(2)(G), (c)(3).

### b. Restrictions on New Chemical Substances

TSCA provides EPA with three tools for regulating new chemical substances. First, if EPA determines a chemical substance presents an unreasonable risk it must take action under § 6(b) or § 5(f). If EPA has sufficient information and time, it can regulate the substance under its general § 6(a) authority discussed above. Second, if EPA has enough data to conclude that the substance will present an "unreasonable risk of injury" to human health or the environment before a § 6(a) rule can be promulgated, it can issue a "proposed rule" or a "proposed order" which temporarily bans or restricts the substance. § 5(f). In most instances, however, EPA's ability to evaluate a new chemical substance is impaired by both scant data and limited time. Nonetheless, § 5(e)—EPA's third tool—may provide a vehicle for regulation under these circumstances.

Before the 2016 amendments, § 5(e) applied if:

- the information available to EPA was insufficient to permit a reasoned evaluation of the health and environmental effects of the substance; *and*
- *either* (1) absent such information, the manufacture, processing, distribution, use, or disposal of the substance might present an unreasonable risk of injury without considerations of costs or other nonrisk factors *or* (2) the substance would be produced in substantial quantities and either would enter the environment in such quantities or may cause "significant or substantial human exposure."

If either of these was met, EPA could issue a proposed order that prohibited or limited the manufacture, processing, distribution, use, or disposal of the new substance. This step initiated a complex procedure, which could culminate in the imposition of restrictions by either a final EPA order or an injunction. The 2016 amendments appear to have broadened the scope of § 5(e) by allowing EPA to regulate based on insufficient information *alone.* § 5(e)(1)(A)(1).

Before the 2016 amendments, the § 5(e) procedure was rarely employed. For example, EPA formally imposed restrictions on only *four* new chemicals out of the roughly 32,000 chemicals it reviewed between 1976 and 2005. Instead, EPA typically used its § 5(e) authority as leverage to negotiate a consent order with the PMN submitter. Such consent orders typically: (a) suspended the 90-day review period; (b) restricted the new substance temporarily; and (c) required the submitter to conduct further testing on the substance and to supply the resulting data to EPA for further evaluation. With its 2016 mandate to make affirmative risk determinations and expanded authority to require testing data, EPA is empowered to change this practice.

### c. Special Rules for Biotechnology Products

Under EPA's biotechnology policy, the standard PMN requirements apply to microorganisms that are intentionally designed to contain genetic material from dissimilar sources. On the other hand, if genetic engineering is used to create microorganisms *other than* from "inter-genetic combinations," then the resulting product is treated as an "existing" chemical substance; thus, it must undergo SNU review if it is a pathogen and, if not, it is only subject to the standard reporting and recordkeeping requirements of § 8.

### d. Control of Nanoscale Material

Nanoscale materials may differ from the same chemical substances with larger scale structures, such as by having enhanced strength, lighter weight, or greater reactivity than their larger counterparts. In turn, these properties may cause nanoscale materials to behave differently. EPA has taken a specific regulatory approach to nanoscale materials by (1) requiring a PMN for new nanoscale materials and (2) adopting an information-gathering rule for new and existing nanoscale materials. 82 Fed. Reg. 3641 (Jan 12, 2017). For purposes of the rule, nanoscale materials are considered "chemical substances" under TSCA when they have structures with dimensions of approximately 1 to 100 nanometers. Pursuant to its § 8(a) authority, EPA adopted a rule that requires companies to provide data on nanoscale material, including:

- Specific chemical identity
- Production volume
- Methods of manufacture
- Processing, use, exposure and release information; and
- Available health and safety data.

## 7. REPORTING AND RECORDKEEPING REQUIREMENTS

Section 8 imposes various reporting duties on manufacturers and processors. For example, § 8(d) requires that studies concerning the effects of certain chemical substances on human health and safety be provided to EPA. In addition, § 8(c) directs manufacturers, processors, and distributors to maintain records of significant adverse reactions which the chemical causes to human health or the environment; this provision includes consumer complaints of personal injury or harm to health, worker reports of disease or injury, and reports of injury to the environment. EPA can use data from these records in deciding whether to regulate a suspect chemical substance. EPA is also now required to review and require substantiation of confidentiality claims for active chemicals on the confidential portion of the TSCA Inventory. § 8(b)(4).

## 8. ENFORCEMENT

Much like FIFRA, TSCA authorizes a range of penalties. The most common EPA response to a TSCA violation is the imposition of civil penalties. Section 16(a) provides that EPA may assess civil penalties of up to $37,500 each day. EPA's policy has been to compute a penalty amount based on the nature, extent, and circumstances of the violation (a "gravity-based penalty"), and then to determine whether to modify this amount in light of various criteria (e.g., ability to pay, any history of prior violations, and degree of culpability). See, e.g., Newell Recycling Co., Inc. v. EPA, 231 F.3d 204 (5th Cir.2000) (upholding $1.345 million penalty based on gravity criteria).

In order to recover civil penalties, EPA initiates an administrative proceeding against the alleged violator by filing a civil administrative complaint. The respondent is entitled to a hearing on the complaint before an administrative law judge, and may appeal an unfavorable ruling to federal court. In practice, however, most EPA civil penalty assessments are resolved through settlement, not litigation. In addition, the government can:

(a) obtain criminal penalties for knowing or willful violations (a power exercised only rarely) (§ 16(b));

(b) secure an injunction in district court to ensure compliance (§ 17(a)); and

(c) sue in rem to seize substances which were illegally manufactured, processed, or distributed (§ 17(b)).

Like most federal environmental statutes, TSCA contains a citizens' suit provision. Section 20 authorizes "any person" to sue anyone who violates any provision of TSCA or any rule issued under §§ 4, 5, or 6, after appropriate pre-filing notice is given. However, this section does not allow citizens to challenge discretionary decisions by EPA. See, e.g., Physicians Committee for Responsible Medicine v. Johnson, 436 F.3d 326 (2d Cir.2006) (citizens could not compel EPA to establish mandatory testing program for high production volume chemicals).

## 9. EVALUATING TSCA

To date, TSCA is more a failure than a success. The original expectation that TSCA would function as a "gatekeeper" statute by blocking dangerous new chemicals from commerce remains unfulfilled. The 2016 amendments were intended to address TSCA's tepid performance. As discussed above, in crafting the amendments Congress strategically addressed areas of weaknesses, by enhancing EPA's testing authority, requiring prioritization and deadlines for evaluation and regulation of chemical substances, and eliminating the "least burdensome" regulatory framework that hampered EPA's ability to impose restrictions on chemical substances after *Corrosion Proof Fittings*. Moreover, Congress authorized new fees to help finance this expanded effort; notably, these fees go directly to a TSCA Service Fee Fund for EPA use, rather than to the general treasury. §§ 26(b)(1), (b)(3)(A). Although Congress has enhanced EPA's authority, whether the agency will fulfill its mission is unclear.

Each of the major new EPA rulemakings under the revised TSCA—the prioritization rule, the risk evaluation rule, and the TSCA Inventory rule—have been challenged by environmental and health advocates as inadequately implementing TSCA's mandate. Nor has TSCA been updated to keep pace with technological changes; for example, little has been done to regulate biotechnology products. Because no other federal statute is even arguably relevant, TSCA has been pressed into service to regulate such products, on the theory that they are "chemical substances." Of course, the resulting regulatory framework does not take into account the unique challenges posed by novel life forms. Similarly, nanoscale materials may face additional scrutiny under EPA's expanded mandate, even though the amendments do not specifically address them. In sum, TSCA's updated framework moves significantly in the right direction, but only time will tell if it fulfills its intended goals.

## E. OTHER CHEMICAL SUBSTANCES: STATE AND LOCAL REGULATION

To what extent can state or local governments regulate chemical substances? The 2016 TSCA amendments sparked controversy over potential preemption of more protective state and local laws. Because EPA imposed scant regulation pursuant to TSCA, preemption was not a significant issue in the past. However, the 2016 amendments generally bar states from imposing new restrictions on a chemical once EPA designates it as high-priority and publishes its risk evaluation.

State actions taken before April 22, 2016, or any later action taken pursuant to a state law that was in effect on Aug. 31, 2003, are allowed to remain in effect. California's Proposition 65, and Massachusetts' Toxics Use Reduction Act are specifically excluded from the scope of preemption. But beyond these exclusions, states cannot adopt or continue to enforce laws that would:

(1) require information already mandated under TSCA §§ 4, 5, or 6 rules, consent agreements or orders;

(2) prohibit or restrict a chemical after EPA has

- made a § 6(i)(1) determination that a chemical substance does not present an "unreasonable risk" under a § 6(b)(4)(A) risk evaluation; or
- applied a requirement imposed by a final § 6(a) rule after finding that a chemical substance poses an "unreasonable risk";

(3) subject a chemical to the same notification of use already established in a § 5 significant new use rule.

The scope of preemption is limited to restrictions relating to the hazards, exposures, risks, and uses or conditions of use that are included in the scope of EPA's risk evaluation. Further, states can act on a chemical substance to address a different health or environmental concern than EPA considers under TSCA, such as a regulation related to air quality. And although states in some instances are preempted from placing restrictions on a chemical substance, they can impose certain reporting, monitoring or disclosure requirements. §§ 18(a)(1)(B), (b)(1), (d)(1)(A)(ii).

The 2016 amendments retain former TSCA provisions on discretionary waivers and add additional waiver provisions. States may seek a waiver to restrict chemical substances. If the waiver is sought before final EPA action on risk evaluation, then EPA *shall* grant the waiver if the conditions are similar to TSCA or the state has enacted a statute or proposed or finalized an administrative action prior to publication of the scope of EPA risk evaluation. § 18(f)(2). If the waiver is sought after a final risk evaluation or risk management rule EPA *may* issue a waiver if certain conditions are met, such as a compelling need to protect health or the environment, or where the state is attempting to address a risk identified consistent with the best available science, using studies conducted with sound and objective scientific practices, and based on the weight of the scientific evidence. § 18(f)(1).

# CHAPTER 4

# REGULATING THE USE OF TOXIC SUBSTANCES

## A. OVERVIEW

After a toxic substance is allowed to enter the stream of commerce, how does federal law regulate its use? Certainly use restrictions may be imposed by EPA under FIFRA or TSCA as a condition of market access, as discussed in Chapter 3. Beyond this gateway, however, the use of toxic substances is governed by a bewildering array of federal statutes, each oriented toward a different aspect of the issue. Moreover, adding to the confusion, each is typically administered by a different federal agency, and thus affected by that agency's agenda, priorities, and constituencies.

Given this fragmentation, it is unsurprising that the resulting regulatory framework is characterized by gaps, overlaps, and inconsistencies. Even the threshold question of which toxic substances merit regulation receives widely disparate answers, depending on the particular statute and agency involved. This chapter surveys the substantive highlights of the most important federal statutes addressing the problem and briefly discusses state regulation in the field as well.

## B. CONSUMER PROTECTION

### 1. HAZARDOUS SUBSTANCES AND CONSUMER PRODUCTS: THE FEDERAL HAZARDOUS SUBSTANCES ACT (FHSA)

The Federal Hazardous Substances Act, 15 U.S.C.A. § 1261 et seq., authorizes the Consumer Products Safety Commission to regulate a wide range of consumer products. As a prerequisite to regulation, the Commission must designate the product a "hazardous substance." The definition of "hazardous substance" under the Act has two components. First, the substance must be toxic, corrosive, flammable, combustible, an irritant, a strong sensitizer, or generate pressure through decomposition, heat, or other means. In this context, "toxic" means a substance which "has the capacity to produce personal injury or illness to man through ingestion, inhalation, or absorption through any body surface." § 1261(g). Second, the substance must have the ability to cause "substantial personal injury or substantial illness during or as a proximate result of any customary or reasonably foreseeable handling or use." § 1261(f)(1)(A). The process for designating a hazardous substance involves a formal rulemaking process. § 1262(f)–(i). Nonetheless, a wide variety of products (e.g., certain chemicals, toy darts, "cherry bomb" fireworks, and children's finger paints) have been classified as hazardous substances under the Act.

### a. Labeling Requirements

The main regulatory tool authorized by the Act is product labeling. All hazardous substances intended for "use in the household or by children" must bear a label which includes: (1) appropriate warning words (e.g., "DANGER" on highly toxic substances); (2) description of the principal hazards (e.g., "Vapor Harmful"); (3) precautionary measures describing actions to be taken or avoided; (4) first aid instructions if appropriate; and (5) handling and storage instructions. § 1261(p). For example, after animal bioassays demonstrated that methylene chloride could cause cancer, the Commission designated it a hazardous substance and mandated labeling for household cleaning fluids, detergents, and various other products which contained it. Much like FIFRA, the Act preempts any state cause of action that challenges the adequacy of product labeling, such as negligent failure to warn, unless the labeling itself violates FHSA. See Richards v. Home Depot, Inc., 456 F.3d 76 (2d Cir.2006).

### b. Product Bans

Labeling alone may not afford adequate protection. Under certain conditions, the Commission may ban from interstate commerce certain hazardous substances intended for household use or use by children. §§ 1261(q)(1), 1274. In order to designate a "banned hazardous substance," the Commission must first find that the degree or nature of the hazard involved in the presence or use of the substance in households is such that public health and safety can be adequately protected only by a product ban. For example, the Second Circuit upheld the Commission's decision to classify children's foam finger paint as a banned hazardous substance in United States v. Articles of Banned Hazardous Substances Consisting of an Undetermined Number of Cans of Rainbow Foam Paint, 34 F.3d 91 (2d Cir.1994). The court reasoned that the paint was intended to be dispensed from a pressurized canister by children too young to understand a label warning; yet the canister was flammable when used upside down, posing the risk of substantial injury. In the Consumer Safety Improvement Act of 2008, Congress adopted the "lead paint rule" to designate lead as a "banned hazardous substances" when above specified limits in children's products. § 1278a.

## 2. CONSUMER PRODUCTS GENERALLY: THE CONSUMER PRODUCT SAFETY ACT (CPSA)

The Consumer Product Safety Act, 15 U.S.C.A. § 2051 et seq., the principal federal statute regulating the safety of consumer products, is also administered by the Consumer Product Safety Commission. Under the Act, a "consumer product" is defined as any article produced or distributed for sale to a consumer for use in and around a household or residence, a school, in recreation, or otherwise. § 2052(a)(5). Thus, for products containing toxic or hazardous substances, CPSA and FHSA overlap awkwardly; both acts may potentially apply to the same product. Despite this substantive overlap, the procedures for regulating under CPSA (informal rulemaking) are far less demanding than those required by FHSA (trial-type hearing), creating an incentive for the Commission to use CPSA.

### a. Consumer Product Safety Rules

The Act empowers the Commission to adopt "consumer product safety rules" for consumer products which present an unreasonable "risk of injury," defined as a "risk of death, personal injury, or serious or frequent illness." § 2052(a)(14). To promulgate such a rule, the Commission must find, among other things, that: (1) the rule is reasonably necessary to eliminate or reduce the risk of injury associated with the product; (2) the benefits expected from the rule bear a reasonable relationship to its costs; and (3) the rule imposes the "least burdensome requirement which prevents or adequately reduces the risk of injury." § 2058(f)(3). There are two basic types of consumer product safety rules. Section 2056 authorizes the adoption of "consumer product safety standards," which consist of performance requirements, product packaging and labeling requirements, or both. If no feasible consumer product safety standard would adequately protect the public, however, the Commission may adopt a rule declaring the product a banned hazardous product under § 2057 and prohibit its distribution, sale, and use. In 2008, Congress specifically adopted a prohibition on the sale of children's toys and child care articles containing specified levels of particular phthalates. § 2057c.

### b. Case Study: The Formaldehyde Saga

Despite its broad authority, the Commission's efforts to regulate consumer products containing toxic substances have been quite limited, as symbolized by the fate of its first attempt to ban such a product. In 1982, following a six year investigation, the Commission banned the installation of urea-formaldehyde foam insulation (UFFI) in homes and schools. Its investigation had revealed that UFFI emitted significant amounts of formaldehyde gas, a toxic substance found to induce cancer in laboratory animals, creating an increased cancer risk to affected humans of up to 1 in 20,000. The Fifth Circuit struck down this ban in Gulf South Insulation v. CPSC, 701 F.2d 1137 (5th Cir.1983), as unsupported by substantial evidence. Though conceding that the Commission's studies "do suggest that UFFI appreciably raises in-home formaldehyde levels," the court found them tainted by poor methodology; it noted, for example, that many of the UFFI-homes studied were chosen because of prior UFFI-related health complaints, rather than through random selection. Similarly, the court found an "element of doubt" in the Commission's dose-response assessment. It observed that the number of rats used in the animal bioassay was too small, and questioned the Commission's assumption that very low doses of formaldehyde were carcinogenic.

### 3. FOOD, DRUGS, AND COSMETICS: THE FEDERAL FOOD, DRUG, AND COSMETIC ACT (FFDCA)

Perhaps the most prominent example of health-based regulation, the Federal Food, Drug, and Cosmetic Act, 21 U.S.C.A. § 301 et seq., empowers the Food and Drug Administration (FDA) to protect the overall safety of food, drugs, and cosmetics. Although the intricacies of the Act are confusing, its central theme is simple: only "safe" food, drugs and cosmetics may be sold in the United States. As the Supreme Court explained in Young v. Community Nutrition Institute, 476 U.S. 974, 106 S.Ct. 2360, 90 L.Ed.2d 959 (1986), the "Act seeks to ensure the purity of the Nation's food supply * * *." Thus, the shipment or receipt in interstate commerce of any "adulterated" food, drug, or cosmetic violates the Act, potentially subjecting the offender to civil and criminal penalties. §§ 331, 333. The discussion below focuses on two of the many subjects regulated under the Act: *food additives* and *pesticide residues*.

#### a. Food Additives

A variety of substances—including flavorings, nutrients, and preservatives—are directly added to food. Other substances may be added to food indirectly, such as by contact with packaging. The starting point through the FFDCA maze is the definition of *food additive*. Under the Act, this is a substance which *both*:

- becomes a "component" of, or otherwise affects the "characteristics" of, any food (other than, e.g., pesticide residues or color additives); *and*

- is not "generally recognized" by qualified experts as having been "adequately shown through scientific procedures" to be "safe under the conditions of its intended use." § 321(s).

The most striking aspect of this definition is that, in a manner reminiscent of FIFRA, it assigns the burden of proving safety to the food additive producer, not to the FDA. For example, a substance which due to scientific uncertainty cannot be proven safe is assumed to be unsafe. Thus, *as a general rule,* any food containing a food additive is considered to be "adulterated"—and thus unsalable—regardless of cost, technology, or other factors. §§ 348(a), 342(a). The FDA maintains a list of additives which are "generally recognized as safe." Any interested person (including an additive manufacturer) can petition for an administrative determination that a substance is or is not a food additive.

This *general rule*, however, is qualified by a major *exception.* Even though a food additive is not "generally recognized as safe," FDA may issue a regulation authorizing its use upon finding that the proposed use is in fact "safe." § 348(a). In reaching this determination, FDA must consider criteria including the probable consumption of the additive, the cumulative effect of the additive in the diet of humans, and safety factors which qualified experts generally recognize as appropriate for the use of animal experimentation data. § 348(c)(5). Thus, for example, even if an additive is not generally safe, FDA may permit its use under special conditions (e.g., allow use only in certain foods, regulate the manner by which the additive is added, or impose labeling or packaging requirements). FDA's principal regulatory tool in this area is a limitation on the quantity of a food additive which may be added to food, known as a "tolerance."

FDA's approach to genetically-modified foods has been controversial. In general, it does not require any special review process for these foods. Thus, genes which are added to a food through genetic engineering are not considered a "food additive" under the FFDCA. Accordingly, the producer does not have the burden of proving that a genetically-modified food is safe. This approach was upheld in Alliance for Bio-Integrity v. Shalala, 116 F.Supp.2d 166 (D.D.C.2000).

Finally, the scope of FDA's regulatory power is limited by the so-called "Delaney clause," in essence an *exception* to the *exception*. Any food additive which "is found to induce cancer when ingested by man or animal" is always deemed "unsafe." § 348(c)(3)(A). The Delaney clause (also found elsewhere in the Act) is widely condemned as the product of unreasoning cancerphobia. In effect, if a substance causes cancer in laboratory animals under any conditions (e.g., extremely high doses), it cannot be authorized for use in food, even if the risk to humans is trivial (e.g., 1 in a trillion). This results in the "Delaney paradox": substances with a trivial risk of cancer are prohibited, while substitute substances carrying a significant risk of a lethal disease other than cancer may be permitted.

In Public Citizen v. Young, 831 F.2d 1108 (D.C.Cir.1987), the D.C. Circuit rejected FDA's effort to circumvent the Delaney clause contained in another FFDCA section; that section required an FDA "listing" (a form of registration) before a "color additive" may be used. The case revolved around two dyes which—though admittedly inducing cancer in laboratory animals—presented trivial risks to humans; one of the additives in question, Orange No. 17, presented an increased cancer risk to humans of only 1 in 19 billion. Although protesting that judges were not "hopeless slaves to literalism," the court refused to adopt the FDA's argument that substances carrying a de minimis risk were impliedly exempted from the Delaney clause.

### b. Pesticide Residues

Under the Act, "tolerances" for pesticide residues are determined by EPA, not FDA. As a general rule, any fruits, vegetables, other "raw agricultural commodities," or processed foods bearing *any* pesticide residues are deemed "adulterated" (and thus unsalable) unless *either:* (1) the amount of the residue is within the limits of a tolerance EPA has established for the pesticide; *or* (2) a special exemption applies. § 346a(a)(1). Thus, growers have an incentive to minimize their use of pesticides so that their produce qualifies for an EPA tolerance.

EPA may normally establish a tolerance for a pesticide residue only if it determines that the tolerance is "safe." In this context, "safe" means that there is a "reasonable certainty" that no harm will result from aggregate exposure to the residue, including all anticipated dietary exposures. § 346a(b)(2)(A). Predictably, the Act provides a major exception to this standard. Even if EPA is unable to identify a threshold level below which exposure to the residue will not threaten human health (e.g., certain carcinogens), it may still set a tolerance for the residue under limited conditions (e.g., where (1) use of the pesticide protects consumers against health dangers which would pose an even greater risk *and* (2) specified quantitative safety margins are used). § 346a(b)(2)(B). Enhanced protection is mandated for foods consumed by infants and children. § 346a(b)(2)(C).

## C. EMPLOYEE PROTECTION: THE OCCUPATIONAL SAFETY AND HEALTH ACT (OSHA)

The workplace is the largest source of human exposure to toxic substances. Concern about the health effects of such exposure helped stimulate the 1970 passage of the Occupational Safety and Health Act, 29 U.S.C.A. § 651 et seq. Although OSHA extends to a variety of worker safety issues (e.g., safety glasses and machinery use restrictions), it particularly stresses the importance of protecting workers from toxic materials and harmful physical agents. The Act creates a general duty in the employer to provide workers with "employment and a place of employment which are free from recognized hazards that are causing or are likely to cause death or serious physical harm to his employees." § 5(a)(1).

### 1. OCCUPATIONAL SAFETY AND HEALTH STANDARDS

The centerpiece of the Act is § 6, which authorizes the Secretary of Labor ("Secretary") to promulgate an "occupational safety or health standard," i.e., rules requiring employers to utilize specific methods to protect their employees. § 6(a). In practice, this responsibility is exercised through the Occupational Safety and Health Administration. The protective methods may include: (1) labels or other appropriate warning devices; (2) protective equipment; (3) control or technological procedures; (4) monitoring and measuring employee exposure; and (5) employee medical examinations. In the context of toxic substance regulation, the most important type of standard is the "permissible exposure limit" (PEL). A PEL restricts the amount of a substance to which an employee may be exposed over a particular time period (e.g., an average of no more than 5 ppm over 8 hours).

### 2. PERMISSIBLE EXPOSURE LIMITS FOR TOXIC MATERIALS

The Supreme Court examined the process for setting occupational safety and health standards in Industrial Union Department, AFL-CIO v. American Petroleum Institute, 448 U.S. 607, 100

S.Ct. 2844, 65 L.Ed.2d 1010 (1980). There, various industry groups challenged the Secretary's decision to reduce the PEL for benzene from 10 ppm to 1 ppm. The Secretary argued that the new PEL was justified under § 6(b)(5), the special provision covering standards for "toxic materials" and "harmful physical agents." This section directs the Secretary to set "the standard which most adequately assures, to the extent feasible, on the basis of the best available evidence, that no employee will suffer material impairment of health or functional capacity even if such employee has regular exposure to the hazard * * *."

Writing the plurality opinion, Justice Stevens concluded that the Secretary had omitted a key step in the regulatory process and accordingly invalidated the PEL. He interpreted § 3(8) as mandating threshold determinations—before *any* occupational safety or health standard could be adopted under the Act—that the work place exposure posed a significant health risk *and* that the new standard was "reasonably necessary or appropriate." Thus, "the burden was on the Agency to show, on the basis of substantial evidence, that it was at least more likely than not that long term exposure to 10 ppm of benzene presents a significant risk of material health impairment."

Justice Stevens concluded that the Secretary had failed to demonstrate any evidence of significant risk which justified lowering the PEL. At one level, his opinion can be viewed as a critique of the rather primitive risk assessment methodology which had been used in the process. More fundamentally, it signaled a renewed judicial willingness to reassess administrative determinations of which risks merit regulation. Still, the opinion provided little guidance as to what constituted a "significant risk." The Court commented:

> If, for example, the odds are one in a billion that a person will die from cancer by taking a drink of chlorinated water, the risk clearly could not be considered significant. On the other hand, if the odds are one in a thousand that regular inhalation of gasoline vapors that are 2% benzene will be fatal, a reasonable person might well consider the risk significant * * *.

Seven years after *American Petroleum Institute,* following extensive epidemiologic studies and animal bioassays which demonstrated that exposure to 10 ppm of benzene created an increased leukemia risk of approximately 88 in 1,000, the Secretary again reduced the benzene PEL to 1 ppm. Yet in the interim, thousands of workers were exposed to the higher benzene levels which the original PEL would have avoided.

In establishing a standard for "toxic materials and harmful physical agents," then, the Secretary must *first* meet the threshold test enunciated in *American Petroleum Institute* and *then* fulfill the specific requirements of § 6(b)(5) set forth above. In this second step, the Secretary must reduce the hazard to the extent "feasible" considering both economic and technological limitations.

- *Economic feasibility:* A standard is considered economically feasible if the costs it imposes "do not threaten the existence or competitive structure of an industry," even if some "marginal firms" are displaced. United Steelworkers of America v. Marshall, 647 F.2d 1189 (D.C.Cir.1980). As the Supreme Court established in American Textile Manufacturers Institute, Inc. v. Donovan, 452 U.S. 490, 101 S.Ct. 2478, 69 L.Ed.2d 185 (1981), the Secretary is not required to justify a new standard through cost-benefit analysis.
- *Technological feasibility:* A standard is considered technologically feasible if "modern technology has at least conceived some industrial strategies or devices which are likely to be capable of meeting the PEL and which the industries are generally capable of adopting." United Steelworkers of America v. Marshall, 647 F.2d 1189 (D.C.Cir.1980).

## D. PUBLIC PROTECTION GENERALLY

### 1. WARNING THE PUBLIC: EMERGENCY PLANNING AND COMMUNITY RIGHT-TO-KNOW ACT (EPCRTKA)

In the wake of the 1984 toxic release in Bhopal, India, which killed thousands of people, Congress enacted the Emergency Planning and Community Right-to-Know Act, 42 U.S.C.A. § 11001 et seq. The Act has two basic objectives: (1) to develop local emergency plans for responding to toxic releases; and (2) to provide citizens and local governments with information concerning hazardous chemicals used, produced, or stored in the community.

### a. Emergency Planning

The Act's emergency planning component focuses on "extremely hazardous substances" (EHS), the substances which Congress deemed the most dangerous to human health. § 302(a). The current list, which includes methyl isocyanate (the substance which caused the Bhopal disaster) and over 350 other toxic substances, is set forth at 40 C.F.R. Part 355, Appendix A. The Act mandates that each state appoint a series of local emergency planning committees; each committee is charged with developing a plan for responding to the release of EHS in its community. § 301. The plan must include items such as: (1) identification of facilities using EHS; (2) identification of likely transportation routes for EHS; (3) methods and procedures to be followed by facility owners and emergency personnel if an EHS release occurs; (4) methods for determining the occurrence of such a release; (5) evacuation plans; (6) training programs; and (7) methods and schedules for exercising the plan. § 303.

To facilitate this process, the Act imposes disclosure obligations on owners and operators of "facilities" where certain threshold amounts of EHS or other hazardous chemicals are present. A "facility" means all buildings, equipment, structures, and other stationary items on a single site or adjacent sites under common control. § 329(4). Initially, in order to prepare and update the local emergency plan, all such owners and operators must notify local and state officials about the types and amounts of EHS and hazardous chemicals present at their facilities. §§ 302(c), 311, 312. If a threshold quantity of EHS actually spills, leaks, or is otherwise "released" into the environment from a facility, the owners and operators must immediately notify government authorities so that the local emergency plan can be implemented. § 304(a). This emergency reporting obligation is also triggered by the release from such a facility of a threshold quantity of a CERCLA "hazardous substance." (See Chapter 7).

### b. Public Information

Do citizens have the right to know what toxic substances are used in their community? Section 313—probably the most significant and controversial portion of the Act—answers this question with a resounding "yes." It requires that industry provide this information annually for public scrutiny. The initial Toxics Release Inventory (TRI) compiled from this information shocked the nation: industry reported that during 1987 it had released over 10.4 billion pounds of "toxic chemicals" into the environment. The resulting firestorm of adverse publicity persuaded many companies to substantially reduce their emissions.

The TRI currently contains nearly 600 "toxic chemicals," placed on the list pursuant to § 313. See 40 C.F.R. § 372.65. In general, owners and operators of certain facilities with 10 or more employees which manufacture, produce, or use specified quantities of toxic chemicals must submit a "uniform toxic chemical release form" to EPA each year. § 313(b)(1)(A). This report must include: (1) an estimate of the maximum amount of each toxic chemical present at the facility; (2) a description of the waste treatment or disposal methods employed; and (3) the amount of each toxic chemical released into the environment. § 313(g)(1)(C). EPA must establish, maintain, and make available to the public a computerized "national toxic chemical inventory" based on the information provided by these reports. § 313(j). Citizens accessing this database through personal computers can readily obtain detailed information on the use of toxic chemicals in their region.

A chemical may be listed on the TRI only if it *directly* causes serious harm to humans. Thus, in American Chemistry Council v. Johnson, 406 F.3d 738 (D.C.Cir.2005), the District of Columbia Circuit invalidated EPA's listing of methyl ethyl ketone (MEK). EPA had listed MEK because it contributed to the formation of ozone, which was clearly a toxic chemical. But the court found that MEK itself did not directly endanger humans, and was at most an *indirect* threat. It noted that EPA's broad interpretation of "toxic chemical" would even allow water to be listed on the TRI.

## 2. TRANSPORTATION OF TOXICS: THE HAZARDOUS MATERIALS TRANSPORTATION ACT (HMTA)

Transportation and handling increase the risks posed by toxic substances and hazardous wastes. The truck carrying hazardous wastes may become involved in a traffic accident; the railroad car containing chlorine may derail. The Hazardous Materials Transportation Act, 49 U.S.C.A. § 5101 et seq., administered by the Department of Transportation (DOT), is the most important federal statute regulating the transportation of "hazardous materials." Other federal agencies also empowered to regulate aspects of such transportation (e.g., EPA and OSHA) have typically deferred to DOT's broader authority.

The Act applies to the transportation in "commerce" (by railroad, highway, air, water, pipeline, or otherwise) of any "hazardous material." If transporting a particular material "in a particular amount and form may pose an unreasonable risk to health and safety or property," DOT may designate it as a hazardous material under § 5103(a). Over 2,000 substances (including toxic, explosive, radioactive, flammable, combustible, and corrosive materials) have been so designated; the current list appears at 49 C.F.R. § 172.101. In particular, all RCRA "hazardous wastes" and all CERCLA "hazardous substances" are also deemed "hazardous materials" under HMTA.

Pursuant to the Act, DOT has promulgated extensive regulations for the safe transportation of hazardous materials in intrastate, interstate, and foreign commerce. Spanning over 1,000 pages in the Code of Federal Regulations, these regulations impose standards for all aspects of transportation, including shipping documents, containers, packaging, labeling, placarding, packing, handling, loading, routing, unloading, temporary storage, inspections, employee training, and emergency preparedness. 49 C.F.R. Parts 171–180. The DOT harmonized these hazardous materials regulations with international standards in 2017. 82 Fed. Reg. 15796–01 (Mar. 30, 2017). In addition to actual transporters, persons who "cause" hazardous materials to be transported or who manufacture or maintain shipping containers are also subject to these requirements. § 5103(b). The Act also mandates that transporters of certain hazardous materials (and persons who "cause" such transportation) file registration statements with DOT. § 5108(a).

## E. STATE REGULATION

The regulatory fragmentation in this area is exacerbated by a hodgepodge of state approaches. In general, the federal statutes governing the use of toxic substances do not entirely preempt state law. For example, CPSA allows states to adopt consumer product standards which are more protective than federal law; this allowed Massachusetts to ban UFFI insulation under state law even after the federal ban was struck down in *Gulf South Insulation*. Borden, Inc. v. Commissioner of Public Health, 388 Mass. 707, 448 N.E.2d 367 (Mass.1983) (upholding state prohibition on UFFI use). Similarly, under OSHA a state may implement its own worker protection plan which is "at least as effective as" the federal standards, subject to various limitations, e.g., that it not unduly burden interstate commerce. At least partial state regulation is also permitted under EPCRTKA, FFDCA, HMTA, and FHSA.

One of the best-known examples of such state regulation is California's Safe Drinking Water and Toxic Enforcement Act of 1986, Cal. Health & Safety Code § 25249.5 et seq. (also known as "Proposition 65"). Approved by a voter initiative, this Act prohibits any business with 10 or more employees from knowingly exposing any person to a chemical substance known to cause cancer or reproductive toxicity in humans or laboratory animals *unless either:* (1) the business proves that the substance is safe; *or* (2) the business provides an appropriate advance warning. The statutory test for safety requires, in part, that the user prove the substance "poses no significant risk assuming lifetime exposure" at the level known to the state to cause cancer; the burden of scientific uncertainty accordingly falls on the affected business. Because this safety standard is difficult to meet, in practice the Act is similar to the "Delaney clause," affecting even the de minimis use of cancer-causing substances. Accordingly, most California businesses using such chemical substances comply with the Act by routinely placing consumer warnings on labels, in billings, in advertisements, on point-of-sale signs, or otherwise. Yet because the warning signs are ubiquitous (e.g., at all service stations, and most bars, supermarkets, and office buildings), they are largely ignored by the public.

# CHAPTER 5

# REGULATING TOXIC POLLUTION UNDER THE CLEAN WATER, CLEAN AIR AND SAFE DRINKING WATER ACTS

## A. INTRODUCTION

### 1. RELATIONSHIP TO OTHER LAWS

Understanding the regulation of toxic substances under the three statutes explored in this chapter develops in three steps. The first step considers the specific provisions addressing toxic substances within each Act. For the Safe Drinking Water Act, 42 U.S.C.A. § 300f et seq., identification of these provisions is easy, as virtually the entire Act addresses such substances. For the Clean Water Act, 33 U.S.C.A. § 1251 et seq., and the Clean Air Act, 42 U.S.C.A. § 7401 et seq., however, that task is more complicated, as provisions governing toxic substances are enmeshed in legislation that addresses a broader range of pollutants. Because of this, for these two Acts a second step must be taken. Understanding their approaches to toxic substances requires some appreciation of the two overall statutory schemes. Accordingly, the following discussion places each statute's treatment of these substances in the broader context of the entire Act in issue. It concludes with a discussion of some features common to the three Acts.

It is not enough, however, to understand each Act in isolation. Rather, for all three Acts, a third step must occur. This entails consideration of the relationship of the particular Acts to other laws governing toxics. In particular, it involves the relationship between these Acts and the two main laws governing cleanup of hazardous wastes: the Resource Conservation and Recovery Act (RCRA) and the Comprehensive Environmental Response, Compensation and Liability Act (CERCLA). Thus, this last step requires consideration of the materials in Chapters 6 through 12.

## 2. CURRENT RELEASES OF TOXIC POLLUTANTS

Despite decades of regulation under the Clean Water, Clean Air, and Safe Drinking Water Acts, Americans continue to release staggeringly large amounts of toxic pollutants into the ambient water and air. For example, according to EPA's 2004 TRI, in that year, 1.55 *billion* pounds of hazardous pollutants were emitted into the atmosphere alone in the United States. (In contrast, surface waters received a substantially smaller 241 *million* pounds of toxic pollutants.) During the period 2005–2015, however, air releases dropped significantly, 56%, to 669 million pounds. This is largely because of electric utilities switching from coal to other sources. These figures reflect both substantial progress *and* substantial challenges remaining in the control of harmful releases of toxic substances into the ambient environment.

Many environmentalists and health advocates believe that the current level of emissions remains excessive. Finding a "safe" level of permitted releases, particularly for atmospheric emissions, is no easy task. Although atmospheric dispersion allows the assimilation of a large volume of these pollutants, and reduces their concentrations to levels near the limits of detection, persons living near the sources may well experience health threatening exposure. This is especially true in urban areas, where large numbers of sources of toxics are often located. Moreover, as described in Chapter 2, particularly for carcinogens, there may be no "safe" exposure level at all, i.e., a concentration level below which exposure produces no risk of additional cancer. In such a scenario, the positive effects of dispersion, while reducing the risk of cancer, never eliminate it entirely.

The explanation for the continued presence of such emissions into the atmosphere is not hard to find. The emitters include an important group of businesses and public activities. Everything from major chemical companies, to municipal trash incinerators, to local dry cleaners is potentially subject to regulation under the Clean Air Act. With such substantial economic and public interests involved, it is no wonder that most regulatory efforts in this arena are met with critical response, and often substantial resistance, from industry. Indeed, the administrative and legislative responses to such resistance have shaped the structure of the current Clean Air, Clean Water, and Safe Drinking Water Acts.

## B. REGULATION OF TOXICS UNDER THE CLEAN WATER ACT

### 1. INTRODUCTION

The Clean Water Act, 33 U.S.C.A. § 1251 et seq., contains three distinct approaches for regulating the discharge of toxic substances into the nation's waterways: (1) technology based standards; (2) water quality based standards; and (3) harm based standards. The principal approach involves technology based standards. These standards require wastewater dischargers to reduce their discharges of toxic pollutants to the levels possible through the use of available treatment technologies. For different toxic pollutants and different industries, EPA first determines what is the "best available technology" for reducing such discharges, and then requires all dischargers to meet those levels.

Where these technology based standards do not reduce toxic pollutants adequately, a second set of standards applies. These water quality based standards are set as part of the Act's required water quality planning process. Generally set by state agencies acting under EPA authority, these standards help each state meet the Act's overall goal of making the nation's waterways "fishable and swimmable." They allow states to impose restrictions on toxic discharges beyond those required solely through the technology based standards.

Finally, the Act contains a third set of standards. These health based standards focus on the risks to human health associated with particular toxic substances. Although largely of historical importance, these standards still remain available to EPA under the Act.

## 2. HISTORY

### a. Pre-1972 Approaches

Prior to 1972, the Clean Water Act (then known as the Federal Water Pollution Control Act (FWPCA)) principally regulated discharges into the nation's waterways through a three step water quality planning process. Toxic discharges were included within this process.

First, states would survey the watercourses within their boundaries, divide these watercourses into segments, and determine the primary uses to which each segment could be placed. For example, the State of Smith might conclude that the stretch of the Smith River above Smithville would be used for recreational fishing and boating; the stretch of the river running through Smithville would be used for harbor and waterfront industries; and the stretch of the river below Smithville would be used for ocean going transportation and municipal wastewater dilution.

Second, the states would develop water quality standards and criteria to protect these designated uses. "Standards" "consist of a designated use or uses for the [state's waters] and water quality criteria for such waters * * *." 40 C.F.R. § 131.3(i). "Criteria" are "elements of [s]tate water quality standards, expressed as constituent concentrations, levels, or narrative statements, representing a quality of water that supports a particular use." 40 C.F.R. § 131.3(b). The designation of a river as "fishable and swimmable" generally required the most protective water quality criteria. For example, to protect the designated recreational fishing use in the stretch of the Smith River above Smithville, the state might establish a criterion for dissolved oxygen (DO), a substance essential for fish respiration. In its water quality control plan, the state could set the DO criterion either numerically or narratively. Expressed numerically, the plan might require there to be "at least 5 parts per million of DO within the relevant river segment at all times." The same criterion for the same river segment expressed narratively might simply state: "at all times there shall be sufficient DO to sustain fish life."

Criteria for toxic discharges were often expressed narratively. Since many of the toxics regulated at the time are insoluble in water, it was believed unnecessary to express them quantitatively (e.g., in parts per million). They simply might not be detectable in the waters themselves. Thus, the state's plan might simply "ban the discharge of toxic pollutants in amounts harmful to fish." (Of course, such narrative criteria did little to address the presence of toxics that *were* water soluble, or that sank and became part of the sediments at the bottom of waterways, later to work their way up the food chain).

The third step, however, was the most crucial. In this step, the state had to figure out how to ensure that its criteria were met. Continuing the above example, the state would have to identify all of the dischargers into the river above Smithville whose discharges might affect the DO or toxics criteria. If the combined discharges reduced DO below the criterion, the state would have to allocate the permissible pollution levels among the various dischargers.

In theory, these efforts could work. In practice, for a variety of reasons, they rarely did. For example, within any given state, politics could play an enormous role in determining the particular allocations of pollution required to meet the use-protecting criteria. States were often unwilling to engage in that political exercise. As a result, there was added pressure to downgrade the protected uses of a given river segment. Even if a given state were willing to protect some of the more environmentally demanding uses, interstate dynamics might leave it disadvantaged. Any given state could simply designate its waters primarily for industrial or wastewater dilution uses. In such a state, little pollution reduction would be necessary, while a state that sought to make its waters "fishable and swimmable" might require its industry to undertake expensive pollution control efforts. Business would flock to the former state, leaving the latter state economically disadvantaged. Critics dubbed this dynamic a "race of laxity," where each state's economic interest lay in undervaluing environmental regulation, rather than encouraging higher water quality.

Even if a state had the desire to preserve its waters for such higher quality uses as fishing and swimming, it faced other enforcement problems. These problems were particularly keen for narratively expressed criteria. For example, assume that the State of Smith's water quality control plan for the Smith River above Smithville stated that "toxic pollutants may not be discharged in amounts harmful to fish." Assume further that, despite this criterion, a fish kill occurred in that portion of the river. State water quality control engineers then determined that lethal amounts of the hypothetical toxic substance DDZ caused the fish to die. State regulators would then have to figure out *who* discharged the DDZ during the relevant time period. If there were multiple dischargers, each might point the finger at the others.

Enforcement problems were even more difficult for toxics that persisted for years, perhaps in river bottom sediments, before reaching toxic levels. Bioaccumulation (the process of increasing concentration of toxics as substances work their way up the food chain) and synergistic effects (where two relatively innocuous materials combine to form a third, more dangerous substance) posed additional substantial enforcement problems under this system.

### b. Post-1972 Developments

In response to these and other problems, since 1972 Congress has enacted three sets of amendments. Collectively, these amendments have substantially changed the regulation of both water pollution in general, and toxic pollutants in particular. The initial efforts to address toxics under the landmark 1972 amendments were a dismal failure. That scheme required a tedious, substance by substance, risk based analysis. For all but the most well documented substances, like DDT or PCBs, the scientific uncertainties attendant to such risk analyses led to inordinate delays and vigorous litigation. See, e.g., Environmental Defense Fund v. EPA, 598 F.2d 62 (D.C.Cir.1978) (upholding EPA's zero discharge standards for PCBs). Indeed, ultimately, EPA regulated only six substances under this scheme.

Although the substance by substance, risk based approach remains in the present statute, in its 1977 and 1987 Clean Water Act amendments, Congress has emphasized two different regulatory approaches to toxic water pollutants. Thus, in the 1977 legislation, Congress adopted a technology based approach. In the 1987 amendments, Congress reinvigorated water quality standards.

## 3. CONTEMPORARY SCHEME

In its 1972 legislation, Congress established as its policy the complete prohibition of the "discharge of toxic pollutants in toxic amounts" into the nation's waterways. § 101(a)(3). Under the current scheme, the Clean Water Act attempts to meet the lofty "zero toxics discharge" goal in two principal ways: (1) technology based requirements; and (2) reinvigorated water quality planning based requirements. In addition, the Act contains a variety of both vestigial and emerging approaches to addressing water toxics.

### a. Technology Based Elements

The Act's technology based elements are the heart of its regulatory scheme. In this regard, the treatment of toxics follows the Act's overall emphasis on technology based discharge standards.

#### *i. Sources of Pollutants*

The Act as a whole divides the sources of water pollutants into two groups: point sources and nonpoint sources. Point sources are defined as "discernible, confined and discrete conveyance * * * from which pollutants * * * may be discharged." § 502(14). The definition expressly excludes "agricultural storm water discharges and return flows from irrigated agriculture." § 502(14). A point source is most easily envisioned as a sewer pipe discharging directly into a watercourse. A nonpoint source is anything that is not a point source. It is most easily envisioned as rain water running off a hillside and draining into a nearby stream. The Act principally regulates point sources, although nonpoint sources have been attracting increasing legislative and regulatory attention in recent years. Separate provisions require pretreatment of industrial wastes sent to a publicly owned treatment plant. In effect, these provisions require such indirect dischargers to adopt the same pollution control efforts as point sources for any pollutant which interferes with, passes through, or is otherwise incompatible with such a public plant. See, e.g., § 307(b).

### *ii. Types of Pollutants*

Within the realm of point sources, the Act divides the pollutants into three different groups: (1) conventional pollutants; (2) toxic pollutants, and (3) nonconventional, nontoxic pollutants. Conventional pollutants include such substances as biological oxygen demanding (BOD) materials, suspended solids, fecal coliform, and pH. § 304(a)(4). Statutorily designated nonconventional, nontoxic pollutants include ammonia, chlorine, color, iron, and total phenols. § 301(g). These nonconventional, nontoxic pollutants are often regulated as if they were toxics, where their presence also indicates the presence of toxics. 40 C.F.R. §§ 122.44(e)(2)(ii), 125.3(h)(1); Rybachek v. EPA, 904 F.2d 1276 (9th Cir.1990). The Act contains provisions by which EPA can add new substances to the lists of conventional and nonconventional, nontoxic pollutants. § 304(g)(4).

Categorization of a pollutant as a toxic pollutant may occur in three ways. First, the Act identifies 65 substances that must be regulated as toxics. § 307(a)(1); 40 C.F.R. § 401.15. Second, it specifies six factors that EPA must consider when revising the list to add or remove particular substances. In such revisions, EPA must "take into account [the] toxicity of the pollutant, its persistence, degradability, the usual or potential presence of the affected organisms in any waters, the importance of the affected organisms, and the nature and extent of the effect of the toxic pollutant on such organisms." § 307(a)(1). This second provision interacts with the third: a broad definition of toxic pollutants as those that "will, on the basis of information available to the [EPA] cause death, disease, behavioral abnormalities, cancer, genetic mutations, physiological malfunctions (including malfunctions in reproduction) or physical deformations, in [any] organisms or their offspring." § 502(13).

### *iii. Discharge Restrictions and Permits*

After categorizing the sources and types of pollutants, the Act imposes substantial, technology based restrictions on discharges from point sources. Each point source must reduce the pollutants in its effluent to a level associated with the adoption of particular pollution control technology and practices. These levels are specified initially by statute, and then, as discussed below, implemented concretely by EPA. EPA's general requirements are then applied to individual dischargers through a permit system. Each discharger must obtain a permit, usually from an EPA authorized state agency, that limits its discharge of particular pollutants to the level permitted under the EPA standards. Collectively, these standards and the permit system are known as the "National Pollution

Discharge Elimination System" (NPDES). Violations of the NPDES are generally enforced by the states. EPA, however, retains backup enforcement authority.

### *iv. Timetables for Required Reductions*

In its 1972 amendments, Congress set up a schedule that required all then existing sources to reduce their pollution to the levels reached by application of the "best practicable control technology [then] currently available" (BPT) within an industry. § 301(b)(1)(A). This was meant to be an "average of the best" pollution reduction efforts in an industrial category. EPA v. National Crushed Stone Ass'n, 449 U.S. 64, 101 S.Ct. 295, 66 L.Ed.2d 268 (1980). Congress then expected that additional reductions would be made in a second round of technological enhancements. Ultimately, completion of this second round was extended until 1989.

As of the 1977 amendments, the efforts required in this second round depended on the type of pollutant involved. For example, for conventional pollutants, Congress required a further reduction to the level reached by application of the "best conventional pollutant control technology" (BCT). § 301(b)(2)(E). For toxics and nonconventional, nontoxics, Congress required a reduction to levels reached by application of "the *best available technology* economically achievable" (BAT) for a given category or class of point sources. §§ 301(b)(2)(A) (emphasis added), 307(a)(2). (Congress also authorized EPA to relax BAT standards for nonconventional, nontoxics, where the discharge of such pollutants would not cause human health or environmental damage. § 301(g)(1), (2).) In setting BAT limitations for toxic discharges, EPA must consider both the six above-described factors relevant to the identification of a substance as toxic and the "extent to which effective control [over a substance] is being or may be achieved under other regulatory authority." § 307(a)(2).

These standards applied to existing sources. Even tougher standards, known as "New Source Performance Standards" (NSPS), apply to new sources of pollution. § 306. Potential sources who first seek to discharge after the promulgation of standards for existing sources are required to adopt the "best available demonstrated control technology" (BADT). These tougher standards recognize that it is easier to require additional investments in pollution control equipment in an unbuilt facility than in an existing facility. In addition, they minimize the chance that new sources will add pollution to any preexisting problem.

### *v. Implementing Technology Based Standards*

EPA determines BAT or BADT for a given pollutant or pollutant class in a four step process. First, for each individual pollutant or class, EPA determines the sources (e.g., factories) that discharge that pollutant. Second, it divides the sources into numerous industrial groups and subgroups. E.g., § 306(b)(1)(A). For example, pulp and paper mills form one category of dischargers, inorganic chemicals manufacturers form another. Subclasses within each such grouping may turn on the particular kinds of paper or chemicals manufactured. Third, EPA surveys specific dischargers to measure their actual discharges of the target pollutants. Fourth, based on the actual practices of dischargers, and the statutory criteria, EPA requires that *all* dischargers within a given industrial grouping meet the same discharge levels as selected "model" dischargers. See, e.g., Waterkeeper Alliance v. EPA, 399 F.3d 486 (2d Cir.2005). Thus, all dischargers within a given classification are treated identically, regardless of their location. American Iron & Steel Institute v. EPA, 526 F.2d 1027 (3d Cir.1975). These uniform national standards remove one of the incentives that led to the "race of laxity" described above.

For each type of pollutant, EPA sets maximum daily and monthly allowances, expressed in terms like the overall volume of wastewater or the concentration of material permitted. The differences among the effluent limitations, with their similar sounding acronyms, depends upon two principal factors: (1) the degree to which the required performance is based upon "cutting edge" technology or practices; and (2) the relationship between costs and benefits of a given standard. Compare §§ 304(b)(1)(B) (factors used to set BPT) and 304(b)(2)(B) (factors used to set BAT). Specifically, in setting BAT, EPA must consider "the age of equipment and facilities involved, the process employed, the engineering aspects of the application of various types of control techniques, process changes, the cost of achieving such effluent reduction, [and] non-water quality environmental impact (including energy requirements) * * *." See Texas Oil & Gas Ass'n v. EPA, 161 F.3d 923 (5th Cir.1998). Additional differences between BAT and the other standards turn upon the availability of variances and the role in pollution reduction played by mandated changes in a discharger's *operations*—as opposed to its treatment *technology*. Finally, for toxics, the Act specifically requires EPA to establish effluent standards that provide "an ample margin of safety." § 307(a)(4).

A comparison of BPT and BAT illustrates these differences. Before it set BPT, EPA and its consultants surveyed the existing water pollution control practices of actual dischargers. EPA interpreted BPT as an "average of the best" results obtained by then existing dischargers of a given pollutant. In determining what was this "average of the best," EPA originally looked only to "end of the pipe" water pollution control technologies; it did not generally require dischargers to change the operations that created the waste stream in the first place. In addition, EPA was required to conduct at least a limited cost-benefit analysis to compare the benefits of these pollution reduction efforts to the costs. § 304(b)(1)(B).

In contrast, BAT reflected the levels of pollution reduction reached by the best single performer within the industrial group at the time of each survey. In setting BAT, EPA considered only the costs required to comply; it did not need to determine specifically that the benefits achieved by the additional increment of pollution control effort outweighed the costs of such additional efforts. EPA v. National Crushed Stone Ass'n, 449 U.S. 64, 101 S.Ct. 295, 66 L.Ed.2d 268 (1980). In addition, in setting BAT, EPA considered the "whole plant," not just the end of the drain pipe. Thus, operational changes that minimized the waste stream in the first place were included. EPA sets BAT knowing that compliance costs may force a segment of the given industry to shut down. See, e.g., Waterkeeper Alliance v. EPA, 399 F.3d 486 (2d Cir.2005). Variances from the BAT standards for toxics are allowed only where a discharger can demonstrate that its discharges differ in some fundamental way from the other members of its industrial class. §§ 301(l), (n).

In establishing these standards, EPA does not generally require a particular permittee to use the exact technology used by the control groups. Rather, a permittee need only make sure that the discharges coming out of its drain pipe do not exceed the concentrations achieved by the control group sources. In practice, however, there may only be one way to achieve the concentrations achieved by the top performers, and that may be to install the same pollution control equipment they use. See, e.g., Rybachek v. EPA, 904 F.2d 1276 (9th Cir.1990).

EPA must resurvey the performances achieved by actual dischargers in each industrial category at least every three years. § 307(a)(3). In theory, as process and treatment technologies improve, BAT standards will be upgraded. Dischargers within a given industrial category will then have to upgrade their own performance to meet any newer BAT standards when their discharge permits are up for renewal. The Act requires such renewals at least every 5 years. § 402(b)(1)(B).

### b. Water Quality Based Elements

While the technology based system represents the heart of the Clean Water Act's approach to toxics, it does not stand alone. Rather, the pre-1972 Act's water quality planning approach remains an important complement to the BAT program. Indeed, as evidenced by the 1987 amendments to the Act, Congress has backstopped the BAT approach by reinvigorating the water quality planning approach. In general, where BAT alone is unable to ensure adequate water quality, EPA and the states can impose whatever additional effluent limitations are necessary to ensure adequate water quality. § 302(a). See, e.g., Friends of the Earth v. EPA, 446 F.3d 140 (D.C.Cir.2006). Both the likelihood and efficacy of these additional limitations, however, remain a matter of debate.

As under the pre-1972 provisions, each state must adopt water quality standards and implementation plans. § 303. The outline of the provisions remains the same as under the prior provisions. Each state must designate the uses of its waterways and promulgate criteria to protect those uses. But the current provisions depart from their weaker predecessors in an octet of respects. Five of these differences reflect general water quality considerations that will have some effect on toxic pollution. The other three specifically address the role of toxics in water quality planning. Collectively, these provisions attempt to respond to the problems inherent in the pre-1972 system.

Three of the five general provisions implore, if not require, the states to dedicate their waters to high quality uses. First, in designating the uses of its waterways, a state must "protect the public health or welfare [and] enhance the quality of water * * *." § 303(c)(2)(A). Second, the states must expressly consider the full range of uses of a given waterway. Water quality standards must consider a waterway's "use and value for public water supplies, propagation of fish and wildlife, recreational purposes, and agricultural, industrial and other purposes [including] navigation." § 303(c)(2)(A) . No longer can a state simply designate its rivers as "open sewers;" it must at least evaluate that use relative to other uses. See, e.g., Ohio Valley Environmental Coalition v. Horinko, 279 F.Supp.2d 732 (S.D.W.Va.2003). Third, the entire designation process proceeds against the backdrop of the twin national goals of ending all discharges into the nation's waterways and making all of the nation's waterways suitable for fishing and swimming. § 101(a)(1), (2). While largely hortatory, these provisions set the tone for the more specific toxics provisions addressed below.

The fourth general provision involves the calculation of the amount of pollutants that a given waterway can assimilate without violating a designated use. Each state must identify the waterways that will not meet the water quality standards despite the application of the technology based effluent standards to point sources. § 303(d)(1)(A). For each of these waterways, it then must calculate the total maximum daily amount ("TMDL") of pollutants that will allow the waterway to meet the standard, considering "seasonal variations and a margin of safety which takes into account any lack of knowledge concerning the relationship between effluent limitations and water quality." § 303(d)(1)(C). "Daily" load means a single day, not a seasonal or annual average. Friends of the Earth v. EPA, 446 F.3d 140 (D.C.Cir.2006); compare Natural Resources Defense Council, Inc. v. Muszynski, 268 F.3d 91 (2d Cir. 2001). A TMDL is the sum of the individual WLA [wasteload allocation] for point sources and LA [load allocation] for nonpoint sources and natural background." 40 C.F.R. § 130.2(i). For those pollutants identified by EPA as "suitable for maximum daily load measurement," § 304(a)(2)(D), the states must include these loads within their plans. In 1978, EPA concluded that "all pollutants" were suitable for TMDL calculation. 43 F.R. 60, 662 (Dec. 28, 1978). Of course, allocation of this maximum daily load continues to raise political problems. For waterways that meet the designated uses, the states must still estimate the maximum daily loads of all EPA designated pollutants. § 303(d)(3). This requirement allows EPA to build up a database for future regulatory efforts. Where a state fails to develop a

TMDL for a waterway, the EPA may issue its own. Pronsolino v. Marcus, 91 F.Supp.2d 1337 (N.D.Cal.2000).

The fifth general provision addresses the contribution of nonpoint sources to water quality problems. § 319. As point sources have been increasingly regulated, Congress has realized that nonpoint sources contribute a substantial portion of the total pollutants that find their way annually into the nation's waterways. Accordingly, the 1987 amendments to the Act contained an entire section devoted to management of these nonpoint sources. These provisions require the states to identify their waters in violation of water quality standards from nonpoint sources and to develop best management practices (BMPs) for controlling such nonpoint source pollution. § 319(a)(1). No specific penalty attaches to a state's failure to submit such a plan; rather, the Act encourages plan development by hinging federal grant eligibility upon its completion. See Pronsolino v. Marcus, 91 F.Supp.2d 1337 (N.D.Cal.2000).

In addition to the five above described water quality provisions, three other provisions expressly address the role that toxics play in allowing a state's waterways to meet their designated uses. First, for each substance listed by Congress or EPA as toxic, EPA must publish water quality criteria. §§ 304(a)(1), 303(c)(2)(B). Among other statutorily required factors, these criteria must address a pollutant's impacts on health and welfare; its ability to concentrate or disperse; and its impacts on biological communities. § 304(a)(1). Once promulgated, the states must adopt these criteria as part of their water quality standards. § 303(c)(2)(B). The Act avoids the problems associated with the use of narrative criteria by requiring the adoption of specific numerical criteria. § 303(c)(2)(B). Where such numerical criteria are not available, the state must adopt criteria based upon biological monitoring. § 303(c)(2)(B). Biological monitoring focuses on the health of fish species found in, or exposed to, waters of the particular water course segment under review. See, e.g., Edison Electric Institute v. EPA, 391 F.3d 1267 (D.C.Cir.2004).

Second, the 1987 amendments to the Act required the states to identify their waterways that, despite the application of BAT, would have levels of toxic pollution from any source—point or nonpoint—that prevented the waterway from meeting the applicable water quality standards. § 304(*l*)(1). (This requirement was in addition to the above-described list necessary to promulgate maximum daily loads.) States had to list separately those waterways in violation of water quality standards solely because of toxic discharges from point sources. § 304(*l*)(1)(B). For each segment of a waterway on this latter list, the states had to identify the point sources responsible for preventing attainment of the applicable standard and the amount of pollutants discharged by each source. § 304(*l*)(1)(C). In addition, the states had to develop an "individual control strategy" to reduce, within three years, the toxic discharges from the identified point sources in quantities sufficient to meet the applicable water quality control standards. § 304(*l*)(1)(D). Because the work required by these provisions largely fell to the states, EPA was quite successful in meeting the statutory deadlines.

Third, the Act specifically integrates the water quality based and technology based effluent limitations in the context of toxics. These two sets of limitations operate in tandem to restrict toxic pollutants. In general, where a technology based limitation alone will not allow a waterway to meet a designated use, the Act *requires* EPA to impose additional effluent limitations on point sources. § 302(a). These additional restrictions are imposed on point sources as part of the NPDES permit process. §§ 402(a)(1), (b)(1)(A). Dischargers of toxics subject to these additional, water quality based effluent limitations may seek a single relaxation of the additional requirements for up to five years. To obtain this five year relaxation, a permittee must demonstrate that it will otherwise undertake the "maximum degree of control [of toxics] within [its] economic capability" and that these maximum efforts will "result in reasonable further progress" beyond BAT toward meeting the water quality objectives.

### c. Additional Provisions

#### *i. Harm Based Criteria*

Although they have lain dormant since the 1977 amendments, the original provisions that allow EPA to regulate a material as a toxic pollutant solely by its impact on human or environmental health remain in the Act. § 307(a)(1). This provision was modeled on the 1970 version of § 112 of the Clean Air Act. Both provisions contemplated a substance by substance analysis of the risk of harm associated with each pollutant. Both provisions required EPA to set a margin of safety to resolve any uncertainties in favor of more protective regulations. The statutes did not require, and arguably did not even permit, EPA to consider the cost to industry or the economy from each of these regulations. See Hercules Inc. v. EPA, 598 F.2d 91 (D.C.Cir.1978). Paralyzed by the near absolute discretion it has to regulate under this provision, in an arena fraught with uncertainties that invite cost, delay and litigation, and reinforced by its similar difficulties under the comparable Clean Air Act provision (see, e.g., Natural Resources Defense Council, Inc. v. EPA, 824 F.2d 1146 (D.C.Cir.1987)), it is very unlikely that EPA will use its power to issue harm based criteria in the foreseeable future.

### *ii. Alternative Criteria*

The 1987 amendments directed EPA to develop information on alternatives to toxic by toxic water quality criteria. Under traditional criteria, EPA determines, one pollutant at a time, the permissible amounts or concentrations. Under the alternative criteria, EPA can look at the combined effects of multiple toxics on individual species or an entire ecosystem. For example, "biological assessment" criteria look to the observed effect on test species of exposure to waste streams or ambient, receiving water. If too many of the test creatures show acute toxicity after being exposed in a laboratory to the sample waste stream or ambient water, the water quality standards will be violated. See, e.g., Edison Electric Institute v. EPA, 391 F.3d 1267 (D.C.Cir.2004).

### *iii. Point Source BMPs*

The Act supplements both the water quality based and technology based effluent limitations with an additional requirement for point sources. For any material regulated as toxic under the Act, EPA must require industrial point sources to adopt "best management practices" (BMPs). § 304(e). Such practices involve the control of toxic "plant site runoff, spillage or leaks, sludge or waste disposal, [or] drainage from raw materials." § 304(e). Like the other effluent limitations, BMPs are imposed through the NPDES permit process. § 304(e).

### *iv. Prohibitions on Certain Toxic Discharges*

In terms that allow for no exception, the Act bans the discharge of any "radiological, chemical or biological warfare agent, any high-level radioactive waste, or any medical waste * * *." § 301(f). The Act separately defines "medical waste." § 502(20). It does not define the other terms.

### *v. Oil and Hazardous Substance Pollution*

Beefed up substantially after the 1989 Exxon Valdez oil spill in Alaska, the Act operates in tandem with the Oil Pollution Act of 1990 (OPA) to regulate spills of oil and hazardous substances into waterways. See 33 U.S.C.A. §§ 2701–2762. The OPA, in turn, draws heavily from CERCLA. In combination, the Acts bar the discharge of oil and other "hazardous substances" into the nation's waterways, shorelines, and abutting seas. § 311(b)(3). Discharges permitted under the NPDES permit system are excluded from the prohibition and resulting liability scheme. § 311(a)(2). The Clean Water Act delegates to EPA the task of defining "hazardous substance." It instructs EPA to include those materials whose discharge "present an imminent and substantial danger to the public health or welfare, including [marine resources]." § 311(b)(2)(A). The Acts require emergency response plans; create a comprehensive liability scheme; authorize reimbursement from responsible parties for cleanup costs; establish a trust to help fund cleanups; require reimbursement for natural resources damages; and address tanker design and operations.

## 4. EVALUATION

The sheer number of different approaches taken by the Clean Water Act to toxic pollutants attests to the difficulties regulators have faced in addressing the problem of toxic discharges. Although the 1987 amendments are now over three decades old, the track record of the multi-faceted approach advanced under that legislation is unclear. On the one hand, the technology based effluent limitations appear to have been successful in reducing point source pollution, at least to the levels associated with BAT.

On the other hand, there were still almost a quarter of a *billion* pounds of toxic materials discharged into surface waterways in 2004 alone. Critics have charged that EPA has set BAT too weakly. Moreover, there are many toxic discharges that are not regulated by the Act, as EPA has been very slow to add to the list of toxics that require BAT.

The water quality planning approach reinvigorated by the 1987 amendments produced a host of state plan amendments and individual control strategies. Within these plans, however, criteria for toxic discharges have varied greatly from state to state. Moreover, the states' and EPA's willingness to enforce these strategies is still largely untested. It is still too early to tell whether these are control strategies that will be enforced in the permit process or simply nicely written pieces of paper. And finally, while regulatory attention to toxic discharges from nonpoint sources has grown, these discharges remain largely beyond the regulatory sphere. For all of the above reasons, Congress will likely revisit the toxic area whenever it next revises the Clean Water Act.

## C. REGULATION OF TOXICS UNDER THE CLEAN AIR ACT

### 1. INTRODUCTION

Like the Clean Water Act's provisions governing the discharge of toxic effluent into the nation's water, the Clean Air Act's provisions governing the discharge of toxic emissions into the nation's air are part of an enormously complex statutory and regulatory system. Both Acts now take a technology based approach backed up by other approaches. As described above, the Clean Water Act principally relies on a water quality based backup, with a health based approach dormant but largely forgotten. In contrast, the Clean Air Act, 42 U.S.C.A. § 7401 et seq., anticipates a health based approach as its principal backup. Because of generous technology based deadlines in the 1990 Clean Air Act amendments, it will still be well into the 21st century before the health based backup will be developed and can be assessed.

With each passing year, the number of cases addressing the 1990 Clean Air Act's toxic provisions increases. Several of these are discussed briefly below. Beyond those cases, students and attorneys interested in greater articulation of the statutory provisions can consult the 1990 amendments' substantial legislative history and EPA's subsequent rulemaking comments. If such sources fail to illuminate a provision under review, they can also consult the case law involving comparable provisions under the Clean Water Act. One must, however, proceed with great caution before importing wholesale the decisions reached under other environmental laws; slight differences in statutory provisions invite substantially different interpretations.

## 2. HISTORY AND OVERVIEW

Although Congress enacted air quality control legislation in 1955 and 1963, it was not until 1967 that federal air quality regulation began to take its current shape. In the Air Quality Act of 1967, Congress required the states to develop enforceable standards (i.e., maximum permissible levels) for air pollutants that were consistent with federal "criteria" and suggested control techniques.

In the landmark 1970 amendments to the Clean Air Act, Congress built upon its earlier legislation. For conventional air pollutants (known as "criteria pollutants" because "criteria" for most of these widespread pollutants had been developed under the 1967 legislation), Congress directed EPA to develop primary and secondary "National Ambient Air Quality Standards" (NAAQS). § 109. Currently, the list of "criteria" pollutants includes such substances as sulfur dioxide, particulate matter, oxides of nitrogen, and lead. Primary standards are meant to protect human health from these criteria pollutants; secondary standards are meant to protect "welfare" values, such as aesthetics or odors, from the effects of criteria pollutants. § 109(b). The states then develop plans, known as "State Implementation Plans" (SIPs), to implement the NAAQS. These plans usually require the states, through complicated computer modeling, to determine how much pollution generated by existing stationary sources (e.g., industrial smokestacks) can be assimilated without violating the NAAQS. See, e.g., Cleveland Electric Illuminating Co. v. EPA, 572

F.2d 1150 (6th Cir.1978). As under the Clean Water Act, new sources were required to meet tough, technology based emissions limitations regardless of a state's degree of compliance with the NAAQS. § 111. If the expected pollutant levels exceed the standards, the state must determine which of the stationary sources must cut back their emissions. Additional provisions address pollution from *mobile* sources, i.e., automobiles. Any emissions restrictions are placed within permits issued to stationary sources by state or local air quality control boards. Extensive amendments in 1977 and 1990 placed additional requirements upon states who had failed to attain the NAAQS for the criteria pollutants.

For toxic pollutants, the 1970 Clean Air Act amendments took a different tack. In enacting § 112, Congress added to the environmental alphabet soup by creating the "National Emissions Standards for Hazardous Air Pollutants" (NESHAPs). Unlike the NAAQS, the NESHAPs were to apply directly to individual emitters. In § 112, Congress required EPA to set up special health based standards for those pollutants (other than the criteria pollutants) which might "reasonably be anticipated to result in an increase in mortality, or an increase in serious, irreversible, or incapacitating irreversible illness." § 112(a)(1) (1970 amendments). Congress further directed EPA to include an "ample margin of safety" when issuing these health based standards. § 112(b)(1)(B) (1970 amendments).

For the same reasons that caused EPA to make painfully slow progress under the 1972 Clean Water Act's health based toxic pollutants provisions, EPA's track record under the 1970 Clean Air Act hazardous air pollutants provisions was abysmal. This is not surprising, since Congress modeled the 1972 water toxics provisions on its 1970 air toxics provisions. Initially, the Supreme Court imposed a hurdle, rejecting EPA's attempt to regulate asbestos emissions by ordering work practice changes. Adamo Wrecking Co. v. United States, 434 U.S. 275, 98 S.Ct. 566, 54 L.Ed.2d 538 (1978). In *Adamo Wrecking*, the court threw out a criminal indictment because it found that EPA's ordered work place changes did not meet the statute's definition of "emissions standards." While Congress rejected the *Adamo Wrecking* holding in the 1977 Clean Air Act amendments (§ 112(h) (current version)), much more fundamental obstacles lay in the path of air toxics regulation.

The three principal problems were: (1) the lack of adequate data about the health effects of most potential toxic air pollutants; (2) the potential to shut down major industries if EPA concluded that the required "margin of safety" allowed *no* releases of carcinogens; and (3) the length of time necessary to complete a substance by substance approach to emissions regulation. Compounding the delays inherent in this apprcach was the near certainty that, given the economic stakes involved and the weakness of much of EPA's data, each health based criterion would be challenged in court. Additional issues arose regarding EPA's authority to consider compliance costs as justification to substitute a technology based approach for the health based approach ostensibly required by § 112. In effect, EPA wished to short cut the regulatory path by requiring the application of something akin to the Clean Water Act's "best available technology" (BAT). Lengthy litigation involving the relationship between the required "margin of safety" and EPA's authority to consider compliance costs in setting its ostensibly health based criteria culminated in Judge Bork's now-famous opinion in Natural Resources Defense Council, Inc. v. EPA, 824 F.2d 1146 (D.C.Cir.1987) (en banc). In that opinion, which addressed the air toxic "vinyl chloride," Judge Bork concluded that EPA *could* consider compliance costs in issuing its criteria, but only after it had determined what was a "safe" exposure level to an air toxic based solely on the risk to health.

Indeed, EPA's attempt to regulate vinyl chloride under the original version of § 112 exemplifies that provision's failures. In 1975, EPA proposed technology based vinyl chloride regulations. Litigation over that proposal led to a settlement where EPA set a goal of zero emissions for vinyl chloride. In 1977, EPA proposed new vinyl chloride regulations. These proposals set lower permissible levels than set in the 1975 proposal, but did not achieve the zero emissions goal sought by environmental groups. In 1985, EPA issued its final vinyl chloride regulations. These marked a virtual return to the original 1975 proposal. Litigation over that proposal led to the above described opinion by Judge Bork. In that decision, he threw out the 1985 regulations because of EPA's failure to consider safety before considering compliance costs. Thus, a full 15 years after the initial enactment of § 112, EPA was virtually back to square one: it still had no enforceable vinyl chloride regulation.

Were the problems associated with vinyl chloride regulation unique or had EPA's overall toxic regulation "learning curve" substantially flattened as a result of its vinyl chloride experiences, even a 10 year delay might be forgiven. But nothing suggested that either situation was true. By 1990, two full decades after the initial enactment of § 112, EPA had promulgated standards for only eight hazardous air pollutants. Moreover, only one—benzene—was added in the three years after the vinyl chloride decision. As a result, by 1990 Congress was ready to overhaul the air toxics statutes completely. Ironically, as the source for much of 1990 Clean Air Act Amendments' toxics provisions, Congress borrowed from the 1977 and 1987 Clean Water Act amendments. Thus, the Act whose toxic regulatory provisions had once been modeled *after* the Clean Air Act now serves as the model *for* the Clean Air Act's current toxic provisions.

## 3. CURRENT PROVISIONS

### a. Technology Based Standards

Like the Clean Water Act, the Clean Air Act's toxic provisions: (1) identify specific substances that must be regulated as toxic; (2) require categorization of sources into various classes and categories; (3) impose technology based standards for emitters of those substances; and (4) contemplate enforcement through a state run permit system.

### *i. Toxic Substances*

Substances can reach the list of regulated toxics in two ways. First, Congress specified 189 substances that EPA must regulate as toxic. § 112(b)(1). Second, Congress provided a revised, harm-based definition. This provision requires EPA to add pollutants that "may present * * * a threat of adverse human health effects * * * or adverse environmental effects." § 112(b)(2). The statute illustrates, but does not exhaust, the broad range of adverse human health effects with references to carcinogens, mutagens, teratogens, and other classes of known toxics. It extends beyond substances harmful to human health to include substances that can cause environmental harms. It further defines such harms as reasonably anticipated "significant and widespread adverse effect[s] * * * to wildlife, aquatic life or other natural resources * * *." § 112(a)(7). It excludes from toxic regulation certain pollutants regulated under the NAAQS or under the stratospheric ozone provisions. § 112(b)(2), (e).

### *ii. Emissions Sources*

The Act hinges its technology based emissions restrictions on the volume of hazardous pollutants emitted by a particular source. It defines "major sources" as a "stationary source or group of * * * sources located within a contiguous area and under common control" that can emit at least "10 tons per year * * * of any hazardous air pollutant or 25 tons per year * * * of any combination of hazardous air pollutants." § 112(a)(1). To place some perspective on this volume, large dry cleaning businesses may well fall within the major source definition. In general, emitters of lower volumes fall within the residual definition of "area sources." Area sources include any other source of hazardous air pollutants, other than motor vehicles. § 112(a)(2). They include wood stoves and such businesses as smaller dry cleaners and gasoline service stations. EPA, however, may reduce the volume of emissions necessary to trigger "major source" treatment below the 10/25 ton levels because of "potency * * * persistence, potential for bioaccumulation" or other factors. § 112(a)(1).

As it had done for nearly 20 years under the Clean Water Act, in the 1990 Clean Air Act amendments Congress required EPA to divide major and area sources into industrial categories. § 112(c). Because the list of area sources was potentially much more diverse than the list of major sources, Congress told EPA how to prioritize its source categorization. It gave EPA five years to develop an area source list that ensured regulation of "area sources representing 90 percent of the area source emissions of the 30 hazardous air pollutants that represent the greatest threat to public health in the largest number of urban areas * * *." § 112(c)(3).

This latter provision lays the groundwork for an urban air toxics program with a goal of reducing by 75% the cancer risks associated with urban air. § 112(k).

### *iii. Emissions Restrictions*

Within a given source category, different technology based emissions requirements apply to the two classes of sources. Major sources must make the "maximum degree of reduction * * * achievable" of hazardous air emissions. § 112(d)(2). In popular terms, this requires emissions reductions to the level reached by application of the "maximum achievable control technology" (MACT). § 112(g)(2) (referencing MACT). (As noted above, since 1977 EPA could require emission reductions not just from technological changes, i.e., from pollution control devices, but also from process changes, ingredient changes, work practices, and operator training. § 112(d)(2).) The statute further distinguishes MACT for new and existing sources. For new sources, defined as sources constructed or reconstructed after the initial proposal of an applicable emissions standard, § 112(a)(4), MACT may "not be less stringent than the emission control that is achieved in practice by the best controlled similar source." § 112(d)(3). For existing sources, MACT can be no less stringent than the average limitations reached by a group of the five best performing existing sources, if there are less than 30 sources within a category, or the best 12 percent of sources, if there are more than 30. § 112(d)(3). In any case, when setting MACT for a particular source category, EPA can consider "the cost of achieving such emission reduction, and any non-air quality health and environmental impacts and energy requirements." § 112(d)(2).

Litigation over MACT-setting has focused on the relationship between the "steps" contemplated by §§ 112(d)(3) and (d)(2). EPA has looked first to the (d)(3) requirements, to determine what has actually been accomplished. These set what have become known as the "floors," or minimum stringency levels. Once these are determined, EPA then looks to the (d)(2) requirements, and considers whether a higher (tougher) standard is appropriate. In interpreting both the (d)(3) and (d)(2) requirements, EPA must deal with a substantial range of source performance variability. Measurements taken from the same source may vary substantially over time; measurements taken from different sources may vary as well. In a series of cases that culminated in Cement Kiln Recycling Coalition v. EPA, 255 F.3d 855 (D.C.Cir.2001), the D.C. Circuit addressed EPA's obligations to consider variability in its MACT setting. It struck down EPA's solution: setting the floors based on the worst emissions level at sources that were using the best pollution control technology. Similarly, in Northeast Maryland Waste Disposal Authority v. EPA, 358 F.3d 936 (D.C.Cir.2004), the court rejected EPA's floor-setting. It summarized, "EPA has once again improperly invoked achievability (incorrectly relying on the emission variability of *all* [sources within the category] that use the technology rather than on the variability of the *best performing* unit) to gloss over the actual achievement requirement."

An open question remains about EPA's discretion to not set MACT standards for very-low risk sources. See, e.g., 67 F.R. 47, 894 (July 22, 2002). EPA has used authority under § 112(c)(9)(B) to "delist" a category of sources if all sources within the category are "low-risk." See, e.g., 69 F.R. 45, 944 (July 30, 2004). These delistings, favored by industry, have been criticized by environmental and health advocates.

Area sources are subject to potentially less stringent reductions. The Act requires area sources to reduce emissions either to levels associated with MACT or in EPA's discretion to "generally available control technologies or management practices" (GACT). § 112(d)(5). EPA must review and revise MACT and GACT at least every 8 years. § 112(d)(6).

The statute permits few variances from MACT. It did allow up to 6 year extensions of compliance with MACT standards for sources that reduced their hazardous air emissions by 90 to 95% before EPA proposed an applicable MACT standard. § 112(i)(5)(A). Additional extensions, up to five years, were authorized for sources that had invested in emissions reductions under provisions applicable in portions of states that had failed to attain NAAQS. § 112(i)(6). Brief, one or two year extensions are also possible if the additional time is necessary to install pollution controls. § 112(f)(4)(B), (i)(3)(B). Beyond these extensions, the principal way to avoid MACT requirements is a presidential exemption. § 112(i)(4). To qualify, a source must demonstrate that the technology to implement such standard is unavailable and that it is in the national security interest to grant an exemption. Each such presidential exemption, while renewable, may last no more than two years.

### *iv. EPA Performance in Setting MACT Standards*

In the 1990 Clean Air Act amendments, Congress attempted to impose some relatively strict deadlines for the EPA to determine MACT. Specific deadlines were set for 1992, 1994, 1997 and 2000. As an incentive for EPA to meet the deadlines, Congress created what became known as the "MACT hammer." § 112(j). Under the hammer, if EPA missed a MACT deadline by 18 months for any source categories, each major source within that category would have to apply for a case-by-case MACT determination. To avoid all of these case-specific determinations, much of whose burden would fall on the state agencies that administer the permit programs, EPA worked to meet the deadlines.

Over a dozen years beginning in the mid-1990's, EPA set initial MACT standards for virtually all of the source categories. In contrast to the extremely slow, pre-1990 regulatory pace (seven standards in 20 years), by the mid-1990's, EPA was promulgating an average of 10 a year. Many of these individual rules involved multiple pollutants. For example, in 1994, EPA promulgated MACT regulations for hazardous organic air pollutants from the synthetic organic chemical industry. 40 C.F.R. § 633.100. These standards covered 111 of the 189 pollutants listed in § 112(b).

As part of the regulation, EPA established an emissions averaging procedure for sources with up to 25 emissions points. This provision is a cousin of the famous—or infamous—"bubble" concept developed under other portions of the Act. Such concepts envision a hypothetical bubble over contiguous emissions points controlled by the same person. As long as the total emissions from all sources under the "bubble" are (in the case of toxics) at least 10% less than the requirements that would otherwise apply to each source were it treated separately, MACT is met for the whole group. These approaches give a source owner some flexibility in choosing where its investments can make the greatest overall contribution to pollution reduction. See also § 112(g)(1) (permitting some pollution reductions to offset some pollution increases and thus avoiding new source MACT and permit requirements).

Still, despite its substantial improvement over its pre-1990 performance, EPA still lagged behind the mandated deadlines. It did not finally complete promulgation of its initial MACT standards for source categories until 2004. And, as of early 2007, despite an eight-year Integrated Urban Air Toxics Strategy, it had only completed rules for 16 of the required 70 area source categories. Pursuant to court orders issued in 2003 and 2006, EPA was to complete rules for the remaining 54 categories by June 2009.

### *v. Permit System*

To enforce its provisions, the Act contemplates a state based permit program. New sources, or existing sources who wish to modify their plants, must apply for a permit. § 112(g)(2), (i)(1). Once a construction permit is granted, the permittee need not comply with any additional, subsequently promulgated residual risk standards (see below) for 10 years. § 112(i)(7). Absent a modification or reconstruction of its plant, an existing source is not expressly required to obtain a permit. Rather, the Act simply prohibits an existing source from operating in violation of a MACT or GACT standard. § 112(i)(3)(A). Still, the Act contemplates that most states will adopt a program that will encompass existing major sources. § 112(j), (*l*). These programs invariably are permit based.

### *vi. Mobile Sources*

In addition to the extensive stationary sources program sketched out above, § 202(*l*) requires EPA to regulate mobile sources of hazardous air pollutants. EPA was to study the need and feasibility for regulation of such sources by 1992, and to promulgate any necessary regulations by 1995. In 2007, EPA adopted the Mobile Source Air Toxics Rule, with the goal to reduce benzene and other hazardous air pollutants by imposing controls on benzene content in gasoline, limits on passenger vehicle emissions, and limiting emissions from portable containers. 72 Fed. Reg. 8428 (Feb. 26, 2007).

### b. Harm Based Elements

Recognizing that even MACT might not eliminate all risks to health from hazardous air pollutants, Congress also established a harm based backup system. Eight years after promulgating MACT, EPA can require additional emissions reductions to avoid any unacceptable residual risks. § 112(f)(2)(A). Before proposing any such additional restrictions, EPA, in consultation with the Surgeon General, must report to Congress on the health risks remaining from hazardous air pollutants. § 112(f)(1). Congress set a 1996 deadline for the initial report. Using 1996 data, EPA released an initial National Scale Air Toxics Assessment in 2002. Using 1999 data, it released a second assessment in 2006. Each assessment considers estimated emissions, concentrations, and risks.

The Act makes some minor improvements on the uncertainties attendant to the harm based approach that inhered prior to 1990; it does not, however, eliminate those uncertainties in any meaningful way. It begins ambiguously by incorporating the pre-1990 language that requires such standards if necessary "to provide an ample margin of safety to protect public health." § 112(f)(2)(A). It is unclear, however, what portion of the pre-1990 case law, if any, this reference is meant to include. In recognition of the impact of hazardous air pollutants on other environmental values, the current statute allows EPA to demand restrictions even greater than necessary to protect human health. Before taking this additional step, however, EPA must consider "costs, energy, safety, and other relevant factors." § 112(f)(2)(A). Arguably, because the statute does not expressly require EPA to consider "cost, energy, safety, and other relevant factors" before providing the "ample margin of safety to protect public health," Congress did not intend EPA to consider such factors when providing the health margin.

The Act does address EPA's risk evaluation for carcinogens. For carcinogens, EPA must promulgate a health based standard if the technology based standards "do not reduce the lifetime excess cancer risks to the individual most exposed * * * to one in a million." § 112(f)(2)(A). Nothing in the Act, however, instructs EPA *how* to make this difficult risk assessment. Nevertheless, other provisions of the Act required EPA to consult with the National Academy of Sciences to assess its risk assessment protocols. § 112(*o*)(1). The National Academy of Sciences issued a report in the early 1990's that generally upheld EPA's risk assessment approaches, but suggested numerous improvements in its procedures.

In 1998, EPA issued guidelines for Ecological Risk Assessment. Under the guidelines, EPA uses a three-phase approach to risk assessment: problem formulation, analysis and risk characterization. Among other matters, it included guidelines for mutagenicity, carcinogenicity, developmental toxicity, reproductive toxicity, and neurotoxicity.

### c. Other Provisions

In addition to the technology and harm based standards discussed immediately above, and the reports and studies described in the concluding portion of this Chapter, two additional provisions merit attention.

#### *i. Emergency Releases*

First, in response to the tragedies at Bhopal, India, and elsewhere, the Act contains extensive provisions to address accidental releases. § 112(r). In 1994, as required by the Act, EPA listed the 100 substances which posed the "greatest risk of causing death, injury or serious adverse effects to human health or the environment from accidental releases." § 112(r)(3). This list was developed in part by reference to the Emergency Planning and Community Right-to-Know Act (see Chapter 4); in part by a list required by statute; and in part by consideration of three factors (severity of acute health effects, likelihood of accidental releases, and potential magnitude of human exposure). § 112(r)(4). For each listed substance, EPA had to determine threshold release quantities. In establishing those thresholds, EPA considered "the toxicity, reactivity, volatility, dispersibility, combustibility, or flammability of the substance." § 112(r)(5).

The Act created a Chemical Safety and Hazard Investigation Board to investigate accidental releases, and recommend risk management and response plans. § 112(r)(6)(C). EPA, in turn, is authorized to require accidental release reports and responses.

### *ii. Incinerator Provisions*

Finally, special provisions apply to waste incinerators. § 129. Incinerators regulated under the Clean Air Act include those not covered under RCRA. § 129(g)(1). See Chapter 6. These provisions require EPA to develop, for new sources, specific numerical limitations for 11 substances commonly found in incinerator emissions. § 129(a)(4). Guidelines were also required for existing sources. § 129(b)(1). Additional provisions govern emissions monitoring, operator training, and state permits. § 129(c), (d), (e).

## 4. EVALUATION

Now more than two decades after Congress last substantially amended the Clean Air Act, the regulatory legacy of the 300 pages added by the 1990 amendments to the United States Code has taken its initial shape. The regulatory battle will likely be rejoined once EPA begins to address the residual risks remaining after application of MACT standards. Most likely, Congress will allow EPA a substantial opportunity to address these residual risks before wading again into the toxic muck itself. It is unlikely, however, that Congress will give EPA the same 20 years it gave it following the 1970 enactment of the original health based regulatory scheme. Indeed, further legislation is likely. Despite substantial scientific and government efforts over the past 30 years, substantial difficulties, expenses, and uncertainties still attend to health based risk assessments. Since so much of risk assessment ultimately presents policy choices, to resolve the likely administrative gridlock, Congress will almost certainly have to intervene.

## D. REGULATION OF TOXICS UNDER THE SAFE DRINKING WATER ACT

### 1. INTRODUCTION

Although not as emphasized in law school as the preceding two Acts, the Safe Drinking Water Act (SDWA), 42 U.S.C.A. § 300f et seq., has an increasingly important role to play in the regulation of toxic substances. Its impact can be substantial. It has threatened many small, rural water systems with bankruptcy, as they have sought ways to spread among their often tiny population bases the costs of the substantial improvements frequently required by the Act. It has forced some large urban water districts to consider billion dollar level investments to change their water treatment methods to avoid toxic byproducts associated with the chlorination of water from certain types of sources. The standards promulgated under the Act may serve as an "applicable or relevant and appropriate requirement" (ARAR) under CERCLA to determine the level to which a contaminated groundwater site must be cleaned. See, e.g., Ohio v. EPA, 997 F.2d 1520 (D.C.Cir.1993). And finally, the Act has required water purveyors whose waters violate applicable standards to notify millions of consumers annually of these violations. These warnings, often tucked away in the back of a water bill, have led to fascinating, even Pulitzer Prize winning, reports of the circumstances triggering the violations.

## 2. HISTORY

The statutes now known as the Safe Drinking Water Act were originally enacted in 1944 as the "Public Health Service Act." The enforceable provisions of this legislation were largely directed at communicable water borne diseases. In 1962, under this Act, the Public Health Service issued nonenforceable guidelines for other drinking water contaminants. In 1974, Congress completely rewrote the law and gave it its current popular name. For convenience, the following discussion and citations will use the popular name, rather than the more formal "Public Health Service Act."

In the first dozen years after the 1974 legislation, EPA issued regulations for only 22 contaminants. Again dissatisfied with this slow pace, Congress substantially amended the law in 1986 and gave it much of its current form. These amendments doubled the Act's length. In particular, the 1986 provisions required EPA to regulate 83 specified contaminants within three years, and an additional 25 contaminants every three years thereafter. In addition, they added new programs to control lead in drinking water.

In 1996, Congress again amended the Act. The 1996 amendments gave EPA greater flexibility in prioritizing the contaminants to be regulated. In place of the "25 contaminants every three years" required under the 1986 amendments, Congress gave EPA five years to choose whether to regulate the five worst contaminants not yet regulated. Additional provisions addressed rising concerns over microbial contaminants; required specified cost/benefit and risk reduction analyses; revised enforcement, notification, exemptions and variances, and citizens' suit provisions; and encouraged water supply protection and conservation. Many of these provisions were designed to ease the regulatory burden placed on small, rural water providers.

In 2002, in response to the September 11, 2001, terrorist attacks, Congress again revisited the Act. In passing the Public Health Security and Bioterrorism Preparedness Response Act, Pub. L. No. 107–188, 116 Stat. 594, it included the "Drinking Water Security and Safety Amendments." Among other matters, it required various assessments of water systems' vulnerabilities to potential terrorist attacks.

## 3. STRUCTURE OF THE ACT

### a. Introduction

In its basic structure, the Act most closely resembles elements of the Clean Air Act, although it also imports the Clean Water Act's technology based standards. Like the Clean Air Act's NAAQS, the Safe Drinking Water Act creates a scheme with federal primary and secondary standards. The primary standards aim to protect health, while the secondary standards address public welfare, in particular, substances that affect color and taste. Like the Clean Air Act's SIPs, the Safe Drinking Water Act looks to the states for primary planning and enforcement of the federal standards, with federal enforcement as a backup. Like the Clean Water Act, the Safe Drinking Water Act requires EPA to use a version of "best available technology" when setting the drinking water standards.

The D.C. Circuit has upheld the constitutionality of the Safe Drinking Water Act under the Commerce Clause. Nebraska v. EPA, 331 F.3d 995 (D.C.Cir.2003).

### b. "Public Water Systems"

The Act applies to "public water systems." Broadly defined, this includes water purveyors with at least 15 service connections or who "regularly" provide service to 25 individuals. § 1401(4)(A). A subclass of "public water systems," known as "community water systems," includes those who serve either 15 or more connections "used by year-round residents of the area served by the system" or 25 year round residents. § 1401(15). Exemptions from the definition of "connection" provide some relief for small or rural water systems. § 1401(4)(B). For waters provided by "public water systems," EPA promulgates appropriate primary and secondary drinking water regulations. § 1401(1), (2).

### c. The Threshold Criteria

Congress has required EPA to promulgate regulations for contaminants that meet three requirements. First, EPA must identify contaminants that "may have an adverse effect on the health of persons." § 1412(b)(1)(A)(i). Under this step, EPA need only find a non-de minimis chance that there could be some adverse health effect. The statute's language requires neither certainty nor even probability of harm. Prior to 1996, this was the only threshold criterion. In the 1996 amendments, however, Congress tightened this open-ended authority. It added two more threshold criteria. Under the first of these new criteria, EPA must find at least "a substantial likelihood that the contaminant will occur in public water systems with a frequency and at levels of public health concern." § 1412(b)(1)(A)(ii). Under the second, in its "sole judgment," EPA must determine that regulation of a contaminant "presents a meaningful opportunity for health risk reduction * * *." § 1412(b)(1)(A)(iii).

### d. The Listing Process

To help EPA prioritize its choice of contaminants to regulate, Congress has created a listing process. The process includes a formally published list, a schedule for regulatory decisions, and specific cost/benefit, health risk assessment, and feasibility analyses. All of these requirements are set forth in the heart of the Act: § 1412(b). This single subsection, with fifteen subparts of its own, occupies multiple pages of the code.

Prior to 1996, Congress had mandated that, every two years, EPA promulgate regulations for 25 previously unregulated contaminants drawn from a list developed after the 1986 amendments. Under the 1996 amendments, Congress has given EPA substantially more flexibility. Beginning in February, 1998, and every 5 years thereafter, EPA must produce a new list of unregulated contaminants. § 1412(b)(1)(B)(i). The list must include the published CERCLA hazardous substances and pesticides registered under FIFRA. Additional substances must include those contaminants that "are known or anticipated to occur in public water systems, and which may require regulation * * *." EPA's decisions to add substances to the list, or keep them off the list, are not reviewable judicially.

Beginning in August 2001, and every five years thereafter, EPA must decide whether to regulate five substances from the list. Unlike the pre-1996 law, EPA does not have to issue regulations for those five substances; it only has to decide "whether or not to regulate such contaminants." § 1412(b)(1)(B)(ii). The decision to regulate must be based "on the best available public health information." A decision not to regulate a contaminant is immediately reviewable in a court. A decision to regulate is only reviewable after the final regulations have been published. Generally, EPA has up to three and a half years to complete the process after deciding that a contaminant needs regulation. § 1412(b)(1)(E).

In selecting substances to regulate, Congress has directed EPA to consider the impacts of a potential contaminant on specified population groups "that are identifiable as being at a greater risk of adverse health effects due to exposure * * *." § 1412(b)(1)(C). For example, infants, children, pregnant women, and the elderly are often considered such "sensitive receptors."

### e. The Regulations

For each contaminant that it decides to regulate, EPA must first establish "maximum contaminant level goals" (MCLGs). § 1412(a)(3). These nonenforceable goals are set "at the level at which no known or anticipated adverse effects on the health of persons occur and which [allow] an adequate margin of safety." § 1412(b)(4)(A). Compliance costs are not considered in setting MCLGs. EPA has now set MCLGs for scores of substances. Approximately two dozen are set at zero; the balance allow the presence of specific concentrations, often on the level of several parts per billion. See 40 C.F.R. § 141.50.

In addition to the MCLGs, for each regulated contaminant, EPA must either establish "maximum contaminant levels" (MCLs) or treatment techniques. § 1401(1)(C). In general, MCLs are maximum permissible concentrations in water delivered to a user. § 1401(3). EPA must set an MCL for each listed contaminant unless it determines that it is neither technically nor economically feasible to set one. § 1401(1)(C). For example, for substances that are insoluble in water, it might not be technically or economically feasible to detect their presence. In such instances, EPA must specify a treatment technique that will ensure that the listed substances are removed sufficiently from the water source. In effect, this requires the application of something akin to "best available technology." For example, EPA might require filtration or disinfection to reduce the contaminants to acceptable levels. See, e.g., § 1412(b)(7). Indeed, these two techniques have been required for such contaminants as giardia lamblia, viruses, certain bacteria, and turbidity. 40 C.F.R. § 141.70.

Although MCLs are ordinarily to be set at "feasible" levels, the 1996 amendments gave EPA limited authority to set stricter than feasible MCLs "if the technology, treatment techniques, and other means used to determine the feasible level would" themselves increase health risks. § 1412(b)(5). Such increases might come from increased concentrations of other contaminants or interference with the effectiveness of treatment processes required to meet other primary drinking water regulations. In such circumstances, the Act allows EPA to balance the costs and benefits from the alternative regulatory approaches.

If technically and economically feasible to detect the level of a given contaminant, EPA must set an MCL "as close to the [MCLG] as feasible." § 1412(b)(4)(B). In the context of setting an MCL, "feasible" means "feasible with the use of the best [available] technology [BAT], treatment techniques and other means * * *." § 1412(b)(4)(D). In some respects, the statutory language used to describe BAT for MCL setting suggests the incorporation of more advanced technologies than required under the Clean Water Act. Indeed, the Safe Drinking Water Act's BAT appears to be somewhere in between two Clean Water Act standards: BAT (required for existing sources) and BADT (required for new sources). As under both the Clean Water and Clean Air Acts, Congress allowed EPA to "consider" compliance costs when setting BAT under the Safe Drinking Water Act. § 1412(b)(4)(D). Unlike the other two Acts, however, Congress specifically suggested that newly emerging technologies, even if not yet adopted, should provide BAT standards. These newly emerging technologies must have been field tested; laboratory demonstrations alone are insufficient. § 1412(b)(4)(D). Moreover, unlike the technology standards in the other two Acts, for one of the largest classes of contaminants—synthetic organic compounds—Congress established a benchmark

BAT standard. It specifically determined that "granular activated carbon" was "feasible" for their control. § 1412(b)(4)(D). Thus, for these chemicals, EPA must set BAT to at least the levels associated with the use of this treatment technology. The 1996 amendments required EPA to publish a list of the technologies or treatment techniques that are feasible for small public water systems. EPA 815–R–97–002 (Aug. 1997). Like the technology standards under the other Acts, EPA must review and revise these technology standards periodically; under the SDWA, it is at least every six years. § 1412(b)(9).

The secondary regulations include MCLs set for nontoxic substances that affect color and taste. Secondary regulations have been set for about a dozen substances, including aluminum, chloride, copper, and silver. (At much higher concentrations, these substances may also pose health hazards). 40 C.F.R. § 143.3. Secondary regulations are goals that are not binding on the states.

### f. Required Cost/Benefit Analyses

While setting the MCLs or treatment techniques, EPA must undertake an extensive cost/benefit analysis. (These are not required if EPA chooses to maintain pre-1986 MCLs. City of Waukesha v. EPA, 320 F.3d 228 (D.C.Cir.2003).) The risk assessment provisions require EPA to consider the "quantifiable and nonquantifiable" health risk reduction benefits and costs associated with each proposed MCL. § 1412(b)(3)(C). In making these assessments, EPA must use "the best available, peer reviewed science and supporting studies," § 1412(b)(3)(A), and ensure that "the presentation of information on public health effects is comprehensive, informative, and understandable." § 1412(b)(3)(B). In general, EPA may set MCLs at the level that "maximizes health risk reduction benefits at a cost that is justified by the benefits." § 1412(b)(6)(A).

### g. Variances and Exemptions

The Act allows several variances and exemptions. To obtain a variance from the primary standards, a water system must show to the enforcement authority's satisfaction that there are characteristics of its raw water supply that, despite the application of BAT, preclude the attainment of MCLs. § 1415(a)(1)(A); 40 C.F.R. § 141.4. In addition, the applicant for the variance must demonstrate that "the variance will not result in an unreasonable risk to health." § 1415(a)(1)(A). Where EPA established treatment techniques in lieu of MCLs, variances are also possible if the applicant can demonstrate that the purity of the raw water source makes the treatment technique unnecessary. § 1415(a)(1)(B).

Although the Act requires the establishment of a "schedule for compliance" whenever a variance is granted, § 1415(a)(1)(A), nothing within the statute directly precludes the periodic extension of such variances. In effect, a variance can become a de facto exemption. EPA, however, has authority to review and reject variances. § 1415(a)(1)(E)–(G).

The 1996 amendments created, in effect, a permanent exemption for small public water systems. Systems with less than 10,000 customers can apply for a variance if they cannot afford to comply with a primary drinking water regulation. § 1415(e)(1), (3). Congress has required EPA to specify approved variance technologies for each regulated contaminant that are appropriate to different sizes of water systems. § 1412(b)(15). Variances are not available for pre-1986 regulations or for microbial contaminants. § 1415(e)(6). Small system variances last indefinitely, although they must be reviewed every five years. § 1415(e)(5).

In addition to the de facto exemptions available as extended variances, the statute creates an express exemption. To obtain an exemption from either an MCL or a treatment technique, the applicant must show three things. First, it must demonstrate that "compelling factors" preclude compliance. § 1416(a)(1). The statute specifically allows "economic factors," i.e., compliance costs, to be such "compelling factors." Second, it must show that it either was already in business when EPA promulgated the relevant MCL or treatment technique, or, if it is a new water provider, it has "no reasonable alternative source of drinking water." § 1416(a)(2). Finally, it must show that "the granting of the exemption will not result in an unreasonable risk to health." § 1416(a)(3). Like the variance procedure, the exemption procedure requires a "schedule of compliance." § 1416(b)(1). Extensions and periodic renewals are possible for some exemptions. § 1416(b)(2)(B), (C). Again, EPA has authority to review and reject exemptions. § 1416(d).

### h. Enforcement

Like both the Clean Water and Clean Air Acts, the Safe Drinking Water Act contemplates that states will receive primary responsibility for ensuring compliance with the national regulations. § 1422. EPA retains backup enforcement authority. §§ 1422(c), 1423(a). The courts, however, retain traditional equitable jurisdiction to weigh and balance the costs and benefits of forcing compliance with an EPA order. See, e.g., United States v. Massachusetts Water Resources Authority, 256 F.3d 36 (1st Cir.2001).

### i. Public Notification

Perhaps the most striking provisions of the Act are its public notification requirements. Each regulated water supplier must notify its customers of violations of MCLs or treatment techniques, as well as its receipt of any variance or exemption. § 1414(c). Required notices "must not contain overly technical language or very small print;" "must not be formatted in a way that defeats the purpose of the notice;" and "must not contain language which nullifies the purpose of the notice." 40 C.F.R. § 141.205(c).

EPA regulations divide the realm of violations into three tiers, according to the seriousness of the violation and the potential adverse health effects. 40 C.F.R. § 141.201. See also Appendices A and B to

Subpart Q of 40 C.F.R. Part 141. Tier 1 includes situations with a significant potential to have serious adverse effects on human health from short-term exposure. Tier 2 includes situations with a potential to have serious adverse effects on human health. Tier 3 covers all other situations.

The severity of the violation determines the timing and placement of the notice. For Tier 1 violations, within 24 hours after it learns of the violation, the water system must immediately contact all persons served. It must either: air its notices on radio and television stations; post conspicuous notices; or hand deliver notices. 40 C.F.R. § 141.202(c). Tier 2 violations must be issued within 30 days, with repeat notices at specified intervals. These violations may be reported through press releases, public posting, internet posting, newspaper ads or individual mailings. Often, these individual mailings are included in a customer's water bill. Curiosity over the meaning of one such mailing led one customer to investigate the circumstances behind the violation. The trail of intrigue uncovered by this inquisitive customer eventually led to a Pulitzer Prize winning newspaper account of local corruption. Tier 3 violations must be reported no later than a year after the water system learns of the violation. It can use a variety of methods, including mailed, posted, published or e-mailed notice. It may also include the notice in the report described in the next paragraph.

The 1996 amendments added an additional notification requirement applicable to "community water systems." Each year, each community water system must provide each of its customers a "consumer confidence report." § 1414(c)(4). These reports must describe the regulatory standards and indicate the contaminants that have been detected in that system's water. In lieu of bulk mailings, small systems may only have to make copies of their annual reports available to their customers.

### j. Other Provisions

In addition to the general provisions, the Act contains several provisions addressing specific drinking water problems. Special provisions govern the regulation of arsenic, sulfate, and radon. §§ 1412(b)(12), (13). Portions of the Act address underground drinking water supplies. Of particular concern in this area are the underground injection wells used to dispose of hazardous wastes. §§ 1421–1428. Standards developed under these provisions interact with the RCRA requirements for such disposal. Additional provisions ban the use of lead in drinking water pipes, § 1417, and water coolers, §§ 1461–1465. Finally, the Act grants EPA unusual powers to ensure that adequate chemicals are available for water treatment. § 1441.

## 4. EVALUATION

Like most major federal regulatory schemes, the now more-than-30 year track record of the Safe Drinking Water Act has been spotty. On the one hand, it has established minimal national standards for many of the most important toxic substances that can be found in the national drinking water supply. Moreover, its ban on lead in drinking water pipes and water coolers is an important protection for the nation's children. Finally, its reporting requirements have increased national awareness of the importance of ensuring an adequate drinking water supply.

On the other hand, at least prior to 1996, some critics charged that it was an unduly expensive and inflexible system, not based on adequate risk or cost/benefit analyses. Moreover, many public water systems complained that their customers were unduly alarmed by the notices that showed minute, virtually undetectable amounts of toxic substances in many of the nation's drinking water supplies. Still other critics charged that EPA was too slow and cumbersome, failed to keep pace with the continuing growth of toxic substances that might end up in the drinking water supply, and permitted too many exemptions or variances.

The 1996 amendments were meant to address all of these concerns. In the first five years after the amendments, EPA did not noticeably pick up the regulatory pace, adding only 8 more contaminants to the cumulative list, while beginning regulation on another 16. By early 2007, there were Primary Drinking Water Standards set for 7 types of microorganisms; 4 disinfectant byproducts; 3 disinfectants; 16 inorganic chemicals; 52 organic chemicals; and 4 radionuclides, for a total of 86 contaminants. Secondary standards had been set for 15 contaminants. Most of the primary and secondary standards, however, had been set before the 1996 amendments. In addition to adding to the list of regulated contaminants, since 2000 EPA has published regulations and guidance in a number of areas, including general analysis and sampling procedures as well as information collection and public notice requirements.

On the surface, the Drinking Water Program seems to be making steady but slow progress. Despite the near overhaul of its statutory framework in 1996, the program acts more like a mature program rather than as an aggressive new program. And it remains dogged by questions about the cost-benefit analyses and risk assessments that are at its health-based heart.

## E. COMMON FEATURES OF THE ACTS

In addition to the specific provisions addressed above, the three Acts share many other features in their approach to toxic pollutants.

### 1. RELATIONSHIP OF FEDERAL AND STATE LAW

Each of the Acts addresses the relationship of federal and state law in three areas: (1) preemption; (2) implementation; and (3) federal compliance.

#### a. Preemption

Each Act contemplates the establishment of minimum federal levels of protection for the relevant resources. After Congress sketches the broad outlines, EPA sets out the basic regulatory scheme. For example, EPA identifies the toxic substances subject to regulation under the specific Acts. It then indicates the level of emissions, discharges, or concentrations permissible in the ambient air or water, or in drinking water. These federal levels, however, serve as floors, not as ceilings. Thus, the states are generally free to set stricter standards. CWA § 510; CAA § 112(r)(11) (accidental release provisions); SDWA § 1414(e). The states may choose to add substances not regulated by EPA, or set tougher standards than required by EPA. They may not, however, impose weaker standards.

### b. Implementation

Each Act offers the states a leading role in implementation, subject to federal oversight and backup enforcement. For example, the Clean Air and Clean Water Acts offer the states the ability to receive federal approval to administer the permit systems required under both Acts. CWA § 402(b); CAA § 112(*l*). Most states have sought and received such approval. Similarly, the Safe Drinking Water Act contemplates that states can receive primary authority to implement that Act. SDWA § 1413. Where the states choose not to assume this authority, or where EPA determines that the state programs are inadequate, EPA assumes primary enforcement authority. See, e.g., SDWA § 1413(b)(1), (c). Finally, EPA retains oversight over approved state enforcement programs, and can step in if it finds state enforcement lax. See, e.g., SDWA

§§ 1414(a)(1)(B), 1431(a). Such a step, however, raises both political as well as practical problems for EPA, and is not frequently taken.

### c. Federal Facilities

Finally, each Act requires the federal government to comply with the requirements of any state program. CWA § 313(a); CAA § 118(a); SDWA § 1428(h). Under the Clean Air and Safe Drinking Water Acts, the President may grant limited exemptions from state requirements regulating toxics. CAA § 118(b), referencing § 112(i)(4); SDWA § 1428. No such presidential exemptions are possible for releases of toxics from federal facilities regulated under the Clean Water Act. CWA § 313(a).

## 2. MONITORING, RECORD KEEPING AND REPORTING REQUIREMENTS

All three Acts impose extensive monitoring, record keeping and reporting requirements. See, e.g., CWA § 308; CAA § 504(b), (c); SDWA § 1445. The regulations implementing these statutory commands are voluminous. See, e.g., 40 C.F.R. Part 63 (Clean Air Act NESHAPs testing and monitoring requirements). Much of the cost of compliance with the Acts comes from these requirements. The information gleaned from the monitoring reports is generally available to the public. Environmental and public health groups often use this information to bring successful citizens' suits against violators.

## 3. ENFORCEMENT PROVISIONS

### a. Public Enforcement Provisions

Each Act authorizes both public and private enforcement of its provisions. Public enforcement options include criminal, civil, and administrative actions. CWA § 309; CAA § 113; SDWA § 1423(b). Criminal sanctions can include substantial fines and lengthy imprisonment. For example, under the Clean Water Act, fines can start at $2,500 per day for negligent offenders and range up to $100,000 per day for repeat "knowing" violators. CWA § 309(c)(1), (2). That same Act authorizes prison terms ranging from a year or less for negligent, first time violators, up to 15 years for knowing endangerment. CWA § 309(c)(1), (3). Repeat knowing endangerment under the Clean Air Act can trigger a 30 year prison term. CAA § 113(c)(5)(A). In few cases, however, have maximum fines or sentences been sought or imposed.

Civil penalties under the three Acts can range up to $25,000 per day. CWA § 309(d); CAA § 113(b); SDWA § 1414(b). The Clean Water Act provides an illustrative list of factors that courts should use in setting any civil penalty. CWA § 309(d). These nonexclusive factors include the seriousness of the violation, the economic benefits of noncompliance, the past compliance history, and the violator's good faith efforts to comply. Although the other two Acts do not include such a provision, courts will likely consider such factors anyway.

Administrative penalties imposed by EPA can range up to $25,000 per day of violation under the Clean Air Act, and $10,000 per day under the Clean Water and Safe Drinking Water Acts. CWA § 309(g)(2); CAA § 113(d)(1); SDWA § 1423(c). Both the Clean Water and Clean Air Acts identify the kinds of factors EPA should use when determining the amount of any administrative penalty. CWA § 309(g)(3); CAA § 113(e). Among the illustrative factors listed are the economic impact of the penalty, the party's compliance history, its good faith in attempting to comply, and the severity of the violation. CAA § 113(e)(1). The Clean Water and Clean Air Acts specifically authorize a court to enjoin violations of each Act. CWA § 309(b); CAA § 113(b). Such authority is implicit in the Safe Drinking Water Act. SDWA § 1414(b) (court may issue "judgment" that protects the public health). All three statutes authorize EPA to issue administrative orders commanding compliance with statutory, regulatory, or permit terms. CWA § 309(a)(3); CAA § 113(a); SDWA § 1414(g). Violation of such a compliance order is a separately sanctionable offense. CWA § 309(d); CAA § 113(c)(1); SDWA § 1414(g)(3)(A).

Each Act also empowers EPA to take emergency actions in response to an imminent and substantial endangerment of the public health, welfare, or the environment. CWA § 504(a); CAA § 303; SDWA § 1431. Actions commenced under similar provisions of other environmental statutes suggest that EPA has enormous discretion to determine the existence of such an imminent and substantial endangerment. See, e.g., CERCLA § 106(a); RCRA § 7003(a).

### b. Citizens' Suits

In addition to the extensive public enforcement actions, each of the three Acts has a citizens' suit provision. CWA § 505; CAA § 304; SDWA § 1449. These provisions authorize suit against both EPA and private parties alleged to be in violation of the relevant Acts. Special provisions in each Act govern judicial actions seeking review of EPA regulations. CWA § 509(b); CAA § 307(b)(1), (d)(8)–(9); SDWA § 1448.

The Acts do not authorize suits against private parties for purely past violations of the Acts. Rather, citizens' suits may only be brought against private parties if, as of the time that the suit is filed, the defendants remain out of compliance with the respective Acts or any applicable regulations or permit requirements. They contain the usual pre-suit notice requirements found in comparable provisions in other statutes. CWA § 505(b); CAA § 304(b); SDWA § 1449(b). For alleged violations of standards governing toxic substances, the usual 60 day waiting period is not required. See, e.g., CWA § 505(b). Each Act authorizes the award of attorneys' fees and costs whenever appropriate. CWA § 505(d); CAA § 304(d); SDWA § 1449(d).

Additional provisions protect "whistleblowers" from retaliation by employers for filing an action or testifying in an action brought under the Acts. See, e.g., CWA § 507(a).

## 4. RESEARCH PROGRAMS AND OUTSIDE ADVISORY GROUPS

In addition to the provisions requiring EPA to set standards governing private conduct, each Act requires EPA to broaden the understanding of toxics in the environment by conducting specified research projects. For example, the Clean Water Act requires EPA to conduct extensive studies of toxic pollution of lakes. CWA § 314(a)(1)(F). The Clean Air Act required special studies of deposition of hazardous air pollutants into the Great Lakes, Chesapeake Bay, Lake Champlain, and coastal waters. CAA § 112(m)(5). It also created a national urban air toxics research center. CAA § 112(p). The Safe Drinking Water Act requires EPA to conduct extensive studies of public drinking water supplies. SDWA § 1442. Where research burdens devolve to the states, the Acts often appropriate funds for research grants. See, e.g., CWA § 314(a)(4); SDWA § 1444.

The three Acts also require EPA to consult or cooperate with special technical advisory boards and commissions. For example, the Clean Air Act created the Chemical Safety and Hazard Investigation Board to address accidental releases of hazardous air pollutants. CAA § 112(r)(6). The Safe Drinking Water Act created the National Drinking Water Advisory Council to advise EPA on toxic pollutants in drinking water. SDWA § 1446. The Clean Water Act created the National Study Commission to report on the implementation of the national effluent standards. CWA § 315. Although politics rather than policy or science likely motivates the creation of most of these commissions, their creation gives their members formal incentives to participate more actively in EPA's formulation of policy. In addition, their recommendations can give EPA additional authority, or political cover, to support more controversial recommendations. As regulation of toxics in the air and water grows more complicated and expensive, expect these boards, commissions, and panels to proliferate.

# CHAPTER 6

# REGULATING DISPOSAL OF HAZARDOUS WASTES: THE RESOURCE CONSERVATION AND RECOVERY ACT (RCRA)

## A. INTRODUCTION

### 1. "CRADLE TO GRAVE" REGULATION

Described by the D. C. Circuit as fraught with "mind numbing complexity" (American Mining Congress v. EPA, 824 F.2d 1177 (D.C.Cir.1987)), the Resource Conservation and Recovery Act (RCRA, pronounced "RICK-ruh"), 42 U.S.C.A. § 6901 et seq., establishes a comprehensive system to regulate the generation, transportation, storage, treatment, disposal, and cleanup of "hazardous wastes." Congress "enacted RCRA to 'eliminate * * * the last remaining loophole in environmental law.' " Ecological Rights Foundation v. Pacific Gas & Electric Co., 713 F.3d 502, 515 (9th Cir.2013). Its extensive statutes, articulated by even more extensive regulations, try to regulate hazardous wastes "from cradle to grave." See, e.g., C & A Carbone, Inc. v. Town of Clarkstown, 511 U.S. 383, 114 S.Ct. 1677, 128 L.Ed.2d 399 (1994).

RCRA imposes substantial duties upon each person who comes into contact with a "hazardous waste" during its life cycle. Using a complicated set of definitions, factory owners and other waste generators must determine if they are producing "hazardous wastes." If so, RCRA requires them to keep records, file reports, and properly handle such wastes. Most RCRA "hazardous wastes" are first stored, then treated, and eventually disposed of at the very site where they were generated. RCRA strictly controls that process. It specifies with excruciating detail the permissible storage, treatment, and disposal methods. In particular, it has greatly restricted the disposal of such wastes in landfills and dumps. For wastes that a generator sends off-site for storage, treatment, or disposal, RCRA establishes a system to track the shipments through the transportation labyrinth to their eventual disposal site. Along the way, both the waste's transporters and its eventual processors must follow strict RCRA regulations. Where, despite all the precautions, hazardous wastes are released into the environment at any stage in their life-cycle, RCRA has provisions to clean up the contamination.

Thus, like the statutes addressed in Chapters 3 through 5, RCRA primarily attempts to prevent environmental contamination. Indeed, RCRA interacts extensively with these other statutes. Unlike those other statutes, however, RCRA also contains extensive provisions to clean up contamination if its prophylactic measures fail. As a result, RCRA also interacts substantially with the CERCLA cleanup provisions addressed in Chapters 7 through 11. These interactions are discussed in Chapter 12.

## 2. HISTORY

Congress enacted the statutes now popularly known as RCRA in 1976 as amendments to the 1965 federal Solid Waste Disposal Act. The 1965 legislation had addressed the nation's waste problem through grants to states and localities, research, and nonbinding guidelines. But it had done little to prevent or remedy the nation's mounting problems with waste generation and disposal. The 1976 RCRA amendments overhauled the original Act almost completely. Although the current statutes continue to bear the formal title of the 1965 Act, they are now known popularly by the name of the 1976 amendments. Indeed, the 1976 name has stuck even after the passage of the "Hazardous and Solid Waste Amendments of 1984" (HSWA).

Although RCRA represented a sea change in Congressional attitudes towards the solid and hazardous waste problem, EPA implemented RCRA quite slowly. In large part this stemmed from the complexity of the subject matter. In addition, regulated industry ceaselessly communicated its awareness of the potentially enormous costs of the regulatory scheme, while environmental interests insisted on maximum reduction of public health risks. Thus, although enacted in 1976, it was not until 1980 that RCRA first bore notable fruit. In that year, two important milestones occurred. First, RCRA's important "hazardous waste" provisions became effective with EPA's promulgation of its first set of hazardous waste regulations. Second, as addressed in Chapter 12, the federal government first used RCRA to clean up hazardous waste disposal sites that had been contaminated and closed prior to RCRA's 1976 passage.

During the next four years, EPA picked up the pace of RCRA implementation. In addition, a body of case law began to develop as RCRA enforcement actions were undertaken. Nevertheless, Congress was still frustrated by the implementation delays and the limits to EPA's cleanup options. Thus, in HSWA Congress substantially beefed up the regulation of treatment, storage, or disposal (TSD) facilities. Among other provisions, it banned the use of landfills for hazardous waste disposal except under very limited circumstances. In addition, as described in Chapter 12, it substantially increased EPA's ability to require TSD facilities to take "corrective action" to clean up contamination at their facilities as a condition of staying in business. The impact of these and other provisions of HSWA virtually shut down the commercial hazardous waste disposal business, as hundreds of facilities closed rather than comply with the new legislation. In addition, it launched the extensive, expensive, and still ongoing program to clean up thousands of contaminated TSD facilities.

## 3. RELATIONSHIP WITH OTHER LAWS

### a. RCRA and CERCLA

RCRA began a decade of Congressional attention to hazardous waste disposal and cleanup. In addition to its RCRA efforts, Congress expressed its concerns with hazardous wastes in the 1980 Comprehensive Environmental Response, Compensation, and Liability Act (CERCLA), and the 1986 CERCLA amendments known as "SARA" (for "Superfund Amendments and Reauthorization Act.") Ultimately, understanding RCRA's role in hazardous waste regulation requires some understanding of the overlap and differences between RCRA and CERCLA. This Chapter focuses on RCRA's principal provisions. Chapters 7 through 11 address CERCLA's provisions. Chapter 12 then completes the study of the two statutes by addressing first RCRA's waste cleanup provisions and then the interrelationship between RCRA and CERCLA.

For now, a simple, frequently made distinction between the two statutes will summarize their differing approaches to hazardous wastes. In general, RCRA is a *prospective* statute. That is, it focuses primarily on the *prevention* of hazardous waste pollution. It requires persons subject to its provisions to minimize the possibility of contamination from hazardous wastes. In contrast, CERCLA is primarily *retrospective.* That is, it focuses on the cleanup of contamination that occurred either before RCRA's effective date or despite RCRA's prophylactic scheme. See United States v. Shell Oil Co., 605 F.Supp. 1064 (D.Colo.1985). Of course, at the extremes, the simple distinction collapses. Thus, the harsh liability imposed under CERCLA is also a powerful inducement to minimize potential contamination.

Finally, the Safe Drinking Water Act also intersects with RCRA. For example, MCLs developed under the Safe Drinking Water Act have several applications to RCRA's cleanup and disposal provisions. In addition, both RCRA and the Safe Drinking Water Act regulate the injection of wastes into deep underground wells.

## 4. ORGANIZATIONAL STRUCTURE

RCRA is so extensive that particular portions of it are often talked about as though they were separate legislative enactments. Congress facilitated this process by its division of RCRA into ten statutory groups. As codified, these ten groups form the ten subchapters of the Solid Waste Disposal Act. The United States Code designates these subchapters with roman numerals. Prior to codification, these ten groups formed the ten "subtitles" of the RCRA bill. They were designated alphabetically. For example, the principal hazardous waste provisions are within "Subtitle C" of the uncodified RCRA, and "Subchapter III" of the codified provisions. In keeping with the authors' conventions, the following discussion refers solely to the uncodified "subtitles."

The ten subtitles run the gamut from Subtitle A's "general provisions" to Subtitle J's "demonstration medical waste tracking program." The most important subtitle addressed here is Subtitle C—the hazardous waste management program. The discussion below will also address briefly provisions of Subtitles F (federal facilities), G (miscellaneous provisions, including whistleblower protection and citizens' suits) and I (underground storage tanks). In addition, Subtitle D, which regulates *nonhazardous* solid wastes, requires mention. The demands made by Subtitle D regulations on waste generators and handlers are minimal compared to the demands placed by the Subtitle C provisions. Accordingly, waste generators and handlers have a substantial incentive to avoid classification of their wastes as Subtitle C wastes.

## B. "HAZARDOUS WASTES"

### 1. INTRODUCTION

The most critical part of RCRA is working through its answers to the threshold question: *is* a waste a "hazardous waste"? *EPA's demanding Subtitle C regulations apply only to substances determined to be "hazardous wastes" under the regulatory definition.* This critical question, however, is often the most difficult to answer. For some wastes, the answer will be obvious. Thus, discarded barrels of highly corrosive chemicals will almost certainly meet the definition. For many other wastes, however, the answer will be extremely hard to determine. For example, are the rocks left over from mining operations a "hazardous waste"? Is a recycled material still subject to RCRA as a "hazardous waste"?

Initial focus on the "hazardous waste" identification process furthers two purposes in understanding RCRA. First, and most importantly, it introduces the definitional axis around which the

RCRA regulated universe spins. Because the Subtitle C program places substantial, even onerous, compliance costs and regulatory responsibilities upon persons who generate, treat, store, or dispose of hazardous wastes, those persons *must* know whether the materials they produce or handle fall within the "hazardous waste" definition. Second, in addition to their substantive import, the hazardous waste identification regulations serve as a convenient way to demonstrate Subtitle C's overall complexity. While dense, the hazardous waste identification regulations are relatively compact. The complexities raised by just this tiny slice of the RCRA regulations, however, graphically demonstrate the complexities awaiting the student or practitioner asked to delve with comparable detail into the hundreds of additional pages of RCRA regulations.

To determine whether a material is a "hazardous waste" appropriate for RCRA regulation, EPA promulgated regulations that created a complicated definition applicable solely to Subtitle C. These definitions are found in 40 C.F.R. Parts 260 and 261. Although RCRA's "general provisions" found in Subtitle A include definitions of "hazardous wastes" (§ 1004(5)) and "solid waste" (§ 1004(27)), these general definitions do not specifically control the critical question of Subtitle C applicability. See, e.g., 40 C.F.R. § 261.1(b). (The general, statutory definition does, however, determine private or governmental enforcement authority under the "imminent hazard" provisions of Subtitle G. See Chapter 12.) Rather, for purposes of its Subtitle C regulations, EPA has interpreted the general statutory definitions of both "hazardous" and "solid" wastes more narrowly. Thus, persons potentially liable under Subtitle C must work through the multiple steps of the regulatory definition to determine if they are handling a waste regulated under Subtitle C.

Since Subtitle C applies only to those "hazardous wastes" that are also "solid wastes," the analysis begins with the regulatory definition of "solid waste." Only if a substance meets the definition of "solid waste" will it then become necessary to ask if it is also a "hazardous waste." In simplest terms, the identification of a substance as a Subtitle C "hazardous waste" involves seven steps:

- Is the substance not a hazardous waste because it has been excluded from the definition of *solid* waste?

- If not excluded from the solid waste definition, is the matter a solid waste because it has been "discarded"?

- If it is a solid waste because it has been discarded, is it nevertheless not a hazardous waste because it has been excluded from the definition of hazardous wastes?

- If it has not been excluded from the definition of hazardous wastes, is it a substance that has been expressly listed by EPA as a RCRA "hazardous waste"?

- If not expressly listed as a hazardous waste, is it nevertheless such a waste because it exhibits one or more "characteristics" shared by hazardous wastes?
- Even if the substance is neither specifically listed nor exhibits a characteristic of hazardous wastes, is it nevertheless considered a hazardous waste by virtue of its combination with another waste, its derivation from another hazardous waste, or its containment in another waste?
- Finally, even though it would otherwise be a hazardous waste, is it excluded from Subtitle C regulations in whole or in part because it is being recycled?

The following discussion will consider the first two steps under the subheading "Solid Wastes," and the remaining steps under the subheading "Hazardous Wastes."

For two principal reasons, the Subtitle C regulations are quite complicated. First, the variety of waste streams, each presenting its own biochemical complexities, makes the subject inherently difficult to translate into uniform rules understandable by ordinary citizens. Second, in formulating its rules, EPA has attempted to further two competing statutory goals: the encouragement of recycling and the protection of human and environmental health. On the one hand, RCRA attempts to "minimize the generation of hazardous wastes by encouraging * * * materials recovery,

[and] properly conducted recycling and reuse * * *." § 1003(a)(6). On the other hand, RCRA reflects great Congressional concern "that hazardous waste management practices are conducted in a manner which protects human health and the environment" and "that hazardous wastes be properly managed in the first instance thereby reducing the need for corrective action at a future date." § 1003(a)(4), (5). While "recycling" enjoys popularity as a near panacea for environmental woes, in practice the recycling of industrial wastes poses many opportunities for leaks, spills, and other types of contamination. In resolving the tension between health protection and encouragement of recycling, EPA has frequently come down on the side of protection. Thus, only certain recycling activities are excluded in whole or part from RCRA regulation.

## 2. SOLID WASTES

As noted above, RCRA's Subtitle C hazardous waste program applies only to those "hazardous wastes" that are first determined to be "solid wastes." The statute defines "solid waste" as "any garbage, refuse, sludge * * * and any other *discarded material* * * *." § 1004(27) (emphasis added). The Subtitle C regulations address in near exhausting detail the statute's general reference to "discarded."

Industry has often complained that EPA has defined its "solid waste" jurisdiction too broadly. These challenges have occurred most frequently over the regulation of recycled or reused materials.

Confronted with such challenges to the regulatory definition, courts have frequently fallen back to the seeming simplicity of the statutory definition. In effect, they have measured the validity of the regulatory definition by comparing it to the statutory requirements. These courts ask whether the regulated materials have ever been "discarded;" if so, they have become part of the "waste disposal problem" addressed by Subtitle C. See, e.g., Owen Electric Steel Co. of South Carolina, Inc. v. Browner, 37 F.3d 146 (4th Cir.1994) (upholding EPA's determination that slag from steel making cured for six months before sale was part of the disposal problem). Several of these decisions are discussed in more detail below, under the subheading, "Is the Material Recycled?"

Throughout RCRA, the reference to "solid" encompasses more than materials commonly believed to be solid. RCRA defines "solid waste" as including "solid, liquid, semisolid, or contained gaseous material * * *." § 1004(27). The Subtitle C regulations incorporate this broad definition. Thus, liquid wastes are "solid wastes" under RCRA. Indeed, *most* RCRA regulated wastes are liquid chemicals stored in the 55 gallon drums that litter so many hazardous waste sites.

If a substance is not a "solid waste," as defined in the Subtitle C regulations, it will ordinarily not be a hazardous waste. (Special attention must be given to some materials that are treated as hazardous wastes, even if not technically solid wastes, under what are known as the "contained in" policy. This policy is considered below, under the "Hazardous Wastes" subheading.) A substance may not meet the regulatory definition of "solid waste" either because a specific exclusion applies, or because the substance has not been "discarded" within the meaning of the regulations. See, e.g., Ecological Rights Foundation v. Pacific Gas & Electric Co., 713 F.3d 502 (9th Cir.2013) (PCB-based wood preservative that escaped from utility poles through normal wear and tear was not a "solid waste" on facts of case because it was not "discarded").

### a. Is the Substance Excluded from the Definition of "Solid Waste"?

Students or practitioners attempting to determine the applicability of the Subtitle C regulations can avoid much grief by examining first the specific exclusions from the solid waste definition. There are three main ways to avoid that definition. First, and most commonly, § 261.4(a) provides 25 express exclusions. Second, a portion of the "derived from" rule excludes certain reclaimed materials from both the hazardous and the solid waste definitions. 40 C.F.R. § 261.3(c)(2)(i). Finally, Part 260 contains procedures for obtaining limited variances from the solid waste definition. Additional provisions exclude from the hazardous waste definition three recycling methods. § 261.2(e)(1). These provisions are considered below, in the discussion of materials that are considered solid wastes even when they are recycled.

### *i. Is There an Express Exclusion?*

Section 261.4(a) provides 25 express exclusions from the solid waste definition. The first four repeat exclusions found within the statute's solid waste definition. These exclude: (1) domestic sewage; (2) point source discharges regulated under the Clean Water Act's NPDES (see Chapter 5); (3) irrigation return flows, and (4) certain radioactive materials. § 261.4(a)(1)–(4). Since these exclusions come from the statute itself, they apply throughout RCRA, not just the Subtitle C provisions. The 21 remaining regulatory exclusions interpret "solid waste" solely for purposes of the Subtitle C provisions. They include exclusions for pulping liquors, reclaimed spent wood preserving solutions, petroleum refinery secondary materials, spent materials, shredded circuit boards and cathode ray tubes. § 261.4(a)(5)–(27).

At least five of the statutory exclusions have received judicial attention. In *Comite Pro Rescate*, the First Circuit construed the "domestic sewage" exclusion. Comite Pro Rescate De La Salud v. Puerto Rico Aqueduct and Sewer Authority, 888 F.2d 180 (1st Cir.1989). The court determined that the exclusion applied to the physical *source* of the sewage, not the *type* of sewage. Specifically, it found that the exclusion applied to waste that actually came from human dwellings, not waste of the same type found in home sewers that might have come from, say, toilets or sinks in industrial plants.

Several cases have construed the exclusion for discharges allowed under NPDES permits. In 1995, the EPA announced that the exclusion should apply to discharges that should have had NPDES permits, even if the proper permits are not in place. Interpretation of Industrial Wastewater Discharge Exclusion from the Definition of Solid Waste, 1995 WL 911821. The courts, however, have not always read the exclusion as broadly as EPA.

In United States v. Allegan Metal Finishing Co., 696 F.Supp. 275 (W.D.Mich.1988), the court found that the exclusion applied only to actual discharges from the point source, and not to the pre-discharge process of wastewater collection, storage, or treatment. In other words, if a wastewater treatment plant has an NPDES permit to discharge into a waterway, the materials are exempt as they flow out of the discharger's sewer pipe and into the receiving waters. According to this court, however, RCRA exempts neither the materials as they are being collected prior to discharge, nor any sludges that accumulate in the pre-discharge treatment process. Thus, the collection of waste materials in a settling pond prior to treatment and discharge can involve the accumulation of RCRA regulated "solid wastes." Of greatest concern to such treatment plants are the RCRA land disposal restrictions addressed later in this chapter.

Building upon *Allegan Metal Finishing Co.*, in Lutz v. Chromatex, 725 F.Supp. 258 (M.D.Pa.1989), the court found the exclusion inapplicable to discharges of chemicals to sewers, drains and trenches. Because these discharges had not been authorized by the defendant's NPDES permit, the court concluded that the exemption did not apply.

In contrast, later decisions have given the exclusion a broader reading. See, e.g., State v. PVS Chemicals, Inc., 50 F.Supp 2d 171 (W.D.N.Y.1998) (exclusion applies to discharges that exceed limits permitted by NPDES permit); Williams Pipe Line Co. v. Bayer Corp., 964 F.Supp. 1300 (S.D.Iowa 1997) (exclusion applies to spills to ground from above-ground tanks of hydrocarbon containing wastewater.)

In American Petroleum Institute v. EPA, 216 F.3d 50 (D.C.Cir.2000), the court upheld EPA's exclusion of recovered oil produced by the petrochemical manufacturing industry.

In Safe Food & Fertilizer v. EPA, 350 F.3d 1263 (D.C.Cir.2003), the court reviewed the exemption for recycled materials sent off-site to make zinc fertilizers. EPA determined that these materials would not be considered "discarded" provided that they were handled properly and the concentration of six contaminants did not exceed limits that would have been identical to virgin zinc sources. (EPA labeled this latter condition the "identity principle.") The rule allowed materials that were previously considered hazardous wastes under the "derived from" rule to be exempt from Subtitle C regulations. The court upheld EPA's rule, including its identity principle.

Finally, in Sierra Club v. EPA, 755 F.3d 968 (D.C. Cir. 2014) the court struck down an exemption for certain hazardous residuals left over from the petroleum refining process. The Gasification Exclusion Rule was challenged as violating the plain statutory text of RCRA. The court ruled that EPA is required to regulate "[h]azardous waste used as fuel" 42 U.S.C. 6924(q). Id. at 978. Accordingly, the rule was invalidated. Id.

#### *ii. Does the "Derived from" Rule Exclude the Materials?*

The "derived from" rule belongs to the "hazardous waste" definition. As described more fully below, under the subheading, "Is the Waste Otherwise Considered Hazardous?", the "derived from" rule defines "hazardous wastes" to include any "solid waste generated from the treatment, storage, or disposal of a hazardous waste." § 261.3(c)(2). A portion of this provision, however, exempts from *both* the hazardous waste *and* the solid waste definition materials "that are reclaimed from solid wastes and used beneficially." § 261.3(c)(2)(i); cf. § 261.1(c)(4) (defining "reclaimed" for §§ 261.2, 261.6). The "derived from" rule's exclusion for reclaimed materials is lost if the materials are "burned for energy recovery or used in a manner constituting disposal." § 261.3(c)(2)(i). The latter provision refers to the application of the reclaimed materials to the land. See § 261.2(c)(1).

#### *iii. Has a Variance Been Granted?*

Another method for avoiding the "solid waste" definition entirely involves the acquisition of a variance. Part 260 allows for variances from the solid waste definition in limited instances. These apply to: (1) materials that are accumulated speculatively without sufficient quantities being recycled within a specified period; (2) materials reclaimed and then reused as feedstocks; (3) reclaimed materials that require additional reclamation; and (4) hazardous secondary materials either reclaimed in a continuous process, indistinguishable from products, or transferred to verified reclamation facilities. § 260.30. The regulations specify additional conditions for these variances. § 260.31. A person seeking such a variance must petition EPA and demonstrate the applicability of the required conditions. § 260.33.

#### *iv. Non-Waste Determination*

The final method for avoiding the "solid waste" definition is to seek a non-waste determination that the hazardous secondary material is not discarded, and therefore not a solid waste. Section 260.34 lists specific criteria related to the management of the material, comparability to commercial products and intermediates, and other factors relevant to whether the material was discarded. If the applicant does not meet these criteria, it may still be eligible for a variance or exclusion. § 260.34.

### b. Is the Material a "Solid Waste" Because It Has Been "Discarded"?

If the material at issue fits within one of the above described exceptions, it is not a "solid waste" for purposes of the Subtitle C regulations. As a result, it is ordinarily also not a "hazardous waste" for those purposes. See § 261.3(a) (treating as a "hazardous waste" only materials that are also "solid wastes"). The principal exception applies to materials addressed by EPA's "contained in" policy. This policy is addressed below, under the last segment of the "Hazardous Wastes" subheading.

If the material is not excluded from the solid waste definition, a student or practitioner must next determine whether the material meets that definition. As noted above, the statute defines solid waste generically by reference to "discarded materials." RCRA § 1004(27). The Subtitle C regulations incorporate this definition, 40 C.F.R. § 261.2(a)(1), and then specify four circumstances in which a material is "discarded." Under the regulations, a material is "discarded" if it is: (1) abandoned; (2) recycled in specified circumstances; (3) considered "inherently wastelike;" or (4) a defined military munition. § 261.2(a)(2). The regulations then detail the meaning of these four circumstances.

### *i. Is the Material a Solid Waste Because It Was "Abandoned"?*

Under the regulations, materials are "abandoned" where they have either been: (1) disposed of; (2) burned or incinerated; or (3) accumulated, stored, or treated (but not recycled) before (or instead of) being disposed of, burned, or incinerated, or (4) sham recycled. § 261.2(b).

The general regulatory definitions shed some light on the meaning of "disposal" and "storage." "Disposal" means "the discharge, deposit, injection, dumping, spilling, leaking, or placing of any solid waste or hazardous waste into or on any land or water so that [it] or any constituent thereof may enter the environment * * *." § 260.10. "Storage" means "the holding of hazardous waste for a temporary period, at the end of which the hazardous waste is treated, disposed of, or stored elsewhere." § 260.10. The usefulness of these definitions, however, is limited. When used to determine if a material is a solid waste because it is *abandoned*, both definitions are virtual tautologies. Because each turns on the presence of "solid" or "hazardous wastes," they beg the question posed by the "abandonment" regulation: *is* the material in question a "solid waste"? Nevertheless, the two definitions demonstrate the kinds of activities by which a material might be deemed a solid waste because of "abandonment."

### *ii. Is the Material a Solid Waste When "Recycled"?*

#### *[a] Table 1*

The most complicated portion of the solid waste definition involves the identification of materials that are solid wastes when they are recycled. Section 261.2(c) summarizes EPA's conclusions about recycling activities in a chart labeled "Table 1."

| Table 1 | Use Constituting Disposal 261.2(c)(1) | Energy Recovery/ Fuel 261.2(c)(2) | Reclamation 261.2(c)(3), except as provided in 261.4(a)(17), 261.4(a)(23), 261.4(a)(24) or 261.4(a)(27) | Speculative Accumulation 261.2(c)(4) |
|---|---|---|---|---|
| Spent Materials | (*) | (*) | (*) | (*) |
| Sludges (listed in 40 CFR part 261.31 or 261.32) | (*) | (*) | (*) | (*) |
| Sludges exhibiting a characteristic of hazardous waste | (*) | (*) | . . . . . . | (*) |
| By-products (listed in 40 CFR part 261.31 or 261.32) | (*) | (*) | (*) | (*) |
| By-products exhibiting a characteristic of hazardous waste | (*) | (*) | . . . . . . | (*) |
| Commercial chemical products listed in 40 CFR 261.33 | (*) | (*) | . . . . . . | . . . . . . |

| | | | | |
|---|---|---|---|---|
| Scrap Metal that is not excluded under 40 CFR 261.4(a)(13) | (*) | (*) | (*) | (*) |

A student or practitioner must first determine if the material fits within one of the seven categories listed in the far left hand column of Table 1. Section 261.1(c) defines these categories. If a recycled material does not meet any of the six other definitions, it will almost certainly meet the "spent materials" definition. After identifying the category of recycled material, the student must next consider the type of recycling activity involved. The four right hand columns of Table 1 correspond to four types of recycling activities addressed in §§ 261.2(c)(1) through (4). Wherever one of the right hand columns of Table 1 contains an asterisk, it indicates that EPA considers the corresponding material identified in the far left hand column of the Table to be a solid waste when it is recycled in the indicated manner.

A quick glance at Table 1 produces three rules of thumb. First, for all of the materials listed in the far left hand column of Table 1, recycling by either "uses constituting disposal" or for "energy recovery or fuel" identifies the material as a solid waste. Second, listed commercial chemical products may be reclaimed or accumulated speculatively without triggering the solid waste definition. Finally, a person may reclaim any sludges that exhibit a characteristic of a hazardous waste, or any similar by-products, without producing "solid wastes." ("Characteristic" hazardous wastes are discussed below, under the "Hazardous Wastes" subheading.) All other materials, however, are solid wastes when recycled by "reclamation" or "speculative accumulation."

*[b] Conditional Exemptions*

A subsequent provision, § 261.2(e), creates three "conditional exemptions" for materials that appear to be more "product-like" than "waste-like" when recycled. These exempt: (1) materials used as ingredients to make a product, such as fly ash to make cement; (2) secondary materials used as effective substitutes for commercial products, such as sludges used as water conditioners; and (3) secondary materials returned in a "closed loop" to the original production process from which they were generated and used there as a substitute for other raw materials. Each of these conditional exemptions can be lost in a variety of ways. For example, activities involving reclamation of wastes, storage of wastes in surface impoundments, speculative accumulation, or burning for energy recovery will void a conditional exemption.

Similarly, "sham" recycling will void a conditional exemption. For example, evidence of sham recycling includes use of secondary materials in amounts much larger than those required for the production process. Similarly, the EPA will suspect a sham operation when the "recycler" fails to handle the material in a manner that suggests it is a valuable substitute for a raw material or a commercial chemical product. EPA codified its long-standing policy on sham recycling by adopting § 261.2(g), in the 2015 Definition of Solid Waste Rule. 80 Fed. Reg. 1694 (Jan. 13, 2015).

#### *[c] Litigation Involving Recycling*

The recycling provisions have sparked a handful of important lawsuits. These cases have focused on the statutory requirement that a solid waste be "discarded." The challenges have occurred most frequently in the mining and petroleum industries. In both industries, the same stage of a given industrial process often may produce both the desired primary products and certain secondary materials. These secondary materials are often valuable, and can be returned at some point to be further processed into different products. This presents the problem of determining whether, in the interim between their initial production and their further reprocessing, these secondary materials are "solid wastes" regulated under Subtitle C. Given the expense and potential liability attendant to such regulation, industry greatly prefers to avoid treatment of these secondary materials as Subtitle C "solid wastes." EPA, however, originally drew the Subtitle C solid waste definition broadly. Only those materials returned to the original production process *without prior reclamation* meet the exclusion for "closed loop" recycling.

In examining whether EPA has extended its jurisdiction impermissibly over material that is not "waste," the courts look to see whether the material in question is "part of the disposal problem" meant to be addressed by RCRA, or, rather, is part of an ongoing production process. In the first *American Mining Congress* case, American Mining Congress v. EPA, 824 F.2d 1177 (D.C.Cir.1987) (*AMC I*), the D.C. Circuit held that "in-process secondary materials employed in an ongoing manufacturing process" were not "solid waste." Although *AMC I* gave industry much hope that the courts would aggressively supervise EPA's broad definition of "solid waste," several subsequent decisions narrowly construed the types of "ongoing manufacturing processes" eligible for exclusion from the solid waste definition. Thus, the Fourth Circuit upheld EPA's determination that slag from steel making cured for six months before sale was part of the disposal problem. Owen Electric Steel Co. of South Carolina, Inc. v. Browner, 37 F.3d 146 (4th Cir.1994). The D. C. Circuit, in the second *American Mining Congress* case, upheld EPA's determination that impounded wastewater sludges were not part of an ongoing production process even though they might be reclaimed at some future date. American Mining Congress v. EPA, 907 F.2d 1179 (D.C.Cir.1990) (*AMC II*).

Subsequently, the court has allowed a broader range of materials and processes to be considered not "discarded," and thus not "solid waste." In Association of Battery Recyclers, Inc. v. EPA, 208 F.3d 1047 (D.C.Cir.2000), the court overturned

EPA's decision to treat as solid waste materials that were stored for any length of time. Provided the materials were not being accumulated speculatively, the court found that the materials in question were still in-process secondary materials and thus "not part of the waste disposal problem." See also American Petroleum Institute v. EPA, 216 F.3d 50 (D.C.Cir.2000) (striking down two EPA applications of the "solid waste" definition).

The D.C. Circuit revisited *AMC I's* definition of "discarded" in Safe Food & Fertilizer v. EPA, 350 F.3d 1263 (D.C.Cir.2003). In a rulemaking, the EPA had concluded that recycled materials sent off-site to make zinc fertilizers would not be considered "discarded" provided that they were handled properly and the concentration of six contaminants did not exceed limits that would have been identical to natural zinc sources. As discussed above, this rule allowed materials that were previously considered hazardous wastes under the "derived from" rule to be exempt from Subtitle C regulations. Upholding EPA's rule, the court concluded that *AMC I's* "closed loop" test did not require EPA to conclude that the shipment off-site meant that the materials had been "discarded." On rehearing it remanded for EPA to explain further how it had applied the identity principle to the virgin and recycled fertilizers. Safe Food & Fertilizer v. EPA, 365 F.3d 46 (D.C.Cir.2004).

In response to some of the decisions described above, as well as continued industry concern, EPA adopted the 2015 Definition of Solid Waste Rule to

(1) exclude legitimately recycled materials from the definition of solid waste and (2) implement specific recycling regulations. In this process, EPA recognized the legitimacy of in-process ("closed-loop") recycling and the importance of widely recognized commodities such as scrap metal. EPA listed four factors in 40 C.F.R. § 260.43 to define "legitimate recycling." These factors are:

1) material must "provide a useful contribution to the recycling process;"

2) the recycling produces a valuable product or intermediate;

3) the hazardous secondary material is managed as a valuable commodity;

4) the product of the recycling is comparable to a legitimate product or intermediate.

The third and fourth "legitimacy factors" were challenged in American Petroleum Inst. v. Environmental Protection Agency, 862 F.3d 50 (D.C. Cir. 2017). Industry petitioners claimed that applying these factors to all recycling allowed EPA to unlawfully regulate non-discarded materials. Under the third factor, as written, firms could meet the standard if they handle hazardous secondary material "in an equally protective manner" to how an analogous raw material would be treated; and if there is no comparable raw analogue, the secondary material would have to be "contained," that is, "held in a unit (including a land-based unit)" that is labeled or otherwise having a system to immediately identify the hazardous secondary materials within. 40 C.F.R. § 260.10. (defining "contained"). The court upheld this requirement, reasoning that it did not go beyond what EPA might otherwise expect of firms engaged in legitimate recycling. Id. at 57–58.

However, the fourth factor did not survive the court's scrutiny. Although EPA explained that its purpose was to prevent recyclers from loading products with hazardous wastes that were simply "along for the ride," the court rejected this as an unreasonable approach to identifying illegitimate recycling. Noting that "even if EPA could technically say that some small excess of hazardous constituents has been left in the final product, the mere fact of their presence would not constitute a reasonable basis for dubbing the product or the process a sham." Id. at 59.

The Definition of Solid Waste Rule also adopted three exclusions to promote safe recycling of hazardous materials. They are: an exclusion for materials legitimately reclaimed under the control of the generator ("generator-controlled exclusion") (§ 261.4(a)(23)); a verified recycler exclusion for transfers of hazardous materials by generators to a RCRA-permitted reclamation facility or to recyclers that have received a solid waste variance from EPA or the authorized state (§ 261.4(a)(24)); and an exemption for hazardous secondary materials containing solvents transferred for remanufacturing (§ 261.4(a)(27)).

In *American Petroleum*, the court vacated part of the verified recycler exclusion. EPA is likely to revise its rules to re-instate the previous transfer-based exclusion provisions, potentially re-working this section's sub-parts. Under this prior 2008 rule, a generator could send materials to any reclaimer it chose after meeting a set of five questions related to the skill, capacity, and enforcement record of the recycler. This generator-based inquiry was replaced in 2015 with the requirement that EPA or a state regulator approve a variance for the recycler.

### *iii. Is the Material a Solid Waste Because It Is "Inherently Waste-Like"?*

The last category of materials defined as "solid waste" are materials considered "inherently waste-like." The regulations identify two classes of materials that meet this definition. First, they specifically identify, by a chemical waste code, several hazardous wastes. § 261.2(d)(1), (2). EPA believed that these materials are always discarded; listing under this section thus obviates any generalized analysis of whether the material has been "abandoned" or "recycled." Second, they provide a two-part formula for listing additional materials as "inherently waste-like." Under this formula, a material can be added to the list if it might "pose a substantial health or environmental hazard when recycled" and either: (1) it is "ordinarily disposed of, burned, or incinerated;" or (2) it contains listed hazardous "constituents" not ordinarily found in raw materials for which the materials substitute. § 261.2(d)(3).

## 3. HAZARDOUS WASTES

A student or practitioner who has identified a material as a solid waste must next determine whether the material is regulated as a hazardous waste under Subtitle C. This analysis involves four steps. First, as with the solid waste definition, exceptions from the hazardous waste definition also exist. Second, if no exception exists, a solid waste will be considered a hazardous waste if it is either specifically listed as a hazardous waste by EPA or if it exhibits one of four "characteristics" of hazardous wastes. Third, certain other materials are treated as hazardous wastes under one of several additional rules and policies. Finally, certain hazardous wastes that are recycled may escape substantial portions of the Subtitle C regulations.

### a. Is the Material Excluded from the Hazardous Waste Definition?

Like the solid waste definition, there are three principal ways for a material to be excluded from the hazardous waste definition. First, § 261.4(b) contains over a dozen express exclusions. Second, the "derived from" rule exempts some materials from the definition. Finally, EPA can exclude wastes produced at particular facilities from portions of the hazardous waste definition. In general, EPA may not base a decision to create an exclusion on the "stigma" that would attach to the material were EPA to regulate it as "hazardous." Hazardous Waste Treatment Council v. EPA, 861 F.2d 270

(D.C.Cir.1988) (striking down EPA decision not to regulate used oil as hazardous).

### i. *Is There an Express Exclusion?*

Section 261.4(b) excludes 18 types of materials from the hazardous waste definition. The most important of these are: (1) household waste; (2) crop residues and manures returned to the soil as fertilizer; (3) mining overburden returned to the mine site; (4) fly ash waste generated from fossil fuel combustion; (5) drilling fluids and produced waters associated with petroleum and natural gas drilling; and (6) twenty specified mining wastes.

The municipal waste exclusion, part of the original 1980 regulations, engendered a statutory counterpart. In 1984 legislation, Congress "clarified" the regulatory exclusion. Under RCRA § 3001(i), a facility incinerating municipal solid waste will not be deemed to be "treating, storing, disposing of, or otherwise managing hazardous wastes" if it treats only household waste or nonhazardous commercial and industrial waste. In Chicago v. Environmental Defense Fund, 511 U.S. 328, 114 S.Ct. 1588, 128 L.Ed.2d 302 (1994), the Supreme Court concluded that this exclusion applied only to the wastes *entering* municipal waste incinerators. For these incoming wastes, municipalities do not have to comply with the Subtitle C regulations. Thus, for example, they do not have to demand a manifest from the waste sources, or comply with the Subtitle C disposal requirements. The Court, however, concluded that the ash created by burning these excluded wastes was *not* excluded from potential treatment as hazardous. Thus, municipal incinerators may become subject to Subtitle C regulation as *generators* of hazardous wastes.

The mining wastes are excluded because of a statutory directive. Enacted in 1980, and known as the Bevill Amendment after its principal Congressional sponsor, the provision commanded EPA to delay regulating mining wastes until after it had studied the "special waste" problems unique to the mining industry. §§ 3001(b)(3), 8002(f). The enormous volume of wastes produced by the mining industry—estimated by EPA in its 1985 study at up to 755 million metric tons—threatened that industry with extremely costly treatment and disposal problems. Indeed, EPA estimated that full Subtitle C compliance would cost over $800 million per year in 1985 dollars. Industry advocates had argued that many of its wastes, although higher in volume, were lower in risk than many other solid wastes. They claimed that these lower risks stemmed partly from the low concentrations of hazardous substances within the wastes and partly from the location of much mining activity in areas far from population centers. Industry greatly preferred regulation of mining wastes under the much less onerous Subtitle D provisions applicable to nonhazardous solid waste. Despite opposition from environmentalists, under the Amendment the mining industry was able to postpone regulation of much of its wastes as hazardous wastes. Additional legislation added in 1984 allowed EPA to modify

Subtitle C regulations for those mining wastes that EPA decided to regulate as hazardous wastes.

The Bevill Amendment has received substantial regulatory and judicial attention. During the 1980's, EPA vacillated over its meaning. In regulations proposed in 1985, it stated that the Amendment applied only to "high volume, low hazard" wastes. A year later, supposedly because it faced overwhelming practical difficulties in drawing the line between high and low hazard mining wastes, it withdrew this interpretation. As a result of that decision, it also withdrew a proposal to list as hazardous wastes six specific wastes produced by the smelting industry. EPA's decision not to regulate these six wastes as hazardous wastes was struck down by the D. C. Circuit. That court ruled that, wherever EPA drew the line, the six wastes were not part of the "special wastes" excluded from hazardous waste regulation by the Amendment. Environmental Defense Fund v. EPA, 852 F.2d 1316 (D.C.Cir.1988) (*EDF I*). The same court, however, upheld EPA's overall decision to regulate much of the mining wastes under the less demanding Subtitle D provisions. Environmental Defense Fund v. EPA, 852 F.2d 1309 (D.C.Cir.1988) (*EDF II*). EPA had concluded that Subtitle C regulation of most mining wastes would be too costly. The *EDF II* court found that the Amendment authorized EPA to consider compliance costs when deciding whether to regulate mining waste under Subtitles C or D.

persistence, and degradability in nature, potential for accumulation in tissue, and other factors such as flammability, corrosiveness, and other hazardous characteristics." § 3001(a). Building on the statute's twin requirements to identify "characteristics" and to "list" hazardous wastes, EPA has divided the world of hazardous wastes regulated under RCRA Subtitle C into two realms. A solid waste will be treated as a hazardous waste if it is either: (1) a specifically listed hazardous waste; or (2) it exhibits one of four "characteristics" of a hazardous waste. These four characteristics are: reactivity, corrosivity, ignitability, and toxicity.

### *i. Is the Waste a "Listed" Hazardous Waste?*

EPA has promulgated regulations that specifically list hundreds of materials as hazardous wastes. §§ 261.30 to 261.33. A substance can become listed for any of three reasons: (1) it exhibits one of the four characteristics of hazardous waste, described below; (2) it has a low lethal dose; or (3) it contains a listed toxic constituent and is capable of causing human health or environmental harm. § 261.11. Substances with a low lethal dose are labeled "acute hazardous wastes." § 261.11(a)(2). Substances listed because of their toxic constituents are known as "toxic wastes." § 261.11(a)(3). The EPA maintains a list of these constituents in Appendix VIII to Part 261. (This list is also used for the "Land Disposal Restrictions" discussed later in this chapter.)

When EPA decides to list a material as a hazardous waste, it indicates the basis for the decision by assigning one or more of six "hazard codes" to the material. These six codes indicate that a waste has been listed because it: (1) is ignitable; (2) is corrosive; (3) is reactive; (4) exhibits the toxicity characteristic; (5) is acutely hazardous; or (6) is toxic. § 261.30(b). A material may be listed under multiple waste codes. See, e.g., § 261.31 (listing waste F007 as both a reactive and toxic waste). The waste codes assigned determine the specific regulatory requirements.

The lists of wastes are grouped by hazardous waste number. Each number begins with one of four letters—"F", "K", "P," and "U"—and is followed by a three digit number. The "F" and "K" wastes are wastes from particular industrial processes. §§ 261.31, 261.32. "F" wastes indicate general industrial processes while "K" wastes are wastes associated with specific sources. For example, waste "F007" identifies "spent cyanide plating bath solutions from electroplating operations." It was listed because of reactivity and toxicity. Waste "K032" identifies "wastewater treatment sludge from the production of [the pesticide] chlordane." It was listed because of toxicity. The "P" and "U" wastes are commercial chemical products. § 261.33. The "P" code indicates acute hazardous wastes, while the "U" code indicates "toxic" wastes. For example, waste "P028" identifies "benzyl chloride" and waste "U061" identifies DDT.

### *ii. Does the Waste Exhibit a "Characteristic" of Hazardous Waste?*

The huge number of different wastes generated by industry makes it impossible for EPA to test and list each one separately. Accordingly, the Subtitle C regulations identify four "characteristics" of hazardous wastes: (1) ignitability; (2) corrosivity; (3) reactivity; and (4) toxicity. Persons who generate, transport, treat, store, or dispose of a solid waste that is not a listed hazardous waste must determine for themselves whether their particular waste meets one of the four toxicity characteristics. They may base their determination either on their own knowledge about the waste materials or upon the results of specific laboratory analysis. § 262.11(c). The "personal knowledge" provision is not meant to encourage wrong guesses about a waste's safety; rather, it allows someone who *knows* that its waste is hazardous to avoid the expense of specific tests.

The first three characteristics are rather easily described. Ignitable wastes are generally materials with a low flash point (i.e., below 140 degrees Fahrenheit). § 261.21. Corrosive wastes are liquids that are either very acid or very base (i.e., have a very high or low pH) or can corrode steel at a specified rate. § 261.22. Reactive wastes display one or more of eight characteristics, such as violent reaction with water or ready capability of detonation. § 261.23.

The fourth characteristic—toxicity—is more complicated. The student or practitioner must first distinguish "*characteristic*" toxic wastes from the *"listed"* toxic wastes described above. The latter wastes are those that contain harmful concentrations of a specific "hazardous waste constituent" listed in Appendix VIII to Part 261. In contrast, to establish that a waste shares the *characteristic* of toxic waste, a person must employ the "toxicity characteristic leaching procedure" (TCLP). See § 261.24 (external reference). Under this procedure, extraction liquids are poured over samples of the waste in a laboratory and the resulting extract, known as "leachate," is analyzed. If the leachate contains one or more of forty materials in amounts that exceed specified concentrations, the waste demonstrates the toxicity characteristic.

In developing the TCLP, EPA assumed a worst-case scenario—i.e., that real world wastes might be mismanaged and leachate would contaminate groundwater. The TCLP thus models the leachate that would result from such assumed mismanagement. Industry objected that these assumptions were unfair, either because mismanagement would not occur, or that their particular waste disposal sites did not overlie groundwater. The D. C. Circuit upheld EPA's decision to develop the TCLP. Edison Electric Institute v. EPA, 2 F.3d 438 (D.C.Cir.1993). Nevertheless, it allowed particular waste sources to demonstrate the inapplicability of the assumptions to their wastes.

### c. Is the Waste Hazardous Under the "Derived from" or "Mixture" Rules, or the "Contained In" Policy?

In three instances, EPA considers solid wastes or other materials to be hazardous wastes even if the solid waste considered alone would not meet either of the hazardous waste requirements. These circumstances apply to: (1) mixtures of solid and hazardous waste; (2) materials derived from hazardous waste; and (3) hazardous waste that is "contained in" contaminated soil or water.

Under the "mixture" rule, EPA treats an entire mixture of a solid waste and a *listed* hazardous waste as a hazardous waste, even if the solid waste standing alone would not be a Subtitle C hazardous waste. § 261.3(a)(2)(iv). If, however, the mixture does not demonstrate any characteristics of hazardous wastes, it is not treated as a hazardous waste.

Under the "derived from" rule, "any solid waste generated from the treatment, storage or disposal of a hazardous waste * * * is a hazardous waste." § 261.3(c)(2)(i). This rule, known as the "derived from" rule, is part of EPA's "continuing jurisdiction" provisions. § 261.3(c)(1). In effect, these provisions say, "once a hazardous waste, always a hazardous waste." Thus, sludges, dusts, spill residues, ash, and leachate from hazardous wastes are automatically considered hazardous wastes. As noted above, the "derived from" rule excepts from the definitions of both solid and hazardous waste "materials that are reclaimed from solid wastes and that are used beneficially * * * [provided that] the reclaimed material is [not] burned for energy recovery or [applied to the land]." § 261.3(c)(2)(i). Otherwise, if not within the exemption for reclaimed materials, a waste "derived from a hazardous waste" will remain a "hazardous waste" until it either no longer exhibits the characteristic of a hazardous waste or has been "delisted" under the above described petition procedure. § 261.3(d).

The "mixture" and "derived from" rules were formally promulgated regulations. § 261.3(a)(2)(iii), (c)(2)(i). Although struck down for irregularities in the procedure originally used to promulgate them (Shell Oil Co. v. EPA, 950 F.2d 741 (D.C.Cir.1991)), they were repromulgated as interim regulations. The final rule went into effect in 2001. 66 F.R. 27, 266 (May 16, 2001). In American Chemistry Council v. EPA, 337 F.3d 1060 (D.C.Cir.2003), the court upheld both the "mixture" and "derived from" rules.

A practical application of the "continuing jurisdiction" rules was challenged in the context of EPA's "land ban" regulations. These provisions, discussed below, preclude the land disposal of Subtitle C hazardous wastes unless the wastes have first been pretreated. Under the land ban, EPA required nonlisted characteristic wastes to be treated to concentrations far below that which led them to be considered characteristic wastes in the first instance. In Chemical Waste Management, Inc. v. EPA, 976 F.2d 2 (D.C.Cir.1992), the D. C. Circuit upheld EPA's decision to order pretreatment to *below* characteristic waste levels. Although the court based its decision on the specific language of the land ban provisions (see § 3004(m)(1)), the case demonstrates the great difficulties in removing a particular waste from the hazardous waste regulatory scheme.

In contrast to the mixture and derived from rules, most of the "contained in" policy is found in EPA guidance documents and a 1996 proposed regulation. 61 F.R. 18, 780 (April 29, 1996). EPA never finalized the proposed regulation but the policy remains in effect. See 63 F.R. 65, 874 (Nov. 30, 1998). This policy treats certain materials that "contain" hazardous wastes as if they themselves were hazardous wastes—even if they are not themselves even "solid waste." The policy most clearly applies to contaminated media, such as soil or groundwater. For example, assume that a storage tank leaks known hazardous wastes onto the soil beneath it. The contaminated soil itself is not a hazardous waste, since it is not first a solid waste: no one has "discarded" it. Nevertheless, because it is contaminated, it requires careful handling.

### d. Is the Waste Excluded from the Hazardous Waste Regulations Because It Is Being Recycled?

Five hazardous wastes are excluded from the operation of the principal hazardous waste regulations if they are recycled under specified circumstances. § 261.6(a)(3). These include reclaimed industrial ethyl alcohol and scrap metal. Additional recycling activities can exempt other hazardous wastes from substantial portions of the Subtitle C regulations. § 261.6(a).

## C. REGULATION OF THE GENERATION, TRANSPORTATION, TREATMENT, STORAGE, AND DISPOSAL OF HAZARDOUS WASTES

A person who generates, transports, treats, stores, or disposes of a RCRA "hazardous waste" must comply with the extensive Subtitle C regulations. The applicability of specific regulations turns on three factors: (1) the kind of activity undertaken in regard to the material; (2) the particular material involved; and (3) the identity of the person undertaking the activity. Separate regulations address generators, transporters, and operators of TSD facilities. 40 C.F.R. Parts 262–268.

The same person may be subject to more than one set of regulations. Indeed, since much industrial hazardous waste is treated on site (i.e., at the place where it was created), the same factory will frequently be subject to both the generator and TSD regulations. Similarly, even the inadvertent storage of hazardous wastes for more than 90 days converts a factory into a RCRA "storage" facility.

### 1. REGULATION OF GENERATORS

In RCRA, Congress specifically directed EPA to develop "standards" applicable to generators of hazardous wastes. § 3002(a).

### a. Classes of Generators

Although RCRA itself does not define "generator," the regulations define it as "any person, by site, whose act or process produces hazardous wastes * * * or whose act first causes a hazardous waste to become subject to regulation." § 260.10. In the mid-1980s, EPA estimated that the 15,000 to 20,000 generators of more than 1000 kilograms (kg) per month of hazardous wastes accounted for over 99% of all the hazardous wastes produced annually in the country. Although this group of large generators then represented roughly 2% of the total number, its monumental contribution to the hazardous waste problem led it to become the focus of EPA's limited regulatory resources. Indeed, EPA originally exempted all generators of less than 1000 kg per month. In 1984, however, Congress directed EPA to regulate generators of between 100 and 1000 kg per month.

In 2016 EPA adopted a Hazardous Waste Generator Improvements Rule. 81 Fed. Reg. 85,732 (Nov. 28, 2016). The rule identifies generator categories based on the amount of hazardous waste generated each month, with the express understanding that the category may change from month to month. Accordingly, EPA has classified RCRA generators into three groups: (1) very small quantity generators; (2) small quantity generators; and (3) large quantity generators. Each generator must determine its category according to the rules in 40 C.F.R. § 262.13. Generators who produce either acute or non-acute hazardous wastes count the total waste, subtracting exempt waste, and then determine their category according to Table 1 below. If a generator produces both acute and non-acute hazardous waste, it must calculate each total separately, subtracting from each total exempt waste, and if the total acute or non-acute calculations yield different categories according to Table 1, the generator must apply the more stringent generator category for accumulation and management of hazardous wastes for that month. § 262.13 (b). Waste exempted from the calculations are identified by § 262.13 (c) and (d), including waste exempted by other sections of RCRA.

| Table 1 to § 262.13—Generator Categories Based on Quantity of Waste Generated in a Calendar Month | | | |
|---|---|---|---|
| **Quantity of acute hazardous waste generated in a calendar month** | **Quantity of non-acute hazardous waste generated in a calendar month** | **Quantity of residues from a cleanup of acute hazardous waste generated in a calendar month** | **Generator category** |
| > 1 kg | Any amount | Any amount | Large quantity generator |
| Any amount | ≥ 1,000 kg | Any amount | Large quantity generator |
| Any amount | Any amount | > 100 kg | Large quantity generator |
| ≤1 kg | > 100 kg and < 1,000 kg | ≤100 kg | Small quantity generator |
| ≤ 1 kg | ≤100 kg | ≤ 100 kg | Very small quantity generator |

The three categories of hazardous waste generators have different obligations under RCRA.

- *"Very small quantity generators"* monthly produce 1 kg or less acute hazardous waste, and 100 kg or less non-acute hazardous waste, and 100 kg or less residues from a cleanup of acute hazardous waste. This class is not subject to most of the generator requirements in 40 C.F.R. parts 124, 262–268 and 270, or RCRA § 3010, provided they meet certain conditions identified in § 262.14, such as staying within the monthly generation limits. They must comply with waste determination and recordkeeping requirements (§ 262.11) and continuing monthly generator category determinations (§ 262.13), and also send off-site shipments to appropriate facilities for management (§ 262.14(a)(5)).

- *"Small quantity generators"* monthly produce 1 kg or less acute hazardous waste, between 100 kg and 1,000 kg non-acute hazardous waste, and 100 kg or less of residues from a cleanup from acute hazardous waste. These generators must comply with most of the RCRA generator requirements. For this class, however, EPA has relaxed some of the reporting and recordkeeping requirements and imposed a lower burden to certify waste minimization efforts. See, e.g., §§ 262.44, 262.27.

- *"Large quantity generators"* include all other types of generators of hazardous wastes. They are subject to the full Subtitle C generator provisions described immediately below.

### b. Duties of Generators and the Manifest System

Perhaps the most important duty placed on those generators who do not treat their wastes on site is the duty to prepare waste shipments properly. § 262.20. This duty is an integral part of EPA's "manifest" system. This system allows EPA to track waste shipments and ensure wastes are handled appropriately once they have left the generator's site. Prior to any such shipment, the generator must fill out a manifest. See 40 C.F.R. Part 262, Appendix. The manifest must identify both the generator, by EPA identification number, and the waste, by hazardous waste code. It must also identify the facility to which the waste is being sent. § 262.20(b). The generator is responsible for ensuring that the treatment, storage, or disposal facility to which the waste is being sent is authorized to receive the particular kind of waste shipped. Once the waste is properly packaged, labeled, and marked for shipment, the generator gives copies of the manifest to the transporter, retaining a copy signed by the transporter for the generator's records. § 262.23.

Generators have five other principal duties.

- They must determine for themselves whether their wastes are Subtitle C hazardous wastes.

- They must notify EPA that they are producing such wastes and obtain an EPA identification number. § 3010(a); 40 C.F.R. § 262.18.

- They must properly store and label any such wastes prior to treatment or transportation. §§ 262.30 to 262.33. Again, generators who accumulate wastes for more than the maximum permitted storage times (generally 90 days for large quantity generators and 180 days for small quantity generators) risk converting themselves into "storage" facilities subject to the EPA storage facilities permit system and requirements unless they meet the exemptions for accumulation provided in § 262.16 (for small quantity generators) and § 262.17 (large quantity generators).

- They must keep records and make periodic reports. §§ 262.40 to 262.44.

- Finally, they must establish waste minimization programs. Indeed, the manifest must certify that the generator has a waste minimization program in place. § 262.27. Congress mandated such programs in its 1984 RCRA amendments. § 3002(b). To date, EPA has issued guidelines to help generators reduce the volume and hazardousness of their wastes. It has also developed its "Resource Conservation Challenge." The RCC is a set of programs to prevent pollution; promote recycling and reuse; reduce priority chemicals and conserve energy and materials. EPA has not yet finalized waste minimization regulations first proposed in 1993. See 58 F.R. 31, 114 (1993).

## 2. REGULATION OF TRANSPORTERS

RCRA commanded EPA to develop, in conjunction with the federal Department of Transportation (DOT), standards applicable to "transporters of hazardous wastes." § 3003. As discussed in Chapter 4, much of the regulation of hazardous waste transportation occurs under DOT regulations. See, e.g., 49 C.F.R. Parts 171–180. These regulations were promulgated under authority of the Hazardous Materials Transportation Act of 1975 (HMTA) and amending legislation. See former 49 U.S.C.A. §§ 1801–1812, now revised 49 U.S.C.A. §§ 5101 et seq. They apply not only to the shipment of hazardous wastes, but also to the shipment of any hazardous "materials" as defined in that Act. Under 1990 HMTA amendments, the DOT regulations preempt inconsistent state law. See 49 U.S.C.A. § 1804(a)(5), moved to § 5125(a) (Preemption). The RCRA-inspired manifest system adopted by the DOT does, however, allow for some state-specific information.

EPA's RCRA transportation regulations are found in 40 C.F.R. Part 263. They incorporate the applicable DOT regulations. 40 C.F.R. § 263.10(a). Accordingly, to prevent duplication of regulations, EPA's transporter regulations are RCRA-specific and correspondingly rather slim.

Although RCRA does not itself define "transporter," EPA regulations define it as "a person engaged in the offsite transportation of hazardous wastes by air, rail, highway, or water." § 260.10. Accordingly, the RCRA transportation regulations do not apply to a person who is moving waste around "on site," i.e., within the same facility. § 263.10(b). (The DOT packaging and labeling regulations, however, might apply to certain onsite movement of hazardous wastes. 49 C.F.R. § 171.2).

EPA regulations place three principal duties upon transporters. First, they must obtain an EPA identification number. § 263.11. Second, they must comply with the manifest system and its record retention requirements. §§ 263.20 to 263.25. In particular, they must ensure that all waste they receive is accompanied by a manifest. The manifest requirement is slightly modified for rail shipments and for bulk shipments by water. §§ 263.20(e), (f). In addition, for small quantity generator wastes, wastes do not need a manifest if they are shipped pursuant to a reclamation agreement. § 262.20(e). Rather, a more informal record of the shipment is permitted. Finally, transporters must take "appropriate immediate action" in the event of a discharge. § 263.30(a). This includes notification of appropriate authorities and assistance in cleanup. §§ 263.30(a), (c), 263.31.

Transporters must be careful not to subject themselves inadvertently to RCRA requirements applicable to storage facilities or generators. Storage by a transporter for more than 10 days may subject the transporter to the TSD permit system. § 263.12. If the transporter either imports waste into the United States, or mixes wastes of different codes in the same container, the transporter subjects itself to the generator regulations. § 263.10(c).

Collectively, EPA and DOT regulations govern the *mechanics* of the transportation of hazardous waste. Once such waste moves across state lines, however, a more fundamental regulatory issue arises. Many states, fearful of becoming dumping grounds for other states' hazardous wastes, have attempted to restrict shipments of such wastes into their jurisdiction. These efforts have engendered a substantial amount of litigation. In general, these suits raise issues under the Constitution's Commerce Clause. To date, the courts have not demonstrated much sympathy for those state restrictions on the importation of hazardous wastes that discriminate against interstate commerce. See, e.g., Chemical Waste Management, Inc. v. Hunt, 504 U.S. 334, 112 S.Ct. 2009, 119 L.Ed.2d 121 (1992) (striking down state fee imposed only on out of state imports to a RCRA permitted TSD facility).

### 3. REGULATION OF TSD FACILITIES AND THE "LAND BAN"

The most complicated RCRA regulations apply to facilities that treat, store, or dispose of Subtitle C hazardous wastes (TSD facilities). There are six basic types of TSD facilities.

- *"Incinerators"* burn hazardous wastes.

- *"Surface impoundments"* are depressions, excavations, or diked areas that can hold liquid wastes or wastes with free liquids. Common examples are wastewater lagoons, settling ponds, and storage ponds.
- *"Land treatment facilities"* are places where hazardous wastes are either applied onto or incorporated into the soil by spraying, spreading, or injection. They are commonly used for petroleum wastes.
- *"Underground injection wells"* deposit hazardous wastes deep beneath the earth's surface in geologically stable, impermeable rock formations. They are the principal exception to the ban on land disposal of hazardous wastes.
- *"Containers, tanks, and waste piles"* permit the temporary collection and storage of hazardous wastes.
- *"Landfills"* belong in a catchall category. They include all placements of hazardous wastes in or on the land under circumstances that do not fit under the other categories.

Particularly in its 1984 RCRA amendments, Congress has required EPA to adopt very specific provisions governing the design and operation of TSD facilities. § 3004. The most important of these 1984 amendments placed a virtual ban on the land disposal of hazardous wastes. See, e.g., § 3004(d). To maximize compliance with these and other regulatory requirements, Congress has required

EPA to develop a permit system for TSD facilities. § 3005. In most instances, the states now implement the permit system, under EPA authorization and supervision. Every TSD facility must have either a permit or, as discussed below, "interim status" to operate.

### a. TSD "Facilities"

Unlike CERCLA § 101(9), RCRA does not separately define "facility." It does, however, define "treatment," "storage," and "disposal." § 1004(34) ("treatment"), (33) ("storage"), (3) ("disposal"); cf. § 1004(29) ("solid waste management facility"). The Subtitle C regulations fill this gap. They contain separate definitions for "facility" and "disposal facility," as well as definitions of "treatment," "storage" and "disposal." 40 C.F.R. §§ 260.10 and 270.2. The first of these two sets of largely parallel definitions applies generally throughout the Subtitle C program; the second set applies specifically to the TSD permit program.

The TSD permit regulations define "facility" tautologically as "any [hazardous waste management] facility or any other facility * * * that is subject to regulation under the RCRA program." § 270.2. This definition is fleshed out by the broader, general definition of "facility" as including: "all contiguous land, and structures * * * used for the treating, storing, or disposing of hazardous wastes." § 260.10. It further specifies that a facility may include "several * * * operational units." § 260.10 ("facility"). Both the TSD permit and general regulatory definitions define "disposal facility" as "a facility or part of a facility at which hazardous waste is intentionally placed into or on any land or water, and at which waste will remain after closure." §§ 260.10, 270.2. Similarly, they contain identical broad definitions of "storage," "treatment," and "disposal." "Storage" means the temporary holding prior to treatment, disposal, or storage elsewhere. "Treatment" means "any method, technique or process * * * designed to change the physical, chemical, or biological character or composition of any hazardous waste [to neutralize, recover energy or material, or make it safer]." Finally, "disposal" means "the discharge, deposit, injection, dumping, spilling, leaking, or placing of any solid waste or hazardous waste into or on any land or water so that such * * * waste * * * may enter the environment * * *."

If an entity's activities meet the regulatory definitions of treatment, storage, or disposal, that entity will become a TSD "facility." Such status triggers requirements to comply with the extensive and complicated TSD regulations. In particular, to ensure their compliance with these regulations, most TSD facilities must obtain a permit, either from EPA or an EPA authorized state enforcement agency. § 3005; 40 C.F.R. Parts 124, 270. In addition, a facility must obtain a post-closure permit if either hazardous wastes or contaminated soil or groundwater will remain on-site after closure. 40 C.F.R. § 270.1(c).

## b. The Permit System

### *i. Exclusions and Special Circumstances*

Nine types of TSD activities are excluded from the permit requirement. § 270.1(c). Notably, these include farmers who dispose of waste pesticides from their own use on their own land in accordance with the label's instructions. § 270.1(c)(2)(ii). In addition, wastes that were disposed of prior to the applicability of RCRA are not regulated under the permit system. See Environmental Defense Fund, Inc. v. Lamphier, 714 F.2d 331 (4th Cir.1983). This exception is lost, however, if the wastes are actively managed after RCRA's effective date. Moreover, leaks from pre-RCRA disposals may be addressed under the RCRA "imminent endangerment" provision discussed in Chapter 12.

In addition to these express exclusions, three sets of special provisions apply to certain TSD facilities. First, three types of facilities regulated under permit schemes established by other statutes will be deemed to have obtained a RCRA permit "by rule." § 270.1(c)(1). Thus, provided they are in compliance with their permit terms, underground injection wells permitted under the Safe Drinking Water Act, publicly owned treatment works permitted under the Clean Water Act's NPDES, and ocean vessels permitted under the Marine Protection, Research and Sanctuaries Act (16 U.S.C.A. § 1431 et seq.) do not have to obtain a separate RCRA permit. Second, TSD facilities that seek to conduct specified trial activities may qualify for special permits. See, e.g.,

§ 270.65 (demonstration activities). Finally, EPA can issue emergency permits if treatment, storage, or disposal is required to allay an imminent and substantial endangerment of human or environmental health. § 270.61.

One additional class of TSD facilities may operate without a full RCRA permit. "Interim status" facilities are "grandfathered in" to the RCRA system under § 3005(e). Interim status is addressed two subsections below.

### *ii. The Process*

Separate regulations govern permit application, conditions, modifications, and termination. An application to construct a TSD facility contains two parts. "Part A" lists fairly simple, basic information about the proposed facility. See § 270.13. "Part B," however, must detail how the proposed facility will meet *all* of the applicable TSD regulations. See, e.g., § 270.14.

Once issued, permits contain general and specific conditions. The general conditions reiterate the facility's duty to comply with specified regulations. The specific conditions are imposed case-by-case. In particular, the permit will specify what "corrective actions" a facility will have to undertake to remedy contamination at the site. (For a discussion of the corrective action program, see Chapter 12.) Including their site-specific supporting documentation, permits may run hundreds of pages long. A permittee who objects to the imposition of specific permit requirements will probably be unable to challenge the conditions until EPA brings an action against the permittee for violation of the disputed conditions. W.R. Grace & Co. v. EPA, 959 F.2d 360 (1st Cir.1992) (finding "unripe" pre-enforcement challenge to RCRA permit condition).

A permittee may need to modify its permit when its circumstances change. To facilitate its review, EPA has grouped proposed permit modifications into three classes. See § 270.42. The classes differ according to the severity of the proposed change. Different procedures govern the different classes.

Unless terminated earlier by EPA action, a RCRA permit may last up to ten years. § 3005(c)(3), (d). Prior to expiration of the permit, the permittee must seek renewal. The facility owner must either renew its operating permit, or obtain a post-closure permit, until the facility is "clean closed." Clean closure means the removal of all hazardous wastes and contaminated soil or groundwater. 40 C.F.R. § 270.1(c)(5). Additional closure duties are discussed below, under the subheading, "Requirements for Permitted Facilities."

### c. Interim Status Facilities

The Subtitle C regulations contain separate but similar regulations for two classes of TSD facilities. The principal regulations applicable to permittees are found in 40 C.F.R. Part 264. Facilities regulated under these provisions—discussed in the following section—are known as "permitted" facilities. Part 265 regulates a second group of facilities, known as "interim status" facilities. RCRA authorized these interim status regulations to "grandfather in" two sets of TSD facilities: (1) facilities that existed at the time the RCRA Subtitle C regulations became effective on November 19, 1980 (§ 3005(e)(1)(A)(i)); and (2) facilities that exist prior to the date that any subsequent statutory or regulatory provision first subjects that facility to the RCRA hazardous waste permit program (§ 3005(e)(1)(A)(ii)). These grandfathered facilities must notify EPA that they are handling hazardous wastes and submit a timely "Part A" permit application. Under the interim status regulations, however, they can continue operations during the time that EPA is reviewing the permit application.

The class of facilities currently subject to the interim status regulations is quite small, but could expand at any time. As a result of the 1984 RCRA amendments, most of the original, pre-1980 interim status facilities shut down in 1985 rather than begin the required (and expensive) process of filing the Part B application to seek full permitted status. Those that continued to operate have long since either closed or obtained full permitted status. See § 3005(c); 40 C.F.R. § 270.73 (requiring final decisions by 1992 on permit applications). The interim status regulations apply now principally to those rare facilities that first become subject to RCRA because of a statutory or regulatory change. For example, a facility handling solid but nonhazardous waste must apply for an interim status permit if EPA amends its regulations to identify the type of waste handled by that facility as a Subtitle C hazardous waste. Indeed, a new EPA *interpretation* of its regulations that makes a substance a hazardous waste may trigger interim status. New Mexico v. Watkins, 969 F.2d 1122 (D.C.Cir.1992). Similarly, process changes might make a facility's formerly nonhazardous wastes exhibit a characteristic of hazardous wastes for the first time. See § 270.10(e)(ii).

RCRA and its implementing regulations describe the time by which an interim status facility must submit its Part A and B permit applications. The deadline for the relatively simple Part A varies between 30 days and 6 months. Where statutory or regulatory changes trigger interim status, the facility has 6 months to submit Part A; where process changes trigger RCRA jurisdiction, the facility has a mere 30 days. § 270.10(e). The deadline for the more complicated Part B extends from 6 months, to one year and beyond. Where statutory or regulatory changes trigger RCRA jurisdiction, Part B is due no later than 12 months after the date when RCRA jurisdiction accrued. § 3005(e)(3). EPA, however, may demand the Part B application "at any time;" once demanded, the application is due within 6 months. 40 C.F.R. § 270.10(e)(4). This open-ended, "6 months after EPA demand" deadline apparently governs Part B applications from facilities newly regulated because of process changes.

One additional group of "facilities" could be subject to the interim status regulations. A person who never complied with applicable interim status regulations may still be prosecuted for violating the regulations. Given the broad definitions of "disposal"—e.g., to include "leaking"—and "facility," RCRA might thus subject a person who owned or operated a contaminated TSD site in the 1980s to liability for failure to obtain an interim status permit. Such an action, however, would raise issues under the five year RCRA limitations period. See, e.g., United States v. White, 766 F.Supp. 873 (E.D.Wash.1991) (applying "continuing violation" approach to uphold criminal enforcement of permit violations). (For a brief additional discussion of the limitations period, see the discussion below of enforcement actions.) To avoid such issues, a cleanup action brought under CERCLA is a more likely response to a newly discovered site that has been leaking hazardous wastes for many years.

The interim status regulations contain many, but not all, of the provisions applicable to permitted facilities. For example, interim status facilities are subject to groundwater monitoring and financial responsibility requirements. See, e.g., § 3005(e)(3). Given this similarity, the specific interim status regulations are not separately discussed here. Ultimately, while interim status facilities receive some relaxation of the regulatory requirements, their reprieve is only temporary. Eventually, they must receive full permitted status under the Part 264 regulations, or shut down.

For an interim status permittee, noncompliance with the regulations triggers the unhappy fate known as "Loss of Interim Status" (LOIS). A LOIS facility must immediately cease operations and begin long term closure. Litigation involving the large numbers of pre-1980 permittees originally subject to the interim status regulations developed a body of case law addressing LOIS. See, e.g., EPA v. Environmental Waste Control, Inc., 917 F.2d 327 (7th Cir.1990) (ordering closure of LOIS facility). Newly added interim status facilities will have this case law to explore if faced with their own LOIS.

### d. Permitted Status Facilities

The extensive Part 264 regulations contain both general provisions applicable to all TSD facilities and specific provisions applicable to particular types of facilities.

#### *i. General Provisions*

Among other matters, the general provisions include requirements governing:

- *EPA identification numbers*—each TSD facility must obtain an EPA identification number. § 264.11.
- *Waste stream analysis*—each TSD facility must physically and chemically analyze a representative sample of the wastes it has received to ensure proper handling. § 264.13.
- *Facility inspection*—owners or operators must regularly inspect their facilities to detect and prevent releases. § 264.15. (Additional regulations governing specific facilities, such as landfills, require the installation of extensive groundwater

monitoring wells to aid release detection. § 264.97.)

- *Emergency release prevention, preparedness, and contingency planning*—where such releases occur, facilities must have emergency response plans in place. §§ 264.50 to 264.56; see also §§ 264.90 to 264.101 (corrective action requirements for TSD facilities, discussed in Chapter 12.)

- *Record keeping and reporting, including TSD facility responsibilities in the manifest system*—as endpoints in the waste stream, TSD facilities play an important role in the manifest system. Facility owners and operators must check for any discrepancies between the waste received and the waste described in the manifest. § 264.72. For example, if a drum of waste listed on the manifest is missing, or if the kind of waste received differs from that listed, the TSD owner or operator must try to resolve the discrepancies. If consultations with the generators and transporters of that waste fail to resolve the discrepancy, the TSD facility must promptly report the matter to EPA. § 264.72(c).

- *Closure and Post-Closure Plans*—permitted facilities must have written "closure" and "post-closure" plans. §§ 264.110 to 264.120. Closure plans address the process for shutting a TSD facility down. During this process, which can take roughly six months, the facility must dispose of all contaminated equipment, soil, and structures. Closure plans must minimize both the need for post-closure facility maintenance and the chance of post-closure releases to the environment. § 264.111. For example, landfills must be "capped" with a virtually impermeable cover. § 264.310(a)(5). Post-closure plans address the supervision of the site *after* closure. Among other matters, they require extensive post-closure monitoring *for thirty years* to ensure that releases do not occur from the closed facility. § 264.117.

- *Financial Responsibility*—the facility owner or operator must demonstrate that it has the necessary funds for its closure and post-closure obligations. §§ 264.140 to 264.151. The owner can meet this obligation in several ways, e.g., a cash fund, a bond, a letter of credit, insurance, a guarantee from a parent corporation, or a demonstration of sufficient corporate assets. § 264.151. In addition, some facilities must maintain sufficient insurance to cover injury to third parties, e.g., landfills must maintain up to $3 million per occurrence for non-sudden accidental leakages, such as leaking into public drinking water systems. § 264.147(b).

### *ii. Provisions Applicable to Specific Facilities*

The facility-specific provisions cover design, operating, and closure requirements for the different types of TSD facilities, such as tank systems, landfills, and incinerators. These requirements make it essential for a TSD owner or operator to classify its facility correctly. See Beazer East, Inc. v. EPA, 963 F.2d 603 (3d Cir.1992) (sanctioning facility mischaracterization). In addition, all facilities must comply with the relevant "land ban" regulations, discussed in the following subsection.

Perhaps the most important provisions applicable to landfills and surface impoundments are the statutory requirements for double liners and a leachate collection system in between them. § 3004(*o*)(1)(A)(i). Liners, made of materials with very low porosity (e.g., compacted clay), retard the movement of hazardous materials from the landfill or impoundment into the environment. Even the best materials, however, will eventually leak; moreover, liners occasionally rupture. For this reason, underlying the initial layer must be a "leachate collection system." In general, these systems intercept the leachate—the liquids that escape the initial liner through seepage—and pump it to a treatment system. The second liner thus traps this leachate, prevents its release to the environment, and facilitates its collection.

If the TSD facility meets these extensive obligations, it will become a fully permitted facility. A permit provides the permittee with its license to operate. In addition, it provides a "shield" to certain enforcement options. In general, compliance with a RCRA permit shields the permittee from enforcement actions taken for violation of provisions not within the permit. 40 C.F.R. § 270.4. The courts have upheld the shield. Shell Oil Co. v. EPA, 950 F.2d 741 (D.C.Cir.1991). It applies not only to EPA and state enforcement actions, but also to citizen suits. Families Concerned About Nerve Gas Incineration v. U.S. Dept. of Army, 380 F.Supp.2d 1233 (N.D.Ala.2005). The shield, however, does not apply to: (1) new statutory provisions; (2) the restrictions on the land disposal of hazardous wastes, known popularly as the "land ban" restrictions (addressed immediately below); and (3) some additional performance standards applicable to specific TSD facilities. § 270.4.

### e. The "Land Disposal Restrictions," a.k.a. the "Land Ban"

Perhaps the most widely known, and certainly the most litigated of the TSD regulations, are the provisions governing the land disposal of hazardous wastes. These provisions ban the disposal of hazardous wastes in landfills, surface impoundments, land treatment systems, and injection wells unless the TSD facility either meets rigorous pre-disposal treatment requirements or demonstrates that the wastes will not migrate for as long as they remain hazardous. Collectively known as "the land ban regulations," or by their acronym "LDRs" ("Land Disposal Restrictions"), these provisions implement one of the most important provisions of the 1984 RCRA amendments. These provisions reflect Congressional recognition that even the best designed and managed landfills eventually leak, contaminating the underlying soil and groundwater. In addition, they reflect Congressional frustration with the slow pace of EPA implementation of RCRA.

In the 1984 legislation, Congress identified land disposal as the "least favored" method of hazardous wastes disposal. § 1002(b). It broadly defined "land disposal" to include "any placement of * * * hazardous wastes in a landfill, surface impoundment, waste pile, injection well, land treatment facility, salt dome [or bed] formation * * * or underground mine or cave." § 3004(k). It then divided the world of hazardous wastes into three separate groups. The first group of wastes became known as the "California list." § 3004(d). In creating this group, Congress borrowed from a list of hazardous waste standards used by California, which California had previously adopted from federal standards developed under the Safe Drinking Water Act. The second group of wastes involved specified solvents and dioxins. § 3004(e). The third group included every EPA regulated hazardous waste other than wastes contained in the first two groups. § 3004(g). Congress subdivided this last group into thirds. The wastes within each of these subgroups became known by their subgroup, i.e., "first third" wastes, "second third" wastes, and "third third" wastes. The "third third" included the characteristic hazardous wastes. An additional provision specifically addressed the disposal of any hazardous wastes by injection into deep wells. § 3004(f).

Congress then prohibited the land disposal of all *untreated* hazardous wastes by specific dates unless EPA made certain findings. § 3004(d)(1), (e)(1), (g)(1). Different waste groups and subgroups had different deadlines, with the latest deadline (for the so called "third third") falling on May 8, 1990. § 3004(g)(4)(C). The findings necessary to avoid the land prohibition required EPA to conduct a complicated risk analysis. Cost of compliance was not one of the listed factors. Instead, the listed factors addressed only such health based matters as the waste's "persistence, toxicity, mobility and propensity to bioaccumulate." § 3004(d)(1)(C). In particular, to avoid the ban, EPA had to find that "to a reasonable degree of certainty, * * * there will be no migration of hazardous constituents from the disposal unit * * * for as long as the wastes remain hazardous." See, e.g., § 3004(g)(5). It was widely believed in 1984 that it would be virtually impossible for EPA to make this last finding. Moreover, an additional provision eliminated a potential loophole by banning storage of wastes subject to the land ban, except while accumulating sufficient quantities to properly treat or dispose of the waste. § 3004(j). Thus, at first glance, the land disposal prohibition appeared absolute.

At the same time that it set up this rigorous prohibition, however, Congress opened the door to continued land disposal in one principal instance. It allowed EPA to avoid the ban by issuing standards for treating hazardous wastes before land disposal. § 3004(m). These pretreatment standards had to specify either "levels or methods of treatment * * * which substantially diminish the toxicity of the waste or substantially reduce the likelihood of migration of hazardous constituents from the waste so that short-term and long-term threats to human health and the environment are minimized." § 3004(m)(1). Several additional provisions further softened the land ban by creating limited variances and special treatment for certain facilities. The most important of these is the "national capacity variance." Under this variance, EPA can postpone the land ban if there is insufficient treatment capacity nationwide for a given class of wastes. § 3004(h)(2). EPA has used this authority repeatedly. Additional variances exist for circumstances beyond permittee's control. § 3004(h)(3). Finally, small quantity generator wastes are not subject to the land disposal restrictions. See 40 C.F.R. § 268.1(e).

In combination, the land ban statutes thus *prohibit* land disposal unless: (1) disposal occurred in an EPA approved "no migration" land disposal facility; (2) a variance was obtained; or (3) the waste is pretreated according to EPA regulations. To meet the "no migration" exception, the permittee must demonstrate that the concentration of hazardous constituents at the boundary of the facility will remain below health levels established by EPA for 10,000 years. The D.C. Circuit upheld this exception in Natural Resources Defense Council, Inc. v. EPA, 907 F.2d 1146, 1159–62 (D.C.Cir.1990). To date, only certain deep injection wells have met EPA's "no migration" test. Given the limited availability of these deep injection wells, and the limited abilities to obtain a variance, in effect, the land ban has required pretreatment of most hazardous wastes before any land disposal.

EPA met its statutory deadlines and issued pretreatment requirements for each of the three main waste groups. 40 C.F.R. §§ 268.40 (and Table 1). A list of "hazardous constituents" is maintained in Part 261, Appendix VIII; see 268.2(b). If the waste stream contains a mixture of wastes, the strictest standard applicable to any of the constituents controls the treatment for the entire mixture. § 268.40(c). The standards contain either numerical levels or a specific treatment method. For example, they specify that waste code K025 must be incinerated. § 268.40 (Table 1). Similarly, they specify that waste code K005 must be treated to reduce the lead within it to .75 milligrams per liter (parts per million). § 268.40 (Table 1). (Because treatment options differ, the same waste code may have separate standards for its liquid and solid forms.) Whether concentration or treatment method based, the pretreatment standards must be met *before* the materials are placed in a land disposal facility; *post*-disposal treatment that might occur within such land disposal facilities does not count towards meeting the pretreatment standards. American Petroleum Institute v. EPA, 906 F.2d 729, 734–36 (D.C.Cir.1990).

Court challenges to several of the regulations have both refined EPA authority under the land ban statutes and helped determine how the LDRs interact with regulations imposed under other environmental schemes. For example, in Hazardous Waste Treatment Council v. EPA, 886 F.2d 355 (D.C.Cir.1989) (remanding for better explanation of EPA decision), the D.C. Circuit generally upheld EPA's authority to set pretreatment standards based on the reductions that can be attained by application of "best demonstrated available technology." At issue was the statute's directive that the pretreatment standards "minimize" harm to human health and the environment from land disposal of hazardous wastes. Industry had argued that such technology based standards led to expensive over-treatment to levels far below those which demonstrate any harm to human health or the environment. The uncertainties inherent in industry's preferred harm-based efforts, however, led the court to uphold EPA's decision to use technology based standards that eliminated such threats to the maximum extent possible.

Similarly, in Chemical Waste Management, Inc. v. EPA, 976 F.2d 2 (D.C.Cir.1992) (superseded by rule as stated in Safe Food & Fertilizer v. E.P.A. (D.C.Cir.2003), the D.C. Circuit upheld EPA's decision to require pretreatment of characteristic wastes to levels even *below* that which made them hazardous in the first instance. Industry had argued that once a characteristic waste no longer exhibited the characteristic for which it met the hazardous waste definition, the waste was no longer "hazardous," even if substantial hazardous constituents remained within the waste. Hence, it argued, the LDRs should not apply to such material that was, by definition, not hazardous. EPA, however, successfully argued that once a waste was hazardous *as generated*, the land ban pretreatment standards applied, even if, as of the time of treatment, the waste no longer exhibited the relevant hazardous characteristic. Otherwise, characteristic hazardous wastes would receive preferential treatment. Moreover, the strict treatment standards helped meet the statutory requirement that no *hazardous constituents* remain that might threaten human or environmental health. Such harmful constituents could remain in waste that formerly exhibited a characteristic of hazardous wastes even if the waste no longer exhibited the characteristic at the time of disposal.

The *Chemical Waste Management* court also considered the role that dilution can play as a pretreatment standard for characteristic wastes. Initially, EPA had concluded that dilution was not an acceptable form of treatment. § 268.3(a). It felt that dilution was too tempting a way for TSD facilities to avoid treatment requirements. It changed its mind, however, when it appeared that certain wastewater facilities regulated under the Clean Water Act would be forced to comply with the LDRs. These facilities often pool untreated wastes from many sources in unlined holding ponds prior to treatment. The "third-third" regulations appeared to subject these facilities to RCRA's LDRs. To prevent the disruption of the Clean Water Act regulatory scheme, EPA allowed such facilities to dilute wastes that demonstrated the characteristics of ignitability, corrosivity, or reactivity, and toxic metal wastes for which pretreatment involved a concentration level, not a particular method. Over environmentalists' objection, the *Chemical Waste Management* court upheld the use of dilution to deactivate characteristic wastes. The court allowed such dilution, however, only where no *hazardous constituents* will remain in amounts that threaten human or environmental health. In its opinion, the court reconciled the LDRs and the Clean Water Act-governed surface impoundments. The court allowed the pretreatment pooling and dilution of characteristic hazardous wastes in unlined ponds so long as the wastewater facilities removed, before ultimate discharge, "the hazardous constituents to the same extent that any other treatment facility that complies with RCRA does." Finally, the court concluded that the existence of Safe Drinking Water Act regulations of deep injection wells did not replace the LDRs.

The LDRs and CERCLA intersect in two important instances. First, as noted above, wastes disposed of pre-RCRA do not become RCRA regulated wastes unless they are "actively managed" after the effective date of an applicable RCRA regulation. See 53 F.R. 31, 149 (1988). Cleanup of a CERCLA site containing RCRA regulated hazardous wastes often involves exhuming and moving RCRA wastes around the site. To minimize the LDR impacts on these intra-site CERCLA activities, EPA created the "corrective action management unit" (CAMU). 58 F.R. 8658 (1993); cf. 67 F.R. 2961 (Jan. 22, 2002). Management of RCRA wastes within a CERCLA CAMU does not trigger the LDRs. Second, the LDRs will often serve as "applicable or relevant and appropriate requirements" (ARARs) for CERCLA. In general, ARARs affect EPA's cleanup options for a CERCLA facility; they are addressed more specifically in Chapter 8. Use of LDRs as CERCLA ARARs has greatly increased the cost and complexity of many CERCLA facility cleanups. In extreme cases, where waste is only being moved on site, EPA may choose to waive the application of LDRs as ARARs.

## 4. STATE AND FEDERAL RELATIONSHIPS UNDER SUBTITLE C

The preceding discussion of the Subtitle C regulations focuses on the federal requirements. This focus stems naturally from the contemporary federal primacy in hazardous waste regulation. But Congressional and EPA efforts to address environmental contamination are not exclusive. Rather, they contemplate extensive, if subordinate, state involvement.

### a. History

The history of the relationship between the state and federal efforts to regulate hazardous wastes fits the general pattern of environmental regulation. Initially, through the 1960s and early 1970s, the states had primary regulatory authority. During this period of state ascendancy, the federal government's role was largely to issue reports, guidelines and, occasionally, grants. Beginning with the passage of the 1970 Clean Air Act, however, the federal government became the primary environmental regulator. States were largely charged with the local implementation of federally set standards. In particular, the major environmental statutes of the 1970s, such as the statutes described in Chapter 5, generally allowed the states to obtain EPA authorization to run the permit systems required by the federal legislation. EPA, however, retained supervisory control over state implementation efforts.

Hazardous waste management has followed a similar pattern of "cooperative federalism." Prior to RCRA's enactment, the states were principally responsible for developing hazardous waste policies, standards, and regulatory programs. Federal hazardous waste efforts were largely hortatory. After RCRA, EPA became the primary agency charged with regulating the national hazardous waste problem. Under RCRA, it is EPA's job to craft the Subtitle C regulations. At the same time, however, Congress preserved important roles for the states. § 1003(a)(7).

### b. State Regulatory Authority Under RCRA

RCRA contemplates two principal ways for states to retain regulatory authority over hazardous wastes within their borders. First, like most other federal environmental statutes, RCRA allows states to impose more stringent requirements. § 3009. As discussed in the last section of this chapter, several states (notably California and New Jersey) have exercised this authority to exceed federal requirements. The scope of the authorization has received substantial judicial attention. Despite § 3009, some courts have struck down local requirements that conflicted with the RCRA regulatory scheme. See, e.g., Ogden Environmental Services v. San Diego, 687 F.Supp. 1436 (S.D.Cal.1988) (overturning city's denial of conditional use permit for RCRA regulated facility). Others, however, have used the clause to uphold state and local requirements. See, e.g., North Haven Planning & Zoning Comm'n v. Upjohn Co., 753 F.Supp. 423 (D.Conn.1990) (upholding local zoning ordinance requiring sludge pile cap despite state and federal approval of an alternative plan).

Second, even if states have not imposed tougher standards, they retain an important implementation role. Like other major environmental statutes, RCRA contemplates that states can, and will, obtain EPA authorization to run the RCRA hazardous waste system. § 3006. Indeed, EPA must authorize a state program unless it finds that the program: (1) is not equivalent to the federal program; (2) is inconsistent with the federal program, or programs in other states; or (3) lacks adequate enforcement authority. § 3006(b). See, e.g., Hazardous Waste Treatment Council v. Reilly, 938 F.2d 1390 (D.C.Cir.1991) (upholding EPA determination that North Carolina program was "consistent" with RCRA). Most states have received at least partial EPA authority to administer RCRA hazardous waste programs.

At a minimum, the state program must include provisions that are equivalent to the five principal Subtitle C components. 40 C.F.R. §§ 271.9 to 271.16. Thus, a state program needs provisions on: (1) hazardous waste identification; (2) generator obligations; (3) transporter obligations; (4) TSD facility obligations; and (5) permitting standards. In addition, the state programs must ensure compliance through inspection and enforcement efforts.

An authorized program operates "in lieu" of the federal program. § 3006(b). The "in lieu" provision has raised some jurisdictional issues in enforcement actions. These issues are addressed in the enforcement discussion below.

## D. SPECIAL PROVISIONS FOR UNDERGROUND STORAGE TANKS (USTs)

### 1. INTRODUCTION

In 1984, over 1.5 million underground storage tanks (USTs) containing petroleum or other hazardous substances were estimated to be made of steel that lacked corrosion protection. In response, Congress' 1984 amendments included then-new RCRA Subtitle I. Subtitle I regulates underground tanks that store petroleum and hazardous substances *other than* RCRA Subtitle C regulated hazardous *wastes*. § 9001(1), (2). (Underground storage of Subtitle C hazardous wastes is regulated, appropriately, under Subtitle C. § 9001(2)(A).) The three principal groups of tanks excluded from Subtitle I regulation are: (1) farm or residential tanks of 1,100 gallons or less containing motor fuel for noncommercial purposes; (2) tanks storing heating oil for consumption on the premises where stored; and (3) septic tanks. Specific provisions require federally owned tanks to comply with the UST program, unless exempted by the President. § 9007.

Combining elements of RCRA and CERCLA, the RCRA UST program establishes a basic national program to regulate such tanks. Most states, however, have their own provisions. Once EPA authorizes a state to administer the UST program, that state's requirements supersede the federal requirements, provided they are at least as tough. §§ 9004, 9008.

## 2. BASIC ELEMENTS

The statute commanded EPA to promulgate release detection, prevention, and corrective action regulations for USTs. § 9003(a). Congress further specified that the regulations were to contain financial responsibility requirements and new tank performance standards. § 9003(d), (e). In addition, Congress created various mechanisms to fund EPA led cleanups of leaking tanks, including CERCLA-like liability and trust fund provisions. § 9003(h). Finally, the statutes contain administrative and civil enforcement provisions, including substantial fines.

Regulations implementing the statutory requirements are found in 40 C.F.R. Parts 280 and 281. In addition to the statutory exclusions, some of which were noted above, principal regulatory exemptions from the program include: (1) tanks that are part of wastewater treatment facilities regulated under the Clean Water Act; (2) UST systems with 110 gallons or less capacity; (3) UST systems with only *de minimis* amounts of regulated substances; and (4) emergency spill containment tanks expeditiously emptied after use. § 280.10(b). Owners of regulated tanks must notify EPA or the appropriate state authority prior to putting a tank into service. § 280.22(a).

The performance standards applicable to new tanks contain four principal elements. Each new tank must: (1) be designed, constructed and installed according to recognized industry standards (§ 280.20(a), (d)); (2) contain corrosion protection (§ 280.20(a)); (3) contain spill and overflow controls (§ 280.30); and (4) contain release detection devices (§ 280.40(a)). Separate release detection requirements apply to petroleum tanks and to hazardous substance tanks. The former may simply use monthly "inventory control" procedures (see § 280.41(a)(1)); the latter must have secondary containment systems, such as double walls, concrete vaults, or liners. § 280.42(b). Additional provisions apply to new underground tank piping. See §§ 280.20(b), 280.41(b)(1). The regulations gave then-existing tank owners 10 years from the promulgation of the regulations to either comply with the new tank performance standards, upgrade as permitted, or close. § 280.21(a). This period expired December 22, 1998.

The release reporting and response requirements mandate prompt notification by tank owners to the appropriate implementing agency. §§ 280.53, 280.61. Tank owners must then undertake specified abatement and corrective action steps. §§ 280.62, 280.64, 280.66. Closure regulations govern permanent and temporary closures. §§ 280.70 to 280.74. Finally, the financial responsibility options required of petroleum tank owners resemble the panoply of options generally applicable to RCRA TSD facilities. See, e.g., §§ 280.90 to 280.116. (Comparable provisions for owners of tanks containing hazardous substances have not yet been promulgated.) If, despite these financial responsibility options, a release occurs whose cleanup the tank owner cannot afford, a special, smaller version of "Superfund" may be tapped. § 9003(h)(2); for discussion of CERCLA's "Superfund," see Chapter 7. This money may also fund cleanups in designated emergencies or where the tank owner refuses to comply with a corrective action order.

## E. PUBLIC AND PRIVATE ENFORCEMENT

### 1. INTRODUCTION

RCRA's extensive enforcement provisions authorize both public and private actions. In general, RCRA authorizes three principal types of enforcement actions. First, violations of the Subtitle

C requirements support administrative, civil, and criminal enforcement proceedings under § 3008. The Subtitle C requirements may be enforced either by EPA (or authorized state permitting authority) or by individuals under citizens' suit provisions. Second, § 7003 authorizes judicial responses to releases of hazardous wastes that pose an "imminent and substantial endangerment" to human health or the environment. Finally, § 3004(u) and (v), and § 3008(h), authorize what are known as "corrective actions;" these involve the cleanup of releases from permitted and interim status TSD facilities.

This chapter considers first EPA's information gathering powers applicable to all three enforcement actions. It then examines the public and private actions involving Subtitle C violations. It concludes with an examination of the problems caused by overlapping federal and state jurisdiction in states with EPA-approved RCRA programs. Because of their interaction with CERCLA, the "imminent endangerment" and "corrective action" provisions are addressed in Chapter 12.

## 2. OBTAINING INFORMATION

Before enforcement can be considered, EPA or an authorized state agency must first know that a violation has occurred. Three principal sources of such information are available to enforcement agencies. First, regulated entities (e.g., generators or TSD facility permittees) may provide information "voluntarily" in fulfillment of their reporting duties. Second, § 3007 authorizes periodic inspections.

According to an influential GAO report, the value of these inspections is compromised in part by lack of quality control. Finally, external surveillance and "whistleblowers" may reveal potential violations. Like many environmental protection statutes, RCRA protects "whistleblowers" from specified recriminations. § 7001. The following discussion focuses on the second option: government information requests and inspections.

RCRA provides two separate information gathering provisions. Section 3007(a) authorizes inspectors to gain access to the premises of generators, transporters, and TSD facilities to obtain information or take samples. Most EPA information gathering begins with a form letter requesting information under this section. If the owner permits it, EPA may then conduct a voluntary inspection of the premises. If the owner refuses, EPA can seek an involuntary inspection by obtaining an "administrative search warrant." EPA need not demonstrate "probable cause" to suspect criminal activity before obtaining an administrative warrant; such a requirement is often impossible where the purpose of an inspection is to see whether an entity is in compliance with the law. See, e.g., Marshall v. Barlow's, Inc., 436 U.S. 307, 98 S.Ct. 1816, 56 L.Ed.2d 305 (1978) (OSHA inspection). To obtain an administrative warrant, the enforcement agency must show either: (1) probable cause to believe that a statutory violation has occurred, or (2) that the site was chosen in a neutral selection program which is a normal component of the agency's regulatory enforcement program. Refusals to comply with an information request under § 3007 are sanctionable themselves as separate RCRA violations. United States v. Charles George Trucking Co., 823 F.2d 685 (1st Cir.1987).

Section 3013 provides an additional important information gathering provision. This provision blends the "inspection" and the "voluntary" reporting requirements. Under the statute, EPA can require a TSD facility owner or operator to monitor, test, and analyze as necessary to determine the nature and extent of a hazard at its facility. In effect, this provision shifts the burden of information production from EPA to the TSD facility; the TSD facility must develop information which EPA may later use against it. To authorize such tests, EPA must determine that the presence or release of a hazardous waste "may present a substantial hazard to human health or the environment." § 3013(a). Although reminiscent of the "imminent and substantial endangerment" standard applicable under the § 7003 enforcement provisions discussed in Chapter 12, the lack of "substantial" under § 3013 demonstrates that a lesser showing is needed under that provision. If the owner or operator is unable to conduct the tests properly, EPA itself may conduct the required tests. § 3013(d). Failure to comply with EPA's request is itself a separate RCRA violation. § 3013(e).

A party to whom EPA has submitted an information request may be caught between a rock and a hard place. Judicial review of such requests will probably be denied. See, e.g., E.I. Dupont de

Nemours & Co. v. Daggett, 610 F.Supp. 260 (W.D.N.Y.1985) (no pre-enforcement review under § 3013). The recipient of a request who wishes to challenge EPA's authority to make the request will have to wait until EPA begins an enforcement action. As noted above, however, should the court uphold EPA's authority, it can impose sanctions for violation of the request itself. If, however, the recipient complies with a request, courts will likely conclude that compliance waived any challenge to EPA's authority. See E.I. Dupont de Nemours & Co. v. Daggett, 610 F.Supp. 260 (W.D.N.Y.1985).

## 3. FEDERAL ENFORCEMENT

If informal efforts fail to resolve a compliance problem, RCRA provides EPA with three formal enforcement options: (1) an administrative sanction; (2) civil penalties and injunctive relief; and (3) criminal prosecution. The first option accounts for almost three quarters of all formal compliance efforts. It can culminate in a compliance order, in a permit suspension or revocation, or fines of up to $25,000 per violation per day. The latter two options require EPA to refer the case to the Department of Justice (DOJ). EPA refers matters involving chronic and intentional violators as well as those in violation of a previously determined compliance schedule or order.

### a. Administrative Enforcement

Administrative enforcement involves EPA's issuance of an administrative complaint. Most of these complaints are settled by negotiation, and the settlement terms are incorporated into a judicially enforceable consent decree. If the matter is not settled, the recipient of the complaint can proceed to a hearing before an administrative law judge. The hearing process is conducted under EPA's uniform enforcement procedures. 40 C.F.R. Part 22. The unsuccessful party can appeal to EPA's Environmental Appeals Board. The Board's decision, in turn, is reviewable in federal district court. See, e.g., Chemical Waste Management, Inc. v. EPA, 649 F.Supp. 347 (D.D.C.1986).

In assessing administrative penalties, RCRA requires EPA to "take into account the seriousness of the violation and any good faith efforts to comply with applicable requirements." § 3008(a)(3). EPA has converted these two requirements into a four-part formula. Under this formula, the penalty amount is the product of a gravity based component and a multi-day component, adjusted first by consideration of six specified factors, and then adjusted again by consideration of the economic benefit of noncompliance. The gravity based component looks to the degree of harm and the extent of noncompliance. This factor can range from $100 per day for minor violations to the full statutory maximum of $25,000 per day for major violations. EPA next multiplies the gravity factor by the number of days of proven noncompliance. EPA then adjusts the product of these first two factors either up or down by considering six more factors: (1) good or bad faith in the permittee's efforts to comply; (2) degree of willfulness; (3) prior compliance history; (4) ability to pay; (5) other environmentally positive efforts conducted by the permittee; and (6) any other unique circumstances. The final adjustment considers the overall economic gain to the permittee from noncompliance. Under EPA policy, the overall penalty should never be less than the benefit received from noncompliance.

The statute and regulatory factors give EPA substantial discretion in assessing administrative sanctions. Courts asked to review the amount of administrative sanctions generally defer to this discretion. See, e.g., Chemical Waste Management, Inc. v. EPA, 649 F.Supp. 347 (D.D.C.1986) (upholding $40,000 sanction).

Administrative compliance orders are not self-executing. If a permittee refuses to comply with such an order, EPA must seek injunctive relief in district court. Failure to obey a compliance order is itself a separate RCRA violation that subjects the recalcitrant party to penalties of up to $25,000 per day. § 3008(c).

### b. Civil Enforcement

For serious, repeat, and recalcitrant violators, EPA will refer the matter to DOJ for potential civil enforcement. If DOJ decides to proceed, it files its action in the district court for the district in which the violation occurred. § 3008(a)(1). Courts may issue injunctions and assess civil penalties. § 3008(a)(1), (g). The defendant probably has a right to trial by jury on the question of liability; the amount of any penalty, however, is probably a matter solely for the courts. See Tull v. United States, 481 U.S. 412, 107 S.Ct. 1831, 95 L.Ed.2d 365 (1987) (Clean Water Act).

Like administrative enforcement proceedings, almost all civil enforcement actions settle after negotiations. Similarly, these settlements are usually incorporated into a consent decree. If a case does not settle, and a violation is proven, the judge will set the amount of any penalty. Penalties may range up to $25,000 per violation per day. § 3008(g). Although EPA routinely urges the courts to apply the same formula EPA itself uses in calculating administrative sanctions, the courts have preserved some independence. Thus, rather than mechanically working through EPA's formula, they tend to apply the statute's directive to consider both the seriousness of the penalty and extent of the defendant's compliance efforts. See, e.g., United States v. Environmental Waste Control, Inc., 710 F.Supp. 1172 (N.D.Ind.1989).

In addition to, or instead of, imposing a penalty, a court can issue an injunction. Such an order can range from a simple command to obey an administrative compliance order, to an order shutting permanently a TSD facility. See, e.g., United States v. Environmental Waste Control, Inc., 710 F.Supp. 1172 (N.D.Ind.1989). In crafting injunctions under RCRA, courts apply traditional equitable principles. See, e.g., United States v. Production Plated Plastics, Inc., 762 F.Supp. 722 (W.D.Mich.1991). Proof of a RCRA violation does not entitle EPA to an automatic injunction, particularly not where the drastic remedy of closure is sought. Nevertheless, courts frequently repeat the Supreme Court's observation that "[e]nvironmental injury, by its nature, can seldom be adequately remedied by money damages and is often * * * irreparable. If such injury is sufficiently likely * * * the balance of harms will usually favor the issuance of an injunction to protect the environment." Amoco Prod. Co. v. Village of Gambell, 480 U.S. 531, 107 S.Ct. 1396, 1404, 94 L.Ed.2d 542 (1987).

Beyond the "permit shield" described above, the only affirmative defense likely to succeed in an appropriate case is the statute of limitations. Notably, an enforcement proceeding defendant may not generally challenge the validity of the underlying regulation. RCRA requires that any challenge to the validity of a regulation be made within 90 days of its date of promulgation. § 7006(a)(1). As for the statute of limitations, because RCRA contains no express limitations period, the general federal five year period governs RCRA civil enforcement actions. See 28 U.S.C.A. § 2462. To date, two issues involving the limitations period for RCRA remain unresolved: (1) when does the claim arise? and (2) do administrative proceedings toll the statute?

### c. Criminal Enforcement

#### *i. Introduction*

For the most serious violations, RCRA contains two sets of stiff criminal penalties. First, § 3008(d) addresses "knowing" violations of RCRA provisions. The meaning of "knowing" in this provision is a matter of some dispute, and is addressed more fully below. Second, § 3008(e) penalizes the "knowing endangerment" of another. As discussed more fully below, "knowing" in this context is specifically defined by statute. § 3008(f).

The most serious RCRA violations support felony convictions. Prison sentences can range up to ten years for repeat violators of the basic provisions, and up to fifteen years for persons who "knowingly endanger" another. § 3008(d), (e). Fines may range up to $100,000 per violation, per day for repeat violators. § 3008(d). In practice, both the fines and prison sentences have tended to be set well below the maximum. The length of prison sentences and amount of fines, however, are now largely controlled by the Federal Sentencing Guidelines. See, e.g., Guidelines § 2Q1.2 ("Mishandling of Hazardous * * * Substances").

### *ii. "Knowing" Offenses*

Section 3008(d) criminalizes seven activities "knowingly" undertaken by "any person." Three of the offenses involve transportation of hazardous wastes. Subsection one bans knowing transportation of waste to an unpermitted facility. Subsection five proscribes knowing transportation of unmanifested wastes. Subsection six prohibits the knowing exportation of hazardous wastes without the agreement of the import country. Two of the remaining four offenses involve knowing violations of reporting and record keeping requirements. § 3008(d)(3), (4). The sixth provision applies only to knowing violations of requirements applicable only to used oil. § 3008(d)(7). The final provision, subsection two, applies to TSD operations. It subjects to criminal penalties "[a]ny person who * * * knowingly treats, stores, or disposes of any hazardous wastes listed [under Subtitle C] (A) without a permit [issued under Subtitle C] * * * or (B) in knowing violation of any material condition or requirement of such permit; or (C) in knowing violation of any material [interim status requirement]."

The provisions in subsection two (TSD violations) and subsection one (knowing transport of hazardous wastes to an unpermitted facility) most frequently form the basis of criminal prosecutions. Consequently, they have also received the most judicial development. Three issues have arisen under these statutes: (1) who is a "person"? (2) to what does "knowingly" refer? and (3) how may scienter be proven?

As to the first question, courts have given a literal meaning to "any person." Thus, they have not limited subsection two's application to owners or operators of TSD facilities. See, e.g., United States v. Johnson & Towers, Inc., 741 F.2d 662 (3d Cir.1984) (foreman and service manager were "persons" under subsection two even though neither could have obtained a RCRA permit for the facility in question). They have, however, refused to extend liability to someone who merely "receives" hazardous waste, without otherwise arranging for its "treatment, storage or disposal." United States v. Fiorillo, 186 F.3d 1136 (9th Cir.1999).

As to the scienter requirement, different results have occurred in different circuits and under different subsections. No dispute has arisen about the required extent of the defendant's knowledge of the waste's hazardous character. The courts agree that the defendant does not have to know that the waste involved is specifically regulated under RCRA Subtitle C. Rather, the defendant need only know that the waste is something potentially harmful. See, e.g., United States v. Goldsmith, 978 F.2d 643, 645 (11th Cir.1992).

Differences have emerged over the other elements to which "knowingly" refers. The principal litigation has occurred under subsection two. The problem arises because, as quoted above, Congress used "knowingly" in the introductory portion of subsection two, and then added "knowing violation" to subsections 2(B) and 2(C), but *not* to subsection 2(A). Accordingly, courts have been asked to determine whether "knowingly" as used in the introductory clause *also* modifies subsection 2(A)'s provision, "without a permit * * *." The difference affects the mental state that the government must prove in order to obtain a conviction under subsection 2(A). The Third Circuit has concluded that "knowingly" *does* also apply to "without a permit" in subsection 2(A). United States v. Johnson & Towers, Inc., 741 F.2d 662 (3d Cir.1984). Under this interpretation, the government must prove that the defendant knew *both* that it was treating, storing, or disposing of a potentially harmful substance, *and* that it needed a permit to do so. In contrast, the Ninth Circuit took the opposite view in United States v. Hoflin, 880 F.2d 1033 (9th Cir.1989). Under the Ninth Circuit's view, the government need only prove that the defendant knew it was treating, storing, or disposing a potentially harmful substance; while the government must still prove that the TSD facility lacked a permit, it need not prove that the defendant *knew* that it lacked a permit.

The Ninth Circuit's subsection two ruling contrasts with its subsection one ruling. Under subsection one, that court concluded that the government must prove that the defendant knew *both* that it was transporting a harmful material to an unpermitted site, *and* that the site lacked a permit. United States v. Speach, 968 F.2d 795 (9th Cir.1992). The court reconciled the two rulings by emphasizing the different language used in the two subsections.

The third question involves the quantum of proof required before the government can establish "knowing" conduct. Courts have only required the government to prove knowledge of the actions taken, and not of the specific RCRA prohibitions against such actions. United States v. Johnson & Towers, Inc., 741 F.2d 662 (3d Cir.1984). Moreover, they have allowed circumstantial or other indirect evidence to prove such knowledge. See, e.g., United States v. Greer, 850 F.2d 1447 (11th Cir.1988). To establish that a corporate official committed a "knowing" violation, the government must show—if only circumstantially—that the official had actual knowledge of the conduct alleged; a conviction cannot rest solely on evidence that the defendant was responsible within the corporation for waste disposal activities. United States v. MacDonald & Watson Waste Oil Co., 933 F.2d 35 (1st Cir.1991).

As with civil liability, few affirmative defenses exist to RCRA criminal prosecutions. The five year statute of limitations applies. Each day of noncompliance triggers a new violation. United States v. White, 766 F.Supp. 873, 886–87 (E.D.Wash.1991); compare People v. Thoro Products Co., 70 P.3d 1188 (Colo.2003) (action time barred where "disposal" held not to include daily passive migration of materials originally spilled more than five years before action commenced). As in civil cases, challenges to the regulatory requirements may generally not be raised in criminal enforcement proceedings. § 7006(a)(1); cf. Adamo Wrecking Co. v. United States, 434 U.S. 275, 98 S.Ct. 566, 54 L.Ed.2d 538 (1978) (noting constitutionally based exceptions to comparable statutory prescriptions). Detrimental reliance on an EPA letter or advice, while possibly relevant in assessing a penalty, will not estop the government from prosecuting a violation. See United States v. Production Plated Plastics, Inc., 742 F.Supp. 956, 961 (W.D.Mich.1990).

### *iii. "Knowing Endangerment"*

In addition to the seven "knowing" violations set out in § 3008(d), RCRA proscribes the "knowing endangerment" of another person. Section 3008(e) applies to the knowing transport, treatment, storage, disposal, or export of hazardous wastes in violation of one of the seven provisions of § 3008(d). If such activities are conducted by "any person * * * who knows at that time that he thereby places another person in imminent danger of death or serious bodily injury," the defendant faces fines of up to $250,000 for individuals and $1 million for corporations, and imprisonment for up to 15 years. "Serious bodily injury" is further defined to include risk of death, unconsciousness, extreme pain, disfigurement, or impairment. § 3008(f)(6). The "knowing endangerment" provisions have survived a challenge that they were unconstitutionally vague. United States v. Protex Industries, Inc., 874 F.2d 740 (10th Cir.1989).

Specific scienter provisions in subsection (f) answer some of the questions left open in subsection (d). The government need only show the defendant's "aware[ness] of the nature of his conduct;" awareness or belief that a circumstance exists; and awareness or belief that "his conduct is substantially certain to cause" the harm. § 3008(f)(1). Actual knowledge is required; knowledge possessed by another may not be attributed to the defendant. § 3008(f)(2). The government, however, may prove actual knowledge circumstantially. § 3008(f)(2). The statute also creates an affirmative defense where the injured party consented to foreseeable harm resulting from conditions of employment, medical treatment, or scientific experimentation. § 3008(f)(3).

## 4. CITIZENS' SUITS

RCRA's citizens' suit provisions offer ample opportunity for nongovernmental enforcement of the Subtitle C provisions. Assuming a plaintiff meets standing requirements (Lujan v. Defenders of Wildlife, 504 U.S. 555, 112 S.Ct. 2130, 119 L.Ed.2d 351 (1992)), § 7002(a)(1)(A) authorizes "any person" to sue "any person * * * who is alleged to be in violation of any [RCRA] permit, standard, regulation, condition, requirement, prohibition, or order * * *." A companion provision authorizes any person to sue EPA "where there is alleged a failure of the [EPA] to perform any [nondiscretionary] act or duty under [RCRA] * * *." § 7002(a)(2). (In addition, § 7002(a)(1)(B) authorizes private actions akin to actions under § 7003's "imminent and substantial endangerment" provision; these are addressed in Chapter 12.) In either class of actions, courts may order compliance with RCRA; in actions against persons other than EPA, the court may also assess civil penalties. § 7002(a).

Proper defendants in a citizens' suit can include the federal government. RCRA specifically waives federal sovereign immunity, even for suits seeking penalties, and subjects federal facilities to state and local laws. § 6001(a). A presidential exemption is possible for specific federal facilities. § 6001(a).

Suits in federal court against states are restricted by the Eleventh Amendment to the United States Constitution. See Seminole Tribe v. Florida, 517 U.S. 44, 116 S.Ct. 1114, 134 L.Ed.2d 252 (1996).

Section 7002 contains specific venue and intervention provisions. Venue for suits against persons other than EPA is proper in the district court for the district in which the alleged violation occurred. § 7002(a). Suits brought against EPA for violations of RCRA may be brought only in the district in which the alleged violation occurred. § 7002(c); but cf. § 7002(a) (also proper in district court for the District of Columbia). Intervention is allowed as of right to "any person" and to the EPA administrator. § 7002(b)(1), (d).

Fueling much privately filed RCRA litigation is the possibility for partial federal funding of the litigation. Like similar provisions in other environmental statutes, RCRA's citizens' suit provisions authorize the court to award a successful litigant costs of suit, including reasonable attorneys' fees. § 7002(e). To recover such fees, a party must demonstrate at least partial success on an issue of more than de minimis or technical import. See, e.g., Dague v. City of Burlington, 935 F.2d 1343 (2d Cir.1991), rev'd on other grounds, 505 U.S. 557, 112 S.Ct. 2638, 120 L.Ed.2d 449 (1992). The court may not enhance an award by factoring in the risk that a case taken on contingency might produce no recovery for plaintiff's attorney. City of Burlington v. Dague, 505 U.S. 557, 112 S.Ct. 2638, 120 L.Ed.2d 449 (1992).

Three principal limitations apply to RCRA's citizens' suits. First, a citizen may seek relief only for an ongoing violation; purely past misconduct is not actionable. See, e.g., Murray v. Bath Iron Works Corp., 867 F.Supp. 33 (D.Me.1994). Second, the plaintiff must give the right notice to the right authorities within the mandated time period. See, e.g., § 7002(b)(1)(A). These provisions give time both to the government, allowing it to take over the litigation if necessary, and to the alleged violators, allowing them to come into compliance. Finally, certain governmental enforcement actions will bar the maintenance of the suit. See, e.g., § 7002(b)(1)(B). These latter two requirements are discussed immediately below.

The notice requirement has received the most judicial attention. Actions brought both against "any person" or against EPA require 60 days advance notice. § 7002(b)(1)(A), (c). EPA regulations specify the content and form of the notice. 40 C.F.R. Part 254. In both instances, the notice, known popularly as the "NOIS" ("Notice of Intent to Sue") letter, must go to the EPA administrator. § 7002(b)(1)(A)(i), (c). In suits against any person other than EPA, notice must also be sent to the state in which the alleged violation occurred and to the alleged violator. § 7002(b)(1)(A)(ii), (iii). These notice provisions are jurisdictional and are strictly construed. Hallstrom v. Tillamook County, 493 U.S. 20, 110 S.Ct. 304, 107 L.Ed.2d 237 (1989). In both instances, however, plaintiffs may file suit immediately after giving the required notice if the action involves a non-frivolous alleged violation of

Subtitle C or its implementing regulations. § 7002(b)(1)(A), (c); cf. Aiello v. Town of Brookhaven, 136 F.Supp.2d 81 (E.D.N.Y.2001). In such cases, plaintiffs must still give the required notice; they simply need not wait to file until some time after giving the required notice. In hybrid cases, involving some claims for Subtitle C violations, and some claims under other RCRA provisions, courts have been willing to let the Subtitle C timing provisions govern. Thus, they will excuse the delay requirement otherwise applicable to the non-Subtitle C claims. See, e.g., Dague v. City of Burlington, 935 F.2d 1343 (2d Cir.1991), rev'd on other grounds, 505 U.S. 557, 112 S.Ct. 2638, 120 L.Ed.2d 449 (1992). Where, however, the plaintiffs voluntarily dismiss even non-frivolous Subtitle C allegations, the exception to the delay requirement no longer applies, and the entire case is subject to dismissal. Atwell v. K.W. Plastics, 213 F.Supp.2d 1294 (M.D.Ala.2002).

The types of government actions that will bar maintenance of a citizens' suit have also received some judicial attention. The statute precludes such suits "if the [EPA] or State has commenced and is diligently prosecuting a civil or criminal action in a court * * * to require compliance with [the applicable RCRA provisions]." § 7002(b)(1)(B). To date, the courts have disagreed over whether nonjudicial, administrative proceedings will preclude a citizens' suit. See Lykins v. Westinghouse Electric Corp., 715 F.Supp. 1357 (E.D.Ky.1989) (summarizing cases). The circumstances that constitute "diligent prosecution" are less easily categorized. Some courts assume that an appropriate action, once filed, is being diligently prosecuted. Orange Environment, Inc. v. County of Orange, 860 F.Supp. 1003 (S.D.N.Y.1994). Others conduct a case-by-case, fact intensive investigation. See Dague v. City of Burlington, 935 F.2d 1343 (2d Cir.1991), rev'd on other grounds, 505 U.S. 557, 112 S.Ct. 2638, 120 L.Ed.2d 449 (1992).

A potential new area of citizen litigation involves emergency preparedness in the face of climate change. Climate change has presented new challenges to the remediation of contaminated sites as sea levels rise and intensifying storms put such sites into the path of hurricanes and flooding that can spread pollutants into waterways and onto uncontaminated lands. In Conservation Law Foundation, Inc. v. Exxonmobil Corp., Case 1:16-cv-11950-MLW (D. Mass. 2017), plaintiffs claimed that Exxon's Everett Terminal, a petroleum storage facility, violated RCRA and the Clean Water Act because the facilities would not be sufficiently secure from the danger of rising sea levels and speculative increases in the severity and frequency of storms that might occur in 2050 or beyond. The district court granted Exxon's motion to dismiss in part, concluding that the plaintiffs could not seek redress based on the speculative claims of future sea level rise because they lacked standing for injuries that were not "imminent." However, as climate change proceeds, it seems likely that at some point courts will find that citizens have standing to bring such RCRA lawsuits.

## 5. SPECIAL PROBLEMS WITH OVERLAPPING STATE ENFORCEMENT

The existence in all but a few states of EPA-approved programs to implement RCRA creates the possibility of overlap and conflict between state and federal enforcement agencies. Among other requirements for obtaining EPA approval of a state Subtitle C permit program, the state must demonstrate adequate authority to enforce the permit provisions. § 3006(b)(3). Upon receipt of EPA approval, the state program operates "in lieu of the Federal program under [Subtitle C] in such State * * *." § 3006(b). In addition, state actions taken under EPA approved programs have "the same force and effect" as EPA actions. § 3006(d). These two provisions have led to two related, still unresolved interjurisdictional disputes.

First, can a citizens' suit be filed in federal court in a state with an approved enforcement program? The courts are divided. See Lutz v. Chromatex, Inc., 725 F.Supp. 258 (M.D.Pa.1989) (finding federal jurisdiction despite authorization of state program); contra, Thompson v. Thomas, 680 F.Supp. 1 (D.D.C.1987). Where courts find such jurisdiction, they tend to restrict it to violations of the state provisions, not of federal law per se. See, e.g., Murray v. Bath Iron Works Corp., 867 F.Supp. 33 (D.Me.1994); cf. Orange Environment, Inc. v. County of Orange, 860 F.Supp. 1003 (S.D.N.Y.1994) (allowing federal citizens' suits to enforce RCRA provisions not superseded by the EPA-approved state scheme).

This particular jurisdictional problem does not arise when EPA itself seeks to enforce a Subtitle C provision in a state with an approved program. Section 3008(a)(2) specifically authorizes EPA to pursue administrative and civil relief in such a state, provided it first notifies the state. Wyckoff Co. v. EPA, 796 F.2d 1197 (9th Cir.1986). Although federal enforcement authority exists, however, it is unclear whether in exercising this authority, EPA is enforcing state or federal law, or both. On the one hand, the permit was issued pursuant to state law which operates "in lieu of" the federal provisions. See United States v. Elias, 2000 WL 489732 (D.Idaho 2000) (finding EPA could only enforce state permit). On the other hand, a person who treats, stores, or disposes of Subtitle C regulated hazardous wastes without a proper state permit is also in violation of RCRA § 3005(a). See United States v. Flanagan, 126 F.Supp.2d 1284 (C.D.Cal.2000) (rejecting *Elias* and finding a violation of federal law); Northside Sanitary Landfill, Inc. v. Thomas, 804 F.2d 371, 381 (7th Cir.1986) (finding violations of both federal and state law).

A second issue is whether EPA can file its own federal enforcement action if it is dissatisfied with the actions taken by the approved state agency. EPA argues that it can so "overfile" at any time despite the "in lieu of" and "same force" provisions. It principally relies on the above described provisions of § 3008(a)(2). Defendants subjected to prior state proceedings, however, insist on a literal interpretation of the "in lieu of" and "same force and effect" provision. Cf. United States v.

Environmental Waste Control, Inc., 710 F.Supp. 1172 (N.D.Ind.1989) aff'd, 955 F.2d 45 (6th Cir.1992) (rejecting defendant's claim where prior state proceeding involved administrative consent order). The issue remains unresolved.

## F. ADDITIONAL PROVISIONS OF SELECTED STATE PROGRAMS

Most state regulatory schemes largely track the federal regulatory program. Some states, however, have gone beyond RCRA's minimum requirements in important ways.

- *Hazardous Waste Identification*: States have frequently regulated as "hazardous wastes" materials that do not meet the EPA definition. This may occur in three ways: (1) the state specifically lists as "hazardous wastes" materials not listed by EPA; (2) the state uses broader criteria than EPA for determining the characteristics of a "hazardous waste;" or (3) the state has a narrower exclusion from the definition of solid or hazardous waste than EPA. For example, several states, such as California and New Jersey, specifically list PCBs as "hazardous wastes" under their state regulatory schemes. As a result, although EPA only regulates PCBs under TSCA, states that regulate PCBs as "hazardous wastes" require generators, transporters, and TSD facilities that handle PCBs to comply with their standard "hazardous waste" regulations.

- *Recycling Requirements*: Some states, notably California and New Jersey, regulate the recycling of hazardous wastes more strictly than EPA. For example, in California, such recyclers must obtain a special permit. Moreover, under California law, all recyclable materials are wastes; accordingly, more materials will potentially meet the definition of "hazardous wastes" than under EPA's definition. Special California requirements apply to such recyclable materials as agricultural wastes, used oil, and spent lead-acid batteries. In addition, California authorities can ask any hazardous waste generator to explain why it disposed of a recyclable waste rather than recycling it.

- *Generator Requirements*: Three examples of state-imposed requirements on generators will illustrate the broad range of additional state law regulations. First, several states, including Illinois, New Jersey, New York and Texas, require generators to file *annual* reports; EPA, however, requires only *biennial* reports. Second, some states, such as California, have required generators to include more information on waste container labels than EPA requires. Finally, several states, including California, New York and

Texas, have less generous exemptions for small quantity generators.

- *Transporter Requirements*: Several states, such as California and New Jersey, have restricted the time that a transporter can store hazardous wastes in transit without converting the transporter into a TSD facility. In addition, New Jersey requires hazardous waste haulers to obtain a special license; to obtain such a license, the transporter must meet financial responsibility and training requirements.

- *TSD Requirements*: For the most part, state TSD requirements do not appear to differ substantially from EPA requirements. One significant difference is the absence of the "permit shield" under the Ohio and Illinois schemes. Some states, such as New Jersey and Texas, require more frequent reports by TSD facilities. New York and New Jersey also impose additional design and permitting restrictions.

- *UST Requirements*: For historical reasons, state UST requirements often differ materially from EPA requirements. Many states have long regulated certain USTs under programs designed to ensure fire safety and explosion protection. Because their focus is on fire safety rather than on groundwater contamination, the state regulations may include a broader range of tanks and may impose different design requirements from the RCRA UST regulations.

# CHAPTER 7

# INTRODUCTION TO THE COMPREHENSIVE ENVIRONMENTAL RESPONSE, COMPENSATION, AND LIABILITY ACT (CERCLA)

The main federal statute governing the cleanup of sites contaminated with hazardous wastes is the Comprehensive Environmental Response, Compensation, and Liability Act, 42 U.S.C.A. §§ 9601 et seq., commonly called "CERCLA." CERCLA is probably the most controversial environmental law ever enacted. Supporters praise it as a vital program to safeguard human health and the environment from the toxic consequences of decades of irresponsible waste handling. In turn, critics deride it as an extraordinarily expensive measure which imposes crippling liability on innocent parties to fund cleanups which are either unnecessary or largely ineffective.

This chapter provides a general introduction to CERCLA, focusing on its history, terminology, and overall structure. It serves as the foundation for Chapters 8–11 which discuss CERCLA's major provisions in depth.

## A. OVERVIEW

Congress enacted CERCLA for two purposes: (1) to promote the prompt cleanup of hazardous waste sites; and (2) to ensure that the costs of such cleanup efforts were borne by "those responsible for the contamination" rather than by taxpayers in general. Burlington Northern & Santa Fe Railway Co. v. United States, 556 U.S. 599, 602, 129 S.Ct. 1870, 173 L.Ed. 812 (2009). Congress was aware that if CERCLA liability was defined only by a party's *conduct* under traditional tort principles, the program would not generate enough money to fund the required national cleanup. In many cases, it was impossible to identify the persons who had actually contaminated a particular site; and when such persons could be located, they were often insolvent. Accordingly, CERCLA departs radically from conduct-based tort rules. It imposes strict liability for cleanup costs—regardless of the person's good faith, ignorance, or inaction—based merely on the person's *status*. Thus, if other liability factors are present, certain site "owners," site "operators," "arrangers," and "transporters" (collectively called "potentially responsible parties" or "PRPs") are strictly liable under CERCLA.

CERCLA is triggered if a "release" or threatened release of a "hazardous substance" has occurred at a "facility" or "vessel;" each of these terms is discussed later in this chapter. Once this triggering event occurs, CERCLA provides four basic mechanisms for cleaning up the site:

- *Cleanup performed by government:* Federal and state governmental entities (primarily EPA) can clean up the site (§ 104, discussed in Chapter 8) using government monies from the "Superfund" or other sources (§ 111), and then sue PRPs for reimbursement (§ 107(a)(4)(A), discussed in Chapter 9).

- *Cleanup mandated by government:* The federal government can mandate under certain conditions that PRPs clean up the site (§ 106, discussed in Chapter 10).
- *Negotiated cleanup:* Government entities can enter into settlement agreements with PRPs under which such parties finance or perform the cleanup (§ 122, discussed in Chapter 9); this is the option most commonly used by government.
- *Cleanup voluntarily performed by private party:* Under some circumstances, a private party can use its own funds to clean up the site, and sue PRPs for reimbursement ((§ 107(a)(4)(B)) or for contribution (§ 113), discussed in Chapter 11).

## B. ENACTMENT OF CERCLA

### 1. BACKGROUND: THE LOVE CANAL TRAGEDY

For decades, American factories, refineries, mines, and other business enterprises disposed of hazardous wastes in the cheapest possible manner, with little or no concern for human health or the environment. Before CERCLA was enacted, EPA estimated that more than 2,000 dump sites across the nation—most of them abandoned—contained hazardous wastes which threatened human health.

EPA concluded that over 90% of the hazardous wastes generated in the United States each year were being disposed of improperly. In addition, spills and other accidental releases of hazardous substances into the environment were common. EPA estimated that about 3,500 chemical spills capable of causing environmental harm occurred each year.

In the late 1970s, Americans became increasingly concerned about this toxic legacy. One incident—the Love Canal tragedy—is widely credited with pushing the issue into the national spotlight and thereby inspiring the passage of CERCLA. The Love Canal saga began in the 1940s, when Hooker Chemical Company started dumping 55-gallon drums of chemical waste into an abandoned canal near Niagara Falls, New York. In 1953, Hooker covered the canal and sold it to the local school board. The board built a school on part of the property, and sold the balance to developers who built modest single-family homes. Investigating Love Canal in 1978, the state health department uncovered an environmental disaster. Toxic chemicals migrating from the canal had contaminated the subsoil and groundwater throughout the entire area, even percolating into houses. Studies demonstrated that Love Canal residents suffered from abnormally high rates of miscarriages, birth defects, epilepsy, liver abnormalities, and other illnesses. In the near panic which ensued, Love Canal became a virtual ghost town.

The Love Canal saga shocked the nation and dominated the headlines for months. Millions of Americans, haunted by the fear of future Love Canals, demanded government action. The tenor of the times is summarized in a 1980 Senate report leading up to CERCLA:

> The legacy of past haphazard disposal of chemical wastes and the continuing danger of spills and other releases of dangerous chemicals pose what many call the most serious health and environmental challenge of the decade. * * * The acceptance of man-made chemicals * * * has become a fact of daily life in the United States. We are dependent on synthetic chemicals for health, livelihood, housing, transportation, food, and for our funerals. * * * But in recent years, there has been a realization what is our meat may also be our poison.

## 2. PRE-CERCLA REGULATION

Love Canal and similar events revealed a major regulatory gap: existing law was inadequate to ensure cleanup of sites contaminated by hazardous substances. State law virtually ignored the issue. Federal law, while somewhat more developed, was still fragmentary. For example, as discussed in Chapter 12, RCRA § 7003 empowered EPA to clean up hazardous waste sites which posed an "imminent and substantial endangerment to health or the environment." But at the time, this section was understood to apply only to *active* hazardous waste disposal sites, not *inactive* or *abandoned* sites like Love Canal. Similarly, a 1978 amendment to CWA § 311 extended the existing comprehensive regulatory framework for oil spill cleanup to cover the cleanup of 300 hazardous substances discharged into "navigable waters" (see Chapter 5). But this provision did not extend to most land-based contamination.

### 3. THE ORIGINAL STATUTE

CERCLA was the product of a three year Congressional effort to craft a comprehensive program for cleaning up the nation's toxic legacy. The broad outline of CERCLA is modeled on CWA § 311, modified by concepts borrowed from RCRA and elsewhere. But the final text stems from a last-minute political compromise, which was enacted into law almost immediately by a "lame duck" Congress with virtually no debate. Because of its hasty passage, CERCLA is one of the worst-drafted federal statutes in decades. As the Ninth Circuit observed in California v. Neville Chemical Company, 358 F.3d 661, 663 (9th Cir.2004), "in the 'maze'-like structure and 'baffling language' of CERCLA, clarity is rare." Other courts have been less restrained, criticizing CERCLA as "a statute notorious for its lack of clarity and poor draftsmanship" Lansford-Coaldale Joint Water Authority v. Tonolli Corp., 4 F.3d 1209 (3d Cir.1993)) and "riddled with inconsistencies and redundancies" United States v. Alcan Aluminum Corp., 964 F.2d 252 (3d Cir.1992)).

In 1980, during the waning days of the Carter administration, four hazardous substance cleanup bills were pending in Congress, two in the House (H.R. 85 and 7020) and two in the Senate (S.B. 1341 and 1480). All the bills shared two features: each (1) established a trust fund to finance government cleanup of hazardous substance contamination; and (2) imposed strict liability on certain parties for cleanup costs. Beyond these points, however, the bills differed widely. For example, S.B. 1480, the most far-reaching of the quartet, included strict liability for personal injury and property damage caused by hazardous substance releases. The House of Representatives passed H.R. 7020 in September, 1980, aware that Senate consideration of the much-stronger S.B 1480 was imminent. During November, 1980, a small bipartisan group of prominent senators met privately to reconcile the two approaches. The resulting compromise (known as the "Stafford-Randolph substitute") was an entirely new bill. When consideration of S.B. 1480 began on November 24, 1980, the Senate promptly amended that bill by replacing all of its text with the Stafford-Randolph substitute text (i.e., retaining only the bill number) and proceeded *the same day* to approve the bill as amended. The House of Representatives approved the substitute measure on December 3, 1980, with no amendments and almost no debate.

Accordingly, the legislative history of CERCLA is remarkably scant. As one judge lamented in Rhodes v. County of Darlington, 833 F.Supp. 1163 (D.S.C.1992), there "is virtually no legislative history to guide the courts in interpreting the Act."

Most major federal environmental statutes emerge from Congress accompanied by a long history of amendments, committee reports, public hearing testimony, floor debate, and other data. The substitute measure which became CERCLA, however, slipped through Congress like a virtual phantom, leaving few traces behind. In particular, the text of the compromise bill was never analyzed in a committee report or subjected to the committee hearing process. This lack of legislative history has profoundly affected the judicial approach to CERCLA.

## 4. AMENDMENTS TO CERCLA

### a. Superfund Amendments and Reauthorization Act of 1986 (SARA)

CERCLA was substantially amended in 1986 by the Superfund Amendments and Reauthorization Act, commonly called "SARA." SARA is best understood as a response to the difficulties encountered during the early years of CERCLA. After the enactment of CERCLA, it soon became clear that Congress had underestimated the scope of the hazardous waste problem, both in terms of the number of contaminated sites and the difficulty of cleanup. Further, despite EPA's expenditure of over a billion dollars, by 1986 the program had cleaned up only *six sites*. Critics attacked the program as slow and ineffective.

SARA did not significantly change the core of CERCLA. The cleanup authority and liability standards set forth in §§ 104, 106, and 107 remained largely intact. Instead, SARA added supplemental provisions governing the cleanup process itself, thereby curtailing EPA's discretion. It imposed a partial cleanup timetable (§ 116), mandated more extensive cleanups (§ 121), and increased the Superfund amount. SARA also made a number of procedural changes designed to streamline the administration of CERCLA, adding provisions designed to: (1) encourage settlement (§ 122); (2) facilitate contribution among responsible parties (§ 113(f)); and (3) enhance public participation (§§ 117, 310).

After SARA, CERCLA is an unwieldy combination of old and new provisions. Broadly speaking, the original CERCLA was short, vague, and poorly-drafted. The SARA amendments, however, were lengthy, specific, and generally well-drafted. Similarly, the legislative history of SARA is extensive, unlike the scant record left by the original CERCLA.

### b. Asset Conservation, Lender Liability, and Deposit Insurance Protection Act of 1996

Additional changes were made in 1996 as part of the Asset Conservation, Lender Liability, and Deposit Insurance Protection Act. These amendments clarify the scope of lender liability and provide new protections for trustees and other fiduciaries, as discussed in Chapter 9. Much like the original CERCLA, however, they slipped through Congress with little scrutiny as part of a 1,900 page omnibus budget act, leaving virtually no legislative history behind.

### c. Small Business Liability Relief and Brownfields Revitalization Act of 2002

More recently, the Small Business Liability Relief and Brownfields Revitalization Act of 2002 made several changes to CERCLA. As discussed in Chapter 9, the most important amendments (a) provide special protections for investors who redevelop contaminated locations or "brownfields," (b) create a new defense for owners whose land is adjacent to contaminated sites, and (c) extend immunity to generators of extremely small amounts of hazardous substances.

## 5. JUDICIAL INTERPRETATION OF CERCLA

The federal judiciary has played a prominent role in shaping CERCLA. As CERCLA's architect, Congress produced a statutory blueprint which was vague and skimpy. Much like a building contractor working from incomplete plans, the courts have used expansive judicial interpretation to erect (and enlarge) the CERCLA framework. In many respects, the modern contours of CERCLA far exceed the expectations of its original proponents.

Congress apparently anticipated the need for judicial development of CERCLA to a certain extent. The scant legislative history suggests that Congress left portions of CERCLA vague with the intent that the judiciary create a body of federal common law, particularly in the areas of joint and several liability, contribution, and corporate successor liability. But many of the gaps, inconsistencies, and other CERCLA flaws were the product of careless drafting, not intentional delegation. As a result, the courts were presented with a larger interpretive role than planned.

Most federal courts have given CERCLA a broad interpretation. The early courts that struggled with CERCLA quickly discovered that its legislative history provided little guidance in discerning Congressional intent on specific issues. Yet even this limited history reflected the two broad purposes underlying CERCLA: (1) to protect the public and the environment by forcing prompt cleanup of hazardous substances; and (2) to ensure that the cleanup costs were borne by "responsible" parties. Deprived of more specific guidance, federal courts have typically construed CERCLA provisions in a manner which would implement these sweeping purposes. As the Second Circuit summarized in B.F. Goodrich Co. v. Murtha, 958 F.2d 1192 (2d Cir.1992): "Because it is a remedial statute, CERCLA must be construed liberally to effectuate its two primary goals * * *." See also United States v. Brothers Enterprises, Inc., 113 F.Supp.3d 907 (E.D.Tex.2015).

## C. MAJOR PROVISIONS OF CERCLA

### 1. KEY CERCLA DEFINITIONS: SECTION 101

Five concepts form the jurisdictional heart of CERCLA. Although the alternative mechanisms in

§§ 104, 106, and 107 differ significantly, they all involve: (1) a "release" or threatened release; (2) of a "hazardous substance;" (3) at a "facility" or "vessel." Once CERCLA jurisdiction is triggered, the ensuing cleanup activity is called a "response" action. There are two types of response actions, each governed by different procedures: (1) "removal action;" and (2) "remedial action." These key concepts are all discussed briefly below.

### a. A "Release" or Threatened Release

Section 101(22) defines a "release" as "any spilling, leaking, pumping, pouring, emitting, emptying, discharging, injecting, escaping, leaching, dumping, or disposing into the environment * * *." Abandoning or discarding barrels or other closed receptacles is also considered a release under this section. The statutory definition excepts a number of actions, largely those regulated under other federal statutes (e.g., releases in the work place, releases of motor vehicle exhaust, and the normal application of fertilizer).

Courts construe "release" broadly. Virtually any movement of hazardous substances into the environment will constitute a release. For example, releases have been found where hazardous substances leaked through a cracked sewer pipe, were sprayed to suppress dust, were blown about by a light wind, or were inside shotgun shells fired at a gun range. But evidence demonstrating specifically how the hazardous substances moved into the environment is generally unnecessary. Most courts conclude that the mere presence of hazardous substances in soil, water, or air is sufficient to establish that a release has occurred. As the court reasoned in HRW Systems, Inc. v. Washington Gas Light Co., 823 F.Supp. 318 (D.Md.1993): "Given the breadth of the definitional language in CERCLA, it seems virtually impossible to conceive of a situation where hazardous substances are found in the soil and not *ipso facto* 'released' into the environment."

The requirement that a release enter the "environment" is easily met in most instances. Section 101(8) defines "environment" as all surface water, groundwater, drinking water supply, land surface or subsurface strata, or ambient air within the United States or under its jurisdiction. The interior of a structure, vessel, or other man-made product is excluded from the definition.

CERCLA also extends to potential future releases, described variously as a "threat of release" (§ 104) or "threatened release" (§§ 106, 107). These phrases are not defined by CERCLA and their meanings are thus less clear. The leading case on the point is New York v. Shore Realty Corp., 759 F.2d 1032 (2d Cir.1985), where the Second Circuit noted that the storage of toxic substances in corroding and deteriorating tanks, the owner's lack of expertise in handling hazardous wastes, and even the failure to license the facility, amounted to a "threat of release." Similarly, in United States v. Northernaire Plating Co., 670 F.Supp. 742 (W.D.Mich.1987), aff'd sub nom. United States v. R.W. Meyer, Inc., 889 F.2d 1497 (6th Cir.1989), the court found a threat of release based on the presence of hazardous substances at the site, combined with the "unwillingness of any party to assert control over the substances."

### b. Of a "Hazardous Substance"

The universe of CERCLA "hazardous substances" is extremely broad; it includes RCRA hazardous wastes and much more. It exceeds the RCRA universe in two key respects. First, the scope of CERCLA is not limited to wastes. As the term "substance" suggests, CERCLA potentially extends to virgin materials, consumer products, manufacturing byproducts, wastes, and everything in between.

Second, § 101(14) defines "hazardous substance" mainly by incorporating lists of substances regulated either under RCRA or three other federal environmental statutes. Any substance which has already been designated as hazardous or toxic under specified provisions of the CAA, CWA, RCRA, or TSCA is automatically designated a hazardous substance under CERCLA. In addition, if a substance "may present substantial danger to the public health or welfare" when released into the environment, EPA may specially designate it as a hazardous substance under § 102(a). The § 102(a) list, containing almost 2,000 hazardous substances, is located at 40 C.F.R. § 302.4, Table 302.4. Substances regulated under CERCLA range from the familiar (e.g., arsenic, lead, mercury, and silver) to the esoteric (e.g., isopropanolamine dodecylbenzenesulfonate, toluene diisocyanate, and 2,3,7,8-tetrachlorodibenzo-p-dioxin).

Moreover, CERCLA extends to mixtures of hazardous and nonhazardous materials. As the Second Circuit observed in B.F. Goodrich Co. v. Murtha, 958 F.2d 1192 (2d Cir.1992): "When a mixture or waste solution contains hazardous substances, that mixture is itself hazardous for purposes of determining CERCLA liability." In the early decision of United States v. Wade, 577 F.Supp. 1326 (E.D.Pa.1983), for example, the court suggested that a penny might be considered a hazardous substance because it is a mixture which includes copper, a toxic pollutant regulated under the CWA and thus a CERCLA hazardous substance.

One of the most controversial aspects of CERCLA is the apparent judicial consensus that any amount of hazardous substance, however minute, is enough to trigger liability. In other words, CERCLA is concerned only with the *presence* of a hazardous substance, not with its *concentration* or *quantity*. Appearing as a defendant in a pair of notable cases—City of New York v. Exxon Corp., 744 F.Supp. 474 (S.D.N.Y.1990), and United States v. Alcan Aluminum Corp., 755 F.Supp. 531 (N.D.N.Y.1991)—Alcan Aluminum Corporation pointed out that the concentration of hazardous substances in its wastes was lower than those found in milk, breakfast cereal, or even the paper and ink which comprised the government's own brief. Although Alcan's wastes were *not actually dangerous* to humans or the environment, they were still *deemed* "hazardous substances" under CERCLA. Under this standard, the book which you are now reading could be considered a "hazardous substance" because its paper and ink contain minute amounts of hazardous substances.

However, the stringency of the "no minimum quantity" approach has been mitigated for one category of potentially liable parties by the 2002 amendments to CERCLA. Under some circumstances, factories or other facilities that generate hazardous substances—and would otherwise be liable as "arrangers"—are immune from liability if the quantity of substances released is extremely small, as discussed in Chapter 9.

### *i. Petroleum Exclusion*

As a practical matter, there are two major exceptions to the definition of "hazardous substance." The first is known as the "petroleum exclusion." Section 101(14) expressly provides that the term hazardous substance does not include either (1) "petroleum, including crude oil or any fraction thereof which is not otherwise specifically listed or designated" as a hazardous substance or (2) various natural and synthetic gas products. Thus, for example, a spill of crude oil into a river would not trigger CERCLA. Petroleum product spills are separately regulated under CWA § 311 and the Oil Pollution Act of 1990, 33 U.S.C.A. §§ 2701 et seq.

But if a hazardous substance is incorporated into a petroleum product, is the product excluded? The limited case law on point suggests that if the hazardous substance occurs *naturally* in the petroleum or is added *during* the refining process, then the product is exempt. For example, the Ninth Circuit held in Wilshire Westwood Associates v. Atlantic Richfield Corp., 881 F.2d 801 (9th Cir.1989) that refined gasoline was within the petroleum exclusion, even though it contained lead, benzene, and other additives which would normally be considered hazardous substances. In contrast, the exclusion does not extend to hazardous substances added to a petroleum product *after* the refining process.

### *ii. Municipal Solid Waste Exclusion*

Each year millions of tons of municipal solid waste (MSW) are generated in the United States, most of which is deposited in municipal landfills. A small fraction of MSW consists of hazardous substances (e.g., discarded paint, cleaning supplies, and pesticides). In the early years of CERCLA, it was unclear whether MSW would be considered a hazardous substance. The issue was important because all local governmental entities which collected and disposed of MSW faced billions of dollars in potential liability as site operators, owners, or arrangers.

Congress brought clarity to this issue with the 2002 amendments, creating an express exemption for MSW under certain circumstances. Technically, the exemption is not found in the definition of "hazardous substance"—rather, it appears in the form of a limitation on CERCLA liability in

§ 107(p)—but it has much the same practical effect. In general, the owner, operator, or lessee of a residential property that generates MSW is exempt from liability for the disposal of such MSW; thus, for example, a homeowner who discards a can of insect spray in the trash cannot be sued under CERCLA. Business entities that employ less than 100 full-time employees are similarly exempt from liability for MSW that they generate, as long as the "relative quantity" is the same as found in the garbage of a typical single-family household.

### c. At a "Facility" or "Vessel"

In practice, the term "facility" is devoid of meaning. Virtually any place a hazardous substance is located constitutes a CERCLA "facility." Section 101(9) states that the term includes not only buildings, landfills, ponds, motor vehicles, aircraft, and the like, but also "any site or area where a hazardous substance has been deposited, stored, disposed of, or placed, or otherwise come to be located." Unsurprisingly, courts have given this "catchall" language a broad interpretation. In United States v. Ward, 618 F.Supp. 884 (E.D.N.C.1985), for example, defendants disposed of PCB-contaminated oil by driving their tank truck along highways with the valve open; the resulting 221 mile long strip was deemed a "facility." However, a "consumer product in consumer use" is not a facility under the statute. Thus, in Kane v. United States, 15 F.3d 87 (8th Cir.1994), the Eighth Circuit held that a house containing asbestos insulation was not subject to CERCLA.

"Vessel" is defined by § 101(28) as "every description of watercraft or other artificial contrivance used, or capable of being used, as a means of transportation on water." Only a few CERCLA cases involve vessels.

### d. "Removal Action"

In general, *removal action* consists of short-term, temporary measures which prevent or mitigate a release. Conversely, as discussed below, *remedial action* consists of measures taken to implement a long-term, permanent cleanup of a contaminated site. Thus, examples of removal action include: (1) installing fences, warning signs, and other site control precautions; (2) controlling drainage to prevent hazardous substance migration; (3) stabilizing berms, dikes, or impoundments; (4) capping contaminated soils to reduce migration; (5) using chemicals and other materials to retard the spread of a release; (6) removing drums, barrels, tanks, and other receptacles containing hazardous substances; (7) providing alternate water supplies; and (8) evacuating threatened individuals. See 40 C.F.R. § 300.415(e) (listing sample removal actions).

The distinction between removal action and remedial action is sometimes blurred. Although CERCLA lacks a definition of "removal action," it does define "removal." Yet the explanation of "removal" produces more confusion than clarification. Section 101(23) provides that "removal" means: "the cleanup or removal of released hazardous substances from the environment," including "such actions as may be necessary" to: (1) deal with a threatened release; (2) monitor, evaluate, and assess a release or threatened release; (3) dispose of removed material; or (4) "prevent, minimize, or mitigate damage to the public health or welfare or to the environment, which may otherwise result from a release or threat of release." On its face, this definition seems to include work which results in a permanent cleanup; if so, it would swallow the concept of remedial action. This difficulty surfaced in General Electric Co. v. Litton Industrial Automation Systems, Inc., 920 F.2d 1415 (8th Cir.1990), where the Eighth Circuit held that excavation work which resulted in a permanent cleanup was merely removal action.

Recognizing that Congress intended removal action and remedial action as separate concepts, however, most courts struggle to delineate the boundary between the two. In close cases, factors such as the cost and duration of the project, the need for immediate action, and the nature of the remedy are useful in distinguishing removal from remedial action.

### e. "Remedial Action"

The second type of response action is *remedial action*—the long-term, permanent cleanup of a contaminated site. Section 101(24) defines "remedial action" as: "those actions consistent with permanent remedy taken [sic] instead of or in addition to removal actions * * * to prevent or minimize the release of hazardous substances so that they do not migrate to cause substantial danger to present or future public health or welfare or the environment."

Examples of remedial action include: (1) excavating and treating soil; (2) treating soil in place; (3) removing and treating groundwater; (4) constructing dikes, trenches, or ditches to prevent migration; (5) collecting leachate and runoff; (6) disposing of hazardous substances offsite; (7) relocating residents permanently; and (8) monitoring to assure that such actions protect public health and the environment.

### 2. CLEANUP PERFORMED BY GOVERNMENT: SECTION 104

Once CERCLA jurisdiction is triggered, § 104 authorizes the President to clean up or "remediate" contaminated sites. The President has delegated this authority to EPA by executive order. The original plan was that EPA would finance such cleanups with monies from a special revolving fund known as the "Superfund," but today this is done with appropriations from the federal budget. The cleanup process is governed by an intricate set of substantive and procedural requirements, most of which are contained in the "National Contingency Plan" (NCP). Section 104 cleanups are discussed in depth in Chapter 8.

## 3. CLEANUP MANDATED BY GOVERNMENT: SECTION 106

In the event of an imminent and substantial endangerment to public health, welfare, or the environment, the federal government may compel "responsible" persons to clean up the site under § 106, either by obtaining an injunction or by issuing an administrative order. Courts have generally construed § 106 as incorporating the liability standards applicable to cost recovery actions in § 107. The § 106 powers are discussed in Chapter 10.

## 4. COST RECOVERY ACTIONS: SECTION 107

The main CERCLA provision establishing the liability of "potentially responsible parties" (PRPs) for cleanup costs is § 107(a). This section imposes strict liability on four categories of "persons" linked to the contaminated site: (1) current site "owners" and "operators;" (2) persons who were "owners" or "operators" at the "time of disposal" of hazardous substances on the site; (3) persons who "arranged" for disposal or treatment of the hazardous substances; and (4) transporters of hazardous substances who "selected" the disposal or treatment site. Although § 107(b) establishes potential defenses to CERCLA liability (e.g., act of God), federal courts construe these defenses narrowly; they have succeeded only in a handful of cases. After a government entity performs cleanup work under § 104, it can sue responsible persons under § 107(a)(4)(A) to recover its cleanup costs and other items. Cost recovery actions brought by government are discussed in Chapter 9.

In addition, to encourage cleanup without government intervention, § 107(a)(4)(B) creates a private right of action. For example, under some circumstances, the owner of a contaminated site can clean up the site herself and then sue responsible persons for reimbursement under this subsection. Both this private right of action and the related issue of contribution rights among responsible persons are discussed in Chapter 11.

### 5. THE SUPERFUND: SECTION 111

The financial heart of CERCLA was the Hazardous Substance Superfund, commonly known as the "Superfund" or "Trust Fund," created under § 111. CERCLA initially authorized a $1.6 billion Superfund, but Congress increased its size to $8.5 billion in 1986 through SARA. Congress was fully aware that even this enlarged amount represented only a small fraction of the tens of billions of dollars which would ultimately be required to clean up the nation's hazardous waste sites. However, the Superfund was exhausted in 2003, and today the program is funded through annual budget allocations from Congress.

#### a. Superfund Uses

In practice, the Superfund was used almost exclusively for one purpose: financing government cleanups under § 104. Sections 104 and 107 were designed to work in tandem with the Superfund in a three step process. Thus, for many years EPA could: (1) finance its § 104 cleanup with Superfund monies as permitted by § 111(a)(1); then (2) file a cost recovery action under § 107 for reimbursement of the cleanup expenses; and finally (3) deposit the proceeds from the action into the Superfund. In this manner, the same Superfund dollars would be reused over time to remediate many different sites.

Superfund monies could also—in theory—be used by EPA for other specified CERCLA purposes, including:

- reimbursing non-liable parties who voluntarily incur response costs, as set forth in §§ 111(a)(3) and 112;
- reimbursing non-liable parties who incur response costs in complying with a § 106 administrative order, as set forth in § 106(b)(2);
- compensating government entities for damages to natural resources caused by hazardous substances, as set forth in § 111(b)(2); and
- other miscellaneous uses listed in § 111(a).

In practice, EPA was reluctant to allocate any of the limited Superfund monies to these alternative uses. For example, during CERCLA's first decade, only *one party* who voluntarily incurred response costs received reimbursement from the Superfund.

### b. Superfund Sources

As reauthorized by SARA, the Superfund was financed by: (1) an excise tax on crude oil and petroleum products; (2) an excise tax on certain chemical feedstocks; (3) an import tax on certain chemical derivatives; (4) an "environmental tax" on certain corporate profits; and (5) general federal revenues. The authority to levy these taxes, however, expired on December 31, 1995, and was not renewed. During the 1990s, an increasingly large share of government cleanup expenses was funded by allocations from the general federal budget.

Since 2003, when the Superfund was depleted, EPA's cleanup program has been financed by (1) general federal revenues plus (2) funds obtained through bringing cost recovery actions against liable parties. Over the last 20 years, more than $21 billion in federal appropriations has been spent to clean up contaminated sites.

## D. THE FUTURE OF CERCLA

CERCLA has been relatively successful to date. EPA reports that site remediation work is complete at many sites. But much remains to be done. To some extent, EPA has tended to work on the easiest sites first: sites where solvent PRPs were identifiable or where the cleanup process was comparatively simple. Thus, many of the remaining sites require complex and expensive work, but are "orphan" sites—that is, sites where no solvent PRP can be found. EPA has estimated that more than

$200 billion may be needed through 2030 to complete the cleanup process. In addition, EPA is still adding new sites to the cleanup list. Due to the slow pace of the cleanup effort, today more than 53 million Americans still live within three miles of a contaminated site.

We can safely predict that CERCLA will be amended in the future. A word of caution is accordingly appropriate before the reader embarks upon the detailed explanation of the current CERCLA contained in the next four chapters.

Few are content with CERCLA in its present form. While lauding its goals, environmentalists complain that CERCLA has been underfunded, slowing the national cleanup effort to a snail's pace. Without a reauthorization of CERCLA financing by Congress, they fear that exhaustion of the Superfund will undermine the entire program. On the other hand, industry groups criticize CERCLA as overly expensive, ineffective, and fundamentally unfair. As the price for supporting reauthorization of funding, they would undoubtedly demand significant changes in CERCLA's basic provisions.

For all its flaws, CERCLA has been surprisingly successful in another important arena. Though somewhat disappointing as a mechanism for the cleanup of contaminated sites, it has proven relatively effective in controlling on-going waste disposal. The specter of unavoidable multi-million dollar CERCLA cleanup liability has given industry a strong incentive to minimize the use or creation of hazardous substances, especially wastes.

# CHAPTER 8

# CERCLA: CLEANUP PERFORMED BY GOVERNMENT

## A. OVERVIEW

CERCLA § 104 authorizes government cleanup of sites contaminated by hazardous substances. If its requirements are met, EPA may itself undertake response action using monies from the Superfund. Alternatively, under § 104(d) EPA can enter into cooperative agreements with states, their political subdivisions, or Indian tribes under which they will conduct cleanup actions using this fund. EPA or the other government entity involved can then obtain reimbursement for its expenditures from responsible parties in a cost recovery action brought under § 107(a). In practice, government agencies usually "perform" response actions by retaining private contractors who actually do the required site work.

CERCLA cleanups are governed by a complex network of substantive and procedural requirements. The heart of this network is a set of federal regulations known as the "National Contingency Plan" (NCP). Broadly speaking, if EPA or another government entity violates the NCP in cleaning up a site, it will be unable to recover its response costs from the responsible parties.

The most dangerous sites are targeted for priority cleanup through placement on the National Priorities List (NPL), which now lists approximately

1,340 sites. EPA's remediation of NPL sites—often used as a yardstick for measuring CERCLA's success—has proven both slow and expensive. From discovery to completion, cleanup of the average site spans over 10 years and costs more than $25 million. Cleanup has been completed on over 1,000 sites, many of which have already been removed from the NPL.

This chapter examines the legal standards concerning cleanups performed by government, focusing on EPA. However, its discussion of the procedural requirements for response actions (e.g., NCP provisions and § 121 minimum cleanup levels) is applicable to all CERCLA cleanups, including private party cleanups mandated by EPA under § 106 (Chapter 10) and voluntary private party cleanups under § 107(a)(4)(B) (Chapter 11). Finally, as a practical matter, most CERCLA cleanups are partially or entirely performed by PRPs—also pursuant to the procedures discussed below—who have entered into settlement agreements with EPA or another government entity (Chapter 9).

## B. SECTION 104 CLEANUP AUTHORITY

Section 104 cleanup authority is most commonly triggered when:

- a "hazardous substance"
- is "released" into (or there is a "substantial threat" of such a release into) the "environment,"

- and, if remedial action is involved, the site is listed on the NPL.

If these conditions are met, the government is authorized to take removal action or remedial action in a manner "consistent with" the NCP. The first two elements above—"hazardous substance" and "release" or threat of release—are discussed in Chapter 7. The requirement of NPL listing, together with the other limitations imposed by the NCP, are discussed in this chapter.

Although rarely exercised, § 104 cleanup authority exists in one other situation. The government may also take response action when there is a release or threatened release of a "pollutant or contaminant which may present an imminent and substantial danger to the public health or welfare," with the same NPL listing requirement for remedial work. The phrase "pollutant or contaminant" is broadly defined by § 101(33) to include:

> any element, substance, compound, or mixture * * * which after release into the environment and upon exposure, ingestion, inhalation, or assimilation into any organism * * * will or may reasonably be anticipated to cause death, disease, behavioral abnormalities, cancer, genetic mutation, physiological malfunctions * * * or physical deformations * * *.

The definition is qualified by essentially the same list of exclusions which apply to "hazardous substance," discussed in Chapter 7. Accordingly, in many instances, the same substance can be characterized both as a "hazardous substance" and a "pollutant or contaminant," allowing the government entity to proceed under either approach. But the distinction between the two concepts is critical for purposes of a later cost recovery action. Under § 107(a), only response costs stemming from a "hazardous substance" can be recovered. As the D.C. Circuit noted in Eagle-Picher Industries, Inc. v. EPA, 759 F.2d 922 (D.C.Cir.1985), "the owner of a facility may be liable for cleanup of a release of a 'hazardous substance,' but not for the cleanup of a release of a 'pollutant or contaminant.'" Accordingly, given the option, government entities have uniformly proceeded under the "hazardous substance" approach.

A special rule applies to three types of releases. Absent a "public health or environmental emergency," § 104 cannot be used to abate: (1) releases of a naturally occurring substance from a location where it is naturally found; (2) releases from products which are part of the structure of residential buildings or business or community structures (e.g., asbestos); and (3) releases into public or private drinking water supplies due to deterioration of the system through ordinary use. § 104(a)(3), (4).

## C. LOCATING CONTAMINATED SITES

The first step in the cleanup process is locating a contaminated site which requires response action. EPA discovers sites through methods including: (1)

required reporting of certain releases by facilities; (2) "whistleblowing" by employees; and (3) reports from the public. EPA maintains a computerized inventory known as the Superfund Enterprise Management System (SEMS), which includes active hazardous waste sites as well as those being considered for inclusion on the NPL. Only a small percentage of such sites however, ultimately require action.

### 1. RELEASE REPORTING BY FACILITIES

If a hazardous substance is released in sufficient quantity from a facility or vessel, § 103(a) requires the "person in charge" to report the release immediately. As the Second Circuit observed in United States v. Carr, 880 F.2d 1550 (2d Cir.1989), this provision ensures "that the government, once timely notified, will be able to move quickly to check the spread of a hazardous release." The threshold "reportable quantity" varies from one to 5,000 pounds, depending upon the hazardous substance involved. EPA has established reportable quantities for many hazardous substances at 40 C.F.R. § 302.4; if a hazardous substance is not included in this list, § 102(b) sets its reportable quantity at one pound. Substantial criminal penalties may be imposed for failing to report. § 103(b). The CERCLA release reporting program overlaps somewhat with the various reporting requirements contained in EPCRTKA (Chapter 4) and RCRA (Chapters 6 and 12).

### 2. EMPLOYEE "WHISTLEBLOWERS"

Employees of culpable parties are another potential information source. Like many federal environmental statutes, CERCLA affords protection to "whistleblowers" who either provide information to enforcement agencies or testify in subsequent proceedings. Section 110(a) bars an employer from firing or otherwise discriminating against an employee who has cooperated in the CERCLA process.

### 3. REPORTS FROM THE PUBLIC

Reports from members of the public comprise a third information source. In particular, § 105(d) permits any person who is actually or potentially affected by a release or threatened release of a hazardous substance (or pollutant or contaminant) to petition the President to conduct a preliminary assessment of the hazard. Within twelve months after receiving such a petition, the President must either complete the requested assessment or explain why an assessment is not appropriate.

## D. PLANNING THE RESPONSE: THE NATIONAL CONTINGENCY PLAN (NCP)

The "blueprint" for cleanup action under § 104 is the National Oil and Hazardous Substances Pollution Contingency Plan, commonly called the "National Contingency Plan" or "NCP." It is a set of federal regulations located at 40 C.F.R. Part 300 "that identifies the methods for investigating contamination and the criteria for determining appropriate cleanup actions." Arc Ecology v. United States, 411 F.3d 1092 (9th Cir.2005). An earlier version of the NCP existed before CERCLA was enacted; it established procedures to facilitate cleanups of oil and hazardous substance spills into navigable waters, pursuant to CWA § 311. Once CERCLA became effective, its § 105(a) directed EPA to revise the NCP. In particular, EPA was required to add a new section to the NCP which established "procedures and standards" for CERCLA response actions, known as the "National Hazardous Substance Response Plan;" this section may be found at 40 C.F.R. §§ 300.400 et seq.

The NCP is important for three basic reasons:

- It establishes procedures which EPA and other government agencies must follow in exercising § 104 cleanup authority. As discussed later in this chapter, it details a step-by-step process for dealing with a contaminated site, from the initial discovery through the permanent cleanup.
- It also sets forth standards for determining the appropriate cleanup technique to use, in connection with § 121. This "how clean is clean?" issue is also discussed in this Chapter.
- Finally, it limits the recovery of response costs by both government and private parties under § 107. Government entities can only recover "costs of removal or remedial action" which are "not inconsistent with the national

contingency plan." § 107(a)(4)(A). Similarly, private parties can only recoup "necessary costs of response" which are "consistent with the national contingency plan." § 107(a)(4)(B). These issues are discussed in Chapters 9 and 11.

## E. EVALUATING THE SITE

### 1. PRELIMINARY ASSESSMENT AND SITE INSPECTION (PA/SI)

Once a suspect site is identified, the first step in the process is the "preliminary assessment and site inspection" (PA/SI). This step has two tiers, one concerning removal action ("removal site evaluation") and one concerning remedial action ("remedial site evaluation").

The entire PA/SI is performed by the "lead agency" selected for the site. The lead agency is normally EPA, but under some circumstances it can be another federal agency, a state or one of its political subdivisions (most commonly, the state agency concerned with regulating hazardous waste), or an Indian tribe. § 104(d). As a practical matter, the PA/SI—and ensuing steps in the process of removal action or remedial action—are normally performed by a private contractor retained by the lead agency. For simplicity, the discussion below assumes that the lead agency is EPA.

The following hypothetical cleanup illustrates the PA/SI process. Suppose EPA learns that a factory explosion has ruptured a large tank containing chemical wastes. EPA's first concern is whether the problem requires immediate action. For example, are these wastes actually DDT-contaminated fluids which will quickly taint the town's drinking water supply? EPA will conduct a *removal site evaluation*, a brief review to determine if removal action is required. It will use readily available information such as personal interviews, review of photographs, and literature searches to perform its preliminary assessment of the situation. If more information is needed, EPA will perform a site inspection. Based on this data, EPA will then decide whether the situation is serious enough to justify removal action.

If it appears that the tank rupture does not require removal action, EPA will next perform a *remedial site evaluation*. This process has three purposes: (1) to eliminate from further consideration those releases that pose no significant threat to public health or the environment; (2) to evaluate more fully whether removal action is needed; and (3) to obtain information for determining whether the site requires remedial action. Initially, EPA performs a preliminary assessment, which consists of a "review of existing information about a release such as information on the pathways of exposure, exposure targets, and source and nature of release." 40 C.F.R. § 300.420(b)(2). If appropriate, EPA will next conduct a site inspection, which must include both on-site and off-site field inspections and collection of soil and groundwater samples from the site. Finally, it prepares a report which recommends whether further action is warranted. If so, the site will be considered for inclusion on the NPL. If not,

EPA will assign the site "No Further Remedial Action Planned" (NFRAP) status, meaning that no further federal action will be taken absent new information.

The principal source of EPA's authority to collect site information is § 104(e). It allows EPA to order any person to furnish information or documents relating to the hazardous substances located at a site, the nature and extent of any release or threatened release, and the person's financial ability to undertake site cleanup. In practice, EPA routinely sends § 104(e) letters to all the PRPs linked to the site. Further, the section authorizes EPA personnel to enter potentially contaminated sites for inspection or sampling.

### 2. NATIONAL PRIORITIES LIST (NPL)

Congress understood at the outset that the magnitude of the national cleanup task far exceeded the limited resources which Superfund could provide for remedial action. It adopted what might be described as a "triage" approach: clean up the most dangerous sites first, and defer action on the rest. Thus, § 105(a)(8)(B) directed the President to create the National Priorities List (NPL), a list of the highest priority facilities qualifying for cleanup funding. The NPL is found at 40 C.F.R. Part 300, Appendix B.

In practice, the NPL is best understood as a limit on EPA's § 104 authority to clean up a contaminated site. Unless a site is listed on the NPL, EPA cannot use Superfund money to finance *remedial action* there. As a practical matter, this means that EPA can perform long-term, permanent cleanup only on NPL-listed sites. Even if a site is not listed on the NPL, however, alternative cleanup methods may be used there. For example:

- EPA can perform *removal action* under § 104 with Superfund financing;
- EPA can mandate cleanup by third parties under § 106;
- State governments, local governments, or private persons may clean up the site and bring a § 107 action to recover their response costs.

### a. Listing Sites on the NPL

The primary method EPA uses to evaluate sites for NPL listing is a complex modeling system known as the Hazard Ranking System (HRS); the HRS is located at 40 C.F.R. Part 300, Appendix A. Applied to data derived from the PA/SI process, the HRS provides a numerical estimate of the overall risk presented by the site. This HRS score is calculated by analyzing four potential "pathways" by which humans or the environment might be exposed to hazardous substances: groundwater migration, surface water migration, soil exposure, and air migration. For each pathway, three categories of factors are considered: (1) the existence or likelihood of a release; (2) the characteristics of the hazardous substance involved; and (3) the human population and environment which are endangered.

A site may be placed on the NPL in two other ways. Section 105(a)(8)(B) allows each state to designate the facility which presents the greatest danger in its state; such sites are included on the NPL regardless of their HRS scores. In addition, if the Agency for Toxic Substances and Disease Registry issues a health advisory recommending that humans be isolated from a release site, EPA may include the site on the NPL under certain conditions. 40 C.F.R. § 300.425(c).

### b. Challenging NPL Listings

Some PRPs attempt to remove particular sites from the NPL by challenging the HRS process. Apparently fearing § 107 liability, they hope that success will enable them to negotiate a more favorable settlement with EPA. Because the listing decision results from a rulemaking procedure, it may be overturned only if proven arbitrary or capricious. Moreover, as the D.C. Circuit expressed in B & B Tritech, Inc. v. EPA, 957 F.2d 882 (D.C.Cir.1992): "Significant deference is also called for because the NPL represents only 'a rough list of priorities, assembled quickly and inexpensively.'" Despite these barriers, several decisions have removed sites from the NPL. See, e.g., National Gypsum Co. v. EPA, 968 F.2d 40 (D.C.Cir.1992) (record did not support EPA's assumption that boron compounds other than boron oxide were present at dump site).

## F. INTERIM SITE CLEANUP: REMOVAL ACTION

Removal action may be undertaken where EPA or another agency finds a "threat to the public health or welfare of the United States or the environment." 40 C.F.R. § 300.415(b). This decision is based on factors including: (1) actual or potential exposure of human populations, animals, or the food chain to hazardous substances; (2) actual or potential contamination of drinking water supplies or sensitive ecosystems; (3) hazardous substances in bulk storage containers which may pose a threat of release; (4) high levels of hazardous substances in soils which may migrate; (5) weather conditions that may cause such migration; and (6) the threat of fire or explosion. 40 C.F.R. § 300.415(b)(2). Once the agency determines that removal action is appropriate, action shall "begin as soon as possible to abate, prevent, minimize, stabilize, mitigate, or eliminate the threat * * *." 40 C.F.R § 300.415(b)(3).

The NCP imposes few procedural limitations on removal action, consistent with the need for a quick and flexible response. For example, it provides an illustrative list of specific removal actions which are "as a general rule, appropriate in the types of situations shown." 40 C.F.R. § 300.415(e). Thus, the installation of fences, warning signs, or other site precautions is appropriate "where humans or animals have access to the release." The removal of drums, barrels, tanks, or other bulk containers is acceptable where it will "reduce the likelihood of spillage; leakage; exposure to humans, animals, or food chain exposure." Similarly, the excavation, consolidation, or removal of highly contaminated soils from drainage or other areas is proper where such actions will reduce the spread of the release.

As discussed in Chapter 7, the definitions of *removal action* and *remedial action* overlap substantially. For example, in many instances the excavation and removal of contaminated soil could fall into either category. See, e.g., General Electric Co. v. Litton Industrial Automation Systems, Inc., 920 F.2d 1415 (8th Cir.1990) (excavation and removal of soil which resulted in permanent cleanup held removal action). In such a situation, two factors may motivate the agency to categorize its response as mere removal action: (1) government monies may be used to finance removal action (but not remedial action) at sites not on the NPL; and (2) the procedures governing removal action are far quicker and more flexible than those regulating remedial action. Accordingly, what prevents the agency from circumventing the restrictions on remedial action by characterizing it as mere removal action? In most instances, § 104(c)(1) provides the only potential check on this decision. Under this section, removal action at a site cannot continue after $2,000,000 has been expended for response work or one year has elapsed from the date of the initial agency response. However, removal action can still proceed beyond these limitations if EPA finds that additional response action is immediately required to deal with an emergency situation, there is an "immediate risk," and assistance will not otherwise be provided in time. As a practical matter, the § 104(c)(1) limitations are ineffective because EPA can make the required findings for most removal actions.

## G. PERMANENT SITE CLEANUP: REMEDIAL ACTION

### 1. REMEDIAL INVESTIGATION AND FEASIBILITY STUDY (RI/FS)

The remedial investigation and feasibility study (RI/FS) is the foundation for selecting the appropriate remedial action. The overall purpose of the RI/FS is to assess site conditions and evaluate alternatives to the extent necessary to select a remedy. 40 C.F.R. § 300.430(a)(2). EPA or the other agency involved follows a two step process. First, the agency performs a remedial investigation, essentially collecting the data necessary to perform the feasibility study. 40 C.F.R. § 300.430(d)(1). The remedial investigation normally includes investigation and assessment of: (1) the physical characteristics of the site; (2) characteristics of air, soil, and groundwater; (3) characteristics of the hazardous substance involved; (4) the extent to which the source can be identified; and (5) actual and potential exposure to the hazardous substance. 40 C.F.R. § 300.430(d)(2). Based on these findings, the agency evaluates whether the site poses a threat to human health or the environment.

Second, using the information collected in the remedial investigation, the agency performs the feasibility study by developing and analyzing appropriate remedial alternatives. 40 C.F.R.

§ 300.430(e)(1). The study lists potential alternative remedies and then analyzes whether they comply with the NCP criteria for remedy selection, as discussed later in this chapter. Preparation of the feasibility study often begins while the remedial investigation is still ongoing. EPA does not always perform the RI/FS itself. For sites where PRPs can be identified, EPA prefers to negotiate for the PRPs to undertake the RI/FS, pursuant to EPA standards. In practice, this means that the RI/FS is usually done by an environmental consulting firm retained and paid by the PRPs. Commentators have criticized EPA's reliance on such PRP-controlled contractors.

Members of the public are entitled to participate in the RI/FS process to a limited degree. Before beginning field work for the site investigation, for example, the agency must normally conduct interviews with local residents, officials, and other interested parties to solicit their concerns and informational needs. 40 C.F.R. § 300.430(c)(2)(i). Following these interviews, the agency must prepare a formal community relations plan which, among other things: (1) ensures opportunities for public involvement in various site-related decisions, including selection of the remedy; and (2) informs the public that grants for technical assistance are available. 40 C.F.R. § 300.430(c)(2).

## 2. THE REMEDY SELECTION PROCESS

Once the RI/FS is completed, the lead agency identifies the remedy which best meets the NCP criteria (discussed later in this chapter), and issues a proposed plan based on that remedy. 40 C.F.R. § 300.430(f)(2). The plan describes the alternative remedies considered by the agency, proposes a particular remedy, and summarizes the information supporting its choice. Pursuant to § 117(a), the agency must notify the public of the proposed plan and provide reasonable opportunities for public comment on the plan, both in writing and at a public meeting. The agency then reassesses its proposed remedy based on any new information provided by the public or other government agencies during the comment period. 40 C.F.R. § 300.430(f)(4). Following this review, the agency selects the final remedy and documents its decision in a "record of decision" (ROD). Among other things, the ROD must: (1) explain in detail how the final remedy complies with the NCP criteria; (2) state the remediation goals for the site; (3) discuss significant changes to the plan made in response to comments; (4) describe whether hazardous substances will remain on the site after remedial action is completed; and (5) if appropriate, commit to further analysis. 40 C.F.R. § 300.430(f)(5).

### 3. IMPLEMENTING THE REMEDY

The final phase in the process is "remedial design/remedial action" (RD/RA), which includes development of the actual design of the selected remedy and implementation of the remedy through construction. 40 C.F.R. § 300.435(a). The remedial design process often requires an entire year or more to complete. Once the design has been finalized, a construction contract is awarded to a private contractor to implement the remedy.

When the remedy has been fully implemented and the affected state has consented, the site is eligible for deletion from the NPL. To ensure public involvement in the process, the NCP mandates that EPA provide notice to the public, solicit public comments on the proposed deletion, and respond in writing to any comments received before the site is removed from the NPL.

## H. HOW CLEAN MUST THE SITE BE? ("HOW CLEAN IS CLEAN?")

The most difficult question arising under CERCLA is "how clean is clean?" In other words, how clean must the site be once remedial action is completed? The answer to this question is complex because, in effect, CERCLA contemplates that this decision will be made on a site-by-site basis. CERCLA could have established a national cleanup goal which was equally applicable to all sites. For example, such a standard might have required sufficient cleanup to attain: (1) a zero contamination level (in effect, pristine condition); (2) the lowest concentration level necessary to protect human health; (3) the lowest concentration level possible with existing technology; or (4) the most cost-effective concentration level. Instead, CERCLA mandates that the cleanup level for a particular site be determined by applying various criteria to its individual circumstances. Thus, the required cleanup level for a particular hazardous substance may differ at each site and cannot be readily predicted. In practice, EPA exercises wide discretion in deciding how much remedial action is appropriate.

The main CERCLA provision addressing the issue is § 121, added as part of SARA. Although awkwardly structured, it lists six factors which must be considered in selecting the final remedy. In response, EPA amended the NCP to provide that nine criteria would be used in remedy selection. The discussion below first examines the statutory framework created by § 121, and then discusses the NCP criteria.

### 1. THE SECTION 121 FRAMEWORK

Section 121 applies to all remedial action carried out under § 104 (abatement performed by government) or "secured" under § 106 (e.g., abatement mandated by administrative order). There is some uncertainty about whether the section also applies to injunctive relief obtained under § 106, as discussed in Chapter 10.

Six principles intended to guide EPA's selection of remedial alternatives are scattered throughout § 121. Assembled and rearranged below, they provide that remedial action should:

- *be cost-effective*, taking into account the total short-term and long-term costs, including the costs of operation and maintenance (§ 121(a), (b)(1));

- *comply with the NCP* "to the extent practicable" (§ 121(a));
- *normally involve permanent treatment* which reduces the volume, toxicity or mobility of the hazardous substance, rather than mere offsite transport and disposal of such material without treatment (§ 121(b)(1));
- *protect human health and the environment* (§ 121(b)(1), (d)(1));
- *utilize alternative treatment technologies or resource recovery technologies* "to the maximum extent practicable" (§ 121(b)(1));
- *normally meet "ARARs,"* that is, attain the cleanup level required by any "legally applicable or relevant and appropriate" standard under federal environmental law (including TSCA, RCRA, SDWA, CAA, and CWA) and any standard required under state law that is more stringent than federal law (§ 121(d)(2)).

Unfortunately, these principles provide little practical guidance to EPA. One major problem is internal inconsistency. A cleanup which ensures a permanent remedy, for example, may not be cost-effective; the section provides no mechanism to resolve such a conflict. Moreover, most of these principles are quite vague. When EPA is directed to assure "protection of human health and the environment," does this imply, for example, that a site must be cleaned up to the point where it presents a zero health risk to every person?

## 2. EPA'S RESPONSE: NINE CRITERIA

EPA responded to the confusing mandate of § 121 by adopting regulations which amended the NCP. Thus, 40 C.F.R. § 300.430(f) identifies nine criteria that EPA will use in selecting a remedy:

(1) overall protection of human health and the environment;

(2) compliance with ARARs;

(3) long-term effectiveness and permanence;

(4) reduction of toxicity, mobility, or volume;

(5) short-term effectiveness;

(6) the ease of implementing the alternative;

(7) cost;

(8) state acceptance of the remedy;

(9) community acceptance of the remedy.

The NCP establishes a three-step process for applying these criteria. Under this approach, some criteria are weighted more heavily than others. First, all proposed remedies must meet the initial two criteria above (known as the "threshold criteria") in order to receive further consideration; thus, *all* remedial action must (1) protect human health and the environment and (2) comply with ARARs. Second, EPA then evaluates the remaining potential remedies using criteria (3) through (7) above (known as the "primary balancing criteria"); EPA selects the remedy which best meets these criteria. Third, after EPA has received state and community input on its proposed remedy through the public comment process, it considers the final two criteria (known as the "modifying criteria"); adverse state or community reaction to the proposed remedy may result in the choice of another remedy.

The most important decision examining this procedure is Ohio v. EPA, 997 F.2d 1520 (D.C.Cir.1993). There, the D.C. Circuit ruled that EPA revisions of the NCP were consistent with the Congressional mandate set forth in § 121. Two facets of the decision illustrate the manner in which EPA has fleshed out the § 121 skeleton.

First, "how safe is safe?" The amended NCP provides that in assessing whether a proposed remedy protects public health from cancer, an increased lifetime cancer risk of 100 in 1,000,000 may be acceptable. The *Ohio* petitioners complained that this standard violated the § 121 requirement that remedial actions be "protective of human health;" they argued that a risk greater than 1 in 1,000,000 was never acceptable. The Court's response was simple: "CERCLA requires the selection of remedial actions 'that are protective of human health,' not as protective as conceivably possible." EPA's resolution of the "how safe is safe?" issue was entitled to "significant deference," and upheld.

Second, when is an environmental standard an ARAR? Because most remedial actions include treating contaminated groundwater, attention has focused on which SDWA standards are ARARs. Section 121(d)(2)(A)(i) expressly designates as an

ARAR: "any standard, requirement, criteria, or limitation" under the SDWA which is "relevant and appropriate under the circumstances of the release." As discussed in Chapter 5, the SDWA establishes both water quality goals (maximum contaminant level goals, or MCLGs) and maximum contaminant levels (MCLs). However, EPA decided that where a MCLG was set at zero, it could not be an ARAR; rather, in this situation the MCL would be the ARAR. In effect, this rule ensures that some remedial actions will fail to clean up substantial amounts of hazardous substances. For example, trichloroethylene (TCE), the most commonly detected contaminant in groundwater, has a zero MCLG but a MCL of .005 milligrams per liter. If the MCL is the ARAR, then a site would be deemed "clean" even though its groundwater contained TCE in concentrations up to .005 mg/l.

EPA justified its position on the basis that it is scientifically impossible to measure whether "true" zero has been attained: "If the measuring device indicates zero, this shows only that the device is not sufficiently sensitive to detect the presence of contaminants." The *Ohio* petitioners challenged this provision, arguing that § 121 directed EPA to require cleanup to the point where contaminants could not be detected, thus approximating a zero level. Although agreeing that EPA could adopt an ARAR premised on detectable limits, the Court concluded that it was not required to do so. It found the conclusion that zero MCLGs were unattainable to be "reasonable given EPA's discretion to determine when ARARs are relevant and appropriate."

# CHAPTER 9

# CERCLA: COST RECOVERY ACTIONS BROUGHT BY GOVERNMENT

## A. OVERVIEW

Section 107 is the heart of CERCLA. It is the basic provision imposing liability for cleanup costs and related damages. Both government entities and private parties are authorized by this section to bring "cost recovery actions" against liable PRPs. This chapter discusses cost recovery actions brought by government, while Chapter 11 discusses cost recovery actions brought by private parties.

Congress envisioned that §§ 104 and 107 would work in tandem to facilitate government cleanup efforts, much like interconnected cogs in a machine. In theory, government would: (1) perform § 104 response action using Superfund financing; (2) sue "potentially responsible parties" (PRPs) under § 107 to obtain reimbursement for its response costs and other damages; and (3) replenish the Superfund with the litigation proceeds. Initially, this system functioned poorly. In fact, EPA recovered only 10% of the $10 billion it spent on cleanups during CERCLA's first 15 years. However, the recovery rate has somewhat improved since then.

Section 107 has proven quite effective, however, as a settlement lever. The liability created under the section (and its counterpart, § 106) is extraordinarily broad, perhaps even draconian. Wielding the threat of such liability, EPA and other government agencies are often able to negotiate settlement agreements by which PRPs undertake to finance or perform response action, with little or no actual government expenditure under § 104.

## B. SECTION 107 LIABILITY STANDARDS

### 1. IN GENERAL

Section 107(a) sets forth the elements of liability for response costs. It is awkwardly structured and requires careful study. The key liability phrase ("from which there is a release, or a threatened release which causes the incurrence of response costs, of a hazardous substance, shall be liable for") appears to relate *only* to § 107(a)(4), which concerns only *one* category of PRPs (transporters). In reality, the phrase applies to *all four* subsections (§ 107(a)(1), (2), (3) and (4)); accordingly, it sets liability criteria for all four PRP categories (current owners and operators; certain past owners and operators; arrangers; and transporters).

The liability standard is easier to understand when the § 107(a) elements are slightly rearranged, as follows:

- The "release" or threat of release
- of a "hazardous substance"
- at a "facility" or "vessel"
- "which causes the incurrence of response costs"
- renders a potentially responsible party (PRP)

- "liable"
- for "all costs of removal or remedial action" incurred by government which are "not inconsistent with the national contingency plan," for "damages for injury" to "natural resources," and for other items.

The first three elements were discussed in Chapter 7. The last four elements are discussed below, together with the defenses to liability created by § 107(b).

## 2. WHAT DOES "CAUSES THE INCURRENCE OF RESPONSE COSTS" MEAN?

The release or threatened release of a hazardous substance at a facility or vessel—standing alone—is insufficient to establish § 107(a) liability. Among other elements, the release or threat of release must also "cause" the "incurrence of response costs."

As discussed in Chapter 7, "response costs" in this context are expenses incurred by government in performing removal action or remedial action under § 104. For example, if EPA performs a preliminary assessment/site inspection at a contaminated site, its expenditures are considered "response costs." Similarly, if EPA retains a contractor to remove leaking barrels, excavate contaminated soil, treat contaminated groundwater, or otherwise remediate a problem site, the costs it incurs are "response costs." The scope of recoverable costs is discussed in more detail below.

Discovering the meaning of "cause" is more difficult. As a preliminary matter, courts universally agree that CERCLA imposes strict liability; a plaintiff need not prove that the defendant's conduct caused the release or threat of release. New York v. Shore Realty Corp., 759 F.2d 1032 (2d Cir.1985). But what linkage is required between the release or threat of release, on the one hand, and the response costs incurred, on the other?

The answer to this question is relatively clear where a threat of release exists. The plaintiff must establish that it incurred response costs because of the threat. Dedham Water Co. v. Cumberland Farms Dairy, Inc., 889 F.2d 1146 (1st Cir.1989) (*Dedham I*) is instructive. Plaintiff, a public water supply system, discovered both heavy metal and volatile organic compound (VOC) contamination in its well field, and retained consultants who recommended construction of a water treatment plant to remove these pollutants. Later, plaintiff discovered that defendant's nearby truck maintenance yard was releasing VOCs. Asserting that defendant's facility was both the source of the present VOC pollution and a threat of future pollution, plaintiff built the treatment plant and sued under § 107 for recovery of the construction cost. The trial court found that defendant's release had not actually contaminated plaintiff's wells, and denied recovery. The First Circuit reversed, observing that CERCLA did not require proof that the "defendant's hazardous waste actually migrated to plaintiff's property." It suggested that plaintiff could recover if it could prove the costs were incurred because of a threat of release by the defendant. As the court explained in a later opinion, to meet this standard the plaintiff must prove: (1) it had a "good-faith belief" that action was desirable to address a "particular environmental threat;" and (2) its response was "objectively reasonable." Dedham Water Co., Inc. v. Cumberland Farms Dairy, Inc., 972 F.2d 453 (1st Cir.1992) (*Dedham II*).

Many courts routinely assume that this same causal standard applies to both a release and a threat of release, and this is the better rule. A few courts have actually applied this standard to releases. See, e.g. Amoco Oil Co. v. Borden, Inc., 889 F.2d 664 (5th Cir.1989) (finding causation in release case after endorsing a "factual inquiry" which "should focus on whether the particular hazard justified any response actions"); but see A & W Smelter and Refiners, Inc. v. Clinton, 146 F.3d 1107 (9th Cir.1998) (criticizing fact-specific *Amoco* approach on basis that "[w]here a party is responsible for a particular release, that party is a cause of any response to that release").

However, a few decisions suggest that the phrase "causes the incurrence of response costs" relates only to a "threatened release." For example, analyzing this portion of § 107(a) in Westfarm Associates L.P. v. International Fabricare Institute, 846 F.Supp. 422 (D.Md.1993), the court observed: "That language imposes liability for releases, and *also* imposes liability for threatened releases which cause the incurrence of response costs. Therefore, only in the case of threatened releases does it appear that a plaintiff must demonstrate any degree of causation." (Emphasis in original).

### 3. WHO ARE "POTENTIALLY RESPONSIBLE PARTIES"?

Section 107(a) imposes liability on four categories of "potentially responsible parties" or PRPs:

- current "owners" or "operators"
- persons who were "owners" or "operators" "at the time of disposal"
- persons who "arranged for disposal or treatment" and
- transporters who "selected" the disposal or treatment site.

It is important to stress that CERCLA creates strict liability—regardless of good faith, ignorance, or inaction—based merely on the defendant's *status*. Congress could have assessed taxpayers in general for site cleanup costs. But it chose instead to impose these costs on persons who, although perhaps not culpable under traditional rules, had at least some link to the problem. The four PRP categories share a common theme: *control*. The PRP normally controlled either the hazardous substance or the ultimate disposal site; accordingly, at least in theory, the PRP had the ability to prevent, minimize, or abate the contamination. Moreover, in most instances, the PRP derived financial benefit from the hazardous substance or the site. As between innocent taxpayers, on the one hand, and

PRPs linked to contaminated properties, on the other, Congress found it both fair and politically expedient to burden the latter.

The scope of these four PRP categories, however, remains somewhat vague. CERCLA provides surprisingly little guidance. Although hundreds of reported decisions have explored the issue, the resulting body of case law is incomplete and often inconsistent.

### a. Current Owners or Operators

Section 107(a)(1) identifies the first PRP category as: "the owner and operator of a vessel or a facility." Courts had little difficulty resolving two early issues which this language created. First, although the phrase "owner and operator" appears conjunctive (i.e., it seems to apply only to persons who are *both* owners *and* operators), courts routinely treat it as disjunctive. Thus, *either* owner *or* operator status confers liability. Second, it was quickly established that the time for determining owner or operator status was when the cost recovery action was filed.

It is important to understand that the current "owner" or "operator" is liable under § 107(a)(1) based *only* on this status. The government need not prove, for example, that the current owner or operator: (1) caused the release; (2) knew about the release; or (3) owned or operated the facility at the time of the release. CERCLA proceeds on the assumption that status as a current owner or operator is a proxy for site responsibility.

But who is an "owner" or an "operator"? The relevant statutory language is confusingly circular. Section 101(20)(A) defines the "owner or operator" of a facility as "any person owning or operating such facility." As the Ninth Circuit lamented in Long Beach Unified School District v. Dorothy B. Godwin California Living Trust, 32 F.3d 1364 (9th Cir.1994), this "is a bit like defining 'green' as 'green.' "

#### *i. Owners*

Given this circularity, most courts use state law principles to define "owner." This process is simple in the most common title situation—the person holding fee simple absolute. Courts universally hold that such a person is an "owner." Beyond this easy case, however, the parameters of "owner" status are less clear. The issue mainly arises in two contexts: (1) the person holding property rights less than fee simple absolute title (e.g., an easement holder); and (2) the fiduciary holding title on behalf of another (e.g., a trustee or executor).

In the first situation—the person holding less than fee simple absolute—liability hinges on the extent to which the defendant had the legal right to control the premises. Most courts, for example, conclude that easement holders are not "owners" because they exercise virtually no control over the site in question. The Ninth Circuit reasoned in Long Beach Unified School District v. Dorothy B. Godwin California Living Trust, 32 F.3d 1364 (9th Cir.1994) that imposing CERCLA liability on an easement holder would unfairly penalize "legitimate, non-polluting actors such as telephone and electric companies which, in running pipelines and cables, have no greater responsibility for the nation's toxic waste problem than the public at large."

The same control theme pervades decisions involving the second situation—the fiduciary holding title for another. For example, the trustee of a testamentary trust was held to be an "owner" in City of Phoenix v. Garbage Services Co., 816 F.Supp. 564 (D.Ariz.1993). However, observing that the power and autonomy of an executor or conservator was much less than that of a trustee, the court in Castlerock Estates, Inc. v. Estate of Markham, 871 F.Supp. 360 (N.D.Cal.1994) concluded that executors and conservators were not "owners" under CERCLA simply because they held legal title to a facility; liability would attach only if they also possessed some other indicia of ownership. (Even if a fiduciary is considered a PRP, however, its liability is limited by special provisions added to CERCLA in 1996; these provisions are discussed below.)

### *ii. Operators*

The term "operator" did not have an established common law meaning before CERCLA was enacted. Thus, courts initially encountered difficulty in defining the contours of "operator" liability, and the resulting case law reflected a major split. One early strand of decisions found operator liability if the defendant had the *authority to control* the premises, even if he never exercised that control. See, e.g., Nurad, Inc. v. William E. Hooper & Sons Co., 966 F.2d 837 (4th Cir.1992). However, most circuits required that the defendant *actually exercise control* over the premises.

The Supreme Court resolved the dispute in United States v. Bestfoods, Inc., 524 U.S. 51, 118 S.Ct. 1876, 141 L.Ed.2d 43 (1998) by endorsing the majority view: "[U]nder CERCLA, an operator is simply someone who directs the workings of, manages, or conducts the affairs of a facility." Under this standard, a defendant will be liable as an operator only if he *actually* supervises, manages, or otherwise controls activities at the facility. For example, the United States was deemed a past "operator" of a World War II rayon manufacturing plant in FMC Corporation v. U.S. Department of Commerce, 29 F.3d 833 (3d Cir.1994). Although the plant had been owned and run by a private company, the Third Circuit concluded that the federal government had "active involvement" in plant activities, and thus exercised "substantial control" over it. There, the government had: (1) determined which product the plant would produce; (2) controlled the price and supply of raw materials; (3) supplied equipment for use in manufacturing; (4) participated in the management and supervision of the work force; (5) controlled the price of the product; and (6) controlled who could purchase the product. But see, e.g., Edward Hines Lumber Co. v. Vulcan Materials Co., 861 F.2d 155 (7th Cir.1988) (designer/builder of a wood processing plant was not an operator).

Similarly, a tenant is normally considered an "operator" of the premises it leases. Although not an owner, a tenant both (1) has the legal right to control and (2) actually exercises day-to-day control over the premises. The same dual themes are found in illustrative cases imposing operator liability on: (1) the grading contractor who supervised excavation on a development site (Kaiser Aluminum & Chemical Corp. v. Catellus Development Corp., 976 F.2d 1338 (9th Cir.1992)); and (2) the city holding a right-of-way which erected a chain link fence around the property to bar trespassers (City of Toledo v. Beazer Materials & Services, Inc., 923 F.Supp. 1013 (N.D.Ohio 1996)).

### b. Past Owners or Operators "at the Time of Disposal"

Section 107(a)(2) describes the second PRP category as: "any person who at the time of disposal of any hazardous substance owned or operated any facility at which such hazardous substances were disposed of." Thus, *past* owners or operators are liable only if they owned or operated the facility *at a particular time*—"the time of disposal." The definitions of "owner" and "operator" are discussed above. But what does "disposal" mean?

The basic rule is simple. Section 101(29) defines "disposal" by expressly incorporating its meaning under RCRA. RCRA § 1004(3), in turn, provides that "disposal" is:

> the discharge, deposit, injection, dumping, spilling, leaking, or placing of any solid waste

> or hazardous waste into or on any land or water so that such solid waste or hazardous waste or any constituent thereof may enter the environment or be emitted into the air or discharged into any waters, including ground waters.

Suppose, for example, that A sold her 100 acre farm to B in 2010, B sold it to C in 2014, and C finally sold to D in 2017; D still owns the land. If EPA now discovers that someone jettisoned a truckload of PCB wastes onto the farm in 2012, who is liable? This act would be considered a "disposal" under the above definition; the wastes were "deposited," "dumped," and "placed" on the land. A is a past owner, but is not a PRP because she did not own the farm at the time of "disposal." B, as a *past owner at the time of disposal,* and D, as a *current owner,* are both PRPs. But is C liable?

The definition of "disposal" is ambiguous when applied to the special situation of "passive" disposal. Passive disposal refers to the "leaking or migration of hazardous substances into the soil following their initial disposal." Idylwoods Associates v. Mader Capital, Inc., 915 F.Supp. 1290 (W.D.N.Y.1996). Continuing the above hypothetical, if the PCB wastes continued to migrate further into the soil during C's ownership, without any further human activity, is this "disposal" which renders her liable as a *past owner at the time of disposal*?

There is a split of authority on the issue. Some courts impose liability for passive migration of contaminants, following the Fourth Circuit's lead in

Nurad, Inc. v. William E. Hooper & Sons Co., 966 F.2d 837 (4th Cir.1992). The *Nurad* court found support for its conclusion in both the plain language of the definition and the public policy underlying CERCLA. It pointed out that, although some of the components in the "disposal" definition appear to contemplate action (e.g., "deposit" and "placing"), others "readily admit to a passive component: hazardous waste may leak or spill without any active human participation." Further, the court observed that a requirement of active participation would frustrate CERCLA's policy of encouraging voluntary private cleanup activity. Absent liability for passive disposal, "an owner could avoid liability simply by standing idle while an environmental hazard festers on his property." Conversely, other courts reason that "disposal" requires some affirmative human activity by the owner or operator, such that liability cannot be imposed for mere passive migration. See, e.g., United States v. 150 Acres of Land, 204 F.3d 698 (6th Cir.2000).

In Carson Harbor Village, Ltd. v. Unocal Corp., 270 F.3d 863 (9th Cir.2001), the Ninth Circuit adopted a compromise approach. The case involved tar-like and slag material originally placed on vacant land when it was owned by A. The property was then sold to B, and during its ownership petroleum hydrocarbons and lead moved from these materials into the subsoil. Refusing to find B liable as a past owner at the time of disposal, the court reasoned that none of the verbs in the statutory definition applied to this situation. Most of the verbs, such as "dumping" or "placing," required active human conduct; and while "spilling" or "leaking" might not require affirmative conduct, these words did not describe the gradual spread of the contaminants involved in the case. This decision suggests that a fact-specific analysis is required to determine if passive migration constitutes "disposal."

### c. Persons Who "Arranged for Disposal or Treatment"

Section 107(a)(3) describes the third PRP category as persons who have "by contract, agreement, or otherwise arranged for disposal or treatment, or arranged with a transporter for transport for disposal or treatment, of hazardous substances" which they "owned or possessed." This language is even more ambiguous than the CERCLA norm, and has sparked extensive litigation. Although this subsection is sometimes characterized as creating "generator" liability, its scope is much broader than that term suggests. Congress somewhat clarified the law in 1999 by adopting § 127, which provides that recyclers are generally not liable as arrangers or transporters.

The most common pattern of arranger liability involves the "generator" defendant—the factory, refinery, smelter, or other industrial complex which generates wastes containing hazardous substances. The generator who hires a transporter to haul its wastes acquires PRP status as an arranger. Similarly, when a generator contracts with a treatment or disposal facility to dispose of its wastes, it also becomes an "arranger." If such hazardous substances are later released—even due to unforeseeable events—the generator who has exercised all due care will still be held strictly liable.

For example, in O'Neil v. Picillo, 682 F.Supp. 706 (D.R.I.1988), aff'd, 883 F.2d 176 (1st Cir.1989), the court found that the defendant chemical manufacturer "took every precaution in the disposal of its wastes," including arranging with a transporter to haul the wastes to licensed disposal sites in Pennsylvania and New Jersey. Without the defendant's knowledge or approval, however, the transporter apparently deposited some of these wastes at a Rhode Island pig farm. Investigators later encountered "large trenches and pits filled with free-flowing, multicolored, pungent liquid wastes" at the pig farm site. The defendant manufacturer was held liable as an "arranger" despite its precautions.

A generator may be liable for a release even absent proof that its own wastes were released. In the leading case of United States v. Monsanto Co., 858 F.2d 160 (4th Cir.1988), Monsanto and other generator defendants argued that the plaintiff United States had failed to establish their wastes were still present at the facility when the release occurred. Noting the "technological infeasibility of tracing improperly disposed of waste to its source," however, the Fourth Circuit recognized that such a burden would cripple the prosecution of CERCLA cases involving multiple generators; it rejected the proposed "proof of ownership" standard. The court held instead that a plaintiff need only prove that: (1) the generator defendant's waste was shipped to the site; and (2) "hazardous substances similar to those contained in the defendant's waste remained present at the time of the release." In theory, the defendant can avoid liability by proving that its wastes were not actually released; in practice, however, this burden is usually impossible to meet.

One of the most troublesome "arranger" issues is distinguishing between the *disposal of a hazardous substance* and the *sale of a product*. Many transactions fall between these two extremes, and some of these qualify as "arrangements" that create CERCLA liability. A manufacturer's sale of a virgin product does not typically trigger liability. But courts will normally scrutinize the sale of a used product containing a hazardous substance to determine if the transaction was, in effect, a disguised arrangement for disposal. For example, arranger liability was imposed where: (1) used auto batteries were sold to a recycling company for lead reclamation; and (2) PCB-contaminated waste oil was sold to a drag strip which sprayed the oil for dust control. Recently, the traditional bright line between virgin and used products has softened. As discussed further below, courts now make intense factual inquiries to determine whether the entity was taking intentional steps to dispose of a product. In general, if a product has little or no remaining value for its original purpose and it contains a hazardous substance, its sale may be deemed an "arrangement for disposal" which creates CERCLA liability. See, e.g., MEMC Pasadena, Inc. v.

Goodgames Indus. Solutions, LLC 143 F.Supp.3d 570, 581 (S.D. Tex. 2015), opinion modified on reconsideration (S.D. Tex., Dec. 18, 2015, No. 4:13-CV-599) 2015 WL 9259088.

What if one party contracts with another party to purchase or process raw materials that ultimately contaminate the processing site? For many years, cases were widely divergent on the range of factual situations that triggered arranger liability. For example, perhaps the most expansive view of arranger liability was found in United States v. Aceto Agricultural Chemicals Corp., 872 F.2d 1373 (8th Cir.1989). This case involved eight pesticide producers which contracted with another company to "formulate" commercial grade pesticides. The United States cleaned up the formulator's contaminated factory site, and then sued the pesticide producers on an arranger theory. The defendants insisted that they had merely contracted for the processing of a valuable product, not the disposal or treatment of a waste. Reasoning that defendants should not simply "close their eyes" to the methods of disposal, a result contrary to the policies underlying CERCLA, the Eighth Circuit concluded that if the generation of pesticide wastes was inherent in this mixing process, as the United States asserted, then the producers would be liable as arrangers. See also GenCorp, Inc. v. Olin Corp., 390 F.3d 433 (6th Cir.2004) (GenCorp, which purchased 50% of chemicals produced at Olin's plant, was liable as an "arranger" because GenCorp representatives were among members of special committee that oversaw construction, operation, and management of plant). But see United States v. Shell Oil Co., 294 F.3d 1045 (9th Cir.2002) (refusing to find the United States liable as an arranger for sites contaminated from military aviation fuel despite the fact that the government was the main consumer of the fuel and its wartime policies influenced fuel production.)

Interpretation of this doctrine was refined in 2009, when the Supreme Court decided Burlington Northern & Santa Fe Railway Co. v. United States, developing what has become known as the "useful product doctrine." 556 U.S 599, 129 S.Ct. 1870, 173 L.Ed. 812 (2009). There, Shell Oil Company sold pesticides to Brown & Bryant (B & B). Shell knew that B & B was a "sloppy operator," resulting in leaks and spills of the delivered pesticides. Although Shell knew that its product was being leaked, the majority insisted that an *intent to dispose* was necessary for a finding of arranger liability—a significant change from pre-*Burlington Northern* jurisprudence. The Court focused on the plain language of the statute to conclude that "the word 'arrange' implies action directed to a specific purpose." Id. at 611. Therefore, under section 9607(a)(3) an entity that takes "intentional steps to dispose of a hazardous substance" may well qualify as an arranger. Id.

After *Burlington Northern*, courts have focused on whether the entity selling the product had intent to dispose of the product and control over the disposal. Evidence of intent to dispose or control is often absent where the pollution occurred in past decades.

Thus, courts have accepted circumstantial evidence of whether there was intent to dispose or control over disposal, looking at value of the material (high or low) and how it was managed (carefully or more like a waste product) prior to the sale.

### d. Transporters Who "Selected" Disposal or Treatment Site

Finally, § 107(a)(4) describes the fourth PRP category as any person who accepts hazardous substances for transport "to disposal or treatment facilities, incineration vessels or sites selected by such person." Although most transporter cases involve the movement of hazardous substances over long distances (e.g., by train, truck, or pipeline), even de minimis movement may create liability.

The Ninth Circuit sculpted the outer limits of transporter liability in Kaiser Aluminum & Chemical Corp. v. Catellus Development Corp., 976 F.2d 1338 (9th Cir.1992). There, a building contractor excavated a development site and spread some of the displaced soil on other parts of the land. This soil contained certain hazardous materials, including lead and asbestos. Noting that § 101(26) defines "transport" to include "the movement of a hazardous substance by any mode," the court found this grading activity to be "transportation" of hazardous substances to a site selected by the transporter.

Mere transportation does not trigger liability. Rather, the transporter must either actually select the site or actively participate in its selection. In

Tippins, Inc. v. USX Corp., 37 F.3d 87 (3d Cir.1994), for example, the transporter surveyed potential disposal sites for hazardous dust, identified two landfills which would accept the dust, gathered financial information concerning both sites, and provided this information to its client; the client ultimately selected one of the sites. The Third Circuit held that these facts established "active participation" in the site selection, rendering the transporter liable.

### e. Special Cases

#### *i. Corporate Officers and Employees*

Corporate officers and employees can be personally liable as "operators," regardless of the traditional corporate shield. The early case law was divided, however, on the standard for imposing liability. Some circuits held the officer or employee liable if he had the *authority to control* hazardous substance handling at the facility, even if he never actually exercised control. For example, a corporate president was declared an operator in United States v. Carolina Transformer Co., 978 F.2d 832 (4th Cir.1992), based only on his deposition testimony that he was "in charge" of the company and "responsible" for its operations. Most courts following this view stressed that CERCLA's remedial purpose could be accomplished only by imposing liability on persons who had the ability to prevent dangerous releases.

Conversely, many circuits imposed operator liability only on the officer or employee who *actually exercised control* over hazardous substance disposal. These courts reasoned that the ordinary meaning of "operator" required affirmative conduct or activity. Thus, in Riverside Market Development Corp. v. International Building Products, Inc., 931 F.2d 327 (5th Cir.1991), an individual who was the corporate secretary, the chairman of the board of directors, and also the majority shareholder was not an "operator" because he was not actually involved with hazardous substance handling; his only corporate activities were visiting the facility on occasion, reviewing financial statements, and attending periodic officers' meetings.

The Supreme Court seems to have resolved this division in favor of the actual control standard. In United States v. Bestfoods, 524 U.S. 51, 118 S.Ct. 1876, 141 L.Ed.2d 43 (1998), it defined an operator as "someone who directs the workings of, manages, or conducts the affairs of a facility." Although the case dealt with the liability of a parent corporation as an operator, the same logic would seem to apply to other types of "operators," including officers and employees.

Officers and employees may also be liable as "arrangers." The best-known case on point is United States v. Northeastern Pharmaceutical & Chemical Co., Inc., 810 F.2d 726 (8th Cir.1986), where a corporate vice-president authorized shipping dioxin and other hazardous production wastes to an unlicensed Missouri farm for disposal. The Eighth

Circuit ruled that the officer "possessed" the wastes within the meaning of § 107(a)(3) because he had actual control over them and was directly responsible for arranging for their transportation and disposal.

### *ii. Parent Corporations*

The leading case exploring when a parent corporation is liable as an "operator" of its subsidiary is the Supreme Court's decision in United States v. Bestfoods, 524 U.S. 51, 118 S.Ct. 1876, 141 L.Ed.2d 43 (1998). The Court acknowledged that anyone who "operates" a polluting facility is liable under CERCLA, and defined "operator" as one "who directs the workings of, manages, or conducts the affairs of a facility." But the Court stressed that a parent corporation's general control of its subsidiary was insufficient to impose operator liability: "The question is not whether the parent operates the subsidiary, but rather whether it operates the facility, and that operation is evidenced by participation in the activities of the facility." Thus, the Court suggested that a parent could be liable (a) if it directly operated the facility in place of the subsidiary or in a joint venture with the subsidiary, (b) if a dual officer or agent departed "so far from the norms of parental influence exercised through dual officeholding as to serve the parent," or (c) where an "agent of the parent with no hat to wear but the parent's hat might manage or direct activities at the facility."

Similarly, a parent corporation may be an arranger. If a parent exercises substantial control over the disposal of its subsidiary's hazardous substances, it will be liable on this theory. United States v. TIC Investment Corp., 68 F.3d 1082 (8th Cir.1995). In addition, the parent is directly liable as an "owner" if the corporate veil can be pierced under state law.

### *iii. Successor Corporations*

Courts universally agree that Congress intended to transfer a corporation's existing CERCLA liability to successors; they disagree on whether the liability standard is governed by state or federal law. Some jurisdictions apply the state law of successor liability, reasoning that CERCLA was not intended to displace it. Most courts, however, utilize a federal common law standard gleaned from general principles of corporate law and this is the better view. The Eighth Circuit explained this emerging standard in United States v. Mexico Feed & Seed Co., 980 F.2d 478 (8th Cir.1992). It stated that a corporation which acquires the assets of another corporation will also inherit its predecessor's CERCLA liability only if one of the following applies:

- the purchasing corporation expressly or impliedly agrees to assume liabilities;
- the transaction amounts to a "de facto" consolidation or merger;

- the purchasing corporation is merely a continuation of the selling corporation;
- the transaction was fraudulently entered into to escape liability.

The most controversial issue in this area is whether the "continuation" rule should be broadened to include a "substantial continuity" standard as a matter of federal common law. The continuation rule applies when: (1) a liable corporation transfers its assets to another; (2) only one corporation remains after the transfer; and (3) there is an identity of stock, stockholders, and directors between the two entities. This rigid rule can be easily circumvented (e.g., by continuing the existence of the selling corporation). In contrast, the substantial continuity test dramatically expands the scope of successor liability by using a much more flexible standard; under this approach, the court evaluates a number of factors in deciding whether a corporation is a successor. Some courts have adopted this test, although disagreeing to some extent on which criteria should be considered.

The best-known decision approving this test is United States v. Carolina Transformer Co., 978 F.2d 832 (4th Cir.1992). There the Fourth Circuit evaluated the following criteria in deciding that a purchasing corporation was liable as a successor:

- retention of the same employees;
- retention of the same supervisory personnel;

- retention of the same production facilities in the same location;
- production of the same product;
- retention of the same name;
- continuity of assets;
- continuity of general business operations;
- whether the successor holds itself out as the continuation of the previous enterprise.

However, the Supreme Court's decision in United States v. Bestfoods, 524 U.S. 51, 118 S.Ct. 1876, 141 L.Ed.2d 43 (1998) casts serious doubt on the viability of the substantial continuity test. Although addressing a different issue, the Court commented broadly that nothing in CERCLA "displaced or fundamentally altered common law standards of limited liability." This language strongly implies that the liability of successor corporations should be measured by state law, not federal common law. See K.C. 1986 Ltd. Partnership v. Reade Manufacturing, 472 F.3d 1009 (8th Cir.2007) (questioning the viability of the substantial continuity test after *Bestfoods*).

### *iv. Lenders*

The evolution of the principles governing the CERCLA liability of lenders is best described as a long roller coaster ride which is finally over. As originally enacted, § 101(20) reflected the broad rule that secured creditors were generally not liable. The section provided that a person who held "indicia of ownership" in a facility primarily to protect his "security interest," without "participating in the management" of the facility, was not considered an owner or operator. Thus, the traditional, passive lender who merely held a mortgage or deed of trust as security for debt would avoid liability. Beyond this basic situation, however, two questions arose: (1) what level of lender activity amounts to enough "participation in management" to trigger liability? and (2) does the exemption end if the lender acquires the property through foreclosure? The courts were divided on each issue. After years of uncertainty, lenders rejoiced when Congress finally amended CERCLA in 1996 to clarify these issues.

Section 101(20)(F)(i)(I) now provides that the term "participation in management" means "actually participating in the management or operational affairs" of a facility. Thus, a secured creditor will be considered to participate in management *only* if it: (1) exercises control over the facility's environmental compliance; or (2) exercises general control over the facility at a level "comparable to that of a manager." § 101(20)(F)(ii). This section rejects the Eleventh Circuit's controversial suggestion in United States v. Fleet Factors Corp., 901 F.2d 1550 (11th Cir.1990) that a lender's mere *capacity to influence* the borrower's operational decisions would create liability; it provides that participation in management does not include merely "having the capacity to influence, or the unexercised right to control, facility operations." § 101(20)(F)(i)(II).

In addition, it is now clear that a lender generally will not become an owner or operator simply by: (1) acquiring the contaminated property through foreclosure on its security; or (2) by undertaking related post-foreclosure activities (e.g., carrying on business activities, taking response action, and winding up operations). § 101(20)(E)(ii). In order to qualify for this protection, however, the lender must seek to resell, release, or otherwise transfer the facility after foreclosure "at the earliest practicable, commercially reasonable time, on commercially reasonable terms * * *."

### *v. Fiduciaries*

Fiduciaries held liable as PRPs receive special protection under § 107(n), added in 1996. Under this section, a "fiduciary" is a person acting for another, including a trustee, executor, administrator, custodian, guardian, receiver, conservator, or personal representative; the term also encompasses a trustee under a financing arrangement, such as a trustee on a deed of trust. § 107(n)(5)(A).

As a general rule, the CERCLA liability of a fiduciary cannot exceed the "assets held in the fiduciary capacity." The section also lists specific activities which a fiduciary can undertake without incurring personal liability under CERCLA, including: (1) conducting response action at the facility; (2) inspecting the facility; and (3) administering an already-contaminated facility. However, these protections do not apply if the fiduciary's negligence causes or contributes to the release or threatened release. § 107(n)(1)–(4).

### *vi. Governmental Entities*

Governmental entities are not exempt from CERCLA liability. Section 107(a) imposes liability on the "persons" in four PRP categories. In turn, § 101(21) defines "person" to include the "United States Government, State, municipality, commission, political subdivision of a state, or any interstate body." Thus, for example, counties, cities, and other local governmental entities are subject to CERCLA.

The United States has partially waived its sovereign immunity in the CERCLA context. Section 120(a)(1) provides that each department, agency, and instrumentality of the United States—including the executive, legislative, and judicial branches—is subject to CERCLA to the same extent as any nongovernmental entity. When the United States acts only in its regulatory capacity (e.g., by performing remedial work pursuant to § 104), however, it cannot be held liable. The waiver of sovereign immunity is "limited only to circumstances under which a private party could also be held liable." In re Paoli Railroad Yard PCB Litigation, 790 F.Supp. 94 (E.D.Pa.1992), aff'd, 980 F.2d 724 (3rd Cir.1992). Special procedures governing the application of CERCLA to facilities owned or operated by the federal government are set forth in § 120.

CERCLA's definition of "person" expressly includes states. Thus, for example, if the federal government incurs response costs it can recover them from a liable state under § 107. But the Eleventh Amendment to the Constitution probably limits the ability of private persons or Indian tribes to bring cost recovery actions against states. It provides that the "Judicial power of the United States" does not extend to any suit prosecuted against a state by "Citizens of another State" or by "Citizens or Subjects of any Foreign State." Initially, in Pennsylvania v. Union Gas Co., 491 U.S. 1, 109 S.Ct. 2273, 105 L.Ed.2d 1 (1989), the Supreme Court held that the Amendment did not bar a private party from bringing a § 107 action against a state in federal court. But seven years later the Court expressly overruled *Union Gas* in Seminole Tribe of Florida v. Florida, 517 U.S. 44, 116 S.Ct. 1114, 134 L.Ed.2d 252 (1996). There, in a non-CERCLA context, the Court held that the Eleventh Amendment barred Congress from abrogating Florida's immunity to suit by an Indian tribe. This decision strongly suggests that private persons and Indian tribes cannot bring cost recovery actions against states in federal court. See, e.g., Burnette v. Carothers, 192 F.3d 52 (2d Cir.1999) (holding that Eleventh Amendment barred CERCLA suit against state officers, based on *Seminole Tribe* analysis).

## 4. WHAT DOES "LIABLE" MEAN?

### a. Strict Liability

Courts uniformly construe § 107(a) as imposing strict liability, regardless of fault. Superficially, the section is silent on the standard of liability. It merely recites that—if the requisite elements are met—a PRP "shall be liable." But "liable" is specially defined in § 101(32) as "the standard of liability which obtains under section 1321 of Title 33;" that section is CWA § 311, which regulates discharge of oil and hazardous substances into navigable waters. Before CERCLA was enacted, most federal courts had interpreted CWA § 311 as creating strict liability. Following this chain of logic, courts reason that CERCLA incorporates the strict liability standard established by judicial construction of § 311.

### b. Joint and Several Liability

Suppose that EPA spends $10 million remediating a site contaminated by hazardous wastes from 100 generator PRPs, and then brings a cost recovery action only against M, the sole solvent generator PRP. Is M "jointly and severally" liable for the entire cleanup cost, even though he contributed only 1% of the waste? The answer is a qualified "yes." CERCLA is silent on the issue. However, virtually all courts interpret CERCLA as permitting—but not mandating—joint and several liability. It is generally accepted that Congress intended the judiciary to determine joint and several liability on a case-by-case basis.

A remarkably uniform body of federal case law has emerged from this process. Following the pioneering approach taken in United States v. Chem-Dyne Corp., 572 F.Supp. 802 (S.D.Ohio 1983), which borrowed heavily from Restatement (Second) of Torts § 433A, courts generally follow two rules in adjudicating joint and several liability:

- *Divisible Harm:* When two or more defendants cause distinct harms or a single harm for which there is a reasonable basis for division according to the contribution of each, each is subject to liability only for the portion of the harm that he has caused; the defendant bears the burden of proving that the harm can be apportioned.
- *Indivisible Harm:* When two or more defendants cause a single and indivisible harm, each is jointly and severally liable for the entire harm.

Accordingly, M can avoid joint and several liability in the example above only if he can prove that: (1) his waste caused a separate, distinct harm; or (2) there is a reasonable basis for determining his contribution to a single harm. It is highly unlikely that M will be able to meet this burden. Most CERCLA sites are contaminated by numerous, commingled hazardous substances. Typically the volume, nature, migratory potential, actual migration, synergistic capacities, and toxicity of the contributions of each PRP cannot be determined. For example, in O'Neil v. Picillo, 883 F.2d 176 (1st Cir.1989), Rhode Island brought a cost recovery action against 35 PRPs whose wastes were discovered in trenches and pits "filled with free-flowing, multi-colored, pungent liquid wastes." The First Circuit affirmed the trial court's judgment holding the defendants jointly and severally liable. In so doing, it explained:

> The practical effect of placing the burden on defendants has been that responsible parties rarely escape joint and several liability, courts regularly finding that where wastes of varying (and unknown) degrees of toxicity and migratory potential commingle, it is simply impossible to determine the amount of environmental harm caused by each party.

In many instances, defendants can minimize the impact of joint and several liability by seeking contribution from other defendants, as discussed below in Chapter 11.

Joint and several liability is inevitable in most multi-generator situations. But a handful of defendants have avoided such liability in relatively simple cases. For example, Matter of Bell Petroleum Services, Inc., 3 F.3d 889 (5th Cir.1993) involved three PRPs who successively operated the same chrome-plating shop and thereby released chromium into groundwater. Because the case involved only one hazardous substance, the Fifth Circuit held that it was reasonable to apportion damages based on the volume of chromium-contaminated water which each operator discharged.

In 2009, the Supreme Court addressed the question in Burlington Northern & Santa Fe Railway Co. v. United States, 556 U.S. 599, 129 S.Ct. 1870, 173 L.Ed.2d 812 (2009). The district court had apportioned the defendant railroad's liability based on the small size of its leased parcel in comparison to the overall site, duration of its lease, consideration of the relative volume of releases on the railroad's parcel, and an upward adjustment to account for calculation error, and the Court concluded that this was a reasonable approach. Although some commentators believed this case would signal an increase in apportionment, those who predicted it would be treated as a restatement of the law on divisibility were proven correct. See e.g., United States v. Iron Mountain Mines, Inc., (E.D. Cal., May 6, 2010, No. 91-0768-JAM-JFM) 2010 WL 1854118, at *3 (concluding that *Burlington Northern* simply reiterated the law as established in 1983 by *Chem-Dyne*).

But how do these joint and several liability standards apply to passive owners and operators? The answer to this question is unclear but intriguing. Suppose that O purchases a contaminated site, is later sued as a "current owner" in a cost recovery action (together with assorted generators, transporters, and past owners and operators), and cannot assert the innocent landowner defense due to inadequate pre-purchase investigation. If O did not "cause" any "harm" under the joint and several liability rules described above, would her liability share be zero? The Third Circuit suggested this result in United States v. Rohm & Haas Co., 2 F.3d 1265 (3d Cir.1993). It noted in dicta that if the current site owner "were able to prove that none of the hazardous substances found at the site were fairly attributable to it, we might well conclude that apportionment was appropriate and [the owner's] apportioned share would be zero." Such a result, however, would be inconsistent with the basic precept that CERCLA imposes strict liability, regardless of fault or causation.

### c. Retroactive Liability

Courts almost universally agree that CERCLA imposes retroactive liability. In other words, PRPs are liable for conduct which occurred before CERCLA's enactment in 1980. Given the circumstances of its passage, this interpretation was both proper and inevitable. CERCLA was enacted, in substantial part, to clean up hazardous waste sites which were contaminated before 1980. This remedial purpose could not be accomplished without retroactive liability. Although defendants have frequently attacked the retroactive application of CERCLA on constitutional grounds, courts have uniformly rejected these challenges. In United States v. Northeastern Pharmaceutical & Chemical Co., Inc., 810 F.2d 726 (8th Cir.1986), for example, the Eighth Circuit ruled that retroactive liability did not violate the defendant's due process rights and was not an unconstitutional "taking" of property.

## 5. WHAT ARE PRPS LIABLE FOR?

### a. "All Costs of Removal or Remedial Action"

A responsible party is liable under § 107(a)(4)(A) for "all costs of removal or remedial action incurred by the United States Government or a State or an Indian tribe not inconsistent with the national contingency plan." Although frustrated in their attempts to avoid CERCLA liability, a few defendants have encountered success in challenging the amount of costs recoverable under this section. Two principal issues arise: (1) what does "all costs" actually mean? and (2) when is a cost "inconsistent" with the NCP?

#### *i. "All Costs"*

In general, courts interpret "all costs" in § 107(a)(4)(A) quite literally. The federal government or another listed plaintiff can recover all payments made to effect removal or remedial action. For example, where the government takes direct action to investigate, evaluate, or monitor a release, its costs are recoverable. Because § 104 remediation work is typically performed by contractors working under agency direction, the government can obtain reimbursement for its payments to such contractors. In addition, most courts allow it to recover a wide variety of overhead expenses, including the salaries of agency personnel involved, travel expenses, legal expenses, and "indirect costs" including rent, utilities, supplies, and clerical support. See, e.g., United States v. R.W.

Meyer, Inc., 889 F.2d 1497 (6th Cir.1989) (EPA's permissible recovery included its payroll costs, travel costs, and indirect costs); United States v. E.I. Dupont De Nemours and Company Inc., 432 F.3d 161 (3rd Cir. 2005) (allowing recovery of oversight costs for supervising cleanup). Finally, § 107(a)(4) also allows the government to obtain prejudgment interest.

The common defense plea that "all costs" cannot include unreasonable costs has largely fallen on deaf judicial ears. Courts typically reason that inconsistency with the NCP is the only limitation on recovery. For example, in United States v. Hardage, 982 F.2d 1436 (10th Cir.1992), the Tenth Circuit observed that this subsection "does not limit the government's recovery to 'all *reasonable* costs;' rather, it permits the government to recover '*all* costs * * *.' " (Emphasis in original). The Fifth Circuit, however, left the reasonableness question unresolved in Matter of Bell Petroleum Services, Inc., 3 F.3d 889 (5th Cir.1993). Although finding no statutory basis for the district court's conclusion that EPA could not recover costs stemming from "gross misconduct," the Fifth Circuit was troubled by the implications of EPA's position that it could recover even "unreasonable and unnecessary costs;" it suggested that Congress did not intend to give EPA such unrestrained spending discretion.

Even under the "all costs" standard, however, the total amount of recoverable costs cannot exceed the limitations listed in § 107(c)(1). The maximum liability of a responsible person for a release from a non-incineration vessel which carries a cargo of hazardous substances (including response costs, natural resource damages, etc.), for example, cannot exceed $300 per gross ton or $5 million, whichever is greater. Most facilities, however, fall under § 107(c)(1)(D), which allows recovery of "the total of all costs of response" plus $50 million for natural resource damages and other items.

### *ii. Inconsistency with the NCP*

Defendants have enjoyed limited success in arguing that certain costs are inconsistent with the NCP and thus not recoverable. Courts agree that consistency with the NCP is presumed when the United States, a state, or an Indian tribe is seeking recovery of response costs. Accordingly, the defendant has the burden of proving that such response costs were inconsistent with the NCP. To meet this standard, a defendant must establish that the government action was arbitrary and capricious, because determining the appropriate response action "involves specialized knowledge and expertise, [and therefore] the choice of a particular cleanup method is a matter within the discretion of the government." United States v. Northeastern Pharmaceutical & Chemical Co., Inc., 810 F.2d 726 (8th Cir.1986).

The government's failure to follow the substantive requirements of the NCP may constitute inconsistency. For example, in Matter of Bell Petroleum Services, Inc., 3 F.3d 889 (5th Cir.1993), the defendant attacked EPA's decision to provide an alternate public drinking water supply during remedial work to clean up groundwater contaminated with chromium. Although the NCP allows such an alternate water supply when there is a "substantial danger to public health or the environment," the defendant argued that the administrative record failed to demonstrate any danger. Applying the arbitrary and capricious standard, the Fifth Circuit held that the EPA decision was unsupported and thus inconsistent with the NCP. It observed: "In vain we have searched the over 5,000 pages of administrative record, and found not one shred of evidence that anyone in the area was actually drinking chromium-contaminated water. Amazingly, the EPA made no attempt to learn whether anyone was drinking the water * * *."

A significant violation of the NCP's procedural standards may also constitute inconsistency. The most egregious example is Washington State Department of Transportation v. Washington Natural Gas Co., 59 F.3d 793 (9th Cir.1995), where plaintiff sought recovery of over $4 million incurred for remedial work in connection with tar waste discovered during freeway construction. The plaintiff "did not refer to the NCP for guidance on how to handle the contaminants on the site." Perhaps unsurprisingly, the Ninth Circuit found that plaintiff failed to meet the NCP requirements; for example, it did not conduct an adequate remedial investigation, evaluate alternative remedies, or provide opportunity for public comment. The court concluded that plaintiff could not recover any of its response costs: "Given the high degree of inconsistency with the requirements set forth in the NCP, [plaintiff's] action is arbitrary and capricious."

### b. Declaratory Relief re Future Costs

In addition, the successful plaintiff in a cost recovery action can obtain a declaratory judgment that the defendants are liable for response costs incurred in the future. Section 113(g)(2) provides that "the court shall enter a declaratory judgment on liability for response costs that will be binding on any subsequent action or actions to recover further response costs or damages." In Kelley v. E.I. DuPont de Nemours & Co., 17 F.3d 836 (6th Cir.1994), the leading decision to interpret this provision, the Sixth Circuit concluded that entry of a declaratory judgment was mandatory. The *Kelley* defendants argued that because the required cleanup had been completed, any future costs were speculative; they claimed that there was no existing "case or controversy" as required by Article III of the Constitution to justify judicial action. The court rejected this claim, stressing that in CERCLA cases: (1) the "probability of subsequent activity * * * is more likely than remote;" and (2) it would waste state, corporate, and judicial resources to require relitigation of liability whenever subsequent response action is taken.

The availability of declaratory relief allows EPA to effect cleanups with minimal use of federal monies. Suppose that complete remediation of a particular site is projected to cost $5 million. EPA could finance the cleanup and then sue under § 107 for reimbursement; but this is a slow and uncertain process, during which the $5 million is not available for reuse elsewhere. Alternatively, EPA might use federal funds to perform minor removal action (e.g., $100,000 for emergency removal of barrels), and then bring an action seeking both recovery of the $100,000 in response costs and a declaratory judgment that the defendants are liable for the remaining $4.9 million in future response costs. In this manner, declaratory relief permits EPA to multiply the effect of its limited budget.

### c. Natural Resource Damages

A responsible party is also liable for "damages for injury to, destruction of, or loss of natural resources." § 107(a)(4)(C). The term "natural resources" is given an extraordinarily broad definition in § 101(16): "land, fish, wildlife, biota, air, water, ground water, drinking water supplies, and other such resources" which are owned, controlled, managed, or held in trust by the United States, other governmental entities, or Indian tribes. Unlike recovery of response costs, there is no requirement that the government expend money before it can seek to recover natural resource damages. However, damages received for such injury may be used only to "restore, replace, or acquire the equivalent of such natural resources." § 107(f)(1). Suppose, for example, F dumps toxic wastes at her factory site and is held liable as an operator for response cost reimbursement. If the release killed plant and animal life in the adjacent national forest, F must pay damages to the federal government for these losses. The federal government, in turn, must apply these funds toward restoring or replacing the natural resources.

Most of the controversy in this area concerns the appropriate measure of damages. Section 107(a)(4)(C) vaguely refers to "damages for injury to, destruction of, or loss of natural resources, including the reasonable costs of assessing such injury, destruction, or loss resulting from such a release." Under this language, is the defendant always liable for the cost of restoring the natural resources (which may amount to millions of dollars) or is a lesser damage standard sometimes proper? The only guidance CERCLA offers is § 107(f)(1), which merely provides that natural resource damages "shall not be limited by the sums which can be used to restore or replace such resources."

Regulations promulgated by the Department of Interior, however, address the issue. Section 301(c) directs the Department to issue regulations "for the assessment of damages" to natural resources in two situations: (1) "simplified assessments requiring minimal field observation" (commonly known as "Type A" rules) and (2) rules governing more complex assessments in individual cases (commonly known as "Type B" rules). A damage assessment made in accordance with these regulations is entitled to a rebuttable presumption of validity. § 107(f)(2)(C).

The initial regulations issued under this authority sparked controversy. They provided that natural resources damages would be the *"lesser of"* restoration or replacement costs *or* "diminution of use values." Finding this standard inconsistent with the intent of Congress, the D.C. Circuit invalidated significant parts of the Type B regulations in Ohio v. U.S. Department of Interior, 880 F.2d 432 (D.C.Cir.1989). The *Ohio* court explained the practical significance of the "lesser of" rule, using a hypothetical hazardous substance spill which killed a rookery of fur seals:

> The lost use value of the seals * * * would be measured by the market value of the fur seals' pelts (which would be approximately $15 each) * * *. Even if, as likely, that use value turns out to be far less than the cost of restoring the rookery * * *, it would nonetheless be the only measure of damages * * *.

The court concluded that Congress "was skeptical of the ability of human beings to measure the true 'value' of a natural resource," and thus intended restoration cost as the basic measure of damages. The revised Type B regulations at 43 C.F.R. § 11.83 eliminate the "lesser of" rule in favor of a standard based on "restoration, rehabilitation, replacement, and/or acquisition of equivalent resources."

Claims for natural resource damages are limited by special rules which do not apply to normal response cost recovery actions. For example:

- *Identity of the Plaintiff*: In general, only the United States, the states, and Indian tribes may sue for such damages. § 107(f)(1). Most courts hold that cities and other local government entities lack standing to sue, unless authorized by a state.
- *EIS Commitment Bars Recovery*: Section 107(f)(1) bars recovery if the resources involved were specifically identified as an "irreversible and irretrievable commitment" of natural resources in an environmental impact statement or similar analysis and the permit or license ultimately issued authorizes this commitment.
- *Limited Retroactivity*: Section 107(f)(1) also bars recovery "where such damages and the release of a hazardous substance from which such damages resulted have occurred wholly before December 11, 1980." Yet if a release occurring before this date causes later damages, at least partial recovery is still permitted.

### d. CERCLA Liens

Section 107(*l*)(1) authorizes a lien to secure payment of "[a]ll costs and damages for which a person is liable to the United States" under § 107(a). According to the section, this lien encumbers real property rights which: (1) belong to a responsible party; and (2) were subject to or affected by a removal or remedial action. But the First Circuit declared this provision unconstitutional in Reardon

v. United States, 947 F.2d 1509 (1st Cir.1991). Observing that the lien could be imposed without prior notice to the property owner and a pre-deprivation hearing, the court concluded that the section violated the owner's right to procedural due process. Although other circuits have not yet addressed the issue, it appears that *Reardon* has effectively annulled this section. However, the 2002 amendments create a new lien for response costs incurred to clean up brownfield sites, under conditions set forth in § 107(r) .

## C. DEFENSES AND EXCLUSIONS

### 1. SECTION 107 DEFENSES

Section 107(b) sets forth the four traditional defenses to CERCLA liability: the act of God, act of war, third party, and innocent landowner defenses. Broadly speaking, all four are designed to protect wholly innocent parties. In order to prevail, a defendant must establish by a preponderance of the evidence that *both* (1) the release or threat of release *and* (2) the "damages resulting therefrom" were caused *solely* by another source (e.g., by an act of God). Thus, if the defendant contributed to the release or the amount of damages incurred (e.g., by a lack of due care), the defense is unavailable. Courts generally construe these defenses narrowly to further the statute's remedial purpose.

The 2002 amendments created three new protections against CERCLA liability: the de micromis (§ 107(*o*)), contiguous property owner

(§ 107(q)), and prospective bona fide purchaser (§ 107(r)) exemptions.

### a. Act of God

An "act of God" is a defense to CERCLA liability. § 107(b)(1). However, defendants asserting this defense have been routinely unsuccessful. Section 101(1) defines "act of God" as "an unanticipated grave natural disaster or other natural phenomenon of an exceptional, inevitable, and irresistible character, the effects of which could not have been prevented or avoided by the exercise of due care or foresight." Interpreting this language narrowly, various courts have held that conditions such as unusually high ocean waves, heavy rainfall, unpredictable winds, and even a hurricane did not support the defense. Courts typically reason that the defendant failed to exercise "due care" in preparing for such an event. Given the pro-CERCLA tenor of such decisions, it seems unlikely that the defense will be effective absent a catastrophic occurrence such as a massive earthquake, a volcanic eruption, an asteroid collision, or the like.

### b. Act of War

The second statutory defense is an "act of war." § 107(b)(2). Although CERCLA does not define the phrase "act of war," the scope of this defense is quite meager. The leading case on point is United States v. Shell Oil Co., 294 F.3d 1045 (9th Cir.2002). The defendants, who manufactured aviation fuel during World War II, had dumped the resulting acid sludge wastes into unlined pits. Defendants asserted the "act of war" defense, maintaining that they contaminated the site only because their wartime contracts with the government required them to produce such large quantities of aviation fuel that they had no other disposal alternative. But the Ninth Circuit adopted the district court's reasoning that an "act of war" necessarily involved: (1) the use of force by one state against another; (2) the seizure or capture of property belonging to an enemy nation; or (3) the wartime destruction of property to injure an enemy. Thus, the government's close regulation of aviation fuel during a war could not itself be considered an act of war.

### c. Third Party Defense

The most commonly asserted CERCLA defense is the "third party defense" found in § 107(b)(3). As its name suggests, the heart of this defense is the claim that the release (or threat of release) and resulting damages were caused *entirely* by a third party. Although the defense has been successful in a handful of cases, most defendants fail to establish its three elements. To prevail, the defendant must prove all of the following:

- the release or threat of release was caused solely by "an act or omission of a third party" *other than* an employee or agent of the defendant *or* a person whose "act or omission occurs in connection with a contractual relationship, existing directly or indirectly, with the defendant";

- the defendant exercised "due care" with respect to the hazardous substance; and
- the defendant "took precautions against foreseeable acts or omissions of any such third party and the consequences that could foreseeably result" from such acts or omissions.

### *i. Act or Omission of Third Party*

The first element is clearly met in those rare instances where the release is wholly attributable to a stranger, such as the maverick truck driver who illegally dumps his toxic cargo on another's land. In the usual case, however, the alleged third party typically has some legal link with the defendant. Accordingly, much litigation has focused on whether the third party's act or omission occurred "in connection with a contractual relationship" with the defendant. The pioneering decision in United States v. Monsanto Co., 858 F.2d 160 (4th Cir.1988) established that a lease between a property owner and tenant constituted a "contractual relationship;" thus, the owner could not use the third party defense to escape liability for the tenant's acts. Many courts continue to follow the Fourth Circuit's suggestion in *Monsanto* that *any* contractual relationship between the defendant and the party at fault will preclude the defense.

However, the Second Circuit charted a different course in Westwood Pharmaceuticals, Inc. v. National Fuel Gas Distribution Corp., 964 F.2d 85 (2d Cir.1992). Noting that the phrase "in connection with" modifies "contractual relationship" in the text of § 107(b)(3), it held that the defendant landowner was precluded from raising the defense *only* "if the contract * * * somehow is connected with the handling of hazardous substances" or "if the contract allows the landowner to exert some control over the third party's actions so that the landowner fairly can be held liable for the release." A number of courts now follow the *Westwood Pharmaceuticals* approach that only *certain* contractual relationships between the wrongdoer and the defendant will defeat the defense.

### *ii. Due Care*

Although the decisions are not uniform on the point, the second element—the exercise of due care with respect to the hazardous substance—primarily concerns the defendant's conduct *after* discovery of the release. CERCLA does not shelter the knowledgeable defendant who remains idle. For example, in Idylwoods Associates v. Mader Capital, Inc., 915 F.Supp. 1290 (W.D.N.Y.1996) the property owner learned that barrels containing PCB-contaminated wastes were present on its land yet took no action. When the owner later asserted the third party defense, the court found that the owner failed to exercise due care; it observed that the owner had failed to erect warning signs, employ a security patrol, fence the site, or take similar protective steps.

### *iii. Precautions Against Foreseeable Acts or Omissions*

The third element—taking precautions against the foreseeable acts or omissions of third parties—mainly focuses on the defendant's conduct *before* discovery of the release. This requirement is well-illustrated by a pair of decisions presenting similar facts: Lincoln Properties, Ltd. v. Higgins, 823 F.Supp. 1528 (E.D.Cal.1992), and Westfarm Associates v. Washington Suburban Sanitary Commission, 66 F.3d 669 (4th Cir.1995). In each case: (1) one or more dry cleaning companies dumped perchloroethylene (PCE) wastes into sewer pipes; (2) sewer pipe leaks allowed the PCE to contaminate groundwater; and (3) the public sewer authority asserted the third party defense when sued. The defense succeeded in *Lincoln Properties,* where the court held that the sewer authority had taken reasonable precautions; the court found: (a) the sewer authority was unaware of the dumping; (b) a local ordinance prohibited such dumping; and (c) the sewer lines were built and maintained in accordance with industry standards.

Conversely, the defense failed in *Westfarm Associates,* where the court found reasonable precautions had not been taken. There, the defendant sewer authority actually knew that: (a) the dry cleaner was pouring hazardous substances into the sewer; and (b) "cracks were present in its sewer." Nonetheless, as the court noted, it "took no precautions—such as mending the pipes or banning the discharge of toxic organics—against the foreseeable result that hazardous substances such as PCE would be discharged into the sewer."

### d. Innocent Landowner Defense

The "innocent landowner" or "innocent buyer" defense is an offshoot of the third party defense. Early CERCLA decisions held that land contracts, deeds, and other title instruments created a sufficient "contractual relationship" to preclude use of the third party defense by an innocent buyer who purchased contaminated property from a culpable seller. Congress remedied this situation in 1986 by adding § 101(35), effectively creating the "innocent landowner" defense. This subsection provides that—if certain requirements are met—deeds and other instruments will *not* be deemed a "contractual relationship." Once having satisfied § 101(35), the innocent buyer can thus escape liability if he proves the remaining elements of the third party defense discussed above: (1) causation solely by the third party; (2) due care by the buyer; and (3) adequate precautions by the buyer.

Section 101(35)(A)(i) provides that the term "contractual relationship" does not include "land contracts, deeds, easements, leases, or other instruments transferring title or possession" if three requirements are met:

- the defendant acquired the property after disposal of the hazardous substance;
- at acquisition the defendant "did not know and had no reason to know that any

hazardous substance which is the subject of the release or threatened release was disposed of on, in, or at" the property;

- the defendant provides full cooperation and assistance for any response action.

Section 101(35)(B) explains the second requirement in more detail. In order to establish that the defendant had "no reason to know" of contamination before buying it, he must meet two tests. First, he must have carried out "all appropriate inquiries * * * into the previous ownership and uses of the facility in accordance with generally accepted good commercial and customary standards and practices." Second, he must have taken reasonable steps to stop any continuing release, prevent any threatened future release, and prevent or limit exposure to prior releases. Cf. United States v. Domenic Lombardi Realty Co., 290 F.Supp.2d 198 (D.R.I.2003) (defendant did not qualify for defense under pre-2002 "due care" test because he failed to warn site visitors about the contamination).

After CERCLA was enacted, it was difficult to determine how much pre-purchase investigation was necessary to satisfy the "no reason to know" standard, because the statutory criteria were somewhat vague. It became common for many buyers to retain a consulting firm to conduct a pre-purchase environmental assessment, especially where commercial or industrial property was involved, but the precise scope of required assessments was unclear.

The 2002 amendments brought more clarity to this area. They establish a key distinction between commercial and noncommercial properties. Thus, if property is purchased for residential use or similar use by a private, noncommercial party, the required assessment is minimal; a facility inspection and title search that "reveal no basis for further investigation" are sufficient.

However, the "no reason to know" standard is complex when applied to the purchase of commercial properties, in part because the requirements established in 2002 differ according to the year of purchase:

- For properties purchased before May 31, 1997, the court must consider five factors in determining whether the defendant had no reason to know of the contamination: (a) the defendant's specialized knowledge or experience, if any; (b) the relationship of the purchase price to the value of the property if uncontaminated; (c) commonly known or reasonably ascertainable information about the property; (d) the obviousness of the contamination at the property; and (e) the ability to detect such contamination by appropriate inspection.

- For properties purchased after May 31, 1997 but before November 1, 2006—a transitional period—compliance with the "Standard Practice for Environmental Site Assessment: Phase 1 Environmental Site Assessment Process," as established by the American

Society for Testing and Materials meets this standard.

- Finally, for properties purchased on or after November 1, 2006, regulations adopted by EPA at 40 C.F.R. § 312.20 et seq. govern the process. These regulations require an extensive inquiry by an environmental professional, which will include: (a) interviews with past and present site owners; (b) reviews of historical sources; (c) reviews of government records; and (d) visual inspections. In addition, the court will consider the five factors set forth above for purchases before May 1, 1997 (specialized knowledge, etc.) in determining whether the defendant had "no reason to know."

There are two exceptions to the requirements of § 101(35)(A)(i) that the buyer be actually unaware and have "no reason to know" of the presence of hazardous substances. Section 101(35)(A)(ii)–(iii) provides that a party will still qualify for the defense if either: (a) it is a government entity which acquired the facility by escheat, other involuntary transfer, or through eminent domain; or (b) it acquired the facility by bequest or inheritance.

Under special circumstances, even a defendant who normally qualifies for the innocent buyer defense will lose its protection. Section 101(35)(C) provides that if a non-liable defendant obtains "actual knowledge" of the release or threatened release during his ownership, but then sells the facility to another without disclosing this knowledge, then the defendant "shall be treated as liable." In effect, this provision imposes a special federal disclosure obligation on certain property sellers.

### e. De Micromis Exemption

Generators who produce extremely small quantities of hazardous substances are immune from liability under § 107(*o*). Subject to various exceptions, a party that produced less than 110 gallons of liquid materials or less than 200 pounds of solid materials (or such other amounts as EPA specifies through regulations) which are disposed of at an NPL site is exempt if all or part of the disposal, treatment, or transport occurred before April 1, 2001.

### f. Contiguous Property Owner Exemption

What happens if hazardous substances migrate from A's contaminated land to neighbor B's pristine land? Section 107(q), added by the 2002 amendments, provides that an owner who purchases land that is contaminated by a release from a contiguous or nearby property is not liable if certain conditions are met. Among other requirements, the owner must show that: (a) it did not cause or contribute to the contamination; (b) it fully cooperated with any response action; and (c) at time of purchase, it did not know and had no reason to know, after the inquiry required by § 101(35)(B), that the land was contaminated.

### g. Prospective Bona Fide Purchaser Exemption

The strict liability imposed by CERCLA made it difficult for EPA to convince investors to purchase, clean up, and redevelop sites that were already contaminated, commonly called "brownfields." Eventually, EPA created a program by which the potential buyer of a contaminated site would negotiate a pre-purchase agreement to obtain both liability protection and financial assistance for the cleanup. This site-specific approach to brownfield redevelopment was replaced in 2002 with a new general defense to liability in § 107(r): the prospective bona fide purchaser exemption. In effect, it provides limited protection for a buyer who actually knows that the site is contaminated.

This exemption applies to a buyer who acquires title *after* both (a) all disposal of hazardous substances on the site and (b) 2002, when the exemption was adopted. See City of Wichita v. Trustees of APCO Oil Corp., 306 F.Supp.2d 1040 (D.Kan.2003). The buyer must also meet portions of the innocent buyer defense, in particular: (a) it completed an appropriate pre-purchase inquiry; and (b) it took reasonable steps to stop any continuing release, prevent any threatened release, and prevent or limit exposure to prior releases. Finally, the buyer must provide full cooperation and assistance for response actions.

## 2. STATUTE OF LIMITATIONS

The Statute of Limitations is another potential defense to CERCLA liability. Under § 113(g), the limitations period for bringing a cost recovery action varies according to the nature of the relief sought.

- *Costs of removal action*: Suit must generally be filed within 3 years after "completion of the removal action."
- *Costs of remedial action*: Suit must be filed within 6 years after initiation of physical on-site construction of the remedial action; if remedial action is initiated within 3 years after completion of the removal action, costs incurred in the removal action may also be recovered in the suit. But see California v. Neville Chemical Company, 358 F.3d 661 (9th Cir.2004) (holding that 6 year period did not begin until final remedial action plan was adopted).
- *Response costs incurred after declaratory judgment*: If the government obtains a declaratory judgment of liability for future response costs, § 113(g)(2) requires that a second suit to collect such costs be filed "no later than 3 years from the date of completion of all response action."
- *Natural resource damages*: In general, under § 113(g)(1), suit must be filed within 3 years of the *later* of the following: (a) the "date of the discovery of the loss and its connection with the release in question;" or (b) the date

upon which regulations are promulgated under § 301(c). The Ninth Circuit has held that the limitations period linked to § 301(c) regulations began running on March 20, 1987, and thus ended on March 20, 1990. California v. Montrose Chemical Corp., 104 F.3d 1507, 43 E.R.C. 1946 (9th Cir.1997).

### 3. EXCLUSIONS FROM CERCLA COVERAGE

CERCLA's impact is blunted somewhat by a variety of exclusions sprinkled throughout its text. Many of these exceptions arise in the statutory definitions of key terms; as discussed above, for example, the definition of "release" in § 101(22) expressly excludes such items as workplace contamination, motor vehicle exhaust, and fertilizer application. In addition, § 107 contains three important exclusions; each rests on the theory that the conduct is already regulated by another federal environmental statute:

- *Application of registered pesticide*: Section 107(i) provides that response costs or damages stemming from the *application* of a pesticide product registered under FIFRA cannot be recovered. The *disposal* of a pesticide product, however, can trigger CERCLA liability.

- *Federally permitted releases*: Similarly, § 107(j) bars the recovery of response costs or damages resulting from a "federally permitted release." As defined in § 101(10), this term refers to a release authorized by a federal permit issued under another statute (e.g., the CAA or CWA).

- *Releases at closed RCRA-permitted TSD facilities*: Finally, owners and operators of RCRA-permitted TSD facilities which are closed pursuant to RCRA standards are insulated from direct CERCLA liability; any such liability is assumed by a special post-closure liability fund. § 107(k).

## D. ENFORCEMENT

### 1. SETTLEMENT

CERCLA is primarily enforced through settlements negotiated between EPA and PRPs, not through litigation. The sweeping CERCLA liability provisions discussed above, coupled with the cost of litigation, give liable PRPs a strong incentive to settle in order to minimize their losses. Even where liability is clear, resource limitations typically motivate EPA to settle CERCLA claims. Settlements can produce reasonably prompt cleanups with minimal expenditure of government monies. Moreover, EPA does not receive enough funding to fully litigate all claims; it accordingly relies on settlements to stretch its enforcement funding for maximum benefit.

Section 122(a) encourages the President (and thus EPA) to enter into settlement agreements with PRPs that are "in the public interest and consistent with the National Contingency Plan in order to expedite effective remedial actions and minimize litigation." This section also establishes guidelines for the CERCLA settlement process. Although EPA typically follows these guidelines, they are not mandatory in most instances.

CERCLA settlements may require one or more PRPs to reimburse EPA or another government agency for response costs, to perform removal or remedial action, or both. For example, suppose EPA spends $100,000 for emergency removal action at a newly discovered site. EPA will then use the lever of future CERCLA liability to negotiate a settlement under which the PRPs will *both*: (1) reimburse EPA for its $100,000 in response costs; *and* (2) undertake responsibility for the remaining work required at the site, either having their own contractors perform the work or by agreeing to finance work by government contractors. Although this chapter discusses EPA's § 107 authority, its § 106 power to compel liable PRPs to perform cleanup work (discussed in Chapter 10) is also a valuable tool in settlement negotiations. Sophisticated PRPs usually prefer to have their own contractors perform the required response action, in order to minimize total response costs.

### a. Settlement Procedures Generally

The cornerstone of CERCLA settlements is collective negotiation. EPA can usually identify between 20 and 100 PRPs for a typical site. Separate settlement negotiations between EPA and each PRP would be extraordinarily difficult. Accordingly, EPA's general policy is to negotiate with all PRPs *as a unit*, not with individual PRPs. EPA usually encourages the PRPs at each site to form an organization (known as a "steering committee") whose representatives can negotiate directly with EPA on behalf of all members.

EPA typically initiates the settlement process by sending a letter to the parties tentatively identified as PRPs at the site. The letter notifies recipients of their potential liability for response costs, describes the site, lists the PRPs linked to the site, and provides other information. It may also invite the recipients to a "PRP meeting" to learn more information about EPA's plans for the site, to organize a steering committee, and to begin settlement discussions.

If appropriate, EPA will next use the "special notice" procedures set forth in § 122(e). These procedures create a special "window of opportunity" for settlement discussions, ranging from 90 to 120 days; § 122(e)(2)(A) imposes a moratorium on further EPA response action during this period. EPA begins this process by sending the PRPs a "special notice" letter, which includes the names and addresses of all PRPs, the volume and nature of substances contributed by each PRP to the site, and a ranking by volume of the substances at the site. The letter requests the PRPs to make a joint proposal within 60 days to perform or finance the required response action. EPA frequently uses an initial special notice procedure for preparation of the RI/FS, and a subsequent special notice procedure for remedial action.

If a settlement is not reached within the 90–120 day period, EPA may perform the required work itself and seek reimbursement in a later cost recovery action. Even with a well-organized PRP steering committee in place, it is often difficult to reach agreement within this short time frame. Usually the most difficult issue concerns the allocation of liability among PRPs. Section 122(e)(3) authorizes EPA to facilitate settlement discussions by preparing a "nonbinding preliminary allocation of responsibility" (NBAR), which tentatively establishes the proportionate liability of each PRP at the site.

### b. Major Party Settlements

EPA's settlement efforts focus on "major parties," that is, PRPs having more than a de minimis role at the site. "De minimis settlements" and "de micromis settlements" are governed by more flexible procedures, as discussed below. In each instance, however, settlement negotiations commonly raise three key issues.

- *Scope of EPA's covenant not to sue*: Suppose that EPA is negotiating a settlement with B, the current site owner. At a minimum, B will want EPA's agreement not to sue him in the future concerning the existing site contamination. EPA will usually agree to a limited "covenant not to sue" a PRP such as B concerning the same site in the future, under conditions specified in § 122(f)(1). EPA normally demands a "reopener" clause, however, which allows it to seek future relief from the PRP under limited circumstances (e.g., problems caused by newly discovered conditions at the site, cost overruns on remedial work, or the failure of remedial work to adequately protect human health and the environment).

- *Protection from contribution claims by other PRPs*: If B settles with EPA, what prevents non-settling PRPs from suing B for contribution? EPA is authorized to provide contribution protection to settling PRPs such as B under §§ 113(f)(2) and 122(h)(4). See Chapter 11.

- *Funding for "orphan shares:"* Suppose that a large share of the hazardous substances sent to the site (e.g., 60%) is linked to insolvent or unknown parties. Who pays for this "orphan share" in a settlement? If B's overall share of liability, for example, is 20%, must B pay 50% of the total settlement amount (i.e., his own 20% share plus half of the "orphan share")? Section 122(b)(1) permits EPA to agree to a "mixed funding" settlement, under which the site remediation costs attributable to the orphan share are ultimately paid with federal funds. (Mechanically, the section requires the settling PRPs to advance the costs covering the orphan share, and then authorizes reimbursement to them from the Superfund.) In practice, mixed funding settlements are rare because EPA prefers to preserve its limited funding.

Once EPA and a PRP group agree to a major party settlement, it must normally undergo a formal approval process. A proposed consent judgment which embodies the settlement terms is usually filed with the appropriate federal district court and made available for public comment for at least 30 days. If ultimately approved by the court, it is then entered as a final judgment. § 122(d)(1). The trial court must independently evaluate the proposed settlement to ensure that it is "reasonable, fair, and consistent with the purposes CERCLA is intended to serve." United States v. Cannons Engineering Corp., 899 F.2d 79 (1st Cir.1990). In practice, courts generally uphold such settlements.

### c. De Minimis Settlements

Section 122(g) encourages prompt "de minimis settlements," that is, settlements with PRPs whose involvement in the site is minimal based on both the volume and toxicity of the wastes. For example, a generator PRP who contributed only a small volume of hazardous substances to the site (e.g., 20 barrels) in relation to the contributions of other PRPs (e.g., 20,000 barrels) will usually qualify for a de minimis settlement. The line between de minimis and non-de minimis parties is determined on a site-by-site basis. Although this cutoff point has varied over time, the most commonly used standard allows a de minimis settlement where the defendant has contributed no more than 1% of the total volume of hazardous substances at the site. Thus, any PRP who contributed 200 or fewer barrels to a 20,000 barrel site would probably be eligible for a de minimis settlement. In addition to these volume standards, a PRP will qualify for de minimis treatment only if its wastes are not significantly more toxic or hazardous than other substances at the facility.

A de minimis settlement offers two distinct advantages over a major party settlement. First, the settlement agreement will normally provide the de minimis PRP with enhanced protection against further government claims. Unlike the normal "reopener" clause inserted into major party settlement agreements, de minimis agreements typically restrict later government action based upon either newly discovered site conditions or the failure of the adopted remediation plan. Also, a de minimis settlement minimizes the PRP's attorneys' fees and other transaction costs because EPA reaches de minimis settlements early in the process.

From EPA's standpoint, however, the early de minimis settlement presents certain risks. The future response action has not yet been chosen; the ultimate cost of remediation is uncertain; and the solvency of other PRPs may be unclear. Thus, EPA normally requires a settlement price which compensates for these risks, in an amount equal to: (1) the de minimis party's anticipated share of actual cleanup costs; *plus* (2) a "premium" payment, ranging from 50% to 100% of the actual anticipated costs. For example, assuming that cleanup will cost

$10 million, the de minimis PRP with a 1% share might pay $200,000 in settlement ($100,000 as his anticipated fair share of the projected cost, plus a $100,000 premium).

### d. De Micromis Settlements

A de micromis settlement is essentially a special subcategory of the de minimis settlement discussed above. It is available only to parties whose contribution of wastes to the contaminated site is extraordinarily minor. For example, suppose a generator defendant cannot qualify for the § 107(*o*) exemption because it contributed 3 barrels (165 gallons) of liquid wastes to the site, while the exemption applies to 2 barrels (110 gallons) or less. The defendant may still qualify for a de micromis settlement depending on factors such as the toxicity of the materials, the effect of multiple de micromis settlements on the remaining parties, and other factors. The de micromis settlement is handled much like the de minimis settlement, except that EPA normally does not demand a "premium" payment as part of the settlement amount; the de micromis PRP need only pay its anticipated share of the cleanup cost.

## 2. LITIGATION

The early procedural steps in a cost recovery lawsuit are comparatively easy. Section 113(b) provides federal district courts with exclusive jurisdiction over controversies arising under CERCLA, regardless of the citizenship of the parties or the amount in controversy. Service of process may be effected anywhere in the United States, under § 113(e).

The typical CERCLA lawsuit, however, presents a case management nightmare. The parties are numerous and mutually antagonistic. The available evidence is often both fragmentary and stale (especially evidence concerning defenses). Finally, the case presents complex technical issues concerning the adequacy of remediation work. As a result, the government frequently moves for summary judgment on liability issues. Alternatively, it may seek bifurcation of the case such that liability issues are resolved first, and remedy issues are determined later. Under this bifurcation approach, an early determination of the defendants' liability may promote settlement. Conversely, if liability is not established, the time-consuming remedy phase can be avoided. (For additional discussion of the procedural complexities of litigation involving hazardous substances, see Chapter 13.)

# CHAPTER 10

# CERCLA: CLEANUP MANDATED BY GOVERNMENT

## A. OVERVIEW

Section 106 provides the federal government with an alternative method for meeting CERCLA's remediation goal: *compelling a responsible person to clean up the contaminated site.* This section is triggered if the President finds there "may be an imminent and substantial endangerment" to public health, welfare, or the environment "because of an actual or threatened release of a hazardous substance from a facility." Although the section refers to action by the President, this authority has been delegated by executive order to EPA. Thus, under § 106 EPA can compel a responsible party to remediate the site, either by obtaining an injunction in district court or by issuing an administrative order. In recent years, EPA has found it more efficient to compel § 106 remediation through administrative orders than through litigation. See, e.g., Chem-Nuclear Systems, Inc. v. Bush, 292 F.3d 254 (D.C.Cir.2002) (EPA order used to compel cleanup of 80 barrels of liquid chemical waste).

This section was partly derived from RCRA § 7003 (discussed in Chapter 12), which authorizes the federal government to order responsible persons to clean up hazardous waste contamination if an "imminent and substantial endangerment to health or the environment" may occur. The early case law interpreting § 7003 indicated that it applied only to spill emergencies at active, RCRA-regulated facilities. The initial § 106 decisions seemed to suggest a similar limitation. Most courts, however, quickly recognized that the language of § 106 encompassed both active and inactive sites.

Section 106 is a powerful weapon in the CERCLA arsenal. It offers several advantages over the standard §§ 104/107 "clean up and sue for reimbursement" approach. First, § 106 cleanups are financed by the "responsible" persons, without the use of scarce federal funds. Second, especially when implemented by an administrative order, the § 106 cleanup process is both more rapid and less expensive than government-led cleanup under § 104. Finally, while remedial action under § 104 is limited to sites on the National Priorities List, EPA can order § 106 remedial action for sites not listed on the NPL. EPA is reluctant to use the § 106 option where: (1) the responsible parties lack the financial resources necessary to clean up the site; (2) there are many responsible parties; or (3) the response action required cannot be clearly and completely defined in advance.

The precise parameters of § 106 are still uncharted. Even for CERCLA, the section is unusually vague and general, offering the reader scant guidance and leaving many issues open for judicial resolution. To date, only a few appellate decisions have construed the section.

## B. SECTION 106 LIABILITY STANDARDS

### 1. IN GENERAL

The first sentence of § 106(a) uses familiar CERCLA terms in describing the conditions which trigger liability: "an actual or threatened release" of a "hazardous substance" from a "facility." But the language of the section is silent on two key issues: (1) *who is liable*? and (2) *what is the standard of liability*? Courts quickly filled this void by finding Congressional intent to incorporate the § 107(a) liability standards into § 106(a). It is now generally acknowledged that the four PRP categories listed in § 107(a) are also liable under § 106(a). Further, most courts interpret § 106(a) as imposing strict liability, like its counterpart § 107(a).

Accordingly, the elements of § 106 liability are as follows:

- An "imminent and substantial endangerment" to the public health, welfare, or the environment because of
- an "actual or threatened release"
- of a "hazardous substance"
- from a "facility" or "vessel"
- justifies an injunction or order against a § 107(a) PRP.

The last four elements have already been discussed in Chapters 7 and 9. Thus, only the first element—

"imminent and substantial endangerment"—is discussed below.

### 2. "IMMINENT AND SUBSTANTIAL ENDANGERMENT"

Courts disagree on whether the "imminent and substantial endangerment" standard applies only to emergency situations. The majority (and better) view is that this language should be liberally construed to include non-emergency conditions. Although the phrase is not defined in CERCLA, the same language is found in other federal environmental laws (notably SDWA § 1431 and RCRA § 7003) and understood to include non-emergency situations. Thus, most courts interpreting the phrase in § 106 actions adopt this meaning.

The leading case exploring the meaning of "imminent and substantial endangerment" under § 106 is United States v. Conservation Chemical Co., 619 F.Supp. 162 (W.D.Mo.1985), where the federal government sought an injunction to force cleanup of a chemical dump site. Defendants asserted that the imminent and substantial endangerment standard was not met because: (1) the site was surrounded by a chain link fence bearing warning notices, thus barring any access; and (2) although hazardous substances from the site were admittedly leaking into both groundwater and nearby rivers, no drinking water supplies had actually been affected.

Applying the meaning which "imminent and substantial endangerment" had acquired in decisions interpreting other statutes, the *Conversation Chemical* court held that the standard was met on the facts before it. The court first observed that "endangerment" did not mean actual harm, but merely a "threatened or potential" harm; it concluded that if the public health or welfare or environment "may be exposed to a risk of harm," then an endangerment might exist. Next, the court reasoned that "imminent" did not mean immediate; "an endangerment is 'imminent' if factors giving rise to it are present, even though the harm may not be realized for years." Finally, it equated "substantial" with a "reasonable cause for concern," not statistical proof. The risk that humans might be exposed to hazardous substances which migrated from the site via groundwater, surface water, or air was sufficient to trigger § 106. The court stressed that a possible endangerment to the public health *or* to the public welfare *or* to the environment would warrant relief. Thus, one of the factors supporting its liability finding was the risk of injury to the non-human species inhabiting the site (e.g., frogs, toads, turtles, lizards, and birds), which would not be deterred by fences or warning signs.

In summary, *Conservation Chemical* held that an imminent and substantial endangerment will be found if:

- there is "reasonable cause for concern"
- that members of the public or the environment "may be exposed to a risk of

harm by virtue of a release or threatened release of hazardous substances"

- "even if the harm may not be realized for years."

This modest standard can be met in most ordinary CERCLA cases. For example, hazardous substances deposited at abandoned dump sites typically leach into groundwater over time, and may affect public drinking water sources in the future. Similarly, surface contamination at these sites often imperils wildlife. As a result, *in most CERCLA cases the federal government can opt to force cleanup under § 106,* avoiding the expense, delay, and uncertainty inherent in the §§ 104/107 process. Some courts, however, still limit the scope of § 106 to emergency situations, effectively restricting its routine use as an alternative cleanup method.

## C. DEFENSES TO LIABILITY

Section 106 is silent on the subject of defenses. At a minimum, most courts acknowledge that the statutory defenses set forth in § 107(b)—act of God, act of war, third party, and innocent landowner—are impliedly incorporated into § 106(a). This conclusion is buttressed by § 106(b)(2)(C) and (D), which authorize parties who remediate a site under § 106 to seek reimbursement from the Superfund *only* if they are not already liable for response costs under § 107.

But courts disagree on whether equitable defenses are also available to § 106 liability. Unlike

§ 107, § 106 expressly refers to equitable principles; it provides that "the public interest and the equities of the case" should be considered in fashioning relief when the government sues for an injunction. Some courts construing this language conclude that it opens the door to the traditional equitable defenses (e.g., laches, estoppel, and unclean hands). Under this view the recipient of a § 106(a) administrative order who reasonably believes he can successfully assert such an equitable defense should have "sufficient cause" for disobeying the order.

## D. ENFORCEMENT BY ADMINISTRATIVE ORDER

Administrative orders which mandate cleanup are authorized by the *second sentence* of § 106(a). It provides: "The President may also * * * take other action under this section including, but not limited to, issuing such orders as may be necessary to protect public health and welfare and the environment." This provision is extraordinarily vague, even for CERCLA. It appears to confer almost unlimited discretion upon EPA, as the President's delegate. Yet it is generally accepted that the liability elements for injunctive relief set forth in the *first sentence* of § 106(a)—including an actual or threatened release of a hazardous substance from a facility—also apply to administrative orders. Still, as EPA acknowledged in a policy memorandum, the § 106 administrative order authority is "one of the most potent administrative remedies available to the Agency under any existing environmental statute."

It is comparatively simple for EPA to order cleanup of a contaminated site. For example, suppose EPA believes that X Corporation is liable under § 106(a) to clean up an abandoned landfill. It will typically send a letter notifying X Corporation of its intent to order cleanup. EPA and X Corporation might then negotiate the terms of a mutually acceptable order, leading to the issuance of a consent order; many § 106 orders stem from negotiation. Assuming that negotiations fail, EPA will compile an administrative record concerning the proposed order. Based upon this record, EPA will then decide whether the liability elements of the section are met; if so, it will prepare a draft order and supporting documents. Although X Corporation will receive notice of these proceedings, and an opportunity to respond in writing, it is not entitled to a hearing.

Assume that EPA issues a unilateral order directing X Corporation to act. If X Corporation reasonably believes itself to be liable, its only realistic choice is to comply with the order. CERCLA encourages liable parties to accept § 106(a) orders by threatening severe monetary penalties for noncompliance. A person who fails "without sufficient cause" to undertake the removal or remedial action mandated by such an order may be liable to the United States both for the resulting *response costs* and for *punitive damages up to three times the response costs.* § 107(c)(3). Thus, the recalcitrant defendant in United States v. Parsons, 936 F.2d 526 (11th Cir.1991) was found liable not only for the government's response costs, but also for over $2,200,000 in punitive damages. In addition, a responsible party who ignores such an order "without sufficient cause" may be fined up to $25,000 for each day of noncompliance. § 106(b)(1).

If, however, X Corporation concludes it may be able to avoid CERCLA liability, it faces a difficult dilemma. Under § 113(h), it cannot litigate the validity of the order at this stage in the proceedings. This section deprives federal courts of jurisdiction to "review any order" issued under 106(a), except in connection with a cost recovery or enforcement action initiated by the government. The Second Circuit explained the rationale for this pre-enforcement review ban in Wagner Seed Co. v. Daggett, 800 F.2d 310 (2d Cir.1986): "To introduce the delay of court proceedings at the outset of a cleanup would conflict with the strong congressional policy that directs cleanups to occur prior to a final determination of the parties' rights and liabilities under CERCLA."

All courts agree that § 113(h) bars any statutory challenge to a § 106 order before EPA brings an enforcement action. But the courts are split on whether this subsection also precludes a constitutional challenge. For example, in General Electric Co. v. Johnson, 610 F.3d 110 (D.C. Cir. 2010), the court held that § 113(h) did not bar a challenge based on the Due Process Clause; but it reasoned that the issuance of a § 106(a) order did not itself deprive a PRP of a constitutionally protected property interest.

Accordingly, as one litigant complained, the innocent recipient of such an order may be "stuck between a rock and a hard place." Solid State Circuits, Inc. v. EPA, 812 F.2d 383 (8th Cir.1987). It must choose between two unattractive alternatives:

- *Comply with the order:* X Corporation can spend its own funds to clean up the site, and then seek reimbursement. Section 106(b)(2) allows the corporation to recover these costs from the Superfund if it can establish that it was not liable. Alternatively, although the law remains unclear here (see Chapter 11), it may be able to recoup its expenses from third parties through a private cost recovery action under § 107(a). Yet the corporation might not be able to secure full reimbursement. Funding constraints may limit recovery from the government; responsible third parties may be either insolvent or impossible to locate. Thus, by selecting this option, X Corporation may ultimately bear the cost of a cleanup for which it is not liable.

- *Disobey the order:* Alternatively, X Corporation can disobey the order and risk incurring the draconian penalties of §§ 107(c)(3) and 106(b)(1) discussed above. Under this scenario, EPA will probably clean up the site and then bring a cost recovery action against the corporation, seeking fines and punitive damages. If the corporation is ultimately found liable for response costs, inquiry will next focus on whether penalties should be imposed. Noncompliance does not automatically trigger punitive damages or fines. Both §§ 107(c)(3) and 106(b)(1) provide only that penalties "may" be imposed. As the *Wagner Seed* court reasoned: "Since awarding the fines and penalties is discretionary, and they may be imposed only after a judicial hearing, obviously that discretion must rest with the judiciary." Under both sections, the key question is whether the party's refusal was "without sufficient cause." Most courts acknowledge that sufficient cause exists where the defendant had an objectively reasonable basis for believing that the order was invalid or inapplicable to it. But United States v. Parsons, 723 F.Supp. 757 (N.D.Ga.1989) suggests that the defendant's financial inability to pay for the required remediation would not be sufficient cause.

The permissible scope of § 106(a) orders is quite broad. Employers Insurance of Wausau v. Clinton, 848 F.Supp. 1359 (N.D.Ill.1994) illustrates the point. There, EPA ordered Employers Insurance of Wausau (EIW) and others to clean up a site contaminated with PCBs and various volatile organic compounds (VOCs). Although EIW arguably was a responsible party as to the PCB-contaminated areas (having arranged for the transportation of PCB wastes to the site), it had no connection to the VOCs problem. EPA's order directed EIW to clean up *all* hazardous substances at the facility, not merely the PCB contamination. In ensuing litigation, EIW asserted that EPA could not order a party to clean up waste for which it is not even potentially responsible. But the court rejected this argument, observing that "it is not inconsistent with the broad goals of the statute to require a party who is potentially liable for some contamination at a particular site to clean up the entire site, and then petition the government for reimbursement of those costs attributable to any portion of the contamination for which the party was not actually responsible."

EPA's § 106(a) enforcement activities focus on administrative orders rather than injunctions. The order offers three advantages over the suit for injunctive relief: cost, speed, and control. EPA can conserve its limited resources through issuance of an order, without the need for litigation; indeed, its orders are not subject to judicial review before the required remediation work is completed. Similarly, absent an emergency which would justify a preliminary injunction, the process for issuing an order is faster than litigation. Finally, the order enhances EPA's ability to control the remediation plan. Federal judges exercise wide latitude in crafting the terms of injunctive relief, arguably even to the point of rejecting EPA cleanup proposals, as discussed below. In contrast, if litigation ensues after EPA-ordered remediation has been completed, courts will accord the order substantial deference. Under § 113(j) it will be upheld unless it is proven arbitrary, capricious, or otherwise not in accordance with law. Absent emergency conditions, remediation work mandated under § 106 generally must comply with both the NCP and the § 121 cleanup standards.

## E. ENFORCEMENT BY INJUNCTION

An action seeking injunctive relief under § 106(a) is governed by the general liability standards discussed above. But if liability is established, who selects the cleanup plan—EPA or the court? The issue arises because § 106(a) contains language which is distinctly different from other CERCLA sections, yet familiar as a general equitable standard. Where liability is found, this section authorizes the district court to "grant such relief as the public interest and the equities of the case may require." Conversely, § 121 seems to circumscribe the court's traditional equitable powers in the context of CERCLA cleanups. It states that "[t]he President" (and thus his delegate, EPA) "shall select appropriate remedial actions" under § 106 which are "in accordance" with: (1) the cleanup standards set forth later in § 121; and (2) "to the extent practicable, the national contingency plan."

Courts are sharply split on the issue. For example, in United States v. Ottati & Goss, Inc., 900 F.2d 429 (1st Cir.1990), Justice Breyer (then on the First Circuit) reasoned that this language vested the remedy selection power in the district court judge, as in any injunctive proceeding; thus, the court was not "legally required to accept EPA's views about remedy." Rather, he reasoned that a court was free to design equitable relief on a case-by-case basis under traditional principles. The opposing view is represented by the Sixth Circuit's opinion in United States v. Akzo Coatings of America, Inc., 949 F.2d 1409 (6th Cir.1991); that court held that the "arbitrary and capricious" standard of review in § 113(j) applied to EPA's proposed remedy. It found congressional intent that "in this highly technical area, decisions concerning the selection of remedies should be left to EPA, and those decisions should be accepted or rejected—not modified—by the district court under an arbitrary and capricious standard." Given the uncertain state of the law on this point, EPA has increasingly shifted its § 106(a) focus from judicial abatement to administrative orders.

EPA's § 106(a) litigation power is now chiefly used in two special settings. First, in the event of a true emergency, it can be utilized to obtain immediate injunctive relief such as a temporary restraining order or preliminary injunction. Second, § 106(a) litigation facilitates settlement; it provides an enforcement vehicle for consent decrees entered into between the federal government and settling parties, as set forth in § 122(d)(1)(A). See Chapter 9.

# CHAPTER 11

# CERCLA: ACTIONS BROUGHT BY PRIVATE PARTIES

The four previous chapters have introduced the CERCLA cleanup process and the elements of liability for the cost of such cleanups. Those chapters focused on the *federal government's* ability to order responsible parties either to clean up a site or to reimburse the costs of a publicly led cleanup. This chapter examines two ways in which *private* parties may themselves bring legal actions under CERCLA. First, it discusses the ability of parties who have incurred response costs or CERCLA liability to shift some or all of these costs to other parties. In particular, it examines: (1) private actions to recover response costs under CERCLA § 107(a); and (2) contribution actions under § 113. Second, the chapter sketches the elements of a CERCLA citizens' suit under § 310, focusing on the limited circumstances where citizens can sue to challenge cleanup decisions made for a particular site.

## A. PRIVATE ACTIONS UNDER § 107 TO RECOVER RESPONSE COSTS

### 1. INTRODUCTION

#### a. Typical Circumstances

As a result of the CERCLA cleanup provisions described in the preceding chapters, a private party may have incurred response costs in three ways.

First, she may have complied with an administrative or judicial cleanup order (or consent decree) issued under § 106. Second, she may have been forced to reimburse the costs of a government led cleanup after the government has brought a cost recovery action under § 107(a)(4)(A). Third, she may have voluntarily cleaned up a site.

Under CERCLA's broad liability provisions, multiple persons are often potentially responsible for a site's cleanup. In many situations, however, only a handful of the potentially responsible parties may have initially incurred response costs. This situation occurs most commonly where a single potentially responsible party—such as the site's current owner—has voluntarily expended funds in cleaning up a site contaminated by someone else (e.g., a lessee or a prior owner). It may also result from the government's decision to proceed under §§ 106 or 107 against only those responsible parties who are the deepest pockets, the most culpable, or the easiest to join. Finally, it can result when some responsible parties sued in a governmental action filed under § 107 settle their liability with the government, while others have neither settled nor had their liability adjudicated.

In most cases where multiple parties are potentially responsible for a site's cleanup, but only some have actually funded that process, the parties who have incurred response costs or have been adjudged liable for those costs will attempt to shift some or all of those costs to other PRPs. CERCLA provides two ways to attempt such a shift. First,

§ 107(a)(4)(B) makes a responsible party liable for "any * * * necessary costs of response incurred by any * * * person [other than a federal or state agency, or an Indian tribe] consistent with the national contingency plan." Second, CERCLA provides two bases for contribution: (1) § 113(f)(1) allows "any person" to "seek contribution from any other person who is liable or potentially liable under [§ 107(a)] during or following a civil action under [§§ 106 or 107(a)]" and (2) § 113(f)(3)(B) authorizes a contribution action by a person who enters into an administratively or judicially approved settlement with the government.

### b. Comparison of Private Cost Recovery and Contribution Actions

The specific elements of a private cost recovery action under § 107 and a contribution action under § 113 are described in more detail below. For the most part, the distinctions between the two are rather inconsequential. Thus, in both cases, liability depends upon: (1) plaintiff's proof that the defendant is a responsible party under the CERCLA liability schemes; (2) plaintiff's proof that there was a release or threat of a release of a CERCLA regulated hazardous substance from a facility that caused the incurrence of response costs, and (3) the defendant's inability to establish any of the statutory defenses.

For three reasons, however, it is important to distinguish whether the plaintiff is proceeding under § 107 or under § 113. First, and most importantly, is the question of whether the plaintiff has the right to sue, as discussed in more detail below. After the Supreme Court decision in Cooper Industries, Inc. v. Aviall Services, Inc., 543 U.S. 157, 125 S.Ct. 577, 160 L.Ed.2d 548 (2004), it is clear that a party who has not been sued under § 106 or § 107 cannot bring a § 113(f) action for contribution. Thus, for example, a PRP who voluntarily cleans up a contaminated site without being sued by, or settling with, the government, cannot seek contribution. However, such a PRP may instead sue to recover its cleanup costs through a cost recovery action under § 107. See United States v. Atlantic Research Corp., 551 U.S. 128, 127 S.Ct. 2331, 168 L.Ed.2d 28 (2007).

The second reason involves the extent of joint liability. Under § 107, liability is joint and several. Thus, the burden is on the defendants in such an action to prove that the injury is divisible; otherwise, each defendant is potentially on the hook for the entire cleanup cost. Given this joint and several liability, in theory, in an action brought under § 107, a plaintiff could shift *all* of its response costs to the defendant(s). In practice, however, the availability of counterclaims for contribution make it unlikely that any but a handful of innocent plaintiffs will be able to use § 107 to shift *all* their response costs to the defendants. In contrast, liability under § 113 is several. Thus, in such actions, the plaintiff must establish each defendant's pro rata share of the cleanup. See, e.g., United States v. Taylor, 909 F.Supp. 355, 364 (M.D.N.C.1995). As a result, the plaintiff may only shift that portion of its response costs that exceed its own pro rata share, and then only to a particular defendant in the amount of that defendant's pro rata share.

The final key basis for distinguishing between the two cost shifting actions involves the applicable defenses. In particular, the limitations period differs substantially. Private actions under § 107 have as long as a six year limitations period. § 113(g)(2)(B). In contrast, contribution actions under § 113 have only a three year period. § 113(g)(3). Moreover, courts are more willing to consider equitable defenses, such as laches or unclean hands, in the context of a contribution action; in contrast, the courts have largely rejected "nonstatutory," common law defenses in cost recovery actions under § 107.

### c. Who Can Bring a § 107 Cost Recovery Action?

As initially enacted, CERCLA did not contain an express provision authorizing a PRP to obtain contribution from other PRPs. Thus, for example, if EPA cleaned up a contaminated site at a cost of $10 million, and then sued A (the past owner at time of disposal) to recover its costs, a question logically arose: could A force other PRPs to share part of this cost? Early CERCLA decisions plugged this gap by holding that a PRP such as A could bring a private cost recovery action against other PRPs, pursuant to § 107(a)(4)(B).

With the passage of SARA in 1986, Congress created an express right of contribution in § 113. As a result, courts had to determine the relationship between (a) the § 107 cost recovery action and (b) the § 113 contribution action. The difference was important because responsible parties trying to shift response costs inevitably preferred to sue under 107, which offers more generous liability provisions with stingier defenses.

For many years, courts held that a PRP could only bring a contribution action under § 113. When private parties relied on § 107 or § 113, in the alternative, courts directed cases involving plaintiffs who were also PRPs to section § 113(f). The rationale for this view was straightforward: allowing a PRP to sue under § 107 is inconsistent with the intent of Congress that § 113 be the PRP's sole remedy. In *Cooper Industries,* the Supreme Court touched on the issue, but refused to decide whether a PRP was eligible to sue under § 107. It observed that: "The cost recovery remedy of § 107(a)(4)(B) and the contribution remedy of § 113(f)(1) are similar at a general level in that they both allow private parties to recoup costs from other private parties. But the two remedies are clearly distinct."

However, in 2007 the Court confirmed that the express terms of § 107(a)(4)(B) allow a PRP to recover costs from another PRP in United States v. Atlantic Research Corp., 551 U.S. 128, 127 S.Ct. 1331, 163 L.Ed.2d 28 (2007). It explained that the provisions of § 107 and § 113 are complementary yet distinct remedies. Incurring one's own costs provides a cost-recovery action under § 107(a).

Reimbursing costs incurred by others, by paying to satisfy a court judgment or settlement, provides a right to contribution under § 113(f).

Recognizing a cost-recovery action under § 107(a) for any PRP who has voluntarily remediated prior to any civil action does justice to the language of § 113(f), but raises additional questions. The Court emphasized that:

> A private party may recover under § 107(a) without any establishment of liability to a third party. Moreover, § 107(a) permits a PRP to recover only the costs it has "incurred" in cleaning up a site, 42 U.S.C.A. § 9607(a)(4)(B). When a party pays to satisfy a settlement agreement or a court judgment, it does not incur its own costs of response. Rather, it reimburses other parties for costs that those parties incurred. Id. at 139.

Two key questions arise in the wake of *Atlantic Research*. First, can a PRP seek § 107(a) cost-recovery following a consent judgment? The Court did not answer the question, merely noting: "We do not decide whether these compelled costs of response are recoverable under § 113(f), § 107(a), or both." Id. at n. 6. The prevailing view is "no," and the PRP has a remedy under § 113(f).

Second, can a party to a Unilateral Administrative Order (UAO) use § 107(a) to recover response costs or does the order qualify as a "civil action" under § 106 or § 107, providing for a 113(f) contribution action? Lower courts are split. The basic issue is that CERCLA has provides distinct remedies for parties in different procedural settings. If PRPs have access to a contribution action offered by § 113(f), the courts that have addressed the issue have found that they must use it. See, e.g., Hobart Corp. v. Waste Mgmt., Inc., 758 F.3d 757 (6th Cir. 2014) (contribution was exclusive remedy following "administrative settlement" for purposes of § 113(f)(3)(B)); Morrison Enterprises, LLC v. Dravo Corp., 638 F.3d 594, 603 (contribution was exclusive remedy for PRP who had been compelled to incur response costs by administrative or judicially approved settlement under § 106 or § 107).

Once again, courts are directing traffic between these two sections, funneling PRPs to § 113(f). It is notable that § 107(a) provides the PRP who voluntarily cleans up with a longer statute of limitations than otherwise provided under section 113(f). Perhaps more significant is the impact on contribution protection provisions, explained in Section 4. Defenses, below. In some circumstances settlement with the government provides protection against *contribution,* but these provisions are inapplicable to cost-recovery actions pursuant to § 107(a), a circumstance recognized by the *Atlantic Research* Court.

Nor did the *Atlantic Research* court confirm or deny the existence of an implied right of contribution pursuant to § 107(a). This issue remains unresolved, although many factual scenarios where a plaintiff may have sought to use an implied right under § 107(a) have been addressed by the *Atlantic Research* holding that allows cost-recovery for voluntary cleanups.

## 2. BASIC ELEMENTS

A private party will only be able to recover under § 107 if the basic elements of CERCLA liability have been met. Thus, as described in Chapters 7 through 10: (1) there must have been a release or threat of a release of a CERCLA regulated hazardous substance from a facility that caused the incurrence of response costs by plaintiff; and (2) the defendant must be a PRP. In addition, the defendant must be unable to fit within any of the statutory defenses to CERCLA liability. If these circumstances are met, for the class of "persons" specified, § 107(a)(4)(B) authorizes recovery of the "necessary costs of response" incurred that are "consistent with the national contingency plan."

### a. "Any * * * Person"

On its face, § 107(a)(4)(B) does not create an express cause of action for recovery of response costs. It simply makes a responsible party liable for the specified costs incurred by "any other person [i.e., other than the persons specified in § 107(a)(4)(A)]." The courts have concluded, however, that these "persons" have an implied right of action under § 107(a)(4)(B). See, e.g., Key Tronic Corp. v. United States, 511 U.S. 809, 114 S.Ct. 1960, 128 L.Ed.2d 797 (1994).

CERCLA § 101(21) defines "person" broadly to include individuals, business organizations, and governmental entities. As described in the prior chapters, § 107(a)(4)(A) provides a cost recovery action for three governmental entities: the United States, states, and Indian tribes. Thus, a party eligible to bring a private cost recovery claim under § 107(a)(4)(B) is anyone within the § 101 definition of "person" *other than* the three governmental "persons" mentioned in § 107(a)(4)(A).

### b. "Necessary Costs of Response"

Section 107(a)(4)(B) authorizes recovery of "necessary" response costs. In theory, the "necessity" of the response costs is a separate element from the "consistency" of the response with the National Contingency Plan. See, e.g., Ambrogi v. Gould, Inc., 750 F.Supp. 1233 (M.D.Pa.1990). In practice, there is a good degree of overlap between the two.

In general, "necessary" means that a threat to human health or the environment required the plaintiff to incur expenses to address that threat. See, e.g., Regional Airport Authority v. LFG, 460 F.3d 697 (6th Cir.2006) (finding that plaintiff did not meet this standard for cleanup of airport runway). Ordinarily, the plaintiff must plead at least one type of recoverable cost as part of its prima facie case under § 107. Ascon Properties, Inc. v. Mobil Oil Co., 866 F.2d 1149 (9th Cir.1989) (finding sufficient an allegation of "cleanup costs" and costs incurred in developing and submitting a remedial action plan). The particular costs recoverable are addressed more fully below, in the discussion of "remedies" under § 107.

### c. "Consistent with the National Contingency Plan"

Chapter 8 described the "national contingency plan" (NCP). Separate portions of that plan address the procedures required in "removal" and "remedial" actions. Chapter 9 noted the requirement that a public entity, seeking cost reimbursement under § 107(a)(4)(A), could only recover costs that were "not inconsistent with" the NCP. Similarly, a private party seeking cost recovery under § 107(a)(4)(B) must establish that its incurred costs were "consistent with" the NCP. In either event, "consistency" is determined under the version of the NCP in effect at the time the plaintiff incurred the response costs. Louisiana-Pacific Corp. v. ASARCO, Inc., 24 F.3d 1565, 1576 n. 3 (9th Cir.1994). Consistency will be determined under the portions of the NCP applicable to the particular type of response taken. Thus, a court will have to characterize the plaintiff's response as either a "removal" or a "remedial" action. See, e.g., Sherwin-Williams Co. v. City of Hamtramck, 840 F.Supp. 470, 475 (E.D. Mich. 1993).

The difference in wording between the public and private cost recovery provisions has led courts to agree that the elements of the plaintiff's prima facie case are different in the two proceedings. As noted in the preceding chapters, the *defendant* in a government led cost recovery action under § 107 bears the burden of establishing that the government's costs were *"not consistent with"* the NCP. In contrast, private *plaintiffs* seeking cost recovery from other potentially responsible parties must establish, as an element of their prima facie case, that their incurred costs were *"consistent with"* the NCP. See, e.g., County Line Investment Company v. Tinney, 933 F.2d 1508, 1514 (10th Cir.1991).

The safer approach may be for the plaintiff to plead such consistency as part of its complaint. But at least some courts only require *proof* of consistency with the NCP, and will not strike a claim for failure to *plead* consistency. Metal Processing Company, Inc. v. Amoco Oil Co., 926 F.Supp. 828, 831 (E.D.Wis.1996). In making that proof, the plaintiff does not have to show that the federal EPA specifically approved the plaintiff's activities. Wickland Oil Terminals v. Asarco, Inc., 792 F.2d 887, 892 (9th Cir.1986).

Ordinarily, failure to comply with the NCP bars any recovery under a cost recovery action. County Line Investment Company v. Tinney, 933 F.2d 1508 (10th Cir.1991). Courts may, however, allow recovery for the initial investigation and monitoring costs, even if the resulting cleanup was not consistent with the NCP. See, e.g., A.S.I., Inc. v. Sanders, 1996 WL 91626, at *6–7 (D.Kan. Feb. 9, 1996); but see Board of County Comm'rs of County of La Plata, Colorado v. Brown Group Retail, Inc., 768 F.Supp.2d 1092, 1115 (D. Colo. 2011) (NCP consistency a prerequisite to recovering investigatory costs). Moreover, courts will likely only insist upon "substantial compliance." See, e.g.,

Sherwin-Williams Co. v. City of Hamtramck, 840 F.Supp. 470, 475 (E.D. Mich. 1993).

"Consistency" with the NCP is ordinarily a question of fact. New York v. Exxon Corp., 633 F.Supp. 609 (S.D.N.Y.1986). Under that standard, a trial court's determination will be upheld unless clearly erroneous. Some courts, however, label "consistency" a "mixed question" of law and fact. Louisiana-Pacific Corp. v. ASARCO Inc. 24 F.3d 1565 (9th Cir.1994). Under that standard, the appellate court will review the overall determination de novo, but the factual underpinning of the decision will be upheld unless clearly erroneous.

## 3. REMEDIES

### a. "Necessary Response Costs"

#### *i. Recovery Allowed*

The courts have approved reimbursement of a wide variety of response costs. While there is not universal agreement on all examples of reimbursable costs, courts have generally allowed claimants to recover the costs incurred in:

- determining if a CERCLA regulated substance was involved in a release (Allied Towing Corp. v. Great Eastern Petroleum Corp., 642 F.Supp. 1339 (E.D.Va.1986));
- preparing a response (New York v. Exxon Corp., 633 F.Supp. 609 (S.D.N.Y.1986));

- finding other PRPs, even where the investigation was done by an attorney for the claimant (Key Tronic Corp. v. United States, 511 U.S. 809, 114 S.Ct. 1960, 1967, 128 L.Ed.2d 797 (1994));
- destroying or removing personal property, although not the *loss of value* of the property (Wehner v. Syntex Corp., 681 F.Supp. 651 (N.D.Cal.1987));
- closing a facility (International Clinical Laboratories, Inc. v. Stevens, 710 F.Supp. 466 (E.D.N.Y.1989));
- securing a facility during cleanup (Amoco Oil Co. v. Borden, Inc., 889 F.2d 664 (5th Cir.1989), contra Woodman v. United States, 764 F.Supp. 1467 (M.D.Fla.1991));
- and relocating a business (Tanglewood East Homeowners v. Charles-Thomas, Inc., 849 F.2d 1568 (5th Cir.1988), contra T & E Industries, Inc. v. Safety Light Corp., 680 F.Supp. 696 (D.N.J.1988)).

### *ii. Recovery Disallowed*

In addition to the specific "contra" authority qualifying the holdings listed in the prior paragraph, courts have generally disallowed recovery of:

- economic losses, lost income or profits, property damage (Ambrogi v. Gould, Inc., 750 F.Supp. 1233 (M.D.Pa.1990));

- medical monitoring, transportation, loss of beneficial use of property (Ambrogi v. Gould, Inc., 750 F.Supp. 1233 (M.D.Pa.1990), contra Williams v. Allied Automotive, 704 F.Supp. 782 (N.D.Ohio 1988));
- provision of an alternative water supply (Werlein v. United States, 746 F.Supp. 887 (D.Minn.1990), contra Lutz v. Chromatex, Inc., 718 F.Supp. 413 (M.D.Pa.1989));
- and punitive damages (Regan v. Cherry Corp., 706 F.Supp. 145 (D.R.I.1989)).

Recovery of attorneys' fees as § 107(a) "response costs" was addressed by the Supreme Court in the *Key Tronic* case. In that case, the court ruled that attorneys' fees incurred in prosecuting a § 107 action are not themselves a "necessary cost of response." Key Tronic v. United States, 511 U.S. 809, 114 S.Ct. 1960, 128 L.Ed.2d 797 (1994). Similarly, the court held that the fees incurred in prior settlement negotiations between the PRP plaintiff and EPA were not recoverable. The court specifically rejected a claim that such fees should be recoverable where they helped EPA shape the ultimate decree. The court, however, did allow recovery of fees incurred by an attorney's efforts to track down other PRPs. By tracking down other solvent polluters, the PRP had "increase[d] the probability that a cleanup will be effective and get paid for." Thus, the court reasoned, reimbursement of these fees "served a statutory purpose apart from the reallocation of costs."

### b. Equitable and Declaratory Relief

Section 107 does not authorize a court to award injunctive relief. Thus, in a § 107 private cost recovery action, a court will not order another PRP to clean up a site. Cadillac Fairview/California v. Dow Chemical, 840 F.2d 691 (9th Cir.1988). In contrast, courts routinely grant declaratory relief. Thus, a § 107 plaintiff *can* get a declaration that establishes the respective parties' obligations to fund future cleanup efforts. Ambrogi v. Gould, Inc., 750 F.Supp. 1233, 1243 n. 14 (M.D.Pa.1990).

## 4. DEFENSES

### a. Statutory Defenses

As noted above, the defendant in a private cost recovery action may avoid liability entirely by establishing one of the limited statutory defenses described in Chapter 9. Beyond those defenses, the only additional statutory defense is the limitations period. That period's length depends upon the type of cleanup activities involved. For "removal" actions, the cost recovery action must be filed within three years after "completion." If a "continued response action" is involved, plaintiff has six years from the date that a waiver was granted under § 104(c)(1)(C). § 113(g)(2)(A). For a "remedial" action, the plaintiff must file its cost recovery action within six years of the *initiation* of on-site construction. § 113(g)(2)(B); see also Schaefer v. Town of Victor, 457 F.3d 188 (2d Cir.2006) (holding plaintiff failed to comply with statute of limitations). Where a remedial action follows within three years of the completion of a removal action, the plaintiff may also recover the earlier incurred removal costs within a timely filed action to recover the remedial action costs.

### b. Non-Statutory Defenses

Beyond these statutory defenses, courts have showed little willingness to create common law, "non-statutory" defenses. For example, the courts have rejected claims that the plaintiff may not recover unless the site is placed on the National Priorities List. New York v. General Elect. Co., 592 F.Supp. 291 (N.D.N.Y.1984). Similarly, while the court in a *contribution* action may consider traditional equitable defenses such as caveat emptor, estoppel laches, or unclean hands in apportioning responsibility, the courts will not consider those defenses in an action to establish a defendant's liability as a responsible party. Westfarm Associates L.P. v. International Fabricare Inst., 846 F.Supp. 422 (D.Md.1993).

The only other way that a defendant might avoid CERCLA liability is by assertion of a valid indemnity agreement, as discussed in Chapter 14. Some courts have allowed an indemnity agreement to shift CERCLA liability. See, e.g., Olin Corp. v. Consolidated Aluminum Corp., 5 F.3d 10 (2d Cir.1993). Others, however, refuse to allow a PRP to invoke an indemnity agreement to shield itself from liability to another PRP. See, e.g., Harley-Davidson, Inc. v. Minstar, Inc., 837 F.Supp. 978 (E.D.Wis.1993).

### c. Constitutional Defenses

In limited circumstances, the federal constitution may provide a defense to CERCLA actions. In particular, where a state has not consented to suit in federal court under CERCLA, the Eleventh Amendment may bar its participation. See, e.g., Thomas v. FAG Bearings Corp., 50 F.3d 502 (8th Cir.1995). However, the Eleventh Circuit rejected a claim that extension of CERCLA liability to clean up an aquifer was barred under the Commerce Clause. United States v. Olin, 107 F.3d 1506 (11th Cir.1997). To date, challenges to CERCLA liability under the Tenth Amendment have been unsuccessful.

## B. ACTION FOR CONTRIBUTION UNDER § 113

### 1. INTRODUCTION

A party who has incurred response costs or has been adjudicated liable for such costs may attempt to shift such costs to other responsible parties through a claim for contribution. As noted above, SARA created an express right to contribution, governed by federal law. Under § 113(f)(1), "any person may seek contribution from any other person who is liable or potentially liable under § 107(a) during or following any civil action under § 106 or 107(a) ." It further provides, "[n]othing in this section shall diminish the right of any person to bring an action for contribution in the absence of a civil action under § 106 or § 107." Further,

§ 113(f)(3)(B) provides a similar contribution right for a PRP who has settled with the government through "an administratively or judicially approved settlement."

### a. Contribution and Actions Under §§ 107 and 106

Contribution claims normally arise in the context of pending or completed litigation. For example, if the federal government sues site owner A under § 107 to recover its response costs, A may seek contribution from other PRPs, either in that case or after its completion. Similarly, if the government brings an action against A under § 106 based on an imminent and substantial endangerment to the public health, welfare, or environment, A has the same contribution rights.

But what happens if a PRP like A cleans up the contaminated site *voluntarily* and then brings a suit for contribution under § 113? In Cooper Industries, Inc. v. Aviall Services, Inc., 543 U.S. 157, 125 S.Ct. 577, 160 L.Ed.2d 548 (2004), the Supreme Court held that contribution was not available in this situation, based on the plain language of the section. Because § 113(f)(1) states that a person "may seek contribution* * *during or following any civil action [under §§ 107 or 106]," the Court reasoned that "contribution may only be sought subject to the specified conditions, namely, 'during or following' a specified civil action." As a practical matter, this holding discouraged current owners and operators from voluntarily cleaning up contaminated sites. As previously discussed, the Supreme Court confirmed in *Atlantic Research* that a PRP who voluntarily cleans up a contaminated site has a cost-recovery action under § 107(a).

### b. Contribution and § 106 Orders

As discussed in Chapter 10, EPA has the power to issue an administrative order under § 106 that compels a PRP to clean up a contaminated site. The PRP's right to contribution under these circumstances, however, is unclear.

#### *i. Existence of Remedy*

In the light of *Cooper Industries*, which provides that a PRP may obtain § 113(f)(1) contribution only "during or following" a civil action, it seems likely that the PRP who merely complies with a § 106 administrative order does not have a right to contribution. Alternatively, such a PRP might have an action for cost-recovery under § 107(a). To date, however, whether the PRP who has voluntarily complied with a UAO may proceed against other PRPs under § 107(a) or § 113(f) is an unresolved issue.

In PCS Nitrogen, Inc. v. Ross Development Corp., 104 F.Supp.3d 729, 741 (D.S.C. 2015), the court ruled that the UAO constituted a "civil action" for purposes of § 113(f)(1) . However, it reasoned that the UAO did not resolve liability, thus foreclosing the availability of a § 113(f)(3)(b) contribution claim. See also Carrier Corp. v. Piper, 460 F.Supp.2d 827, 840–41 (W.D. Tenn. 2006) (reasoning that UAO put similar burden on a party as a civil action, and thus was trigger for § 113(f) contribution rights). Other district courts have rejected this interpretation of UAOs. See, e.g., Raytheon Aircraft Co. v. United States, 435 F.Supp.2d 1136, 1142–43 (D.Kan. 2006) (UAO was not a "civil action" for purposes of § 113(f)(1) ); Emhart Industries, Inc. v. New England Container Co., Inc., 478 F.Supp.2d 199 (D.R.I. 2007) (administrative order was not a "civil action," but in the alternative plaintiff had an implied right of contribution under § 107(a)).

An alternative protection for the PRP served with a § 106 order may be to enter into a consent decree with EPA, and then seek contribution from other PRPs under § 113(f)(3)(B). EPA revised its § 106 terminology in 2005, in response to *Cooper Industries*, from UAO to "Administrative Settlement Agreement and Order on Consent" to support the use of these agreements to create a right of contribution under § 113(f)(3)(B) and protection against contribution actions by other PRPs.

### *ii. Elements of Claim*

Assuming a right to contribution exists, the elements of an action following a § 106 order are also unclear. The main issue involves the contribution defendant's ability to contest the reasonableness of the cleanup. At least two main options exist. First, the courts could simply take the contribution claimant's documented costs at face value, and allocate them under their equitable discretion. Alternatively, the courts could allow the defendants to contest the reasonableness of the response costs. This, in turn, could occur in two ways. First, the courts could make the contribution plaintiff bear a burden of establishing such reasonableness, much like the burden imposed in private cost recovery actions under § 107(a)(4)(B). Second, the courts could make the defendants establish the *unreasonableness* of the costs, much like they must do in government led cost recovery actions under § 107(a)(4)(A).

Ultimately, the courts must accommodate two conflicting policies: encouragement of prompt cleanup and fairness to the defendants. Forcing the contribution plaintiff to bear the burden of establishing the reasonableness of EPA's order seems unduly harsh. Thus, the better approach should be to put the same burden of establishing *unreasonableness* in the contribution context as is placed in the cleanup order process itself, i.e., upon the *challenger*. Such a rule would encourage prompt cleanup, and provide some element of fairness to contribution defendants.

## 2. PROCEDURAL OPTIONS FOR RAISING CONTRIBUTION CLAIMS

There are five different ways that a contribution claim can be raised. Of course, it can support its own lawsuit, under the circumstances set forth above. It can also be raised within a previously filed lawsuit as:

- a third party claim (United States v. R.W. Meyer, Inc., 932 F.2d 568 (6th Cir.1991));
- a cross-claim (United States v. Cannons Engineering Corp., 899 F.2d 79 (1st Cir.1990));
- a counterclaim (Pneumo Abex Corp. v. Bessemer & Lake Erie R.R. Co., 921 F.Supp. 336 (E.D.Va.1996)); or
- a claim in intervention (i.e., to protect contribution rights from being extinguished by a settlement of a government brought § 107 cost recovery action, non-settling persons have attempted to intervene. See Fed.R.Civ.P. 24).

The intervention claims have received the most judicial attention, and demonstrate the most judicial disagreement. Courts are split as to whether a non-settling person may intervene "as of right" in a § 107 action. Compare Arizona v. Motorola, Inc., 139 F.R.D. 141, 146–47 (D.Ariz.1991) (intervention as of right denied) with United States v. Union Electric Co. 64 F.3d 1152, 1170 (8th Cir.1995) (intervention as of right permitted) and United States v. Aerojet General Corp., 606 F.3d 1142, 1153 (9th Cir. 2010) (same). Most courts have denied permissive intervention. E.g., United States v. ABC Industries, 153 F.R.D. 603, 606 (W.D.Mich.1993).

## 3. ELEMENTS

### a. Basic Requirements

To establish its right to contribution, a party must establish the basic elements of liability under CERCLA. Thus, as described in Chapters 7 through 9: (1) there must have been a release or threat of a release of a CERCLA regulated hazardous substance from a facility that caused the incurrence of response costs; and (2) the defendant must be a potentially responsible party. In addition, contribution will not be allowed if the defendant can establish any of the statutory defenses to CERCLA liability. Unlike a cost recovery action under § 107, liability in a § 113 contribution action is several. Thus, if a contribution defendant is found severally liable, the burden is on the contribution claimant to prove the defendant's share of the damages. United States v. J.M. Taylor, 909 F.Supp. 355 (M.D.N.C.1995). Once a party is determined to be a responsible party, it is liable for its share, as determined by § 113(f), of any and all response costs, not just those caused by its release. Control Data Corp. v. S.C.S.C. Corp., 53 F.3d 930 (8th Cir.1995).

### b. "Necessity" and "Consistency"

In theory, a party opposing a contribution claim should have the same opportunity to dispute the reasonableness of the costs incurred as a defendant in a § 107 cost recovery action itself would have. Thus, in a cost recovery action brought under

§ 107(a)(4)(A) by the federal government, a state, or an Indian tribe, a defendant has the opportunity to show that the expenses were either not "costs of removal or remedial action," or were "not consistent with the national contingency plan." Alternatively, in a cost recovery action brought under § 107(a)(4)(B) by "any other person," the defendant can show that the expenses incurred were either "unnecessary" or were "inconsistent with the national contingency plan." Similarly, a party defending a contribution claim should be able to raise the same arguments. Thus, for example, one appellate court has stated that inconsistency with the NCP may well bar recovery in a contribution proceeding. County Line Investment Co. v. Tinney, 933 F.2d 1508 (10th Cir.1991).

In practice, the extent of a contribution defendant's ability to "relitigate" these issues will depend upon the procedural posture in which the claim arises. Thus, if the contribution claim is raised as part of an underlying action under § 107, then, under "law of the case" or "issue preclusion," the underlying action's determination of "necessity" and "consistency" will ordinarily be binding when the court moves on to resolve the contribution claims. If, however, the contribution claim is raised against persons who were not parties to a prior action under § 107, then, unless the rules of "issue preclusion" dictate otherwise, the contribution defendant should be able to challenge the basis for the original determination of response costs. An administrative cleanup order, a court injunction or a negotiated consent decree—the contribution defendant should also be able to challenge the basis for the original determination of response costs.

## 4. DEFENSES

### a. Statutory Defenses

As with private cost recovery actions under § 107, a contribution defendant can attempt to establish the narrow statutory defenses to CERCLA liability. Beyond those, only two other affirmative defenses apply: (1) the three year limitations period; and (2) the contribution protection provisions.

Under § 113(g)(3), a party has three years to seek contribution. That period is calculated from one of two separate starting points: (1) the date of a judgment in a cost recovery action; or (2) the date of any administrative or judicial order approving a settlement of a cost recovery action.

Under § 113(f)(2), "[a] person who has resolved its liability to the United States or a State in an administrative or judicially approved settlement shall not be liable for claims for contribution regarding the matters addressed in the settlement." Section 122(g)(5) offers similar protection to parties to "de minimis" settlements. Settling parties may still seek contribution from nonsettling parties. See, e.g., United States v. Cannons Engineering Corp., 899 F.2d 79 (1st Cir.1990). Nonsettlors, however, may not seek contribution from settlors.

To encourage CERCLA settlements, some courts have refused to give a narrow reading to the statutory contribution protection. Thus, the First Circuit ruled that settlement also bars claims for indemnification against settlors. United States v. Cannons Engineering Corp., 899 F.2d 79 (1st Cir.1990). A district court concluded that a responsible party's settlement with EPA barred cross-claims for contribution against that party even though the cross-claimants had styled their cross-claims as "cost recovery" actions under § 107. United States v. ASARCO, Inc., 814 F.Supp. 951 (D.Colo.1993). Finally, at least one district court has also extended contribution protection to settlements solely between *private* parties, i.e, ones involving neither the United States nor a state. United States v. SCA Services, 827 F.Supp. 526 (N.D.Ind.1993).

The particular extent of the contribution bar depends upon the specific subject of the settlement. Courts will broadly construe the scope of the matters addressed in the settlement to encourage settlement and finalize liability. United States v. Colorado & Eastern R.R. Co., 50 F.3d 1530 (10th Cir.1995). Nevertheless, under the terms of some agreements, some non-settling defendants may still be able to seek partial contribution against settling defendants. Thus, one district court refused to dismiss such a claim where the settlement covered only liability for the costs of EPA's initial site work. Transtech Industries, Inc. v. A & Z Septic Clean, 798 F.Supp. 1079 (D.N.J.1992).

The effect of settlements on the allocation of liability is addressed below, in the discussion of apportionment.

## b. Equitable Defenses

As in private response cost actions under § 107, courts have generally been unwilling to recognize nonstatutory, equitable defenses as complete bars to recovery. For example, courts have rejected "unclean hands" as a complete defense. They acknowledge that since plaintiffs will frequently bear substantial responsibility for the contamination, recognition of the defense would make contribution largely unavailable. See, e.g., United States v. R.W. Meyer, Inc., 932 F.2d 568 (6th Cir.1991). Nevertheless, unlike § 107 actions, in contribution claims, courts *will* consider traditional equitable defenses such as caveat emptor, estoppel, laches and unclean hands, as *factors* in the apportionment of liability. See, e.g., Western Properties Service Corp. v. Shell Oil Co., 358 F.3d 678 (9th Cir.2004) (laches). These matters are considered below, in the discussion of "apportionment."

## c. Constitutional Defenses

As described above in the discussion of defenses to private cost recovery actions, in very limited circumstances the federal constitution may provide a defense. By implication, such Eleventh Amendment or Commerce Clause defenses might also apply in a contribution action.

## 5. APPORTIONMENT

### a. General Provisions

Section 113(f)(1) grants the courts broad discretion to apportion responsibility among responsible parties. It states: "In resolving contribution claims, the court may allocate response costs among liable parties using such equitable factors as the court determines are appropriate."

As a convenient grouping of such equitable criteria, courts frequently cite what are known as the "Gore" factors. These are named after then-Representative Albert Gore, Jr., who introduced them during the legislative discussion leading up to the adoption of CERCLA. These factors are:

- "the ability of the parties to demonstrate that their contribution to a discharge release or disposal of a hazardous waste can be distinguished;"

- "the amount of the hazardous waste involved;"

- "the degree of toxicity of the hazardous waste involved;"

- "the degree of involvement by the parties in the generation, transportation, treatment, storage, or disposal of the hazardous waste;"

- "the degree of care exercised by the parties with respect to the hazardous waste concerned, taking into account the characteristics of such hazardous waste;"

- "and the degree of cooperation by the parties with Federal, State, or local officials to prevent any harm to the public health or the environment."

United States v. A & F Materials Co., Inc., 578 F.Supp. 1249, 1256 (S.D.Ill.1984).

These factors, however, do not exhaust the possibilities. As the Sixth Circuit stated in one oft cited case,

> the court may consider any factor it deems in the interest of justice in allocating contribution recovery. * * * No exhaustive list of criteria need or should be formulated. However, in addition to the [Gore factors] the court may consider the state of mind of the parties, their economic status, any contracts between them bearing on the subject, any traditional equitable defenses as mitigating factors and any other factors deemed appropriate to balance the equities in the totality of the circumstances.

United States v. R.W. Meyer, Inc., 932 F.2d 568 (6th Cir.1991). That court also approved an apportionment decision based not only on the defendant site owner's *physical* contribution to the contamination "but also its moral contribution as the owner of the site."

Regardless of the particular factors used by the trial court, appellate courts will reverse only for "abuse of discretion." United States v. R.W. Meyer, Inc., 932 F.2d 568 (6th Cir.1991).

### b. Voluntary Apportionment

Although the courts thus have broad discretion in considering a variety of factors when allocating CERCLA responsibility in a contribution proceeding, many contribution claims never test that discretion. Like most other suits, contribution claims are usually settled by the parties themselves. In many such settlements, the principal factor used to allocate responsibility is a party's volumetric share of the waste contributed to the site.

### c. Allocation of Orphan Shares

In many of the cases where the courts are asked to exercise their discretion, some responsible parties will be insolvent, deceased, dissolved, or beyond joinder. Such circumstances force the courts to address allocation of the absent or insolvent parties' pro rata shares among the solvent parties to the contribution action. These shares are generally called "orphan" shares.

Two different approaches to this problem are possible. First, under the traditional rule, contribution defendants are liable only for their own share. Thus, the party seeking contribution bears the risk of loss if it fails to join all tortfeasors, or if a tortfeasor is insolvent. Restatement (Second) of Torts, § 886A. Second, under § 2(d) of the Uniform Comparative Fault Act (UCFA), the court can apportion orphan shares among *all* the viable parties. So far, CERCLA courts have followed the UCFA solution. Thus, for any orphan share of an indivisible harm for which joint and several liability was imposed, the solvent parties pick up the orphan shares in amounts corresponding to the solvent parties' relative equitable shares. See, e.g., Action Manufacturing Co., Inc. v. Simon Wrecking Co., 428 F.Supp.2d 288 (E.D.Pa.2006).

### d. Reduction for Effect of Settlement

A second apportionment problem arises from the prior settlement of CERCLA liability by some parties. Prior to SARA, courts had disagreed over whether to reduce nonsettling parties' contribution liability by the amount of settlement, or by the amount of the settling parties' equitable shares, if greater. The difference might be substantial in cases where a nonsettlor believes that the settling party received a generous deal. The former method, preferred by EPA, was similar to the position adopted by the Uniform Contribution among Tortfeasors Act. The alternative approach, favored by many pre-SARA courts, was the position adopted by the Uniform Comparative Fault Act.

As added by SARA, §§ 113(f)(2) and 122(g)(5) state that any settlement "does not discharge any of the potentially responsible persons unless its terms so provide, but it reduces the potential liability of the others by the amount of the settlement." Since SARA, courts have generally reduced the share of nonsettling parties' liability only by the amount of the settlement, not by the settling parties' equitable share of the cleanup. See, e.g., United States v. Cannons Engineering, 899 F.2d 79 (1st Cir.1990). Thus, the nonsettlors bear the risk that the settlement was too generous. This position is in keeping with the overall CERCLA policy of encouraging settlement.

## C. CITIZENS' SUITS

While the discussion in this and much of the preceding four chapters has focused on the obligations of the parties potentially responsible for cleaning up a site, CERCLA's impact extends far beyond those parties and into the general public. As a consequence, in the formulation of both general CERCLA policy and specific site cleanups, the public will often demand substantial participation.

CERCLA recognizes the importance of public input in numerous ways. For example, where EPA promulgates regulations to interpret CERCLA, there is opportunity for public participation on these proposals through the "notice and comment" provisions of the federal Administrative Procedures Act. 5 U.S.C.A. §§ 551–559; see, e.g., CERCLA § 105(a). Alternatively, where EPA and responsible parties devise a removal action to remediate a particular contaminated site, the NCP often provides opportunity for public participation in such decisions. E.g., § 113(k).

Ultimately, however, the public may be dissatisfied with either the regulations promulgated or the specifics of a site cleanup plan and its implementation. For example, environmental or public health advocates may believe that a regulation or a chosen cleanup plan does not go far enough to protect human health and or the environment. Alternatively, they may believe that an otherwise adequate plan is not being implemented properly. In contrast, business organizations and individual PRPs may well believe that a regulation or a chosen cleanup plan goes *too far*, i.e., it demands remedial actions beyond that required by statute.

Where such dissatisfaction is based on the well-founded belief that CERCLA, or its implementing regulations and orders, has been violated, CERCLA provides a limited remedy: the citizens' suit. In providing such a remedy, CERCLA is no different than the other major federal environmental statutes. Citizens' suits under CERCLA, however, have a major limitation. Because such suits can greatly delay site cleanup, Congress has *greatly* restricted the federal courts' jurisdiction to entertain actions that challenge the specifics of a particular site cleanup plan.

## 1. GENERAL PROVISIONS

Section 310(a) authorizes two classes of such suits. Subsection (a)(1) allows suits "[a]gainst any person * * * who is alleged to be in violation of any standard, regulation, condition, requirement, or order which has become effective [under CERCLA]." Subsection (a)(2) allows suits "[a]gainst the President or any other officer of the United States where there is alleged a failure to perform any act or duty under [CERCLA] * * * which is not discretionary."

As is typical for such statutes, additional provisions restrict the right to sue to cases where plaintiffs have given the requisite pre-suit notice and where the government is not otherwise "diligently prosecuting" a similar action. § 310(d)(2). At least 60 days before suing under § 310(a)(1), the plaintiff must have given notice of the alleged violation to the President, to the state in which the alleged violation occurs, and to the alleged violator. § 310(d)(1). For the latter, notice to the alleged violator's plant manager will suffice. Lutz v. Chromatex, Inc., 718 F.Supp. 413 (M.D.Pa.1989). Similarly, at least 60 days before suing under § 310(a)(2), the plaintiff must notify EPA or the other federal department, agency, or instrumentality alleged to be in violation of CERCLA. § 310(e). In either instance, the plaintiff may not sue for purely *past* violations; rather, the defendant must still be "in violation." See, e.g., Coalition for Health Concern v. LWD, Inc., 60 F.3d 1188 (6th Cir.1995). Allegations that the violations are continuous or are likely to recur in the future may also suffice.

The statute addresses venue and remedies. Actions under (a)(1) must be brought in the district court for the district in which the alleged violation occurred. § 310(b)(1). Actions under (a)(2) "may be brought" in the district court for the District of Columbia. § 310(b)(2). The court may make any orders necessary to enforce the relevant permit conditions, statutes or regulations. § 310(c). A successful plaintiff may recover its litigation costs, including reasonable attorneys' and expert witness' fees. § 310(f).

## 2. LIMITATIONS ON REVIEW

Depending upon the specific basis of the citizens' suit, additional statutory provisions may apply.

### a. Challenges to Regulations

Where a citizens' suit challenges a regulation issued under CERCLA, the suit must be filed in the D. C. Circuit. § 113(a). Plaintiffs must file such challenges within 90 days of the promulgation of the regulations. The statute precludes review of the validity of the regulations in any subsequent enforcement action for all challenges that could have been brought within the 90 day period. § 113(a).

### b. Challenges to Site Cleanup Decisions

Because of the potential to slow down greatly the site cleanup process, § 113(h) restricts the federal courts' jurisdiction to hear challenges to decisions regarding the cleanup of specific sites. That statute allows challenges in only four instances:

- in § 107 cost recovery actions;
- in actions to enforce administrative cleanup orders issued under § 106, or actions to compel a cleanup brought under the same statute;

- in actions against the Superfund where a party who obeyed a § 106 order seeks reimbursement;
- and in certain citizens' suits.

This last provision, set out in § 113(h)(4), authorizes citizens' suits "alleging that the removal or remedial action *taken* under [§ 104] or *secured* under [§ 106] was in violation of [CERCLA]." (Emphasis added.) These citizens' suits, however, may not challenge a "removal" action where a "remedial action is to be undertaken at the site." § 113(h)(4).

The scope of the § 113(h) restrictions has received substantial judicial attention. For the most part, concerns over potential cleanup delays have compelled the courts to read the restrictions broadly. Thus, courts have routinely barred challenges to particular remedial decisions before EPA has implemented them completely. See, e.g., Schalk v. Reilly, 900 F.2d 1091 (7th Cir.1990). Such courts have seized on the emphasized portion of the citizens' suit provision quoted immediately above; that language, speaking in the past tense, convinced the courts that the remedial actions must have been *completed* before the courts may entertain a suit to challenge those actions. Indeed, some courts have gone even farther, and barred pre-*enforcement* review of cleanup decisions. For these courts, a site's PRPs could not challenge even a fully *implemented* cleanup decision until EPA had filed a cost recovery action against them. Voluntary Purchasing Groups, Inc. v. Reilly, 889 F.2d 1380 (5th Cir.1989). The bar extends not only to actions filed under CERCLA, but also to actions that assert *any* federal law to challenge the remedial decisions. See, e.g., Boarhead v. Erickson, 923 F.2d 1011 (3d Cir.1991).

The harshness of these decisions, both to PRPs who believe that a cleanup strategy is too costly, and to citizens groups who believe it inadequate, is readily apparent. In either case, the decision cannot be challenged until it may be too late to have much effect. Where only a PRP is involved, and the claim is simply that the government conducted a "Cadillac cleanup" where only a "Volkswagen" would have sufficed, the PRP has some remedy in theory. It can demonstrate, in a § 107 action, that the desired reimbursement includes matters that are either not "costs of removal or remedial action" or that such costs are "inconsistent with the [NCP]." In practice, however, these provisions offer little real compensation for the PRP; the courts will uphold EPA's actions unless they are "arbitrary and capricious or otherwise not in accordance with law." § 113(j)(2). In any event, where only money is at stake, Congress may well have concluded that the harm caused to the few PRPs who may have to pay for an excessive cleanup pales in contrast to the costs the public would have to bear from the inevitable delays attendant to broader pre-implementation or pre-enforcement review.

Where, however, a citizens' group argues that the remedial measures are inadequate to protect public health, the equities are different. For example, remedial plans that call for the exhumation and transportation of buried wastes may endanger the public more than a decision to isolate those wastes in place. In such a case, a bar to judicial review of the decision to exhume until after the exhumation has occurred means that the citizens have no real remedy at all.

In recognition of these harsh consequences, some courts have retreated slightly from an absolute ban on pre-implementation review of site cleanup activities. Thus, in one case, the Sixth Circuit allowed non-settling PRPs, and, by extension, other affected citizens, to examine the appropriateness of any remedies incorporated into consent decrees. United States v. Akzo Coatings of America, Inc., 949 F.2d 1409 (6th Cir.1991). Since, as Chapters 7 through 10 demonstrated, the negotiated § 106 consent decree is EPA's favorite cleanup strategy, the Sixth Circuit's decision opens a major hole in the ban on pre-implementation or pre-enforcement review. In another case, the Tenth Circuit concluded that § 113(h) did not bar a state from enforcing its RCRA authorized hazardous wastes program against an NPL site. United States v. Colorado, 990 F.2d 1565 (10th Cir.1993).

In one other area the courts have reached conflicting results over the extent of the pre-enforcement review ban. Where a party raises a *constitutional* challenge to a remedial action taken under CERCLA, application of the pre-enforcement review ban may itself pose constitutional problems under due process doctrine. Some courts, such as the Sixth Circuit, have held that the ban does apply to these challenges, and that such application does not itself deny due process of law. See, e.g., Barmet Aluminum Corp. v. Reilly, 927 F.2d 289 (6th Cir.1991). In contrast, the First Circuit has concluded that at least facial challenges to such CERCLA decisions may well hurdle the § 113(h) bar. Reardon v. EPA, 947 F.2d 1509 (1st Cir.1991). That court also concluded that, absent prior notice and a hearing, due process precluded EPA's filing of a lien against a PRP's property to secure possible CERCLA liability. See also General Electric Co. v. EPA, 360 F.3d 188 (D.C.Cir.2004) (holding that § 113(h) did not prohibit pre-enforcement challenge based on Due Process Clause).

# CHAPTER 12

# ADDITIONAL HAZARDOUS WASTE CLEANUP OPTIONS UNDER RCRA AND CERCLA

As described in detail in Chapters 7 through 11, many hazardous waste sites are cleaned up under the CERCLA remediation and cost shifting provisions. While CERCLA frequently provides EPA and others with their preferred cleanup option, two RCRA provisions also provide substantial hazardous waste cleanup authority.

First, RCRA § 7003, with its citizens' suit counterpart under § 7002, authorizes administrative and judicial action against hazardous waste sites that pose an "imminent and substantial endangerment to health or the environment." The passage of CERCLA relegated these RCRA provisions to a less prominent role in hazardous waste cleanup. Nevertheless, they still play an important "gap filling" role in cases where CERCLA does not apply.

Second, RCRA §§ 3004 and 3008 authorize EPA to take "corrective action" against any TSD facility that has, or should have obtained, either a RCRA permit or interim status. The substantial leverage provided by these statutes has made them EPA's preferred cleanup option for contaminated TSD sites. Together, these provisions make RCRA's "cradle to grave" regulation of hazardous waste, described in Chapter 6, a system better described as "cradle to grave, and beyond"!

Chapter 6 addressed administrative, civil, and criminal enforcement of the RCRA hazardous waste *management* requirements. This chapter begins by addressing enforcement actions brought under the two RCRA *cleanup* provisions. It then concludes with a discussion of the interactions between RCRA and CERCLA.

## A. "IMMINENT AND SUBSTANTIAL ENDANGERMENT" ACTIONS: RCRA §§ 7003 AND 7002(a)(1)(B)

### 1. HISTORY AND OVERVIEW

As originally enacted in 1976, § 7003 was the only RCRA provision which empowered EPA to clean up hazardous waste contamination. Indeed, prior to the enactment of CERCLA, § 7003 provided almost the entire federal statutory authority for such cleanups. (Comparable "endangerment" provisions did exist under TSCA, see Chapter 4, and the Safe Drinking Water Act, see Chapter 5, but these had limited applicability to solid waste contamination and were rarely used.) Nevertheless, RCRA § 7003 lay dormant for three years because its original language led EPA to opine that it authorized cleanup of only *active* TSD facilities. 43 F.R. 58,984 (Dec. 18, 1978). Eventually, EPA reinterpreted the provision to authorize federal cleanups of both active and *inactive* facilities. 45 F.R. 33,170 (May 19, 1980). In its 1984 amendments, Congress codified the latter interpretation. See United States v. Waste Industries, Inc., 734 F.2d 159 (4th Cir.1984). For a brief period after this reinterpretation, § 7003 provided the principal authority for government led cleanups of pre-CERCLA contaminated sites.

Section 7003 received its first major federal use in 1979. In that year, the Justice Department used it to force cleanup of several contaminated inactive TSD facilities in New York, including the infamous Love Canal. Several dozen additional filings over the next year led to the development of a modest body of case law that fleshed out the principal elements of a § 7003 action. The 1980 passage of CERCLA and the 1984 addition of the "corrective action" provisions to EPA's RCRA arsenal, however, combined to reduce the section's importance. Nevertheless, it remains an important cleanup option in the few cases where CERCLA is inapplicable. Thus, § 7003 is useful where an express exclusion from CERCLA jurisdiction exists (e.g., the petroleum exclusion) or where the waste in question, while dangerous, otherwise does not qualify as a CERCLA "hazardous substance." Its citizens' suit counterpart might also be used by a person who does not have a property interest or liability sufficient to seek recoupment of "response costs" incurred in a voluntary CERCLA cleanup. See Pennsylvania Urban Development Corp. v. Golen, 708 F.Supp. 669 (E.D.Pa.1989) (subsequent purchaser lacked standing to seek recoupment of pre-purchase "due diligence" efforts). Thus, it might allow "Good Samaritans" to seek an injunction ordering cleanup even though such plaintiffs might not be able to recover response costs under either CERCLA or RCRA.

## 2. ELEMENTS

### a. Key Terms

Under § 7003(a) (and its citizens' suit counterpart in § 7002(a)(1)(B) ), the plaintiff must establish that the defendant's handling or treatment of waste has contributed to a dangerous condition. More specifically, the plaintiff must show that: (1) an "imminent and substantial endangerment" exists to "health or the environment;" (2) "the past or present handling, storage, treatment, transportation, or disposal of any solid or hazardous waste" has triggered the endangerment; and (3) the defendant has "contributed" to the activities that created the endangerment. Liability is strict, joint and several. See, e.g., United States v. Northeastern Pharmaceutical & Chemical Co., 810 F.2d 726 (8th Cir.1986). Thus, the plaintiff need not prove that the defendant was negligent, reckless, or intended harm. See United States v. Ottati & Goss, Inc., 630 F.Supp. 1361, 1401 (D.N.H.1985).

The few cases that have construed these elements have made a plaintiff's case relatively easy. As to the first element, courts have concluded generously that "imminent and substantial endangerment" includes cases where harm is merely threatened, even if as yet unrealized. See, e.g., United States v. Conservation Chemical Co., 619 F.Supp. 162, 191–97 (W.D.Mo.1985). Thus, plaintiff need not show that an "emergency" exists. United States v. Waste Industries, Inc., 734 F.2d 159 (4th Cir.1984). As to the second element, the actionable wastes are not restricted to the hazardous wastes regulated under RCRA Subtitle C. (For a discussion of the definition of "hazardous waste" under the Subtitle C regulations, see Chapter 6). Section 7003 is not part of Subtitle C ("Hazardous Waste Management"); rather, it is found in Subtitle G ("Miscellaneous Provisions"). Thus, when determining the scope of EPA's authority under § 7003, courts apply the broad, general *statutory* definitions of "solid" and "hazardous" wastes found in RCRA § 1004(5) and (27). See, e.g., Connecticut Coastal Fishermen's Ass'n v. Remington Arms Co., 989 F.2d 1305 (2d Cir.1993). Judicial use of the broader statutory terms avoids the complicated analysis triggered under the Subtitle C regulatory definitions. Moreover, since there are no EPA regulations governing "solid" and "hazardous" waste for purposes of § 7003, the courts are theoretically less deferential to EPA's interpretation of the statutory definitions. Finally, as to the third element, courts have broadly construed "contributing." Indeed, in perhaps the most famous case under § 7003, the Eighth Circuit initially concluded that it encompassed the president and principal shareholder of a close corporation because of his overall authority to control the corporation's disposal of hazardous substances. United States v. Northeastern Pharmaceutical & Chemical Co., 810 F.2d 726 (8th Cir.1986). More recently, however, that court has required more involvement than just "capacity to control." See United States v. Gurley, 43 F.3d 1188 (8th Cir.1994).

### b. Public Enforcement

Section 7003(a) gives EPA two principal enforcement options. First, it may issue "necessary" administrative orders to protect "health and the environment." The statute makes a willful violation of such an order punishable by fine. § 7003(b). Second, it may sue either to enjoin the defendant from continuing its harmful waste handling activities or to obtain an order "to take such other action as is necessary." Appropriate equitable relief may include orders to investigate or remediate a site. Because of the equitable nature of such actions, defendants have been able to raise equitable defenses; these, however, have generally proved unsuccessful. See, e.g., United States v. Hardage, 116 F.R.D. 460, 464 (W.D.Okl.1987) (laches and unclean hands). Before settling any claim under § 7003, the government must notify the public, hold a public meeting, and provide a "reasonable opportunity for public comment." § 7003(d).

EPA's authority under § 7003 to force defendants to reimburse publicly funded cleanup costs remains somethat uncertain. The Supreme Court rejected such restitutionary awards in citizens' suits brought under § 7002. Meghrig v. KFC Western, Inc., 516 U.S. 479, 116 S.Ct. 1251, 134 L.Ed.2d 121 (1996). Although the public nature of a § 7003 action leaves room to distinguish *Meghrig*, the lack of express statutory authorization for such restitutionary awards may well lead to a similar result under § 7003.

### c. Private Enforcement

As noted above, § 7002—the RCRA citizens' suit provision—authorizes a private party to file an "imminent and substantial endangerment" action. § 7002(a)(1)(B). The key terms are the same under both §§ 7003 and 7002. As discussed in greater length in Chapter 6, RCRA imposes two procedural impediments to the filing of a citizens' suit. First, the plaintiff must give the right persons the right notice sufficiently far in advance of filing. Second, certain governmental enforcement actions will preclude the maintenance of a citizens' suit. In addition, § 7003 may not be used by nongovernmental plaintiffs to challenge the siting or permitting of a TSD facility. § 7003(b)(2)(D).

The notice provisions require a private party who wishes to sue to first communicate that intent to EPA, to the state in which the endangerment may occur, and to the alleged contributors to the endangerment. § 7002(b)(2). The United States Attorney General must also receive notice. § 7002(b)(2)(F). For most endangerment actions, the notice must occur at least 90 days before the plaintiff sues. This appears counterintuitive, as plaintiffs who do *not* allege "imminent endangerment" usually need only wait 60 days before filing their citizens' suit. Compare § 7002(b)(1). The irony of the greater delay applicable to the endangerment provisions is tempered somewhat if plaintiffs allege endangerment as a result of violations of the Subtitle C hazardous waste provisions. Any suit involving such an allegation may be filed immediately after the giving of notice. §§ 7002(b)(1), (2). As with the other citizens' suit provisions discussed in Chapter 6, citizens' suits that combine allegations under multiple parts of RCRA complicate the calculation of the necessary presuit delay. See, e.g., Zands v. Nelson, 779 F.Supp. 1254, 1259–61 (S.D.Cal.1991) (allowing plaintiff to maintain suit on unrelated 60 day claim prior to expiration of 90 day period on a different "imminent endangerment" claim).

RCRA lists several governmental enforcement actions which, if "commenced" and "diligently prosecut[ed]," will preclude a citizens' suit. These actions include: (1) a public "imminent endangerment" action under § 7003; and (2) listed activities taken under CERCLA. § 7002(b)(2)(B), (C). For additional discussion of the preclusive effects of such actions, see Chapter 6.

The remedies available under § 7002 include abatement orders. They do not, however, include reimbursement for the plaintiff's *past* (i.e., pre-judgment) expenditure of private funds to clean up a facility. Meghrig v. KFC Western, Inc., 516 U.S. 479, 116 S.Ct. 1251, 134 L.Ed.2d 121 (1996). In *Meghrig*, however, the Supreme Court left open the ability of a private party to obtain an order requiring the defendant to pay *future* cleanup costs incurred by someone other than that defendant. Of course, as discussed more fully in Chapter 6, a successful plaintiff may also receive an award of litigation costs, including reasonable attorneys' fees.

## B. "CORRECTIVE ACTIONS:" RCRA §§ 3004(u) AND 3008(h)

### 1. INTRODUCTION

The 1980 passage of CERCLA shifted the federal hazardous waste cleanup program from RCRA § 7003 to the multiple cleanup options available under CERCLA. By 1984, however, Congress realized that CERCLA had some serious limitations. The number of potential sites was staggering; the pace of cleanups was slow; and the cleanup costs threatened to devour quickly the limited monies available in the Superfund itself.

Congress responded to these limitations in two legislative steps. Eventually, as addressed in Chapter 7, Congress directly amended CERCLA in 1986 with the passage of SARA. But, two years earlier, Congress had already taken the first, indirect steps to respond to the CERCLA cleanup bottleneck. In the 1984 amendments to RCRA, Congress greatly expanded EPA's limited "corrective action" program applicable to TSD facilities.

As a condition to receiving a RCRA permit, EPA had already required defined "regulated [TSD] units" to clean up releases of hazardous wastes within their boundaries. See 40 C.F.R. § 264.100. The 1984 RCRA amendments, and their implementing regulations and policy documents, broadly expanded the number of TSD facilities potentially required to complete such corrective actions. While the program remains limited to TSD facilities, EPA estimates that over 5,000 such facilities, containing up to 80,000 "Solid Waste Management Units," are potentially subject to the corrective action requirement. Of these, well over half may have to undergo some corrective action, at a total cost in the tens of billions of dollars. Thus, in both the number of potential sites and the projected cleanup costs, the corrective action program now rivals CERCLA.

The corrective action program contains separate provisions applicable to permitted facilities (§ 3004(u), (v)) and interim status facilities (§§ 3005(i), 3008(h)). (For a discussion of the distinction between these two types of facilities, see Chapter 6.) Because of the decreased contemporary importance of the interim status facilities, the following discussion will focus first on the requirements for permitted facilities, then conclude with a brief summary of the interim status requirements.

## 2. KEY TERMS

Section 3004 contains two separate corrective action requirements. First, § 3004(u) mandates that any TSD permit issued after November 8, 1984, require "corrective action for all releases of hazardous waste or constituents from any solid waste management unit at a [TSD] facility * * * regardless of the time at which waste was placed in such unit." The permits must contain a compliance schedule and an assurance that the TSD owner has adequate funds to complete the cleanup. The corrective action requirements also apply to facilities that closed rather than obtain further operating permits. To ensure that facilities could not avoid corrective action by simply closing, EPA required facilities that either received waste after July 26, 1982, or did not officially certify closure by January 26, 1983, to obtain a "post-closure" permit. 40 C.F.R. § 270.1(c). Ordinarily, these post-closure permits require corrective action. § 270.14. The D. C. Circuit upheld these requirements in American Iron & Steel Institute v. EPA, 886 F.2d 390, 397 (D.C.Cir.1989). A second provision, § 3004(v), requires TSD facilities to take corrective action for releases that extend "beyond the facility boundary where necessary to protect human health and the environment * * *." A TSD owner may only avoid this extraterritorial cleanup requirement if it proves its inability to obtain the adjoining landowner's permission to access the site.

The statute does not define the critical terms "release," "hazardous waste constituent," or "solid waste management unit." Through a series of regulations, regulatory proposals, and guidance documents, EPA has broadly read each of these three terms. To date, the courts have generally upheld the expansive reading EPA has given them.

### a. "Hazardous Waste or Constituents"

The statute addresses a release of "hazardous waste or constituents." "Hazardous waste" is defined according to the complicated Subtitle C regulations addressed at length in chapter 6. As discussed in that Chapter, that definition, in turn, depends on the regulatory definition of "solid waste."

The inclusion of "hazardous waste constituents" potentially broadens the corrective action jurisdiction beyond those materials that specifically constitute "hazardous wastes." EPA maintains a list of such constituents. 40 C.F.R. Part 261, Appendix VIII. This is the same list used to apply the RCRA LDRs discussed in Chapter 6.

### b. "Release"

Surprisingly, the corrective action regulations use, but do not define, "release." See, e.g., §§ 264.90 to 264.101; compare § 280.12 (defining "release" for UST corrective action program). In its 1985 comments to the regulations that initially implemented the 1984 statutory amendments, EPA concluded that "release" for the corrective action program had to be "at least as broad as the definition under CERCLA." 50 F.R. 28,702 (1985). According to those comments, the RCRA definition, however, is *not* constrained by the statutory exemptions from CERCLA. Moreover, EPA has concluded that its corrective action authority extends not only to *actual* but also to *threatened* releases, as long as such future releases are "likely." See 50 F.R. 30,874 (1990) (proposed regulation). Consistent with the broad CERCLA definition of release, see Chapter 7, EPA also includes within the RCRA corrective action definition the abandonment of closed containers that contain hazardous substances, at least where leaks are likely to occur.

In one frequently encountered circumstance, however, a "release" will not be deemed to have occurred. EPA does not consider the isolated leakage from raw material or finished product storage a "release" unless the leaks are "routine and systematic." 55 F.R. 30,808 (1990). Nevertheless, EPA may assert its residual authority under the "omnibus" permit provision to require cleanup of such leaks or spills where they occur in designated "areas of concern" (AOC). Under this "omnibus" provision, EPA can impose any term necessary to protect health and the environment. § 3005(c)(3). EPA will require cleanup of an AOC where: (1) a nexus exists between the AOC and the facility's waste management activities; and (2) harm from the AOC appears sufficiently threatening.

#### c. "Solid Waste Management Unit" and "Facility"

The corrective action statute addresses releases from "solid waste management units [SWMUs] at a [TSD] facility seeking a permit * * *." Although Congress did not define "SWMU," EPA has a definition. Under the corrective action regulations, a SWMU is: "Any discernible unit at which solid wastes have been placed at any time * * *." 55 F.R. 30,798. Under this definition, a typical SWMU is a portion of a larger "facility," e.g., a particular landfill, a surface impoundment, or incinerator.

Although it left "SWMU" undefined, the statute implies that TSD facilities may often be composed of multiple SWMUs. In some such facilities, post-

RCRA TSD activities that require a permit might only be occurring in some of these units; many of the other units may have been inactive for many years. Indeed, for purposes of the corrective action requirements, EPA broadly defines "facility" to include all contiguous property owned by the relevant TSD facility's owner. 40 C.F.R. § 260.10. It includes both adjoining parcels and property separated by a roadway. Over industry objections, EPA concluded that whenever a TSD facility owner or operator applied for a permit, EPA could require corrective action for *any* release from *any* SWMU within the facility, including those units not actively managed. The D. C. Circuit upheld this broad interpretation in United Technologies Corp. v. EPA, 821 F.2d 714 (D.C.Cir.1987). Reinforcing the breadth of the corrective action program is the statutory requirement, noted above, that TSD facility owners extend their cleanup activities off site, unless they are unable to obtain an adjoining landowner's permission. Thus, given the broad number of active SWMUs, the duty to clean up inactive units, and the duty to clean up waste offsite, the corrective action program has monumental potential impacts on TSD permitees.

### 3. PROCESS AND STANDARDS

In 1990, EPA proposed regulations to govern the corrective action process and cleanup standards. 55 F.R. 30,798 (July 27, 1990). In 1999, EPA withdrew most of the proposed regulations. 64 F.R. 54,604 (Oct. 7, 1999). Instead, it has developed a series of guidance and policy documents. The process employed resembles the CERCLA "National Contingency Plan," albeit with different acronyms.

Permitted facilities are required to monitor and sample the groundwater and soil beneath their SWMUs in order to detect any release. If a release is detected, or otherwise comes to EPA's attention, a five part corrective action process begins. First, an EPA contractor will have conducted a "RCRA Facility Assessment" (RFA). This report describes the facility, its SWMUs and its AOCs, and the extent of known releases. Second, the facility prepares a "RCRA Facility Investigation" (RFI). This resembles the "Remedial Investigation" component of a CERCLA "RI/FS." During the RFI, the facility owner investigates known or potential releases in detail. Third, the facility owner may need to take Interim Actions to protect against ongoing risks to public health and safety pending the outcome of the RFI. Fourth, the facility owner must undertake a "Corrective Measures Study" (CMS). The CMS resembles the "Feasibility Study" component of the CERCLA "RI/FS." Indeed, like the RI/FS interplay, many owners begin CMS work while still completing the RFI. Unlike the RI/FS process, EPA, however, has demonstrated greater willingness to tailor the required CMS efforts to the magnitude of the risk presented by the given release. In any event, during the CMS, the facility must identify and evaluate alternative remedies. Eventually, the preferred remedy is incorporated into permit terms or corrective action orders. Finally, the last stage of the process involves the completion of the chosen cleanup option. EPA has proposed public participation at specified stages of the process.

Like the CERCLA cleanups described in Chapter 8, RCRA corrective actions raise questions about "how clean" must the facility become. Unlike CERCLA, with its insistence that cleanup meet ARARs, however, RCRA largely leaves the required cleanup standard to EPA's discretion. EPA believes that corrective action cleanups should protect both current and reasonably anticipated future uses. It has proposed establishing "trigger" and "target" levels. Trigger levels will determine *when* a release will require a CMS; target levels will determine the level to which the site must be cleaned. The latter will likely be set case by case, using a variety of factors. For example, where groundwater contamination is possible, the MCLs set by the Safe Drinking Water Act will likely be the RCRA corrective action target levels. Unlike CERCLA, where compliance is measured at the property's boundary, compliance for RCRA corrective actions will ordinarily be measured at each point where exposure may occur. This approach is theoretically more demanding, as it reduces the possibility for "in situ" containment as a remedy.

## 4. INTERIM STATUS FACILITIES

Two statutes address corrective action requirements for interim status facilities. Section 3005(i) applies to any such facility that received hazardous waste after July 26, 1982. It requires such interim status facilities to take the same corrective actions applicable to permitted facilities, including groundwater monitoring to detect releases. Section 3008(h) applies to any interim status facility. It authorizes EPA to order corrective actions, or to seek an injunction commanding the same. EPA has broadly construed its authority under § 3008 to apply to any facility that should have obtained interim status, even if it did not. At least one district court has upheld this interpretation. United States v. Indiana Woodtreating Corp., 686 F.Supp. 218, 223 (S.D.Ind.1988). In addition, generators or transporters who inadvertently become subject to the TSD requirements (e.g., by storing wastes beyond the permissible limits, mixing wastes, or voluntarily remediating a site) also subject themselves to the corrective action requirements. The only facilities excluded are those that filed for interim status but never used their authorization.

Unlike § 3004(u), which speaks of releases of "hazardous waste or constituents," § 3008(h) speaks only of releases of "hazardous waste." Nevertheless, EPA has concluded that both sections address the same materials and circumstances. See 52 F.R. 45,795 (Dec. 1, 1988).

## C. AREAS OF OVERLAP BETWEEN RCRA AND CERCLA

The existence of separate cleanup programs and regulatory requirements under both RCRA and CERCLA prompts four questions. First, at what point do these two statutes diverge? That is, are there circumstances where a contaminated site can be cleaned up only under one of the two? Second, within the broad area of overlap, what circumstances will prompt EPA, or another party to a cleanup, to choose one statutory scheme over another? Third, does the availability of a RCRA remedy preclude EPA from proceeding under CERCLA, or vice versa? Finally, are there areas, other than cleanup authority, where the two regulatory systems overlap?

## 1. JURISDICTIONAL OVERLAP

As discussed in Chapter 7, CERCLA applies to a "release" or threat of a release of a "hazardous substance" from a "facility." Each of these terms has a counterpart under RCRA. Subtle distinctions between the two sets of definitions create the possibility that some cleanups may only proceed under one, but not the other, of the two statutes. In practice, however, most contaminated sites may be cleaned up by EPA under either statute.

At first glance, the most meaningful distinction between the respective jurisdictional definitions appears to be that between CERCLA's "hazardous substances" and RCRA's "hazardous wastes." The CERCLA term seems to cover a broader range of substances than the RCRA term. Indeed, CERCLA "hazardous substances" expressly include RCRA Subtitle C regulated hazardous wastes. In addition, they include other substances regulated under the Clean Air, Clean Water, and Toxic Substances Control Acts. CERCLA § 101(14). Thus, materials excluded from RCRA's definitions of solid and hazardous waste, or simply not within those definitions because they have not been discarded, may still be subject to CERCLA. Finally, in theory anyway, CERCLA applies to hazardous substances regardless of their concentration in contaminated environmental media; a substantial portion of RCRA hazardous wastes, however, are regulated under Subtitle C only because they exist in specific concentrations that are dangerous.

In several areas, however, RCRA can authorize a cleanup where CERCLA cannot. Most prominently, CERCLA excludes "petroleum" from its "hazardous substance" jurisdiction; no such exclusion, however, applies under RCRA. Moreover, RCRA § 7003 authorizes cleanup of "solid waste" that poses an "imminent and substantial endangerment;" in theory, it could require cleanup of waste that, while "dangerous," was neither "hazardous" under RCRA, nor a "hazardous substance" under CERCLA.

Except for the areas where CERCLA or RCRA exclusions apply, the practical differences between a CERCLA "hazardous substance" and a RCRA Subtitle C "hazardous waste" are not very meaningful. The realm of RCRA Subtitle C regulated substances has grown through the addition of the "hazardous constituents" added under the TCLP and LDRs discussed in Chapter 6. Similarly, the RCRA corrective action program also extends beyond "hazardous waste" to "hazardous constituents." Moreover, while CERCLA theoretically authorizes cleanup of hazardous substances regardless of their concentrations, at least some courts have been willing to require proof that the substances existed in sufficient concentrations to require EPA or another responsible party to incur response costs. See, e.g., Amoco Oil Co. v. Borden, Inc., 889 F.2d 664 (5th Cir.1989); contra, United States v. Alcan Aluminum Corp., 755 F.Supp. 531, 538–39 (N.D.N.Y.1991).

Additional apparent differences exist between the RCRA and CERCLA definitions of "release" and "facility." In these areas, the RCRA definitions may be slightly broader. Under RCRA's corrective action definition, "facility" extends from fence line to fence line, and sometimes beyond. In contrast, a "facility" in CERCLA may be limited to the areas of contamination. As for differences between the RCRA and CERCLA definitions of "release," again, the RCRA corrective action definition may be marginally broader. As noted above, EPA does not believe that the statutory exclusions from the CERCLA definition of "release" apply to the RCRA corrective action definition. However, EPA also ordinarily does not apply the RCRA corrective action definition of "release" to isolated spills; the CERCLA definition, however, requires no suggestion of systematic releases. Again, however, in practice, most of these possible distinctions are probably unimportant except in the most unusual case. For example, as discussed above, EPA may well require cleanup of "spills" at AOCs on RCRA corrective action sites, even though they may not meet the "release" definition, under EPA's omnibus authority to impose any necessary condition upon a permittee.

## 2. REMEDIAL CHOICES AND LIMITATIONS

### a. EPA Policy

The areas of overlap between RCRA and CERCLA are most pronounced where the contaminated site is a RCRA regulated TSD facility. In such areas, EPA could use either CERCLA or RCRA to compel a cleanup; moreover, within RCRA, EPA could choose either to proceed under either the imminent endangerment or the corrective action provisions.

EPA has issued a formal policy document to guide its remedial choices in such areas. In general, where the TSD facility owner or operator is financially solvent, EPA will proceed under the RCRA corrective action program rather than CERCLA. In some circumstances, however, EPA will choose to clean up a RCRA TSD facility under CERCLA. This is likely to occur where EPA wishes to pursue off-site generators, or where the areas contaminated by the TSD facility are only a part of the overall contaminated area. In both such instances, it is usually easier for EPA to go after all of the potentially responsible parties under CERCLA. Of course, RCRA standards may still play an important role in such CERCLA cleanups as ARARs.

The existence of these parallel cleanup provisions has led some parties to dispute EPA's choice. In particular, they have argued the availability of RCRA remedies precludes EPA's use of CERCLA.

These challenges have been unsuccessful. With somewhat more success, however, other parties have argued that the decision to proceed under CERCLA precludes the recovery of some costs attributable to the RCRA corrective action program.

### b. Does RCRA Limit CERCLA?

In situations where EPA has chosen to proceed under CERCLA rather than the RCRA corrective provisions, the TSD facilities face the potential of a more stringent, more public, and less flexible NCP cleanups. Occasionally, facility owners have challenged EPA's decision to use CERCLA to clean up their facility. Similarly, private parties who have sought to recover CERCLA response costs incurred to clean up TSD facilities have run into objections that RCRA precluded the CERCLA cost recovery action. To date, however, courts have not been sympathetic with efforts to limit CERCLA's applicability to RCRA TSD facilities. Thus, in one case, the D. C. Circuit upheld EPA's decision to list a RCRA regulated TSD facility on the NPL. Apache Powder Co. v. United States, 968 F.2d 66 (D.C.Cir.1992). In another case, a district court allowed a TSD facility that itself was potentially in violation of RCRA requirements to seek a cost recovery under CERCLA. Chemical Waste Management, Inc. v. Armstrong World Industries, Inc., 669 F.Supp. 1285 (E.D.Pa.1987). In the latter instance, the plaintiff's responsibility for the contamination simply affected the extent of its ability to recover CERCLA response costs; it did not preclude such recovery.

In one additional area, parties regulated under RCRA have argued unsuccessfully that RCRA precludes a CERCLA cost recovery action against them. As discussed in Chapter 6, the RCRA municipal waste exclusion excuses municipalities from much RCRA regulation. Such municipalities have argued that the RCRA exclusion also precludes a CERCLA action seeking recovery of response costs incurred in cleaning up landfills to which the municipalities sent their waste. Reasoning that the relaxation of RCRA manifest requirements for the generation of such wastes did not excuse CERCLA liability for the cleanup of such wastes, the courts, however, have refused to engraft the RCRA exclusion onto CERCLA. B.F. Goodrich Co. v. Murtha, 958 F.2d 1192 (2d Cir.1992).

### c. Does CERCLA Expand RCRA?

In several instances, EPA and private parties have used CERCLA to attempt to recover costs incurred in RCRA corrective actions. Several district courts have allowed at least some recovery of such costs. See, e.g., Chemical Waste Management, Inc. v. Armstrong World Industries, Inc., 669 F.Supp. 1285 (E.D.Pa.1987).

## 3. OTHER INTERACTIONS

RCRA and CERCLA overlap in two additional areas. First, both RCRA and CERCLA require prompt reports to EPA's National Response Center when a regulated hazardous material is released into the environment. CERCLA § 103; 40 C.F.R.

§ 264.56(d) (RCRA). Thus, reportable releases from a RCRA TSD facility would likely also need to be reported under CERCLA. To preclude such duplicate reports of the same release, CERCLA exempts any release reported under RCRA.

Second, both CERCLA and RCRA potentially apply to leaks of CERCLA hazardous substances (other than RCRA hazardous wastes) stored in underground tanks. Chapter 6 described the RCRA underground storage tank (UST) regulations. That program contains its own corrective action program and its own mini-"Superfund." In theory, leaks from a RCRA regulated UST might also be eligible for cleanup under CERCLA.

# CHAPTER 13

# COMMON LAW APPROACHES TO HAZARDOUS WASTES AND TOXIC SUBSTANCES

## A. INTRODUCTION

For good reason, this book focuses on the complex statutory schemes that govern the manufacture, use, disposal, and cleanup of hazardous wastes and toxic substances. Congress enacted these statutes in large part because of the common law system's limitations in addressing such materials. In particular, five aspects of the common law create special problems for the control of hazardous substances. First, judges often know little about the complexities of hazardous substances. Second, the common law is reactive: courts do not generally act until after harm has occurred and someone has sued. Third, the common law develops slowly, case-by-case, with prior decisions, even if questionable, often followed by later judges under *stare decisis*. Fourth, the common law is riddled with disagreements, as different courts sometimes reach different results on virtually the same facts. Finally, the "preponderance of the evidence" burden of proof poses a substantial hurdle for plaintiffs; in effect, it requires them to prove that the defendant's substance or conduct is *unsafe*, rather than forcing the defendant to prove that it is *safe*.

In response to these inadequacies, Congress has largely placed EPA in charge of the legal efforts to clean up hazardous wastes and prevent harm from exposure to toxic substances. In theory, drawing on its technical expertise, EPA can promptly and efficiently create and apply uniform standards. Of course, the statutory and regulatory responses to the problems of hazardous substances raise their own technical, legal, and policy questions. Nevertheless, they represent a qualitatively different approach to the problems than possible under the common law.

Despite the contemporary importance of such statutes as TSCA, FIFRA, EPCRTKA, CWA, CAA, SDWA, RCRA and CERCLA, and the perceived limitations of the common law system, the common law continues to play an important role in responding to harms created by hazardous wastes and toxic substances. Indeed, for the most part, in enacting its statutes, Congress did not supplant the common law liability system. Rather, Congress built upon it. Where, despite the regulatory schemes, a person suffers injury from the use or improper disposal of hazardous substances, common law liability for personal injury or property damage remains an important legal remedy. For example, while CERCLA provides property decontamination help, only the common law will reimburse the land owner either for a decline in property value or for personal injuries caused by the contamination. Similarly, while OSHA limits work place exposure to toxic substances, only the common law provides a worker compensation for injuries that result from such exposure. As a result, despite the citizens' suit provisions in the federal statutes, common law actions seeking compensation for personal injuries and property damage remain the numerical majority of lawsuits filed that present issues of hazardous waste contamination or toxic substance exposure.

Over the last quarter century, a branch of common law has developed known as "toxic" or "environmental" torts. Collectively, these cases apply traditional tort principles to remedy injuries incurred through contamination by hazardous wastes or exposure to toxic substances.

The development of this branch of the law demonstrates two of the principal strengths of the common law system: its endurability and its adaptability to novel circumstances. In assigning liability for injuries allegedly caused by hazardous waste and toxic substances, courts have adapted traditional tort claims, causation principles, and remedies to the unique problems created by such materials. The adaptation, however, has faced substantial problems. Along the way, courts have had to wrestle with such matters as: (1) scientific uncertainties over the toxicity of the materials at issue; (2) often long lag times between exposure and manifestation of injury; and (3) multiple exposure pathways, whereby a party manifesting injury may have been exposed to different sources of the same toxic. In addition, the presence of multiple parties, sometimes numbering in the thousands on the plaintiff's side and the dozens in the defendant's side, has forced the courts to adopt new procedures for the conduct of toxic torts suits. These substantive and procedural accommodations remain ongoing as new cases raise new challenges to the common law system.

This chapter briefly introduces students to the principal common law liability issues presented by hazardous wastes and toxic substances. It assumes some familiarity with basic tort concepts of fault, causation, remedies, and judicial procedure. It focuses on the unique problems for the tort system caused by claims of injury allegedly resulting from contamination by hazardous wastes and exposure to toxic substances.

## B. CLAIMS AND DEFENSES

The common law has not yet developed unique claims for relief for injuries caused by hazardous wastes and toxic substances. Rather, it simply applies the classic common law grounds for liability to the hazardous wastes and toxic substances context. The following discussion highlights the most frequently litigated claims and some of the principal defenses.

For convenience, the discussion breaks the claims into the most common grounds for recovery for property damage (including cleanup costs) and personal injuries, respectively. In practice, there is no rigid distinction between these grounds for recovery. Thus, in a proper case, a nuisance or trespass action can also support recovery for personal injuries received from the property contamination. Similarly, negligence and strict liability in tort may also support recovery for property damage (including cleanup costs), either as independent grounds for recovery, or as part of the proof sequence for a nuisance action.

## 1. CLAIMS FOR PROPERTY DAMAGE

### a. Nuisance

Nuisance law provides the most important ground for recovery of property damage and clean-up costs. In its varying forms it best exemplifies the adaptability of the common law tort system to changing times.

Two kinds of nuisance claims exist: private and public nuisance. The essence of a private nuisance claim is the defendant's substantial and unreasonable interference with the plaintiff's *use and enjoyment* of plaintiff's property. Restatement (Second) of Torts, § 822. Public nuisance is somewhat more broadly stated as an unreasonable interference with a right common to the general public. Restatement (Second) of Torts, § 821(b). It can involve any activity that is detrimental to the public health, welfare, or safety. Public nuisance has been used to abate everything from houses of prostitution to diseased trees. In many cases, the maintenance of activities that contaminate property with hazardous wastes or toxic substances ordinarily qualifies easily as a nuisance under either theory. See, e.g., Evanston v. Northern Illinois Gas Co., 229 F.Supp.3d 714 (N.D.Ill. 2017).

A threshold issue involves the plaintiff's standing to raise a nuisance claim under either theory. To raise a private nuisance claim, plaintiff must have an appropriate possessory interest in the real property whose use is allegedly impacted by the defendant's conduct. For example, lessees and mortgagees ordinarily have standing. Most jurisdictions, however, refuse to allow a current land owner to sue a former owner under nuisance theory. Philadelphia Electric Co. v. Hercules, Inc., 762 F.2d 303 (3d Cir.1985); Mayor and Council of Borough of Rockaway v. Klockner & Klockner, 811 F.Supp. 1039 (D.N.J.1993); compare Ronald Holland's A-Plus Transmission & Automotive, Inc. v. E-Z Mart Stores, Inc., 184 S.W.3d 749 (Tex.App.2005) (former owner was potentially liable to former lessee, now current owner). Similarly, nuisance claims have not generally been permitted against the generators of hazardous substances and their wastes, unless those manufacturers had control over disposal activities. See, e.g., City of Bloomington v. Westinghouse Electric Corp., 891 F.2d 611 (7th Cir.1989).

Standing is more often a problem with public nuisance claims. Public officials charged with law enforcement or health and safety regulation easily meet the standing requirement. To determine whether a private party has such standing, however, the courts determine if the plaintiff has suffered an injury that is different in kind from that suffered by the public at large. See, e.g., Armory Park Neighborhood Ass'n v. Episcopal Community Services, 148 Ariz. 1, 712 P.2d 914 (Ariz.1985). In effect, courts require a showing that the defendant's activity is allegedly both a public *and* a private nuisance to the plaintiff. Thus, private plaintiffs who can show physical injuries or private property damage from the alleged nuisance will ordinarily have standing to raise public nuisance. See, e.g., Anderson v. W.R. Grace & Co., 628 F.Supp. 1219 (D.Mass.1986). Because of its importance to both standing and individual recovery, the following discussion focuses on the elements of private nuisance.

Once standing has been demonstrated, the private nuisance plaintiff must demonstrate two additional matters: (1) an interference with use; and (2) an appropriate mental state. In addition, as described further below, plaintiff must show causation and damages.

The interference requirement focuses on the degree and type of impairment of plaintiff's property use. The defendant's activities must *substantially* and *unreasonably* interfere with the plaintiff's use of its property. Casual or minor interferences will not support a nuisance action. Where hazardous wastes contaminate plaintiff's property, the substantiality of the harm will ordinarily not be in issue. Indeed, the invasion of dust and odors alone may be enough to support a finding of substantial harm. See, e.g., Village of Wilsonville v. SCA Services, Inc., 86 Ill.2d 1, 55 Ill.Dec. 499, 426 N.E.2d 824 (Ill.1981). Where exposure to toxic substances threatens personal injury, courts will examine the extent of the risk presented. See, e.g., Lamb v. Martin Marietta Energy Systems, Inc., 835 F.Supp. 959 (W.D.Ky.1993).

As for the "unreasonableness" of the interference, the authorities are still split over the appropriateness of considering the utility of the defendant's conduct. Under the Restatement's approach, the defendant may raise the utility of its conduct as one factor for the court's determination of the unreasonableness of the interference. Restatement (Second) of Torts § 826. Thus, the Restatement considers the "unreasonable" interference element different from the "substantial" interference requirement. For others, however, the "reasonableness" inquiry does not focus on the social utility of defendant's conduct. Rather, it focuses solely on the burden placed on the plaintiff. Under this approach, the two elements, "substantial and unreasonable," are flip sides of the same coin. The defendant's conduct will be a "substantial *and* unreasonable" interference when an ordinary possessor of land would consider the conduct unduly burdensome. Of course, if the court *finds* a nuisance, the utility of defendant's conduct is relevant to a determination of the appropriate remedy. See, e.g., Madison v. Ducktown Sulphur, Copper & Iron Co., 113 Tenn. 331, 83 S.W. 658 (Tenn.1904).

In most nuisance cases involving hazardous wastes or toxic substances, the more important requirement will likely be proof of the requisite mental state. The mental state requirement allows recovery for three types of activities: (1) intentional; (2) negligent; or (3) abnormally dangerous. The first two types require proof of some fault; the last imposes strict liability. The existence of grounds of recovery, under nuisance law, for "negligent" and "abnormally dangerous conditions" has led to some blurring of legal theory. Courts are often unclear if they are considering "negligence" and "strict liability for abnormally dangerous condition" as independent tort actions or as subsets of nuisance law. In practice, for a person who has standing to bring any type of nuisance action, the distinctions are unimportant. The following discussion focuses on these activities solely as bases for establishing nuisance. They are then addressed briefly below, as independent grounds to obtain compensation for personal injuries.

For an intentional nuisance, plaintiff must show that the defendant either desired to interfere with the plaintiff's property use, or knew to a substantial certainty that such interference would result from defendant's conduct. Restatement (Second) of Torts § 825. Plaintiff may prove either ground with circumstantial evidence. Thus, while the "desire" ground is unlikely to be proven, the "substantial certainty" ground may be easily established by the length and notoriety of the activity at issue.

For a negligent nuisance, plaintiff must establish a breach of a duty of care owed to the plaintiff. In most circumstances, the limitations of negligence will encourage plaintiffs to proceed under the more easily established intentional nuisance or strict liability nuisance. For example, nuisance actions based on negligence often allow a defendant to raise the social utility—i.e., reasonableness—of the defendant's own conduct. Moreover, where the conduct occurred in the relatively distant past, the defendant may succeed in using the standards of the past in assessing the reasonableness of its conduct. Occasionally, however, negligence law may provide an easy proof sequence for plaintiff. For example, where defendant's conduct violates a statutory or regulatory standard, courts may find breach of duty under the "negligence per se" case law. (Some courts arrive at the same result under a different name, "nuisance per se.") See, e.g., Newhall Land and Farming Co. v. Superior Court, 19 Cal.App.4th 334, 23 Cal.Rptr.2d 377 (Cal.App.1993). Similarly, negligence may prove easily established where defendant's conduct implicates *res ipsa loquitur* principles. See, e.g., Reynolds Metals v. Yturbide, 258 F.2d 321 (9th Cir.1958). Finally, in an appropriate case, a failure to warn theory may support a finding of negligence.

To establish strict liability for maintenance of the nuisance, many courts use the "abnormally dangerous conditions" factors of the Restatement (Second) of Torts. Restatement (Second) of Torts, § 520. These factors include:

- the existence of a high degree of risk of some harm;
- the likelihood that the harm will be great;
- the inability to eliminate the risk of harm by the exercise of reasonable care;
- the extent to which the activity is not a matter of common usage;

- the inappropriateness of the activity to the place where it is carried on;
- and the extent to which the activity's value to the community is outweighed by its dangerousness.

Application of the strict liability factors to contaminated property cases has not been automatic. For example, some courts have refused to allow recovery under the theory in actions involving leaking petroleum tanks. These courts emphasize the common nature and overall utility of the defendant's sales of petroleum products. See, e.g., Arlington Forest Associates v. Exxon Corp., 774 F.Supp. 387 (E.D.Va.1991); cf. Biniek v. Exxon Mobil Corp., 358 N.J.Super. 587, 818 A.2d 330 (N.J.Super.Ct.Law Div.2002) (gasoline storage and transportation not an ultrahazardous activity). Other courts, however, find virtually the same conduct to be an appropriate topic for a strict liability based nuisance claim. These courts focus on the great harm that results from contamination and the near impossibility of designing a leak proof storage or piping system. See, e.g., Yommer v. McKenzie, 255 Md. 220, 257 A.2d 138 (Md.App.1969).

Many defenses have been raised to nuisance actions. The most commonly encountered defenses in cases involving hazardous wastes are the limitations period, the permit defense, and the notion of "coming to the nuisance." Unless the nuisance theory is grounded on negligence, "state of the art" or "industry practice" will be largely irrelevant. See, e.g., State of New York v. Schenectady Chemicals, Inc., 117 Misc.2d 960, 459 N.Y.S.2d 971 (N.Y.Sup.Ct.1983); cf. T & E Industries v. Safety Light Corp., 123 N.J. 371, 587 A.2d 1249 (N.J.1991) (reserving question whether "state of the art" is relevant to proof of defendant's knowledge of the risk).

Calculation of the limitations period for long standing nuisances, such as underground property contamination, is often a critical issue. It may turn on the characterization of the nuisance as a "permanent" or "continuing" nuisance. The line between the two is blurry, but the distinction has crucial impact. In general, courts ask whether the effects of the offending conduct could have been cured or interrupted during the running of the limitations period. If so, a "continuing" nuisance will be held to exist. Each separate invasion of plaintiff's use of its property will give rise to a separate action. Where, however, the injury is fixed, constant, and not easily abated, a permanent nuisance exists. See, e.g., Beck Development Co. v. Southern Pacific Transp. Co., 44 Cal.App.4th 1160, 52 Cal.Rptr.2d 518 (Cal.App.1996). Upon the expiration of the limitations period, a plaintiff faced with a permanent nuisance will lose the right to sue entirely. In contrast, the expiration of the limitations period only limits the amount of damages recoverable for a continuing nuisance.

For example, assume that a given jurisdiction allows a three year period to bring a nuisance action. The limitations period for actions to abate a permanent nuisance begins to run at the initiation of the nuisance. Thus, plaintiffs have three years from the initiation of the nuisance to sue. In contrast, each day that a continuous nuisance exists begins a new limitations period. Thus, at worst, the plaintiff who establishes a continuing nuisance will still be allowed to recover for the damages suffered during the most recently concluded limitations period. Under our hypothetical statute, the plaintiff could always recover for the three most recent years that the nuisance existed.

Calculation of the limitations period for nuisance actions involving hazardous substances may also be affected by federal law. Under CERCLA § 309, a state law claim for personal injuries or property damage from such substances does not begin to run until "the date the plaintiff knew (or reasonably should have known) that the personal injury or property damages * * * were caused * * * by the hazardous substance * * *."

The permit defense raises governmental approval of defendant's conduct to avoid characterization of that conduct as a nuisance. While superficially appealing, it is almost always ineffective. The statutory or regulatory criteria for issuing a permit often do not consider the full range of factors and local impacts that are appropriate to a nuisance analysis. Moreover, the statutory and regulatory schemes often set merely the floor for a defendant's conduct, not the ceiling. Thus, unless preempted, the common law may impose tighter requirements on a defendant than the statutory or regulatory minimums.

Finally, the "coming to the nuisance" defense has often been raised where the defendant's conduct has been long standing and the plaintiff's sensitivities only recently impaired. Again, while superficially appealing, the defense amounts to a claim of prescriptive rights to export noxious or harmful activities beyond the defendant's property. Still, courts in private nuisance cases may accept the defense; in public nuisance cases, however, the defense is less available. See, e.g., Spur Industries, Inc. v. Del E. Webb Development Co., 108 Ariz. 178, 494 P.2d 700 (Ariz.1972). In many states, a statutory version of the defense exists. Lobbies for powerful agricultural interests have enacted "right to farm" statutes and ordinances. These provisions shield farmers from many nuisance actions including, presumably, those involving the application of agricultural chemicals and pesticides.

Although there is a lot of practical overlap between public and private nuisance, the public nuisance action provides important benefits to private plaintiffs. Such a plaintiff may avoid some of the defenses—such as prescription, the statutes of limitations, and coming to the nuisance—that might bar a private nuisance claim. In addition, a plaintiff who is seeking equitable relief to abate the nuisance may influence the court's "balance of the equities" by demonstrating the broad, negative public impacts of the defendant's conduct. See, e.g., Spur

Industries, Inc. v. Del E. Webb Development Co., 108 Ariz. 178, 494 P.2d 700 (Ariz.1972).

### b. Trespass

Where nuisance focuses on plaintiff's *use* of property, trespass focuses on plaintiff's right to *possession*. To prove trespass, plaintiff traditionally had to show defendant's direct and intentional invasion of plaintiff's right to exclusive possession. See, e.g., Borland v. Sanders Lead Co. Inc., 369 So.2d 523 (Ala.1979). To prove intent, plaintiff need only show that the defendant intended to do the act which invaded the property; plaintiff need not, however, show that defendant intended to *enter* the property. In those jurisdictions where indirect trespasses—i.e., those facilitated by movements of air or water—are actionable, plaintiffs may prove intent under the "knowledge to a substantial certainty" standard also applicable for intentional nuisances. See, e.g., Restatement (Second) of Torts, § 158, cmt I. Under the Restatement view, adopted in many jurisdictions, a negligent or reckless entry may also support a trespass action. Restatement (Second) of Torts, § 165.

Where plaintiff establishes the requisite invasion, defendant will be liable unless the defendant establishes some privilege to enter the property, or some other affirmative defense. The privilege may come from the plaintiff's actual or implied consent. Alternatively, it may be supplied by the law. For example, many jurisdictions allow an entry where defendant demonstrates personal necessity, such as in avoidance of a robbery or assault. See, e.g., Ploof v. Putnam, 81 Vt. 471, 71 A. 188 (Vt.1908). Necessity, however, is unlikely to arise in trespass action involving hazardous waste.

Traditionally, courts have drawn supposedly sharp lines between nuisance and trespass claims. For example, to bring a trespass action, plaintiff had to show a direct physical invasion of plaintiff's possession of real property. Plaintiffs could only challenge indirect invasions or incorporeal invasions—from, e.g., light, smoke, odors and vibrations—under nuisance law. See, e.g., Born v. Exxon Corp., 388 So.2d 933 (Ala.1980). More recently, some courts have been willing to entertain trespass actions for deposition of airborne particles or underground contamination. Thus, increasingly, hazardous wastes liability actions can be based on either nuisance or trespass. See, e.g., Greenfield MHP Associates, LP v. Ametek, Inc., 145 F.Supp.3d 1000 (S.D.Cal.2015). Courts that allow trespass actions for indirect invasions, however, often require the plaintiff to show "actual and substantial damages." See, e.g., Borland v. Sanders Lead Co., Inc., 369 So.2d 523, 529 (Ala.1979). Cf. Public Serv. Co. of Colo. v. Van Wyk, 27 P.3d 377 (Colo.2001) (plaintiff must prove physical damage).

The practical differences between the two theories may be important. Historically, courts have been more protective of possessory interests than use interests. Indeed, to prevent an invasion of a possessory interest from ripening into a prescriptive right, nominal damages are presumed from the very invasion. Moreover, courts will frequently enjoin a trespass without conducting a rigorous equitable balancing of the competing interests of plaintiff and defendant. Finally, certain defenses applicable in nuisance are either irrelevant or weaker in trespass actions. For example, neither the permit defense nor the coming to the nuisance defense have any application in trespass. Similarly, the limitations period for trespass actions is often longer than for nuisance actions. Unfortunately, the same muddled distinction between "permanent" and "continuing" torts found in nuisance, however, also applies in trespass actions. E.g., Graham Oil Co. v. BP Oil Co., 885 F.Supp. 716 (W.D.Pa.1994).

## 2. PERSONAL INJURY CLAIMS

### a. Negligence

Negligence remains an important tool for those personal injury claims involving exposure to toxic substances that do not arise out of contaminated property. The nuisance discussion mentioned the possible applicability of "negligence per se" and *res ipsa loquitur*. In appropriate cases, these theories are also available for a personal injury claim. In addition, many cases arising out of occupational exposures to toxic substances have involved a defendant's failure to warn plaintiffs of the hazards to workers. Asbestos cases provide a classic example of the theory's application in this context. Indeed, the asbestos industry's knowledge of the dangers of asbestos exposure, coupled with its failure to warn its workers, has supported large punitive damages awards. See, e.g., Fischer v. Johns-Manville Corp., 103 N.J. 643, 512 A.2d 466 (N.J.1986). In these cases, courts have found that the defendant's failure to warn went beyond mere negligence to reckless, even intentional conduct.

Three principal issues arise in the "failure to warn" cases. The first involves the adequacy of the warning itself. In resolving that issue, courts consider multiple factors. These include:

- "the dangerous nature of the product;"
- "the form in which the product is used;"
- "the intensity and form of the warnings given;"
- "the burdens to be imposed by requiring warnings;"
- "and the likelihood that the particular warning will be adequately communicated to those who will foreseeably use the product."

Dougherty v. Hooker Chemical Corp., 540 F.2d 174, 179 (3d Cir.1976). The second issue involves the extent to which the manufacturer must notify all the potential handlers and users of the product. A subsidiary question involves the manufacturer's ability to delegate the duty to warn to intervening purchasers. See, e.g., Borel v. Fibreboard Paper Products Corp., 493 F.2d 1076 (5th Cir.1973). The final issue involves the preemptive effect of state or federal statutory labeling requirements.

### b. Strict Liability in Tort

Strict liability has three potential applications in personal injury cases involving toxic substances. First, as discussed above, a nuisance claim can be based on strict liability for abnormally dangerous activities. Second, strict liability for abnormally dangerous activities can support an independent tort action, even if the other requirements for nuisance, e.g., standing, are not met. Third, in an appropriate case, the user of a product injured by a hazardous substance contained within that product may sue under strict liability for manufacture of a defective product.

### c. Infliction of Emotional Distress

Finally, personal injury plaintiffs often raise emotional distress claims. For example, the ingestion of well water contaminated by carcinogens normally prompts well founded distress and fear of future disease. See, e.g., Potter v. Firestone Tire & Rubber Co., 6 Cal.4th 965, 25 Cal.Rptr.2d 550, 863 P.2d 795 (Cal.1993). Where emotional distress accompanies a physical injury, recovery is generally allowed as an individual item of damages under the tort theory used to remedy the physical injury. Where, however, the plaintiff has not suffered an actionable physical injury, yet still suffers from emotional distress resulting from defendant's actions, modern tort law recognizes two separate actions: (1) intentional infliction of emotional distress; and (2) negligent infliction of emotional distress. Additional discussion of recovery for such distress can be found below, in the discussion of compensatory damages.

To recover for intentional infliction of emotional distress, plaintiff must generally show two matters. First, the defendant's conduct must be "extreme and outrageous." See, e.g., Restatement (Third) of Torts, § 46. Second, the plaintiff's distress must be severe. This, in turn, requires a twin showing: (1) that no reasonable person would have endured the distress; and (2) the distress is "reasonable" under the circumstances.

To recover for negligent infliction of emotional distress, plaintiffs traditionally have had to establish physical injury. See, e.g., Payton v. Abbott Labs, 386 Mass. 540, 437 N.E.2d 171 (Mass.1982). Given the long lag time between exposure to a toxic substance and manifestation of disease or injury, the "physical injury" requirement has effectively limited many plaintiffs' recovery. Recently, some courts have been willing to accept medical testimony about cellular or subcellular damage as proof of physical injury. See, e.g., Buckley v. Metro-North Commuter Railroad, 79 F.3d 1337 (2d Cir.1996). Other courts have required only proof of a physical *impact* upon the plaintiff. See, e.g., Wilson v. Key Tronic Corp., 40 Wash.App. 802, 701 P.2d 518 (Wash.App.1985). Some have gone further and allowed recovery by all plaintiffs within the "zone of danger" created by defendant's conduct. See, e.g., Consolidated Rail Corp. v. Gottshall, 512 U.S. 532, 114 S.Ct. 2396, 129 L.Ed.2d 427 (1994). Finally, a few courts have abandoned any special requirements and simply apply standard negligence principles. Gerardi v. Nuclear Utility Services, Inc., 149 Misc.2d 657, 566 N.Y.S.2d 1002 (N.Y.Sup.Ct.1991).

## C. CAUSATION

### 1. INTRODUCTION

Perhaps the most challenging aspect of toxic torts litigation from the plaintiff's perspective is proof of causation. The causation analysis asks simply enough: did exposure to the hazardous wastes or toxic substances released by defendant harm plaintiff in a legally recognizable way? Behind the apparent simplicity of the question, however, lies a complicated analysis. Although prevalent to some degree in all toxic torts litigation, the causation issue is most pronounced in personal injury cases. Accordingly, the following discussion focuses on proof of causation in such cases.

In more conventional torts cases, causation is often only a minor issue. For example, in a medical malpractice case, the plaintiff's alleged injuries can usually be traced to the doctor's conduct. In such cases, the principal issue tends to be whether the doctor breached a duty of care owed to the patient when performing the actions that injured the plaintiff. In contrast, in litigation involving personal injuries from toxic substances, causation is frequently a case dispositive issue. Moreover, the causation analysis can turn on any of up to four separate sub-issues. In addition, causation cannot generally be proven (or disputed) without liberal use of expert witnesses. As a result, in most personal injury cases arising from toxic substances, and even some property damage cases involving hazardous wastes, causation becomes the linchpin around which the entire case turns. Indeed, as discussed at the end of this chapter, many courts have tailored the procedures employed to develop and try the case to focus on the causation issues.

Causation in toxic torts involves up to four steps. First, the plaintiff must demonstrate that the substance or waste in question is capable of causing harm of the type plaintiff suffered. In short, this asks whether the material *is* toxic. Second, the plaintiff must show that he or she was exposed to some release of the material into the environment. This is known as the "exposure pathway." Third, the plaintiff must show that the *defendant's* release of the material caused the plaintiff's injury, not someone else's release or the plaintiff's exposure to the substance from naturally occurring "background" releases. This is known as the "indeterminate plaintiff" problem. Finally, in cases involving multiple manufacturers of an identical product, the plaintiff must demonstrate that the particular defendants sued were responsible for the plaintiff's exposure. This is known as the "indeterminate defendant" problem. The current section addresses the first three causation issues. The last problem is addressed further below, in the discussion of "multiple defendants."

## 2. PROOF OF TOXICITY

Plaintiff's causation analysis begins with proof that the substance or waste in question was capable of causing harm of the type that plaintiff suffered. In conventional torts litigation, the capability of the defendant to cause harm is usually not in issue. For example, in a medical malpractice case, no one will likely dispute that the slip of the surgeon's knife could have cut the plaintiff in a harmful way. Similarly, in an automobile collision case, the ability of a high speed impact to harm the plaintiff is taken for granted. A particular case may turn on whether the injuries plaintiff suffered were attributable to *this* collision, or, rather, represented a pre-existing condition or a subsequent injury. But no dispute usually arises over the defendant's *ability* to have injured the plaintiff.

In contrast, proof of the toxicity of the substance in dispute is often a central issue in cases involving an allegedly toxic substance. Indeed, failure to make this initial showing has proved fatal for many plaintiffs, particularly those claiming birth defects from exposure to certain drugs. See, e.g., Brock v. Merrell Dow Pharmaceuticals, Inc., 874 F.2d 307 (5th Cir.1989). The difficulties adhere in the very nature of these torts. In high enough doses, virtually anything ingestible may prove toxic, even water and table salt. But acute poisoning from high doses is not the norm in personal injury cases involving toxic substances or hazardous wastes. Rather, as noted in Chapter 2, these cases frequently involve long term exposure to low doses.

In addition, they may involve intergenerational injuries (e.g., birth defects). In such cases, laboratory or field data may not exist to determine whether the material in question is capable of causing the harms suffered.

For a few substances, such as asbestos, good data exists that shows the substance's ability to cause such injuries as asbestosis. But asbestos is the exception. For most substances, scientists or governmental regulators may simply not have studied the substance's effects *upon humans* at the dosage levels and through exposure pathways similar to the circumstances by which plaintiff was exposed. As a result, data on toxicity will have to be extrapolated from the available bioassays or epidemiological studies. Chapter 2 noted the problems that such extrapolations pose. At best, a battle of the experts will ensue, where different scientists take the same data and reach polar opposite conclusions on a substance's toxicity at given dose levels and through given exposure pathways. See, e.g., Daubert v. Merrell Dow Pharmaceuticals, Inc., 509 U.S. 579, 113 S.Ct. 2786, 125 L.Ed.2d 469 (1993); Ruff v. Ensign-Bickford Industries, Inc., 168 F.Supp.2d 1271 (D.Utah 2001) (insufficient evidence that compound caused relevant disease in humans, but sufficient evidence that compound's breakdown products could).

Thus, uncertainties abound at the very threshold of a plaintiff's case. A defendant can often capitalize on this uncertainty and have the case dismissed on summary judgment, or on a directed verdict motion.

### 3. PROOF OF EXPOSURE PATHWAY

If a plaintiff is able to provide at least a prima facie showing that the substance is toxic, plaintiff will next have to demonstrate how he or she became exposed to the substance in question. For example, a plaintiff claiming birth defects from prenatal exposure to a toxic substance must show that his or her mother was exposed during pregnancy, and that the mother could have transmitted the substance to the plaintiff while in utero. Similarly, a worker claiming a job related injury must show an occupational exposure to the substance in question. Absent such proof, plaintiff's case fails.

Proof of the exposure pathway is the one causation issue that may prove critical in cases involving damage to real property from hazardous wastes. Plaintiffs must show how the contaminating wastes traveled from defendant's operations to plaintiff's property. With spills that simply ooze from one parcel to another, proof is simple. Where, however, the case involves either airborne deposition or groundwater contamination, the linkage between the defendant's operations and plaintiff's property may be more difficult to establish. This is particularly true for groundwater contamination, where long buried tanks from long forgotten businesses may not leak for many years.

### 4. INDETERMINATE PLAINTIFF

Assuming that plaintiff has survived the first two causation hurdles, a third challenge awaits: plaintiff must demonstrate that her injury was caused by defendants' conduct, and not from natural means. This is particularly difficult where plaintiff seeks to recover for cancer or birth defects. These injuries are linked to naturally occurring toxic substances or conditions. For example, naturally occurring background radiation may be responsible for plaintiff's birth defects, not defendant's product. Or, the natural aflatoxin in the peanut butter sandwiches plaintiff ate as a child may have caused her cancer. With rare exceptions, the causes of cancer, still poorly understood, do not leave their fingerprints over the plaintiff's injury. In cases involving long term exposure to low doses of carcinogens, it is ordinarily impossible to determine whether a given plaintiff's cancer was caused by exposure to a natural or an artificial release of the carcinogen in question. In other words, a plaintiff will frequently have great difficulty in meeting the conventional burden of persuasion, i.e., demonstrating that it is more likely than not that defendant caused her cancer.

Faced with these uncertainties and the harsh consequences of a strict application of the burden of persuasion, courts have disagreed over the plaintiff's required showing. One of the best discussions of these issues is the district court's opinion in the *Agent Orange* litigation. In re Agent Orange Product Liability Litigation, 597 F.Supp. 740 (E.D.N.Y.1984). In that opinion, Judge Weinstein identified two different judicial approaches to the problems presented by the burden of persuasion.

The first approach involved what Judge Weinstein called the "strong" version of the preponderance of the evidence standard. Under that version, courts require that plaintiffs first show that defendant's conduct more than doubled plaintiffs' likelihood of getting cancer. For example, assume that the background incidence of a given cancer is, say, 10 in 100,000 people per lifetime. Plaintiff would have to prove that the toxic substances released by defendant increased her chance of contracting cancer to at least 21 in 100,000. Such a showing would mean that for any given cancer in the population group it was more likely than not that defendant caused it. If, however, plaintiff can only show that defendant increased the cancer risk from 10 in 100,000 to 15 in 100,000, she would not be able to recover.

For all of the reasons discussed in Chapter 2, such probabilistic evidence is difficult to obtain. But even if it were available, courts using the "strong" version of the preponderance standard demand even more. They also require plaintiff to introduce particularistic proof that links her cancer to defendant's conduct.

The strong version is greatly favorable to defendants. It ensures that defendants will not be forced to compensate a plaintiff who may be suffering only from a naturally occurring injury. But, while protective to defendants, it is harsh upon plaintiffs. The difficulty of disproving a naturally occurring injury means that many plaintiffs who *were* injured by a given defendant will be unable to recover.

In recognition of the harshness of this rule, some courts have modified it. Under Judge Weinstein's terminology, these courts employ a "weak" version of the preponderance theory. For these courts, plaintiff need only show that defendant's release of the substance in question more than doubled the chances that plaintiff would suffer the injury, e.g., cancer. See, e.g., Cook v. United States, 545 F.Supp. 306 (N.D.Cal.1982). These courts do not further demand that plaintiff introduce particularistic evidence to trace her cancer to defendant's conduct. Cf. In re Hanford Nuclear Reservation Litigation, 292 F.3d 1124 (9th Cir.2002) (plaintiffs not required to show a greater-than-doubled risk).

The weak version is more favorable to plaintiff. It will force a defendant, however, to provide compensation for many naturally caused cancers, as there is still no way to determine whether the particular plaintiff's cancer was one that the defendant induced, or was one that would have occurred anyway. But this result is consistent with the principle that a defendant who is a "substantial factor" in the plaintiff's injury is fully responsible for the injury, even if other actors might also be responsible.

Still, both the strong and weak versions fail to compensate plaintiffs who cannot show that the defendant more than doubled the background incidence of cancer. In response to these inadequacies, several courts have traced different approaches entirely. In a famous case involving exposure to radiation from the federal government's desert testing of nuclear weapons, the judge took a multi-factored approach to create particular affiliating links between the defendant's conduct and the plaintiff's cancer or leukemia. Allen v. United States, 588 F.Supp. 247 (D.Utah 1984), rev'd on other grounds, 816 F.2d 1417 (10th Cir.1987). In *Allen*, the plaintiff had to show: (1) membership in an identifiable group put at increased risk of injury by defendant's conduct; and (2) an injury consistent with the type of risks created by the defendant's conduct. This second step required a showing of "substantial, appropriate, persuasive and connecting factors." Once the plaintiff made this showing, the burden shifted to the defendant to offer persuasive proof of noncausation. But see Merrell Dow Pharmaceuticals, Inc. v. Havner, 953 S.W.2d 706 (Tex.1997) (plaintiff must also offer evidence excluding, with reasonable certainty, other possible causes of disease.)

Judge Weinstein's opinion in the *Agent Orange* litigation took an entirely different tack. In place of *Allen*'s particularized, burden shifting approach, Judge Weinstein adopted a collective approach based on a nationwide class action. In re Agent Orange Product Liability Litigation, 597 F.Supp. 740 (E.D.N.Y.1984). He first determined that no one veteran within the proposed class was likely able to demonstrate particularized proof of an injury resulting from Agent Orange exposure. Nevertheless, he approved settlement of a class action that provided partial compensation to all class members with symptoms possibly caused by Agent Orange, but possibly caused by other factors. In approving the settlement, the court explicitly balanced the interests of defendants and plaintiffs. The court's order protected defendants from paying full compensation for the "background" injuries. At the same time, it insured that all veterans with the same injuries got the same compensation, even though no one veteran could tell whether his or her injury was "caused" by Agent Orange.

Finally, the New Jersey Supreme Court in Landrigan v. Celotex Corp., 127 N.J. 404, 605 A.2d 1079 (N.J.1992) allowed both plaintiffs and defendants to use particularistic evidence to counter otherwise unfavorable statistical evidence. On the one hand, a plaintiff who could not demonstrate a statistical doubling of his chance of getting cancer nevertheless could show that *other* circumstances made it more likely than not that defendant's conduct caused his cancer. For example, an asbestos worker suffering from a non-signature cancer might show the presence of asbestos fibers near the tumor to help prove that his cancer was attributable to asbestos exposure. On the other hand, under the same opinion, a defendant could rebut evidence that showed its conduct had more than doubled plaintiff's cancer risk. For example, the defendant might introduce lifestyle or family history evidence to show that the particular cancer involved was probably caused by something other than the defendant's conduct.

## D. MULTIPLE DEFENDANTS

Assuming plaintiff has leaped the first three causation hurdles, a final hurdle involves the problem of multiple potential defendants. Multiple defendants raise two separate problems. The first involves the frequently encountered problem of apportionment of liability among concurrent, independent tortfeasors. Each of these tortfeasors is at least a partial, separate cause of plaintiff's injuries. The common law has long had rules for allocating responsibility among such tortfeasors. The second problem, encountered in some toxic substances cases based on product liability law, involves the "indeterminate defendant." Such cases involve the manufacture of the identical product, such as a prescription drug, by many defendants. Only *one* of the defendants, however, will have manufactured the *particular* dose that harmed plaintiff. Courts have not yet agreed upon rules allocating responsibility among all the potential manufacturers of the harmful product.

### 1. JOINT AND SEVERAL LIABILITY

Where multiple parties, acting independently, are each a substantial factor in plaintiff's injury, the law must find a way to apportion liability. For example, assume that each of two industrial neighbors releases hazardous wastes that contaminate plaintiff's property. To determine the defendants' share of liability, courts use two principal approaches: (1) joint and several liability;

and (2) several liability. Additional approaches are possible where the plaintiff is also partially at fault.

"Joint and several" liability results where courts make each defendant responsible for plaintiff's *entire* injury. In such cases, plaintiff may seek a *full* recovery against any *one* defendant. After such a defendant has made plaintiff whole, the law of "contribution" allows that defendant to seek partial reimbursement from the other defendants who are also jointly and severally liable. Equitable principles will govern this apportionment. In contrast, a defendant who is only "severally" liable will only have to pay plaintiff for the specific proportion of injury that that defendant caused. As a general matter, in recent decades states have increasingly shifted toward imposing only several liability. For additional discussion of joint and several liability and apportionment issues, see Chapters 9 and 11.

### 2. THE "INDETERMINATE DEFENDANT"

A more complicated issue, known as the "indeterminate defendant" problem, occurs in some personal injury cases based on product liability law. Often in such cases, multiple defendants will have each manufactured a "generic" product that later proves toxic. For example, dozens of pharmaceutical companies may have manufactured a drug, like DES, that later is linked to birth defects. In such cases, plaintiffs will often have great difficulty in establishing that a particular defendant manufactured the particular item that actually harmed plaintiff.

In response to these problems, courts have considered four solutions: (1) alternative liability; (2) concerted action; (3) enterprise liability; and (4) market share liability. See, e.g., Smith v. Cutter Biological, Inc., 72 Haw. 416, 823 P.2d 717 (Hawai'i 1991); In re Methyl Tertiary Butyl Ether (MTBE) Products Liability Litigation, 379 F.Supp.2d 348 (S.D.N.Y.2005). They have not yet, however, settled on any one theory.

"Alternative liability" imposes joint and several liability upon each of two or more actors who, acting simultaneously, might have been the sole cause of plaintiff's injury. The classic example, illustrated by the famous case of Summers v. Tice, 33 Cal.2d 80, 199 P.2d 1 (Cal.1948), is when two hunters negligently fire their rifles towards plaintiff. A bullet from one strikes plaintiff, but it is impossible to tell which hunter fired the wounding shot. In such circumstances, courts will shift the burden of proof to the defendants to prove that their shot was *not* the cause of plaintiff's injury. Absent such proof, each is fully liable for all of plaintiff's injuries. But see Spencer v. Baxter Intern., Inc., 163 F.Supp.2d 74 (D.Mass.2001) (producers not liable under theory).

"Concerted action" involves proof that defendants, while nominally acting individually, acted in a consciously parallel manner. To recover under this theory against *all* the parties who were acting in concert, plaintiff must show evidence of an implicit agreement among the defendants. Such evidence may come from similar patterns of design, manufacture, or marketing of the material in question. The theory works best where there is a small number of defendants and a short time between the injury and the discovery of harm.

"Enterprise liability" combines the alternative liability and concerted action theories. Underlying the theory are notions of joint risk control by all participants in the industry that produced the material in question. It best fits where plaintiff shows that the defendants delegated to an industry wide council the authority for responding to product safety concerns. See, e.g., Hall v. E.I. Du Pont De Nemours & Co., Inc., 345 F.Supp. 353 (E.D.N.Y.1972); Thomas ex. rel. Gramling v. Mallett, 285 Wis.2d 236, 701 N.W.2d 523 (Wis.2005).

Finally, "market share liability" is the most recently developed response. Brought to prominence by the famous *Abbott Laboratories* decision, the theory combines burden shifting and assignment of liability in proportion to market share. Sindell v. Abbott Laboratories, 26 Cal.3d 588, 163 Cal.Rptr. 132, 607 P.2d 924 (Cal.1980). Under *Abbott Laboratories* and its progeny, a plaintiff must sue a "substantial share" of the manufacturers of the generic material in question. Once the plaintiff demonstrates culpable conduct in the material's design, manufacture or marketing, the burden shifts to each defendant to prove that that defendant did *not* manufacture the particular unit that harmed plaintiff. Each defendant who is unable to disprove manufacture is held liable for the percentage of plaintiff's damages that corresponds to that defendant's share of the market for the material. Courts further presume that each defendant has equal market share; individual defendants may prove that their market share was lower than the presumed per capita share. See, e.g., Suffolk County Water Authority v. Dow Chemical Co., 987 N.Y.S.2d 819 (N.Y.Sup.Ct.2014) (applying market share theory in action by municipal water supplier against chemical manufacturer).

Because each of these theories has its limitations, the courts are currently in disagreement over the preferred response. For example, the "alternative liability" theory requires clear evidence that at least one of the defendants joined is liable. Thus, it may be difficult to apply if plaintiff does not join all potential defendants simultaneously. The "concerted action" theory is simply difficult to prove. The "enterprise liability" theory fails absent joint, industry-wide control of product safety standards. The "market share" theory raises important questions about the scope of the relevant market (national, regional or local), the proof of individual share within the relevant market, and the number of defendants that plaintiff must join to invoke the theory. Indeed, absent joinder of all the defendants from the relevant market, any given verdict may be imposed upon a manufacturer who did not actually produce the material that injured plaintiff.

Because each of the first three theories imposes joint and several liability, some courts have favored the market share theory. See, e.g., Smith v. Cutter

Biological Inc., 72 Haw. 416, 823 P.2d 717 (Hawai'i 1991). That limits an individual defendant's potential liability to an individual, or "several," share. Other courts, however, have found that the market share theory's problems are too much to justify its use. See, e.g., Smith v. Eli Lilly & Co., 137 Ill.2d 222, 148 Ill.Dec. 22, 560 N.E.2d 324 (Ill.1990). Absent the applicability of one of the other three theories, such courts may well insist that plaintiff establish that defendant actually manufactured the material in issue.

## E. REMEDIES

### 1. DAMAGES

#### a. Compensatory Damages

Plaintiffs who leap the causation hurdles and overcome any affirmative defenses can expect a full measure of traditional compensatory damages.

#### *i. Real Property Contamination*

For example, in real property contamination cases, courts traditionally award the plaintiffs the cost to restore the property. In addition, they have awarded damages for loss of use. They have frequently capped plaintiff's recovery, however, at the pre-contamination value of the property. More recently, some courts have been willing to award full remediation damages, regardless of the property's pre-contamination market value. See, e.g., In re Paoli R.R. Yard PCB Litigation, 35 F.3d 717 (3d Cir.1994); but see Bower v. Westinghouse

Elec. Corp., 206 W.Va. 133, 522 S.E.2d 424 (W.Va.1999) (eliminating one of *Paoli's* requirements).

### *ii. Personal Injury*

Similarly, a personal injury plaintiff damaged by a toxic substance can recover traditional, nonspeculative damages for medical expenses, lost earnings, pain and suffering, and reduced quality of life. In addition to these conventional items, plaintiffs have sought recovery for several new items. In particular, three types of damages have received substantial judicial attention: (1) fear of cancer; (2) increased risk of cancer; and (3) medical monitoring.

Where a defendant's conduct has exposed plaintiff to a carcinogen, plaintiff will frequently suffer from a fear of contracting the disease. (Such fears are often inaccurately described as "cancer phobia.") As noted above, courts are currently split over the recoverability, if any, for such fears. Some courts have denied recovery absent proof that plaintiff has suffered some physical injury. See, e.g., Brewton v. Reichhold Chemicals, Inc., 707 So.2d 618 (Miss.1998) (no cause of action in Mississippi). Other courts find such injury in any cellular or subcellular damage shown to have occurred as a result of the exposure to the carcinogen. Other courts, notably the California Supreme Court in Potter v. Firestone Tire & Rubber Co., 6 Cal.4th 965, 25 Cal.Rptr.2d 550, 864 P.2d 795 (Cal.1993), do not require proof of physical injury at all.

Nevertheless, ordinarily, they only allow recovery if plaintiff can show that it is more likely than not that plaintiff will contract cancer. Under *Potter*, however, where plaintiff can show that defendant has acted with "oppression, fraud, or despicable conduct" toward plaintiff, then, plaintiff need only show a significant increased risk of cancer.

A second and distinct issue involves recovery for the increased *risk* of contracting a disease, such as cancer, from plaintiff's exposure to materials released by defendant. In contrast to the preceding item, this item focuses on the increased *risk* of disease itself, not the *fear* induced by that risk. Some courts have allowed such a recovery, at least where the plaintiff can quantify the extent of the enhanced risk. See, e.g., Bocook v. Ashland Oil, 819 F.Supp. 530 (S.D.W.Va.1993). Others, however, refuse to allow the recovery. For these courts, plaintiffs can recover only if they actually contract the disease. Mauro v. Raymark Industries, Inc., 116 N.J. 126, 561 A.2d 257 (N.J.1989).

In part because of the difficulties of proof of causation where a long time exists between exposure and manifestation of disease, courts have been more generous in allowing recovery for a third new item of damage: medical monitoring costs. Where defendant has exposed plaintiff to a toxic substance, courts have not insisted on rigid proof that plaintiff will *likely* contract some disease or condition in response. Rather, decisions like *Potter* increasingly employ a multi-factored approach to determine whether defendant should pay for regular medical examinations. These courts consider:

- the significance and extent of plaintiff's exposure;
- the relative toxicity of the substances involved;
- the seriousness of the disease for which plaintiff is at increased risk of contraction;
- the relative risk, compared to background levels, that plaintiff will contract the disease;
- and the medical value of early detection of the disease or condition.

The New Jersey courts have developed an additional wrinkle with medical monitoring expenses. To ensure that plaintiffs actually use the award for medical examinations, defendants can pay into a court supervised fund. Ayers v. Township of Jackson, 106 N.J. 557, 525 A.2d 287 (N.J.1987). Plaintiffs are allowed payment from this fund for demonstrated medical expenses covered by the award. Defendants are also given credit for collateral payments made to plaintiffs by others, such as medical insurers, who would otherwise pay for such expenses.

### b. Punitive or Exemplary Damages

In appropriate cases, courts have awarded substantial punitive or exemplary damages for injuries caused by hazardous wastes or toxic substances. Typical language requires plaintiffs to prove "malicious, oppressive or despicable" conduct. For example, defendants in some asbestosis cases have been ordered to pay substantial punitive damages upon proof that they ignored for decades known risks to their workers from occupational exposure to asbestos. See, e.g., Fischer v. Johns-Manville Corp., 103 N.J. 643, 512 A.2d 466 (N.J.1986). Ultimately, punitive damages awards are limited by the Eighth Amendment. In recent years, the Supreme Court has used that provision, which prohibits "cruel and unusual punishment," to first review and then cap punitive damage awards. See BMW of North America, Inc. v. Gore, 517 U.S. 559 (1996); State Farm Mutual Automobile Insurance Co. v. Campbell, 538 U.S. 408 (2003).

The imposition of punitive damages in mass torts contexts raises important policy concerns. On the one hand, such damages serve the traditional functions of all punitive damages. They punish, they deter similar conduct, and they make sure that a defendant who acts with impunity is not left in a better position (because it can better *plan* responses to liability) than a defendant who merely acted negligently. On the other hand, they may provide the first plaintiffs who sue a substantial windfall. Moreover, if too severe, they may limit the defendant's ability to pay compensatory damages to victims whose injuries do not manifest themselves as early.

## 2. EQUITABLE RELIEF

In limited cases, particularly those involving intentional nuisance or trespass to property, equitable relief may be appropriate. That is, courts may order a defendant to change its conduct in order to remedy or prevent injury. But equitable relief raises a host of policy and enforcement issues that limit its availability in many cases involving personal injury from toxic substances. It is rarely available in product liability cases involving personal injury claims. In property contamination, damages are often an adequate remedy. Moreover, courts must consider a variety of public and private factors before shaping their remedies. In particular, courts are not likely to involve themselves in solutions that require long term judicial supervision of a defendant's conduct. For these reasons, courts infrequently order defendants directly to clean up contaminated property; rather, they simply award damages for the cost of that cleanup, and leave the parties to figure out who will actually conduct the cleanup. Finally, courts will rarely intervene to prevent harm that might occur, i.e., from the threat of a future leak of a hazardous substance. A rare example of a trial court that ordered closure of a waste dump principally because of such threats was upheld by the Illinois Supreme Court in Village of Wilsonville v. SCA Services, Inc., 86 Ill.2d 1, 55 Ill.Dec. 499, 426 N.E.2d 824 (Ill.1981).

## F. PROCEDURAL RESPONSES

### 1. INTRODUCTION

In addition to the complexities hazardous wastes and toxic substances present for tort law, they pose substantial challenges to the courts' ability to process the complicated lawsuits. In particular, the number of parties and the complexity of the proof process have led courts to experiment with different approaches to managing a lawsuit.

Tort cases involving hazardous wastes or toxic substances often involve many parties. For example, groundwater contamination cases may present challenges by dozens, or even hundreds, of owners of property overlying the polluted aquifer. At the extremes, in personal injury cases arising out of exposure to toxic substances, plaintiffs may number in the tens of thousands. For example, the *Agent Orange* class action involved tens of thousands of veterans. Similarly, tens of thousands of separate asbestosis claims are pending in *each* of several states. Cases of such size or in such number can easily swamp a court system.

Even if a lawsuit involves a more manageable number of parties, the complexities of the proof process challenge the courts' ability to do substantial justice. The expense and time involved in developing the parties' respective claims and defenses have forced courts to more aggressively manage their cases. Such case management can keep cases moving through the system while reducing waste of public and private efforts on matters that ultimately prove nondispositive.

In response to these and other concerns, courts have developed a number of case management options. The following discussion introduces five ways in which the judicial system has attempted to address the procedural complexities of toxic tort litigation: (1) polyfurcation orders; (2) case management orders; and (3) case consolidations; (4) test cases; and (5) class action certifications.

## 2. "POLYFURCATION"

Rules of procedure generally grant courts broad discretion to divide a case into different segments for separate trial. A court will exercise that discretion in two principal circumstances. First, the court may conclude that separate trial will be more efficient, considered from the perspective of either the parties, the witnesses, or the court itself. Second, particularly where the case is tried to a jury, the court may want to prevent trial of one claim or issue from biasing or confusing the jury's understanding of other claims or issues.

When the courts exercise this traditional discretion, they are said to "sever" or "bifurcate" the case. Traditionally, courts might "sever" one (or more) of several claims for a completely separate trial. Alternatively, courts might "bifurcate" a single case into two separate components. For example, trial might be held first only on liability. Only if the jury returns a verdict of liability will the parties spend the time to address the claimed items of damage. In such cases, bifurcation prevents the jury's liability decision from being influenced by evidence of the damages that plaintiffs have suffered. In addition, it obviates a possibly wasteful introduction of damages evidence in those cases where the jury finds no liability. See, e.g., Pinal Creek Group v. Newmont Mining Corp., 218 F.R.D. 652 (D.Ariz.2003) (bifurcating CERCLA contribution trial into liability and damages/allocation phases).

In toxic torts cases, courts are increasingly using these powers. Indeed, they have frequently gone beyond the simple bifurcation of a case. Instead, in appropriate cases, there may be a split of the case into three or more parts. This process of segmentation is known as "trifurcation" when the case has three parts, or generically as "polyfurcation."

A typical polyfurcation order would divide a personal injury toxic torts case into up to four parts. First, the court would divide the case into liability and damages segments, reserving damages for trial after determination of liability. Second, the court would subdivide the liability phase into up to three separate parts. The initial trial would address toxicity matters: i.e., was the substance capable of causing the harm plaintiffs suffered? If the jury returned a verdict in the plaintiff's favor on the substance's toxicity, the court would then address in two more trial segments the causation issues described above as the "indeterminate plaintiff" and "indeterminate defendant" problems. In so doing, the court can keep the complicated, conflicting expert testimony focused on each potentially case dispositive issue, one issue at a time.

Polyfurcation orders generally favor defendants over plaintiffs. Many plaintiffs' attorneys complain that the segmentation of their cases reduces the case's overall impact on the trier of fact. In particular, they strongly prefer to try damages and liability issues together.

### 3. CASE MANAGEMENT ORDERS

A second procedural development spurred by toxic torts litigation is the use of "case management orders." "Case management orders" are also known both by their acronym—CMOs—and as "Lone Pine" orders. The latter name stems from the title of an unpublished New Jersey decision that was one of the first to employ CMOs in a toxic torts case. Among other matters, these orders address the conduct of the pretrial process.

In their broadest context, CMOs are just one instance of the increasing judicial regulation of the adversary system of litigation. The past few decades have shown a greater judicial insistence upon case management. This insistence has replaced the traditional, laissez-faire approach under which the courts allowed the adversaries themselves to determine the shape of the pretrial process. Traditionally, the courts allowed the parties to bombard each other with discovery requests and pretrial motions, intervening only when asked by one party to correct an alleged abuse by another party. In recent years, courts have intervened routinely in even simple litigation. For example, they have limited the amount of discovery the parties may undertake without prior judicial approval. In addition, they have insisted that the parties plan the discovery that will be permitted. Such planning not only avoids potential scheduling conflicts, it also allows discovery to be scheduled more efficiently. In particular, the time and expense needed for discovery on some matters may be avoided entirely if potentially case dispositive matters are developed first and resolved on summary judgment motions.

In this light, CMOs are just another example of pretrial orders. Thus, courts will typically employ CMOs to schedule discovery more coherently. But one aspect of CMOs developed in toxic torts cases has stood out. As part of the CMOs, the court may require the plaintiff early in the lawsuit to put on a prima facie case *before* permitting full discovery. Only if the plaintiff's initial presentation to the court demonstrates sufficient grounds to suggest that the case is meritorious will the court allow the parties to employ the full range of discovery otherwise permissible. See, e.g., Avila v. Willits Environmental Remediation Trust, 633 F.3d 828 (9th Cir. 2011) (district court did not abuse its discretion in issuing Lone Pine order that required plaintiffs to produce proof of causation during pretrial phase after case had been pending for five years).

## 4. CASE CONSOLIDATION

The converse of "polyfurcation" is "consolidation." Again, courts have traditionally enjoyed broad discretion to consolidate separate cases. Many court rules require only that there be some common issue of law or fact before two cases may be tried together. The court must decide whether the benefits of consolidation outweigh the costs. The benefits include more efficient use of public and private litigation resources and greater conveniences to the witnesses and, often, the parties. In addition, there is a reduced chance for similar cases to be resolved inconsistently. The costs of consolidation include the inefficiencies, jury confusion, and possibly unfairness that results when the *dissimilar* portions of the case are tried together.

Mass toxic torts cases, such as those involving the contamination of a large number of people or properties, present arguments for partial case consolidation. On the one hand, these cases generally present a lot of overlap of basic questions involving such matters as the defendant's conduct, the toxicity of the material in question, and the exposure pathways. On the other hand, the items of damage will often differ markedly between one plaintiff and another.

In such circumstances, courts may take advantage of the benefits of consolidation in two ways. First, cases may be consolidated for pretrial purposes. This will allow much greater efficiencies in the conduct of discovery and pretrial motions. Second, courts can combine polyfurcation and consolidation by ordering joint trial only on the common matters. For example, a consolidated trial could determine first whether the defendant released the material into the environment and whether that material is capable of causing the plaintiffs' harm. If the jury answered yes on both counts, then the court could proceed to separate trials on the individual causation and damages issues.

Consolidation often works to both parties' advantage, but it may be more friendly to the plaintiffs than polyfurcation or CMOs. Plaintiffs may well benefit from pooling resources during discovery and during trial. These potential efficiencies, however, require individual plaintiffs to sacrifice some of their independence. Thus, the courts will often require the respective sides to organize themselves into litigation committees and divide the court and discovery work among themselves. Any given plaintiff thus has no assurance that his or her personal attorney will be the one chosen by committee to handle a particular matter during discovery or trial.

## 5. TEST CASES

Another approach to the problem of mass toxic torts litigation has been the development of the "test case." Test cases can work to both parties' advantage. Under this approach, cases may be consolidated for pretrial purposes, but are tried separately. Subject to judicial supervision, the parties decide which of the myriad cases will be heard in its entirety first. This may involve only a single plaintiff, or, more frequently, a small group of plaintiffs. The jury's verdict will then be used by all to evaluate the settlement prospects for the remaining cases. In addition, depending upon the jurisdiction's law of issue preclusion, a test case that is favorable to the *plaintiffs* may be used by later plaintiffs to preclude the test case defendant, or one in privity with that defendant, from relitigating identical matters determined adversely to the defendant in the test case. Cf. In re TMI Litigation, 193 F.3d 613 (3d Cir.1999) (defense verdict in mini-trial test case, under CMO, would not be extended to remaining plaintiffs).

### 6. CLASS ACTIONS

No discussion of mass toxic torts litigation could be complete without at least mention of the role that class actions play in resolving such claims. A class action is a device that allows multiple parties to sue or be sued jointly, as a class. The litigation is conducted in the name of class "representatives." Under each jurisdiction's standards, the courts must certify that the lawsuit is properly brought. Typically, the certification process involves two steps. First, there are prerequisites applicable to all class actions. These are often expressed as "numerosity," "commonality," "typicality," and "adequacy of representation." See, e.g., Fed.R.Civ.P. 23(a). "Numerosity" requires the existence of so many parties that joinder of all in a single, non-class action suit would be impracticable. "Commonality" requires the existence of some common questions of law or fact. "Typicality" requires that the class representatives' claims be "typical" of the class' claims. And "adequacy" looks to the representatives' ability to protect the class' interests. Compare O'Connor v. Boeing North American, Inc., 184 F.R.D. 311 (C.D.Cal.1998) (requirements met) with Rink v. Cheminova, Inc., 203 F.R.D. 648 (M.D.Fla.2001) (requirements not met).

In addition to these four prerequisites, a class action must fit within one of the permitted types of suit. Under the federal rules, applicable in the federal courts and about half of the states, three separate types of classes are permissible. See, e.g., Fed.R.Civ.P. 23(b). These include cases where: (1) individual cases might lead to inconsistent judgments or practically impair nonparties' interests; (2) cases seeking the imposition of equitable relief; and (3) cases where both the common questions "predominate" *and* the class action is "superior to other available methods." Additional provisions address how potential class members are to be notified of the suit's pendency, and their options in response to that notice.

At first glance the class action would seem to be an especially suitable device for mass toxic tort litigation. The device ensures that there would be a single pool of funds available to all class members. This prevents those parties who first sue from exhausting the defendants' ability to compensate all similar victims. It also allows for extensive economies of scale. Finally, it provides a self financing mechanism, as, contrary to normal practice in the United States, attorneys' fees are routinely awarded to winning plaintiffs.

Indeed, some notable toxic tort cases have been successfully brought as class actions. Perhaps the most notable is the *Agent Orange* decision. That case involved the settlement of a class action. In a now famous opinion, the court approved a settlement under circumstances where it believed that the class members would not have been able to succeed individually. In re Agent Orange Product Liability Litigation, 597 F.Supp. 740 (E.D.N.Y.1984). Since each class member could not demonstrate that it was more likely than not that it suffered its injuries as a result of exposure to the defendant's product, individual lawsuits would not have succeeded. Yet, the court felt that it was proper to approve the class to settle the dispute, because the class's numerosity assured that many individuals who likely *had* been harmed by the defendant would receive some compensation. And, since it was impossible to tell which of the plaintiffs had been harmed by the defendants, and which suffered from other exposure pathways, *all* of the class members would get some compensation. In short, the court found that the class action device was a proper way to solve the indeterminate plaintiff problem.

Nevertheless, out of respect for the enormous power of the class action device to disrupt the lives of both defendants and the courts, courts have scrutinized carefully proposed mass toxic torts classes. Claims seeking only injunctive relief are more readily approved than claims seeking damages. For the same reasons that courts rarely consolidate for trial damages matters, however, they infrequently approve mass tort class actions seeking damages. The differences among class members' individual exposure pathways and damages are considered to outweigh the similarities among their claims. Thus, for example, courts have not generally been sympathetic to class actions in the asbestosis context or in tobacco injury litigation.

# CHAPTER 14

# AVOIDING LIABILITY FOR HAZARDOUS SUBSTANCE CLEANUP COSTS

## A. OVERVIEW

The law provides no invincible shield against cleanup liability. Yet prudent planning can minimize the liability risk. A buyer's due diligence property inspection, for example, may trigger the "innocent landowner" defense to CERCLA liability, as discussed in Chapter 9. Similarly, a parent corporation can structure its relationship with its subsidiary in order to avoid inheriting the subsidiary's cleanup obligation, also discussed above. This chapter discusses the three other principal methods for minimizing cleanup liability: (1) indemnity and hold harmless agreements; (2) insurance; and (3) bankruptcy.

Ultimately, the only sure strategy for avoiding liability is to avoid any link, direct or indirect, with hazardous substances. Indeed, one of CERCLA's implicit purposes is to discourage the generation of such substances. The risk of multimillion dollar liability, for example, might provide a waste generator with a financial incentive to alter its operating procedures to minimize or eliminate hazardous wastes. Ironically, however, this avoidance strategy may impair cleanup efforts in some instances. As the growing "brownfields" program suggests, the basic CERCLA liability structure deters the purchase, cleanup, and redevelopment of contaminated facilities.

## B. INDEMNITY AND HOLD HARMLESS AGREEMENTS

Indemnity and hold harmless agreements are frequently used to minimize cleanup liability, particularly in connection with asset sales. Suppose that A, holding title to contaminated land, negotiates the sale of the property to B. As part of the sales contract, A and B might agree that A will indemnify B to the extent that B incurs liability for cleanup costs. Alternatively, B might agree to release and hold A harmless from any claims which B might have against A relating to potential cleanup liability.

Indemnity and hold harmless agreements concerning hazardous substance cleanup liability under CERCLA and RCRA are generally enforceable between the parties, but not against the government. See Smith Land & Improvement Corp. v. Celotex Corp., 851 F.2d 86 (3d Cir.1988) (interpreting CERCLA § 107(e) as authorizing such clauses); Hanlin Group, Inc. v. International Minerals & Chemical Corp., 759 F.Supp. 925 (D.Me.1990) (assuming validity of indemnity clause concerning corrective action expenses under RCRA). For example, if both A and B are liable under CERCLA as responsible parties, the indemnity or hold harmless agreement between them will not shield them from liability to the government. However, as the Third Circuit explained in

SmithKline Beecham Corp. v. Rohm & Haas Co., 89 F.3d 154 (3d Cir.1996), they "can lawfully allocate CERCLA response costs among themselves while remaining jointly and severally liable to the government for the entire cleanup."

The enforceability of such liability allocation clauses hinges on the specificity of the language used. Clauses which expressly provide for indemnity against CERCLA and RCRA liability are typically enforceable. See, e.g., City & County of Honolulu v. Churchill, 167 F.Supp.2d 1143 (D.Hawai'i 2000). Even sweeping provisions which shift liability for any and all claims, without mention of particular environmental liabilities, may be effective. In Purolator Products Corp. v. Allied-Signal, Inc., 772 F.Supp. 124 (W.D.N.Y.1991), for example, a provision indemnifying for "all liabilities and obligations arising out of the Assets" was held broad enough to include CERCLA liability which arose out of the assets sold. In contrast, a mere "as is" clause in a real property sales contract may not release the seller from CERCLA and RCRA liability. Compare Bonnie Blue, Inc. v. Reichenstein, 127 S.W.3d 366 (Tex.App.2004) (clause ineffective) with Velsicol Chemical Corp. v. Reilly Industries, Inc., 67 F.Supp.2d 893 (E.D.Tenn.1999) (clause enforced).

## C. INSURANCE

Can a liable party recover cleanup costs from its insurance carrier? The sweeping new liability created by RCRA and CERCLA prompted a wave of insurance claims which stunned the insurance industry. Over the years, insurers had issued millions of standard form policies without contemplating liability for hazardous substance cleanup costs. As a result, most existing policies did not either clearly cover or clearly exclude such claims. The resulting deluge of litigation has produced a substantial (if somewhat inconsistent) body of state law on the subject. Some insured parties have been successful in recovering cleanup costs; most have failed. Litigation based on these early policy forms will continue in the future. However, during the 1980s, standard insurance policy forms were amended to expressly exclude coverage for hazardous substance cleanup costs, effectively barring such claims.

## 1. COMPREHENSIVE GENERAL LIABILITY INSURANCE

Most insurance disputes concerning cleanup costs have involved the pre-1986 comprehensive general liability (CGL) policy, the type of liability policy then customarily held by businesses. Four basic interpretation issues have arisen concerning this standard form: (1) are cleanup costs covered "damages"? (2) are cleanup costs "caused by an occurrence"? (3) does the "pollution exclusion" bar recovery? and (4) does the "owned property exclusion" bar recovery?

### a. "Damages"

The key coverage clause in the CGL policy requires the insurer to indemnify the insured for "those sums that the insured becomes legally obligated to pay as damages because of bodily injury or property damage to which this insurance applies." Insurers found early success in arguing that "damages" in this context was limited to money judgments in favor of injured tort claimants, and thus did not extend to the insured's cost of reimbursing government agencies or performing mandated remediation work. See, e.g., Certain Underwriters at Lloyd's of London v. Superior Court, 24 Cal.4th 945, 103 Cal.Rptr.2d 672, 16 P.3d 94 (Cal.2001) (insurers had no duty to pay cleanup costs ordered by state administrative agency). Other recent decisions, however, reason that "damages" is an ambiguous term and interpret it to include cleanup costs in accordance with the reasonable expectations of the insured. The Maryland Supreme Court's decision in Bausch & Lomb, Inc. v. Utica Mutual Insurance Co., 330 Md. 758, 625 A.2d 1021 (Md.1993) reflects this view:

> [I]nsurance policy-holders surely do not anticipate that coverage will depend on the mode of relief, i.e. a cash payment rather than an injunction, sought by an injured party. Policy-holders will, instead, reasonably infer that the insurer's pledge to pay damages will apply generally to compensatory outlays of various kinds, including expenditures made to comply with administrative orders * * *.

This can even extend to voluntarily incurred cleanup costs. See, e.g., Central Illinois Light Co. v.

Home Ins. Co., 213 Ill.2d 141, 290 Ill.Dec. 155, 821 N.E.2d 206 (Ill.2004).

### b. "Occurrence"

In addition, only damages caused by an "occurrence" are covered under a CGL policy. Until the mid-1980s, "occurrence" was typically defined as "an accident, including continuous or repeated exposure to conditions, resulting in bodily injury or property damage neither expected nor intended from the standpoint of the named insured." For example, in American Mutual Liability Insurance Co. v. Neville Chemical Co., 650 F.Supp. 929 (W.D.Pa.1987) a chemical company continued dumping hazardous waste materials into its unlined lagoon in the regular course of business, despite repeated notice that its wastes had contaminated nearby wells. In later litigation, the court found that the ensuing damage was "expected" by the company, and thus not a covered occurrence. But see, e.g., New Castle County v. Continental Casualty Co., 725 F.Supp. 800 (D.Del.1989) (finding that the migration of contaminants from an unlined county landfill was an "occurrence" because, based on the limited scientific knowledge concerning leachate migration at the time of the landfill's design and operation, there was not a "substantial probability" that damage would occur).

### c. Owned Property Exclusion

Insurance companies frequently assert the "owned property" exclusion, which bars recovery for damage to property owned, rented, or occupied by the named insured. Accordingly, even if the owner of a contaminated CERCLA facility vaults the other CGL policy hurdles, as a general rule he will not secure reimbursement for cleanup costs. But two evolving exceptions have somewhat eroded the rule, as Patz v. St. Paul Fire & Marine Insurance Co., 817 F.Supp. 781 (E.D.Wis.1993), aff'd, 15 F.3d 699 (7th Cir.1994) demonstrates. In *Patz*, plaintiff deposited industrial waste on its plant site, contaminating both soil and groundwater. Ordered by the state of Wisconsin to remediate the site, plaintiff then successfully sued its CGL carrier for indemnity, despite the owned property exclusion. The *Patz* court noted that the exclusion did not apply to groundwater contamination because in Wisconsin groundwater is owned by the public, not by the surface owner. Further, citing the danger that the contamination might reach off-site property, the court allowed recovery for remediation of the soil (admittedly owned by the insured) in order to prevent harm to third parties. But see R & D Maidman Family L.P. v. Scottsdale Ins. Co., 4 Misc.3d 728, 783 N.Y.S.2d 205 (N.Y.Sup.2004).

### d. Pollution Exclusion

Finally, insurance companies have routinely invoked the pre-1986 "pollution exclusion" in response to hazardous substance cleanup claims. The version of this exclusion involved in most cases provides that the policy does not apply:

> To bodily injury or property damage arising out of the discharge, dispersal, release or escape of smoke, vapors, soot, fumes, acids, alkalis, toxic chemicals, liquids or gases, waste materials or other irritants, contaminants or pollutants into or upon land, the atmosphere or any watercourse or body of water; *but this exclusion does not apply if such discharge, dispersal, release or escape is sudden and accidental*; * * * (Emphasis added).

The *sudden and accidental* exception to this exclusion has fueled substantial controversy. Some events are clearly "sudden and accidental"—as where PCB-laden waste oil gushes from a tank ruptured by an earthquake—and thus not excluded from coverage. But is the classic CERCLA scenario involving gradual, long-term leakage within the exclusion? A substantial minority of jurisdictions, reasoning that "sudden" is ambiguous, interpret the term as meaning only unexpected or unintended; they accordingly allow recovery by most insureds. The weight of authority, however, holds that "sudden" has a clear and unambiguous temporal meaning. As the court explained in ACL Technologies, Inc. v. Northbrook Property & Casualty Insurance Co., 17 Cal.App.4th 1773, 22 Cal.Rptr.2d 206 (Cal.App.1993), "[t]he word must, if it is to be anything more than a hiccup in front of the word accidental, convey a 'temporal' meaning of immediacy, quickness, or abruptness." Thus, in most jurisdictions the pre-1986 CGL policy does not cover gradual, long-term leakage.

Recovery of remediation expenses under post-1985 CGL policies is unlikely. These policies include a redrafted pollution exclusion known as the "absolute pollution exclusion." This revised exclusion avoids the "sudden and accidental" controversy discussed above by flatly refusing coverage for: "Bodily injury or property damage arising out of the actual or threatened discharge, dispersal, seepage, migration, release or escape of pollutants * * *." Courts have uniformly found the absolute pollution exclusion to be clear and unambiguous.

## 2. TITLE INSURANCE

It is now well-settled that hazardous substance cleanup costs are not covered by standard title insurance policies. The leading case is Chicago Title Insurance Co. v. Kumar, 24 Mass.App.Ct. 53, 506 N.E.2d 154 (Mass.App.1987). It held that the release of hazardous substances on the insured's land was not covered by the insuring clauses of his policy as a "defect in or lien or encumbrance on" his title. The court observed that the protection under this standard policy clause extended only to title defects, liens, or encumbrances which existed on the date the policy was issued, not to "the mere possibility that the Commonwealth may attach a future lien." Similarly, the court reasoned that the mere contamination of the insured's property did not trigger the policy clause insuring against unmarketability of title; it noted that this clause insures only title, not the physical condition of the land. Standard title insurance policies issued after the early 1990s normally contain a provision embodying this non-liability rule; it expressly excludes any damages which arise from "any law, ordinance or government regulation * * * relating to * * * (iv) environmental protection, or the effect of any violation of these laws, ordinances or government regulations * * *."

### 3. ENVIRONMENTAL IMPAIRMENT LIABILITY INSURANCE

The environmental impairment liability (EIL) policy is a special insurance product designed to protect against the environmental contamination normally excluded under the CGL "pollution exclusion." EIL coverage was also intended to meet the TSD financial responsibility requirements mandated by RCRA. Although EIL policy forms vary widely, the coverage provided is typically quite narrow. For example, CERCLA and RCRA cleanup costs can be recovered *only* where the insured is liable for post-policy contamination of another party's property (so long as the property is not a licensed waste handling facility). No coverage is provided for past contamination or for future contamination of the insured's own property or of any waste handling facility. In addition, the premium charged for an EIL policy is quite high. The combination of limited coverage and high cost renders EIL policies undesirable to most potential customers; moreover, insurers are generally reluctant to underwrite this type of risk. Accordingly, EIL policies are not widely available.

## D. BANKRUPTCY

As a last resort, can a liable party escape cleanup obligations by filing bankruptcy? And can the bankrupt's estate itself avoid liability by abandoning contaminated property? Federal courts have struggled valiantly to reconcile the inherent conflict between bankruptcy law and hazardous substance regulation. The Bankruptcy Code is designed to give the beleaguered debtor a "fresh start" by discharging as many debts as possible. The cleanup provisions of CERCLA and RCRA, in contrast, are designed to remediate contaminated facilities, regardless of traditional liability rules. As the Ninth Circuit summarized in In re Jensen, 995 F.2d 925 (9th Cir.1993), the intersection between these two bodies of law "is somewhat messy." Although a few relatively clear rules have emerged from this conflict, many issues remain unresolved and courts continue to approach this volatile area cautiously.

### 1. DISCHARGE OF DEBTOR

In general, liability for hazardous substance cleanup can be discharged in bankruptcy. The landmark Supreme Court decision recognizing this rule is Ohio v. Kovacs, 469 U.S. 274, 105 S.Ct. 705, 83 L.Ed.2d 649 (1985). *Ohio* involved a hazardous waste disposal site operated in violation of state environmental laws. The state of Ohio obtained an injunction directing the corporate owner and respondent Kovacs, its chief executive officer, to clean up the contaminated site. When Kovacs filed bankruptcy instead, the state argued that his obligation under the injunction was not a "debt" subject to discharge under the Bankruptcy Code. However, emphasizing that a receiver now controlled the property, such that in effect the only performance sought from Kovacs was the payment of money to defray cleanup costs, the *Ohio* Court concluded that this obligation constituted a dischargeable debt. See also Mark IV Industries v. New Mexico Environment Dept., 459 B.R. 173 (S.D.N.Y. 2011).

The central question left unresolved by *Ohio* is when a "debt" for cleanup liability arises. A fundamental bankruptcy precept is that only debts which arise before the date of the debtor's discharge are dischargeable. *Ohio* presents the easy case; it teaches that a money judgment stemming from a cleanup obligation is an existing, dischargeable debt. But at what point before a judgment has been rendered does a potential cleanup obligation mature into a "debt"? In the wake of *Ohio,* a few courts held that a dischargeable CERCLA claim arose as soon as a hazardous substance was released; other courts insisted that such a claim arose only when all elements of CERCLA liability (including the incurrence of response costs) were met. Finally, many courts have followed the "fair contemplation" approach, first developed in In re National Gypsum Co., 139 B.R. 397 (N.D.Tex.1992), as a middle course between the two prior standards. Under this approach, cleanup costs arising from the bankrupt's pre-petition conduct are dischargeable only if they were within the "fair contemplation" of the parties before the end of the bankruptcy proceeding. In resolving this issue, courts typically consider five factors: (1) knowledge by the parties of a site for which the bankrupt may be liable as a PRP; (2) site listing on the NPL; (3) notification from EPA or a state agency to the bankrupt; (4) commencement of investigation and cleanup activities; and (5) incurrence of response costs. See, e.g., Signature Combs, Inc. v. United States, 253 F.Supp.2d 1028 (W.D.Tenn.2003).

### 2. ABANDONMENT OF FACILITY

The traditional liquidation bankruptcy requires the appointment of a trustee to collect, manage, and sell the debtor's assets. Although charged with the obligation to maximize recovery by creditors, the trustee may abandon property of the debtor's estate which is "burdensome" or "of inconsequential value." Suppose that the debtor, liable under CERCLA as a current facility owner, files a bankruptcy petition and is discharged. Can the bankruptcy trustee then abandon the contaminated facility in order to prevent the estate from incurring liability for cleanup costs?

The Supreme Court explored this issue in Midlantic National Bank v. New Jersey Department of Environmental Protection, 474 U.S. 494, 106 S.Ct. 755, 88 L.Ed.2d 859 (1986). There, Quanta Resources Corporation accepted toxic PCB-laden oil at its New Jersey and New York waste oil processing facilities in violation of state environmental laws. Stored in deteriorating containers, this waste oil contaminated the subsoil, presenting risks which included "genetic damage or death through personal contact." After Quanta filed bankruptcy, the trustee abandoned the facilities despite the protests of the affected states that abandonment would endanger the public. Reasoning that Congress did not intend for the abandonment power to abrogate state and local laws designed to protect public health and safety, the Supreme Court held that the abandonment was improper. It warned, however, that the "abandonment power is not to be fettered by laws or regulations not reasonably calculated to protect the public health or safety from imminent and identifiable harm." *Midlantic National Bank* thus establishes the rule that a trustee cannot abandon a contaminated site which presents an "imminent and identifiable harm" to public health or safety. The burden is on the party opposing abandonment, however, to demonstrate the existence of such a harm. In re St. Lawrence Corp., 248 B.R. 734 (D.N.J.2000); cf. In re Unidigital, Inc., 262 B.R. 283 (Bankr.D.Del.2001) (trustee allowed to abandon 15 ton printer even though it contained chemicals which must be drained).

# TABLE OF ACRONYMS

| | |
|---|---|
| AEA | Atomic Energy Act |
| AOC | Area of concern |
| ARAR | Applicable or relevant and appropriate standard, requirement, criteria, or limitation |
| BADT | Best available demonstrated technology |
| BAT | Best available technology |
| BCT | Best control technology |
| BMP | Best management practice |
| BOD | Biological oxygen demanding |
| BPT | Best practicable technology |
| CAA | Clean Air Act |
| CAMU | Corrective action management unit |
| CERCLA | Comprehensive Environmental Response, Compensation, and Liability Act |
| CFR | Code of Federal Regulations |
| CGL | Comprehensive general liability |
| CMO | Case management order |
| CMS | Corrective measures study |
| CPSA | Consumer Products Safety Act |
| CPSC | Consumer Products Safety Commission |

| | |
|---|---|
| CWA | Clean Water Act |
| DO | Dissolved Oxygen |
| DOT | Department of Transportation |
| DDT | Dichloro-diphenyl-trichloroethane |
| EHS | Extremely hazardous substance |
| EIL | Environmental impairment liability |
| EPCRTKA | Emergency Planning and Community Right-to-Know Act |
| EPA | Environmental Protection Agency |
| FDA | Food and Drug Administration |
| FFDCA | Federal Food, Drug, and Cosmetic Act |
| FHSA | Federal Hazardous Substances Act |
| FIFRA | Federal Insecticide, Fungicide, and Rodenticide Act |
| FWPCA | Federal Water Pollution Control Act |
| GACT | Generally available control technology |
| HMTA | Hazardous Materials Transportation Act |
| HRS | Hazard Ranking System |
| HSWA | Hazardous and Solid Waste Amendments |
| ITC | Interagency Testing Commission |
| LDR | Land disposal restriction |

| | |
|---|---|
| LOIS | Loss of interim status |
| MACT | Maximum achievable control technology |
| MCL | Maximum contaminant level |
| MCLG | Maximum contaminant level goal |
| MSW | Municipal solid waste |
| NAAQS | National Ambient Air Quality Standards |
| NCP | National Contingency Plan |
| NESHAP | National emissions standards for hazardous air pollutants |
| NFRAP | No further remedial action planned |
| NOIS | Notice of intent to sue |
| NPL | National Priorities List |
| NPDES | National Pollutant Discharge Elimination System |
| NSPS | New source performance standards |
| OPA | Oil Pollution Act of 1990 |
| OSHA | Occupational Safety and Health Act; also Occupational Safety and Health Administration |
| PA/SI | Preliminary assessment/site investigation |
| PCBs | Polychlorinated biphenyls |
| PEL | Permissible exposure limit |
| PMN | Premanufacture notice |

| | |
|---|---|
| PRP | Potentially responsible party |
| RCRA | Resource Conservation and Recovery Act |
| RD/RA | Remedial design/remedial action |
| RFA | RCRA facility assessment |
| RFI | RCRA facility investigation |
| RI/FS | Remedial investigation/feasibility study |
| ROD | Record of decision |
| SARA | Superfund Amendments and Reauthorization Act |
| SDWA | Safe Drinking Water Act |
| SEMS | Superfund Enterprise Management System |
| SIP | State implementation plan |
| SNUN | Significant new use notice |
| SNUR | Significant new use rule |
| SWDA | Solid Waste Disposal Act |
| SWMU | Solid waste management unit |
| TCE | Trichloroethylene |
| TCLP | Toxicity characteristic leaching procedure |
| TRI | Toxic Release Inventory |
| TSCA | Toxic Substances Control Act |
| TSD | Treatment, storage, or disposal facility |

| | |
|---|---|
| UAO | Unilateral Administrative Order |
| UCFA | Uniform Comparative Fault Act |
| UFFI | Urea formaldehyde foam insulation |
| UST | Underground storage tank |
| VOC | Volatile organic compound |

# INDEX

**References are to Pages**

---